What Planners Do: Power, Politics, and Persuasion

What Planners Do: Power, Politics, and Persuasion

Charles Hoch

PLANNERS PRESS
AMERICAN PLANNING ASSOCIATION

Chicago, Illinois   Washington, D.C.

Contents

ACKNOWLEDGMENTS

The idea for this book emerged from breakfast conversations with John Forester and Howell Baum that started in 1980 in a Cincinnati restaurant. We talked about studying planners and planning. Several years later, Howell initiated an informal study group of planning analysts at the annual meetings of the American Collegiate Schools of Planning. We shared notes, criticisms, and questions.

In 1987, John Forester obtained grant funds to bring together a portion of this group (Sy Adler, Linda Dalton, Norman Krumholz, Howell, and me from the United States, and Judith Allen and Patsy Healey from Britain) to review and comment on early drafts of *Making Equity Planning Work,* which he wrote with Norman Krumholz. John's agenda was much more ambitious than Howell's. He asked us each to spend a day with a practicing planner and report what we found. He hoped our conversations would stimulate a research agenda on planning practice tied to the sort of participant observation he favored. I dutifully fulfilled my obligation and was hooked. The meetings inspired Linda Dalton to conduct a pathbreaking survey of the research literature (Dalton 1989a), while Patsy Healey published her detailed account of one planner's work day in the *Journal of the American Planning Association* (Healey 1992).

My sabbatical from the School of Urban Planning and Policy at the University of Illinois at Chicago enabled me to conduct my field research. I received generous and useful advice from colleagues who reviewed my research proposal including Seymour Mandelbaum, John Bryson, Sue Hendler, and Ernest Alexander. Along the way I received reviews from Howell Baum, John Forester, Bruce Stiftel, Sumner Sharpe, Beth Howe, Jerome Kaufman, Rob Mier, Doug Gills, and Stuart Meck. I am especially indebted to George Hemmens and Linda Dalton for their careful and detailed editorial review of the entire manuscript. Finally, I am grateful to the many planners who talked with me and let me observe them at work. I learned a great deal from their experience and hope this book will help others do the same. I enjoyed the excellent editorial services of Linda Mandeville, whose tactful advice has saved me from numerous errors in composition and style.

Portions of this book have been published elsewhere. Chapter 9, "Racism and Planning," was published in the *Journal of the American Planning Association.* The two setback stories of George and Bruce in chapter 6, as well as the story of Andrew in chapter 12, first appeared in an article entitled, "The Paradox of Planning and Power," in the *Journal of Planning Education and Research.* Portions of chapter 3 appeared in *Values and Planning,* edited by Huw Thomas (Avebury Press).

1

Planning and Professional Authority in a Liberal Society

WHAT DO PLANNERS DO?

We all make plans, usually our own. Professional planners, however, get paid to make plans for others. Working mainly for local government, planners advise public officials on how to cope with such various uncertainties as population growth, land use disputes, environmental problems, and job loss. Most planners complete two years of graduate planning education, during which they learn how to analyze the origins and patterns of human settlements and assess the individual and institutional activities that form communities. Planners learn theories of city decline, suburban expansion, neighborhood change, and regional balance. They use these ideas to shape their advice on specific proposals, complaints, and conflicts.

Professional planners face a serious problem in our liberal democratic society. Their professional judgment relies on theoretical and specialized knowledge of social, economic, political, and geographic relationships. However, most of the problems that planners analyze and assess are practical. Officials, advocates, lobbyists, and citizens possess specific attachments that make them feel as if they are experts on the practical matter at hand. When professional planners offer advice that challenges the tacit expertise of those involved, they frequently inspire suspicion and resentment among the very clients they hope to serve. To defend themselves, professional planners assert that they are offering a public good—advice that serves the public interest. Many planners understand this dilemma and work hard to solicit and include in their professional advice the ideas and opinions of the citizens involved. However, the pursuit of widespread consensus through compromise and negotiation often seems to undermine the integrity of expert judgment. If people can figure out what they want and how to get it on their own, who needs professional planners?

Planners inhabit a precarious institutional and professional position in the United States, stemming from the tension between individual purposes and the common good and between professional judgment and citizen preferences. As liberal citizens, we want to have our way, but we also expect others to cooperate and respect our freedom. These two desires often clash. As democratic citizens we take pride in our opinions and yet still look to expert knowledge for support. Conflict follows when opinion and expertise disagree. How professional planners respond to the conflict determines how they do their work. Consider the stories of two professional planners who respond very differently to these demands. The first planner celebrates the wisdom of expertise; the second praises the virtue of mobilized public sentiment.

Tim: Public Design and Professional Autonomy

Tim is well-polished. He is thoughtful and careful about his appearance. He works for a large international consulting architectural firm, but was trained as a planner. He loves cities, travels extensively in European cities whenever he can, and prides himself on his knowledge of urban design. We talk in his tower building office, which affords a view of the nearby metropolitan business district.

> Compared to most European cities, our cities are ugly. In Europe they take design seriously and regulate strongly to protect and enhance the beauty of the buildings. Here we let developers rule without ensuring good design.
>
> In my job I sometimes solicit work from large corporate clients and develop RFPs that match their expectations. The big clients like these can impose their ideas about design. More frequently I review RFPs from smaller clients. In these cases I can select which ones to do and shape expectations about the design.
>
> For instance, we recently completed a design plan to guide the physical redevelopment of an old suburban industrial town—Dover. It was one of the first projects I worked on after getting my job here. I was brought on board to write the urban design guidelines for the project.
>
> Downtown Dover is located on a river front. The basic design uses the river front as the central focus. Many of the older buildings that abut the

river are of similar height and were produced at about the same time. The design attempts to enhance and expand the continuity—the historical feel of this period. But at the moment there is a developer who wants to build a power strip mall on a vacant lot adjacent to the river. The design sets the commercial structure back from the river with lots of parking between the commercial building and the river. This design violates the basic integrity of the proposed design and I urged the city planners to pressure the developer to put the building next to the river with the parking in the rear.

Unfortunately, the Dover planning commission already approved the developer's plans, so getting him to change may be difficult, but I think they should try. If you hope to create a beautiful waterfront then you need to use strong regulations to control developers.

The Dover planners have their own strong ideas of good design. One local city council member wants to create a vault of Italian lights across the river. He saw this somewhere and could not give the idea up. He inserted the idea in every draft of the design plan. It was not a good idea.

The planning director is reasonable and worked well in coordinating the relationship between the planning commission and our firm. He helped link my proposals with preexisting guidelines, and he gave useful comments on the draft proposals. The director of development, however, was less supportive. For instance, in the case of the power mall developer, the director of development insisted that the developer's plan be approved because the city had already promised him that it was OK. He didn't want to pressure the developer to change. The planning director was more willing to consider such a move. My own belief is that a sympathetic corporate counsel could find a legal way to pressure the developer into conforming with the new design.

Of course, the planning director has to juggle competing interests. While I can focus exclusively on design as a consultant, he has to balance the benefits of good design against the potential loss of development. But I keep pushing in favor of design because I believe the long-term economic value of the downtown will be enhanced by protecting and enhancing the existing character of the present river front design.

I have never had a job where I had to balance design and development. I like working in the design environment. I don't think I'd be happy trying to do both, unless I had the power of a dictator. I have strong notions of design. When someone says they want Italian lights over the river front and I think this is a bad design proposal, I want to be able to stop it.

I don't like compromise in design. This all too frequently leads to mediocre results. Many times it is better to have no design than just part of a design. A partially designed project can be worse than no project at all, or a project that is homely but makes no pretense of being designed.

Sometimes I run into resistance from my colleagues at work. Many times a coworker will suggest cutting corners or comply with a foolish proposal from a client "just to get the job done." For instance, in the Dover project, local officials suggested putting the city logo on the benches planned for the waterfront. I thought the idea was provincial and would quickly become dated. I felt the bench design should be more timeless. My colleague was less concerned and was willing to go along.

The Dover officials also proposed that the benches be made of large wooden slabs so as to be vandal proof. I opposed this as shortsighted. I wanted them to adopt a more neutral design that would not clash with the Victorian style of the surrounding structures. My landscape colleague said, "Let's not fight them on this. Let's just do what they want and get it done."

In the end we offered a choice of three different bench designs. This seemed silly to me—offering a choice about a matter of taste. I didn't protest too much, though, and deferred to my colleague initially. But over time I won over the other staff involved on the project. In effect, I adopted an Italian approach to the overall design and the selection of the bench type. The Italians keep the heritage of earlier periods by introducing neutral design elements when they add new features to the landscape. Instead of favoring a particular historical period, you seek to achieve a sort of aesthetic balance of styles. The bench style I proposed was just this sort of approach and my colleagues eventually agreed.

Urban design draws on the skill and artistry of the professional. Tim works hard to make a plan that meets code, functions well, and looks good. He wants his plan to be adopted, without compromises to its compositional integrity. For instance, he believes the elected officials of Dover should take legal steps to rescind approval of the developer's plans, which break up his design scheme. He feels that following democratic procedures in matters of design produces banal compromises. Politicians, bureaucrats, and citizens should leave design to the professionals. To Tim, professional autonomy—the artistic freedom to create a beautiful plan that commands respect—offers a personal reward, even if its public fate may be doomed. He believes that planners derive power and authority from the competent exercise of their talent, skill, and judgment—the image writ large of the modern architect.[1]

Fred: The Responsible Professional and the Public Good

Fred has been planning director for about three years for the aging industrial river town of Burgess. He took me on a tour of the old and new portions of the city. He is a native who takes pleasure in the diversity of the city's people and the successful efforts to improve the physical infrastructure that holds the city together. He possesses the energy and commitment of the civic cheerleader, but without the narrow focus of the conventional business booster.

The biggest issue for me and my department is to communicate and get people on our side. When I hire new employees I pay attention to the applicants' ability to communicate and to their values. We have a small department and do a lot of work together. We do a lot of zoning type stuff and cope with a lot of neighborhood squabbles. The key is to figure out ways to get employees and citizens and clients to work together.

I take a very honest approach and attempt to speak with all those involved with an issue. I tell them the same basic story and act on it. This builds respect, even with those who disagree. I'm in the trenches all the time.

We're almost like social workers here. We have lots of people contact us all the time for a variety of services and complaints. I imagine big city planners work mainly on technical stuff. Here, we deal with all the little stuff. When we put forward a plan we have to carry out every step of the project. This is difficult when we confront new planning issues every week.

The downtown of the city has been depressed for years. We wanted to prepare a concept model that would change peoples' perception of what the downtown could be. We first developed a physical model. We did most of the work in-house and spent a good deal of effort getting the input of local residents. I didn't want to get consultants involved too early, because they tend to use ideas from elsewhere without taking local ideas into account.

After substantial groundwork, we eventually did hire a consultant to help us prepare a downtown development plan. The plan combines substantial improvement to the river front with a prominently located riverboat gambling commercial center and the preservation of several historically significant commercial buildings.

For about a year, my staff and I visited schools, churches, and meetings of all sorts to explain the concept. I preached. I felt the major barrier to a successful downtown plan was the misperception of residents that nothing could be done.

I would ask people where they had lived and visited. I then asked them to compare these places with our city. Invariably people talk about things they like here and focus on what they consider to be important. Especially popular are churches, the river that runs through the downtown, and the large houses. I build on this sense of pride for the town.

I worked with teachers to have the school kids write letters to kids in schools elsewhere telling about our city. We supply all sorts of materials to local school teachers to stimulate interest in the kids about the city in which they live. We visit seniors as well and address their fears and negative assessments right up front. We know they feel a loss for what they had before, and I establish my credibility by pointing out the problems, but then I try to show how things could be different and improved.

Especially helpful is the fact that I am a third generation native. I initially feared that residents would cynically mock me when I used this fact to show my commitment to the town. They didn't. People find this reassuring, especially the seniors.

Every Saturday we do bus tours subsidized by the local newspaper that include the proposed renewal area downtown. We give the participants the opportunity to be on the inside of some of the details we are undertaking to get the plan underway.

I am a booster and a salesman for the downtown planning concept. We don't want to be like Oakdale or Forest Hills, fancy homogenous suburbs. We're not a bedroom community, but an old industrial town with a diverse population.

Marketing the plan is crucial. We must attract new commercial tenants. We used to do this in planning, but now the marketing has been allocated to a countywide nonprofit economic development [ED] agency. Of course, in planning we can still do plenty to attract the attention of developers. I go out of my way to meet with prospective developers, but all the media type stuff will be done by the ED nonprofit.

I emphasize the informal approach and make direct contacts with potential investors and developers. I take them on tours of the "bad" neighborhoods and explain what we're doing to make improvements and control gangs. I point out the good and the bad. I don't think you can fool people about this stuff. Establishing an honest relationship opens the door to the future.

I know about a lot of the development going on nearby and how people are treated. I ask developers about what's going on elsewhere and try to get them to recognize the value and opportunity of downtown renewal. Their feelings and impression of long-term regional growth are positive. I build on that and explain what we could do; how we could work together.

Fred focuses on the creation of feasible and fair-minded plans—plans that inspire consensus and produce tangible and far-reaching improvements in living conditions, especially for the disadvantaged. To Fred, good professional planning means responsible planning that informs and advises democratic leaders about the just, efficient, and orderly use of public goods in the city's many different communities.

Fred's allegiance to the city is not only as an employee, but as a member of the community. He uses his position to advocate plans that will meet the needs of different citizens and interest groups. Planning, for Fred, includes organizing, educating, and motivating others to understand, embrace, and act together on the plan. If modifying the planning document will enhance its legitimacy for a wider portion of the public, Fred changes the plan. The good plan reaches out and incorporates the public's desires and commitment.

The Planning Paradox

Tim emphasizes the primacy of professional expertise and judgment in making good plans. On design issues, citizens should adopt the preferences of the experts. By contrast, Fred seeks to make plans with broad public appeal. He listens to the desires and interests of the city's many different citizens and then develops the plan. Although Tim takes the side of design and Fred the side of public wishes, both are committed to the efficacy of professional action. The two stories illustrate the contradictions within the liberal paradox with which professional planning is always grappling.

When planning professionals in the United States do their jobs they rarely take sides, as do Tim and Fred, but rather they search for ways to straddle the dilemma between professional freedom and social justice. The professional protocol promises that expert knowledge will produce advice that serves the public interest and will therefore obtain public consent. Research studies through the decades on professional planning practice, however, pose serious questions about the efficacy of professional action. Early studies of comprehensive planning (Altshuler 1965) and recent studies of progressive advocacy planning (Hoffman 1989; Krumholz and Forester 1990) have found evidence of persistent tension between the authority of the professional and the politics of the public good. How do professionals meet both claims?

What would Tim and Fred say to each other? Tim might warn Fred that the pursuit of public consensus tends to compromise design quality. Tim might say, "You may get the plan approved, Fred, but only at the expense of your professional integrity." Fred would probably warn Tim that any design that elevates professional vision above the public's desires not only risks public veto, but is also likely to fail to serve the public good. Fred might say to Tim, "What good does it do to preserve your professional status, yet sacrifice the efficacy of building political support for your plans?"

I suspect Tim and Fred would argue for some time and come to a stalemate. No matter the outcome, however, this imaginary debate is only possible because both use the paradoxical dualism to interpret their everyday work. The necessity of planning in our complex urban society and its absence as an important institutional and cultural tradition inform the dualism. Professional planners, as members of our liberal culture, respond in complicated and ambivalent ways to this persistent paradox between individual freedom and public responsibility. Despite the complexity of their practical actions and their failure to resolve the paradox, they end up measuring their practice against professional standards that expect a synthesis. Why?

WHAT IS PROFESSIONAL PLANNING?

Professional planning developed in response to the Progressive reform movements of the early twentieth century. Architects, landscape architects, and engineers sought to change the physical, social, and economic patterns of settlement, especially in the rapidly growing cities, to reduce social disorder and injustice, while enhancing the efficiency and beauty of daily life. As national institutions and corporations were rapidly gathering strength, this tiny group of designers banded together to institutionalize planning in the United States as a profession, but then later as an indispensable function of civic order. These reformers were confident that the rational principles of professional action could be institutionalized within government. The reformers advanced comprehensive planning schemes that they believed would crosscut the frequently antagonistic priorities of powerful corporate, union, and government organizations and would meet the needs of the area's citizens.

Professional planners in the United States take on the problems that private organizations not only avoid, but tend to aggravate or cause. These collective problems, such as congestion, pollution, land use conflict, residential displacement, and flooding, defy simple and unilateral treatment by a single agency. They are problems that markets often create and cannot solve (Boyer 1983; Fogelsong 1986). The complexity and interdependence of these problems' causes and effects make even identifying them a difficult and contested task. As members of the Progressive reform tradition, professional planners try to classify and analyze these messy problems and propose solutions. Central to the solutions that planners propose is the assumption that an active and involved government is committed to planning.

Professional planning, however, has never succeeded in obtaining significant political power and cultural standing in the United States, nor has the federal government ever adopted planning as a central institutional activity. As a result, official public planning holds a subordinate organizational position at the local level. Planners are pushed to the margins of civic life and public culture in the United States. This lack of institutional authority handicaps professional planners when they offer advice from their government offices. When planners expose the conflicts between private purposes and the public good, they receive little institutional support. Planners are left to cope on their own with the conflicts that public planning engenders when it tackles some of the paradoxical problems of a liberal, capitalist society.[2]

Planning's lack of status, however, does not mean that the problems the professional seeks to remedy lack importance. The activities of professional planners are absolutely crucial for the successful maintenance and development of advanced industrial societies. Unfortunately, in the United States, these efforts are rarely popular, especially among the small minority with great wealth and political power. Mainstream culture rarely celebrates, usually ignores, and frequently attacks the activities of professional planners. High school students consider careers as architects, lawyers, and doctors. But as planners? Television dramas portray lawyers struggling for justice and doctors battling disease. But planners, what do they do?

The public's indifference and occasional hostility to professional planning is based less on ignorance than on its commitment to individualism, which fosters (from the view of public planning) a perverse, but powerful desire to be a perpetual free rider. The public enjoys the benefits it receives from government, but sees no reason to give up anything for the public good. The conflict can be seen in the bread-and-butter activity of local land use planning. Professional planners use government regulations to tame uncertainties in the local land economy. Some of these uncertainties are inevitable—congestion and spatial conflict—and others are unnecessary, but commonplace—exclusion, free riding, and waste. Landowners usually resent the regulations that reduce their own discretion and favor those that curb the discretion of others. Hence, they respond ambivalently to planning.

Ironically, the New Deal planning reformers urged the profession to include the public's views so that planning could become a powerful guide for action. This fantasy, however, is one-sided. When freedom-loving citizens must follow a plan that involves others and requires reciprocation, they balk and cry foul. Of course, the dynamic is more complex than this. People subscribe to individualism in inconsistent and contradictory ways. All sorts of groups, movements, sects, and other solidarities modify, support, and even undermine individualism.[3]

PROFESSIONAL PLANNING IN A LIBERAL SOCIETY

A wide variety of institutional planning activities are conducted throughout the modern world. Large-scale organizational life would be impossible without making and assessing plans for future action. Military operations, manufacturing production, product innovation, marketing schemes, election campaigns, trade shows, and thousands of other organized activities are based on plans that show foresight and provide guidance. Perhaps the most vivid (and ancient) planning prototype is the military organized to fight a war. The general staff share a commitment to defeat the enemy. They prioritize objectives and propose various strategies for achieving them. The threat of attack inspires solidarity and support of the military among the vulnerable citizens. The basic goals—protect the nation and defeat the enemy—enjoy widespread consensus. The top brass formulate strategic plans, which are then articulated down the chain of command into a coherent set of operations and tactics for the many specialized units that will fight the battles. Planning strategy addresses how the military conducts the war, not whether the war is worth it.

The military prototype reveals a unified consensus, a broad and diverse assortment of military means, and a rational command hierarchy that binds together the interdependent and functionally specialized activities by fitting means to ends. Strategic planning in other settings, such as corporations or government, tacitly refers to this prototype.

Expanding on this concept of planning, Melville Branch (1983; 1990; 1992) argues that this kind of rational strategy deserves more recognition and respect. Branch asserts that the strategic component resides in all modern bureaucracies, which means that planning is a functional prerequisite for all kinds of modern development. Drawing on the biological sciences, he characterizes these institutional practices as natural prerequisites for successful adaptation and development. He believes that planning is an inevitable and benign, if difficult, necessity for the growth and maintenance of advanced industrial societies. No planning, no progress.

This functional concept of planning is reassuring. The massive deployment of technological and scientific know-how in the pursuit of growth and prosperity will eventually accommodate everyone's needs and desires in their diverse roles as employees, students, citizens, consumers, and managers. The organic metaphors project our individual experiences of growth and maturation onto the evolution of organizational relationships. Just as we actively adapt to our social environment in ways that enable us to get where we want to go, so too do organizations adapt to the uncertainties of interorganizational competition.

This nifty merging of the military prototype and the organic metaphor unfortunately glosses over the many tensions and paradoxes that make modern liberal societies so uncertain. The processes and products of modern capitalist economies expand our individual powers, but also increase our vulnerability to each other in the organizational settings whose rules and relations we use to get ahead. The functional approach treats power as an instrument rather than as a relationship, and so ignores how the institutions that mediate, amplify, and accelerate individual preferences also change the meaning of these preferences. What if the strategic planning principles and practices of one organization prove incompatible with the principles and practices of other organizations? What if corporate and government agencies take antagonistic and even perverse actions?

The concept of planning I draw on in this book does not rely on the military and developmental metaphors. Strategic and functional plans rank and order our purposes—elevating some, subordinating others, and ignoring most. I am interested in democratic plans that sanction individual purposes based on public deliberation that involves those who will bear the consequences. Planning requires the rational assessment and anticipation of shared uncertainties. We study, design, and argue about different schemes to alleviate and remove the social, economic, and political uncertainties we face together. Planning in this sense goes beyond individual efforts to prepare a scheme for achieving a personal goal to include what people do together to avoid shared risks and pursue common goals.

Our discussions in the United States about shared uncertainty use the language of individual liberty and rights—the language of modern liberalism. Our favorite institution is the market. We believe that the pursuit of individual gain will produce the common good through competitive market exchange. This liberal image of solidarity is pluralistic: Society consists of diverse competitors who rely on a neutral state to compensate for failures to get along. The neutral state tames, if not eliminates, the free rider problem of individuals expanding their liberty at others' expense. The state must be neutral in the absence of an agreed-on common good. The state allows individuals to pursue their private goals, while protecting against harm the liberties and rights of others.[4]

Our freedom-loving liberal society promotes mobility within all domains: the economic, social, political, and cultural. We learn to organize our preferences within each domain, balancing our shifting priorities with customs of fair-minded negotiation and bargaining. The achievement of success and fulfillment in each sphere is defined by the individual's mobility in relative prosperity, status, and honor. The pursuit of upward mobility in the United States has fostered geographic mobility and induced pervasive social change. The almost universal reliance on the automobile offers vivid testimony to the importance of individual mobility. The decentralized landscape of the modern metropolis makes possible the pursuit of a vast diversity of discrete, yet commensurable preferences.

It is more difficult for the individual on the move to create and maintain a coherent and stable sense of identity than the popular images of self-improvement promise. As preferences shift, so too do the particular emotional attachments that give them meaning. Many find that the successful pursuit of fulfillment at work, at home, at play, at worship, at market, or any of the many other distinct domains of modern life does not necessarily translate to success in other domains. The self-regulating give-and-take that is so compelling to liberal analysts of the aggregate population turns out to be less obvious for individuals. The successful pursuit of our individual preferences in each domain does not tell us how to form a coherent sense of these different accomplishments. Ironically, success can burden us with serious doubts about our own identity.[5]

When access to and participation in the institutional domains of work, home, and school are restricted by class, race, ethnicity, nationality, and other kinds of hierarchical social relations, the prospects for a divided self are even greater. While ideological blinders can minimize or even gloss over such differences, many of the urban and community problems that planners seek to remedy are the product of divisive relationships. The consequences of inequality are not evenly distributed, but tend to concentrate both geographically and socially. Efforts to make something of myself and to find fulfillment prove more complex than anticipated.

This collective pursuit of individual fulfillment on uneven social and economic terrain creates frustrating and pervasive problems. All those automobile trips produce unintended congestion, waste, pollution, injury, and storage problems from which we each suffer, but for which no one of us can be held responsible. Some argue that these problems are the temporary and minor side effects of mobility. Those who hold such views, especially those whose purposes are well served by the status quo, dismiss the disenchanted and ridicule the need for democratic planning. Faith in the bond between economic growth and social progress, however, appears increasingly tenuous in the late twentieth century as large corporate and government bureaucracies with enormous power founder and fail.

If we expand the scope and scale of corporate and government authority in hopes of spurring growth and making progress more predictable, many of us would face serious restrictions to our own personal agenda. However, relying solely on our individual skills and initiative places each of us at a profound disadvantage. What can individuals do to change things in the face of such concentrated economic and political power? What sorts of institutions could we use to render the future less uncertain without sacrificing our limited autonomy? These are the questions planners try to answer, not only for others, but also for themselves.

PROFESSIONAL PLANNING AS A REFORM TRADITION

Like Tim and Fred, most professional planners undertake their work as a moral journey—a vocation rather than an occupation. They offer a necessary and important service, but often to a largely unsympathetic clientele. Most find ways to adapt public planning to the constraints inherent to institutions and organizations, compromising planning's holistic claims about reducing and redistributing the burdens of uncertainty. This is a difficult task for professionals. In reaction to their institutional weakness, planners seek respect—a quest that many hope to satisfy through their expertise and prowess in one form or another, perhaps unaware of the irony of their quest. Many adopt the reassuring concept of functional inevitability, offered by theorists like Branch, which reduces the liberal paradox to a one-way road leading from rational professional to needy consumer. However, the lumpy and risky qualities of practice and the ambivalence practitioners witness as they try both to be right and do good make such efforts self-defeating in the long run.

Many neoconservatives argue that do-good professionals, whose positions proliferated over the past forty years with the expansion of government employment during the growth of the welfare state, instituted misguided policies and fostered perverse self-serving programs. The neoconservatives are wrong. Government programs produced paradoxical and perverse outcomes, not because of the machinations of a new class of professionals that includes planners, but because of the tensions that accompanied capitalist expansion and social development in the United States. Planners have an elaborate toolkit for handling some of these tensions, but the lack of political authority and popular support made proper and careful use of these tools much too rare to wreak so much damage. Planners sometimes produced plans that failed and even occasionally backfired, but more often than not their advice went unnoticed or unheeded. Professional planners have been as much victims of social change as the neoconservatives imagine themselves to be.

I am writing about professional planners rather than the general activity of planning because I want to describe and evaluate what people do who choose to be part of a particular reform tradition. I am writing about the professional planners who want to inform and serve the public, defined as being more inclusive than the officials, employees, and clients of particular organizations. Millions of people, working as developers, engineers, managers, politicians, contractors, builders, bankers, investors, and realtors, make decisions and take actions that produce settlements, distribute goods, and offer services. They make plans for themselves or their organizations. The independent pursuit of individual and organizational plans in the marketplace and elsewhere does not always yield beneficial social consequences. Even if we presume consensus about what counts as beneficial, inefficiencies, externalities, and inequalities often result that few want, but many endure. Professional planners in liberal societies deserve study because they try to anticipate and remedy what the multitude of individual and organizational plans frequently ignore—the social and public problems generated by the pursuit of private plans.

METHOD AND OVERVIEW

During 1990 and 1991, I interviewed and observed thirty-two planners. Three participants dropped out after the initial interviews. I have not included their stories. All but two of the complete group were alumni of the School of Urban Planning and Policy at the University of Illinois at Chicago; two-thirds were former students. I did not sample. However, I selected planners from different sectors (private, public, not-for-profit); at different scales (national, regional, central city, suburb, small town);

and in different functions (transportation, environment, land use, housing, economic development, and regulation). In addition, I included a disproportionate share of women (ten) and minorities (three African-Americans and three Hispanics), relative to their share of the professional planning population, on the supposition that sex, race, or ethnic discrimination might affect how these groups would discuss and perform their work.[6]

I would explain to the subjects that my purpose was to study what planners do. I would then promise anonymity.[7] I defined planning: the use of reason and understanding to reduce collective uncertainty about the future. I asked the subjects to give their views on planning and the public good, planning and politics, and the relationship between professional autonomy and responsibility. I would occasionally probe for more details, especially about their feelings and actions in particular episodes they considered important. These details illustrated situations that were typical, difficult, successful, unsuccessful, or indicative of their ambitions.

After the interview, I would schedule an observation in which the planners would be interacting and communicating with staff, citizens, or officials. I asked the subjects to choose a situation in which they would be the central actor. Occasionally I went to several events in a single day, but I did not conduct in-depth sustained ethnographic research. My observations follow the methods used by Patsy Healey in her research on a day in the life of a planner in Britain (Healey 1992). I did not tape record conversations. I took detailed notes, but did not keep a detailed log of every meeting, conversation, and event. I selectively recorded conversations and events that addressed the relationships among politics, planning, and the public interest.

Upon completing a draft of a chapter, I sent a copy to the featured participants. I asked them to make sure that my efforts at protecting their anonymity were successful and that the relevant facts of their interview stories were correct. I invited them to offer commentary on my interpretation of their stories and work. Some offered useful suggestions for protecting their anonymity. Only a few commented on my interpretations. I have included these comments either parenthetically or in footnotes. I had expected more disagreement and criticism from participants. Although I purposely wrote sympathetic and faithful accounts of what the planners did, some of the stories are not flattering. While I had a collegial and cordial relationship with all the participants (including the three who withdrew), most were not close friends.

My selection of participants was purposeful from the outset. I had no intention of drawing inferences from the interviews and observations of the participants as representatives of the larger universe of professional planners. I had initially imagined conducting a more detailed and structured content analysis. However, my early field work experience convinced me to give up trying to analyze the words and deeds of the respondents using conventional analytical techniques (see Hoch 1988). Instead of trying to record and recast the ideas, beliefs, and events that I witnessed according to a set of predetermined categories, I tried to make sense of their words and actions by composing stories (Coles 1989). The crucial research questions I asked were: How do planners cope in their work with the competing claims of individual autonomy and social responsibility? How do they deal with the moral and political relationships that dominate planning in a liberal society? How do they describe their experiences, justify their actions, and make sense of their work as planners seeking to serve the public interest through their professional skills and talents?

My analysis and interpretation methods draw on the important empirical work of John Forester (1989), Peter Marris (1974; 1982b), Donald Schon (1982; 1983), and Howell Baum (1983a; 1987). Using detailed notes, interview records, and observations, I constructed stories of practice, which describe and evaluate how planners interpret, cope with, and justify what they do.

I urged respondents to tell stories about the relationship between planning and politics that focused on their identity as planners. I wanted them to relate episodes that illustrated meaningful practice and how they made sense of it. What sort of stories did they make up, not only for me, but for others? What sort of character did they become in the story and who was their audience? Of course, in the interviews I was the audience, but each participant spoke with me in a distinct fashion. Each relationship was different. Did I trust them? Yes, even though the events they narrated probably did not unfold just as they claimed. Our memories select and shape our accounts of past events. I expected the participants to do this and had no desire to adopt methodological schemes to get the real story. My observations were not a skeptical check on the participants' narrative accounts, but rather were a way to capture some of the complex detail of the social and political relationships of each planner's work.

I did not pay special attention to particular planning policies, programs, or strategies that the participants used and described. I focused instead on the actions the participants took and their account of these actions. Because context (e.g., regional planner or municipal planner) and content (e.g., transportation or zoning) greatly affect the actions planners take, I include information on these distinctions, but leave them in the background. I emphasize the relationship between the planner and these elements, not the elements themselves.

Storytelling as a research device has several desirable qualities. First, the open interviews enabled the planners to fashion their own account of what they do. The interviews and observations were not an imposition, but rather provided an opportunity for the participants to take stock of their careers. Many described their planning activity in the context of a brief personal history. Rarely did anyone offer heroic accounts of great deeds. Most described not just what they did, but who they were. Second, the stories provide the sorts of details the reader needs to grasp the meaning of individual action in particular contexts. Readers can form judgments about the merits and efficacy of what each planner said and did by attending to the details in light of their own experiences.

Each story explores how practitioners address issues of power, politics, and persuasion in their efforts to use their professional autonomy and craft to pursue the public good. The book will disappoint readers seeking an inventory of activities and strategies that promise more and better results on the job. I avoid toolkit talk because it tends to overemphasize the instrumental powers of individual planners. The efficacy of planning craft involves political and organizational savvy, as well as technical skill. I wrote the book for students curious and worried about doing professional work: Will I lose my ideals? Can I make a difference? What will happen to me after five years in a public bureaucracy? I wrote the book for practitioners reflecting on their work, having doubts, feeling alone, and perhaps facing political pressure and threats: The plan I worked on for years was shelved, am I a failure? What's the use? Am I beating my head against a brick wall? Does anyone else doing this job face what I'm facing? How can such a simple thing as (fill in the blank) get so complicated and generate so much political heat? Why don't people respect my profession and honor what I do?

Part 1 of this book argues that professional planning and planners rarely face a supportive audience. Most officials, lobbyists, advocates, and citizens who encounter professional planning ignore or tolerate its presence, but a growing number express hostility and contempt. The enemies of planning enjoy a variety of cultural and institutional supports that professional planners have long sought, but have rarely received. Professional planning in the United States has long endured a precarious institutional standing. Chapter 2 details how twentieth-century efforts to institutionalize planning as a powerful function of government in the United States have been largely unsuccessful.

What do planners do in the face of such obstacles? Part 2 addresses this question through planners' stories. Chapter 3 considers the implications of the institutional dilemmas professional planners face. What sorts of political threats do planners face when they do their jobs? How do planners respond to the often ambiguous, self-centered, and conflicting demands of the public comprised of planning commissioners, city council officials, mayors, city managers, other department heads, and advocacy groups? Many planners adopt the rational protocol of expertise to protect them from political conflict, but this strategy may not be fully effective. Warfare in the trenches inflicts heavy casualties on planners who do not possess much in the way of political artillery and whose protective rhetoric discourages the political and social reciprocity needed to negotiate a cease-fire.

The next three chapters reflect the major elements of the professional planning process: research (chapter 4), plan making (chapter 5), and regulation (chapter 6). The next chapters go beyond the bounds of conventional professional practice to discuss how planners engage in negotiation (chapter 7) and organizing (chapter 8) and cope with racism (chapter 9). The stories in each chapter point to modest, but important, accomplishments when understood within the context of planning's cultural marginality and political weakness. Some planners in the trenches carry on better than others, but they all seek to do good for others. How they do this merits close attention.

The stories I tell provide positive examples of public service based on individual resistance and innovation in difficult circumstances. The diverse ways in which planners conduct and interpret some of the most commonplace planning activities should give reason for hope among even hard-core cynics. There are many ways planners can do their jobs. We need not worry about neoconservative criticisms. The planners I interviewed and observed were neither dreary, unimaginative bureaucrats nor power mongers serving the state. They represent a variety of organizations, some small and some large, but very few of the planners identified with their occupational role. Most pushed against the margins of institutional constraint and political custom, some on their own, others in collaboration.

Were they effective? Do these planners really plan well? It all depends on your point of view. The entire book argues for the value of what these planners attempt to do. I tried to avoid classifying the participants, although I wrote their stories with an emphasis on how they cope with some of the salient paradoxes of planning practice. The comparisons and conclusions I make about different beliefs and actions are based on the pragmatic tenets I hold. I did not use a uniform standard, however, to frame comparisons. I tried to provide enough detail in each account to allow careful and critical readers to draw their own conclusions about the meaning of particular episodes and interviews.

There are many forms of success because there are many sets of standards. Some planning professionals, analysts, and theorists, in their efforts to make planning appear more credible, have argued for uniform standards and theory to guide practice. I do not support this effort. Useful and meaningful planning can take many forms, fit many contexts, and serve many different kinds of clients without losing its coherence and authority. This coherence requires, however, that the kind of planning that professionals do become a more widespread and popular practice.

In part 3, I reflect on planning research and theory. What information and insights do these planning stories offer concerning good planning practice? Chapter 10 reviews studies of planning effectiveness in the United States conducted over the past half-century. Research expectations and methods have changed in response to the rapid and uneven institutional growth of planning. During the twenty years (1954–1974) of greatest planning employment growth, case study and survey research found few plans or planners meeting the demands of rational comprehensive planning. Planners were busy making plans that few read and giving rational advice that few followed. The rational model became a casualty of the search for efficacy. Chapter 11 tells how the criticisms of a growing cadre of skeptical planning academics in the 1970s and 1980s undermined the theoretical belief in the efficacy of rational planning, while simultaneously practitioners were adapting the elements of the rational model to serve as the basic protocol for professional planning.

The book's conclusion describes the relationship between craft, character, and community, which forms the nucleus of planning practice. The behavior and beliefs of the planners whose stories I tell offer practical lessons on the arts of resistance, innovation, and persuasion in the bureaucratic trenches of local government and politics. Although efforts to reshape the social, political, economic, and cultural landscape of neighborhoods, cities, and regions are limited by institutional obstacles and misleading professional beliefs, these good public works are neither unimportant nor trivial.

To overcome the institutional and cultural limits on their work professional planners will need to revise their beliefs to enhance the value of political and social collaboration in their work. Planners should embrace and foster democratic planning, which requires public support strong enough to challenge the institutional and cultural marginality of contemporary professional planning. Professional planners should join the public in making this challenge, but as political participants, not as objective experts. Planners should no longer treat the problems of liberal society as paradoxes they can master. Rather, they need to find better ways to invent and expand the repertoire of democratic responses to the externalities, inefficiencies, and inequalities that our society produces. However, neither a cadre of professionals nor the university intelligentsia can script these ways ahead of time.

For plans to take hold, they need be thought up and tried out by a democratic community of experts and citizens—those who will put them into practice and bear their consequences. The stories in this book show how a variety of U.S. planners are doing just this. Making planning more effective, popular, and widespread will require a significant redistribution of resources, power, status, and respect and the democratic reform of organizational life. Professional planners can play a small, but important part in this larger drama.

NOTES

1. In this respect, Tim believes that the moral judgments guiding physical design should be primarily aesthetic. He also projects an American version of romantic individualism: the heroic designer standing up to the self-serving interests of vote-counting elected officials, money-grubbing developers, and dissembling lawyers.

2. In this respect, I differ from the postmodern critics of planning (Boyer 1983; Ligget 1991; Milroy 1991), who emphasize that planners perpetuate relations of domination and subjection with the public in their efforts to do good. See my essays on planning and power (Hoch 1990; 1992). I also disagree with those critics on the right who blame

planners for all sorts of problems associated with government intervention. A good critique of the conservative position is Albert Hirschman's *The Rhetoric of Reaction* (1991). Mary Hommans in her *City Planning in America* (1993) takes a similar tack as I do on the institutional obstacles to planning, but then spends much of her book trashing planners.

3. My communitarian sympathies are showing here. I do not believe for a minute that Americans always act on the basis of this individualism. I agree with Bellah et al. (1985; 1991) that possessive individualism represents the major ideological voice, while other competing notions of shared responsibility and community remain secondary, but important. The challenge for planners is to identify these notions and tap them as a source of legitimacy and support for what they do.

4. I am offering here a simple version of liberal belief that critics like Bellah et al. (1985) characterize as an undesirable and inappropriate form of possessive individualism. The institutional reality offers a more complex assortment of ideas and beliefs. Herbert Gans (1991) offers a contemporary sociological assessment of these ideas as held by the American middle class. Theodore Lowi (1979) conducts a compelling political review of interest group liberalism in government institutions. My own views reflect what Charles Anderson calls pragmatic liberalism:

Orthodox liberalism holds that performance is best enhanced by stimulating competition among individuals. Pragmatic liberalism believes that creative effort is naturally collaborative and cooperative and is best promoted by systematic deliberation and argument about the purposes, practices, and responsibilities of a cooperative undertaking. For pragmatic liberalism, such discussion is necessarily a public matter, and it calls for the exercise of practical political reason (1990, 4).

5. Conservatives have long complained about the burdens or handicaps of liberal individualism, using the perversity argument. The free choices individuals make ensnare them. See Hirschman (1991) for a delightful critique of conservative rhetoric. I have deep sympathies for liberal values, but only if they are tamed by communitarian values. See Fowler (1991) for a sample of communitarian critiques of liberalism.

6. I did not specifically probe for racial or gender issues. In speaking about the relationship between planning and politics, minority planners referred to their experiences with racial and ethnic injustice. I describe many of these in chapter 9. However, the women I spoke with seldom offered such stories. They did not frame their accounts in terms of gender differences. I suspect my being male may have discouraged them from taking this avenue of interpretation, but it may also reflect the profession's not

having yet taken a clear position on gender equality in planning employment and education, in spite of the profession's long-proclaimed strong stance against racism. The women may not have been exposed to the concepts of gender equality to be able to give voice to their experiences and may worry about the legitimacy of their complaints in public settings. In any event, the absence of such stories here does not mean that gender differences do not matter in the conduct of planning, but rather that my method fell short of capturing these experiences.

7. I changed the names of the respondents, significant coworkers, and, where relevant, the type of agency. The final manuscript included stories for twenty-four of the twenty-nine participants.

2

The Quest for Institutional Authority

Liberal governments cannot plan. Planning requires the authoritative use of authority. Planning requires law, choice, priorities, moralities. Liberalism replaces planning with bargaining. Yet at bottom, power is unacceptable without planning (Lowi 1979, 67).

PLANNING AS A PROFESSIONAL REFORM MOVEMENT

Planning in twentieth-century America emerged as a derivative professional activity. Architects, landscape architects, and engineers developed schemes for the physical improvement of cities in service to Progressive reform. Muckrakers dramatized the injustices and inefficiencies of rapid city growth and perceived these urban problems to be susceptible to treatment and reform. Reform advocates politicized efforts to solve these problems as elements of a moral crusade. Reform-oriented design professionals defined these urban problems as objects of physical improvement.[1] Some professionals advanced the efficacy of playgrounds, parks, monuments, civic buildings, and parkways as uplifting reprieves from industrial squalor. Others focused on the redesign and redevelopment of slum housing to reduce the density and congestion of urban life for the poor. Increasing numbers of professionals focused on the design and provision of regional and local infrastructure that would increase the efficiency and predictability of the interdependencies and externalities generated by the growth of the industrial city.

The design professionals, however, soon realized the limits of their craft. The rapid growth of the industrial cities of the United States, set by the tempo of a relatively unconstrained capitalist economy, had overwhelmed the capacity of local governments to maintain order and relieve social distress. The first National Conference on City Planning in 1909 was an offshoot of a series of earlier conferences on the problems of urban congestion. The speakers did not offer disciplinary techniques, but rather discussed the practical issues of taming speculation and instituting government reforms to improve prosperity for all Americans. Benjamin Marsh, Frederick Law Olmsted, and John Nolen drew on European forms of city governance as models for taming and directing the excesses of American laissez-faire capitalism. These reformers believed that executing plans capable of anticipating the fragmented interdependencies of city growth, of relieving congestion, and of promoting order required strong public authority. The notion, however, of a civic public interest that bound together the prosperous and the poor, the newcomer and the native, and the center and periphery challenged popular American notions of social and economic individualism. Planning reforms were part of the larger Progressive movement seeking to change the institutions of government to prevent partisan politics from organizing the governance of municipalities (Hays 1964; Hofstadter 1955; Weinstein 1968).

All planning histories of the Progressive era acknowledge the tension between the planners' notion of a deliberately designed civic order and the prevailing concept of the public good emerging from the sum of competing interests (Boyer 1983; Fogelsong 1986; Hall 1988; Scott 1969). The more militant proponents of city planning began to abandon the profession as its members focused more on the elements of craft and design in service to efficient commerce, rather than on social improvement. The major models of city planning at that time were sponsored not by government, but by business and philanthropic organizations.

For example, Burnham's Plan for Chicago was financed by the city's commercial leaders who recognized the economic benefits of publicly planned and funded transportation and infrastructure improvements (Burnham and Bennett 1909). Organized business offered to support planning consultants who could provide schemes to improve the flow of goods, lay out parks, reduce land use conflicts, and otherwise rationalize the physical order of city growth to protect property and enhance its economic and social value. The radical planning schemes urging slum clearance, worker housing, garden cities, and other redistributive reforms that challenged the primacy of private property went unsupported, even within the profession (Kravitz 1970; Marsh 1953).

Planning professionals after World War I worked hard to turn local boosters' hopes for increased growth and prosperity into a practical reality (Ackerman 1919; Beard 1927; Walker 1941). Patronage and support for planning by philanthropy and business not only promoted a conservative profession, but one removed from politics.

PROFESSIONAL PLANNING AS CIVIC EXPERTISE

The government adoption of planning occurred piecemeal with the development of the more technical aspects of the profession. Planners celebrated New York City's adoption of zoning as a professional victory: Government regulation of commercial space reduced the contentiousness of land development conflicts among industrial and commercial property owners by making land use more predictable. As Marsh and Olmsted had anticipated, zoning could be an instrument for taming the urban speculation of the few to increase the overall gains of the many. City planning spread throughout the United States in the 1920s with the passage of local zoning ordinances and the adoption of local planning commissions. The Department of Commerce, directed by Republican Herbert Hoover, developed model zoning and subdivision ordinances and distributed them to the nation's cities. By 1927, 525 cities had adopted zoning ordinances, while 390 had planning commissions (Scott 1969, 248–49).

Zoning and subdivision ordinances proved a mixed blessing. Initially greeted with enthusiasm by professional planners seeking government powers to implement their plans, these regulations soon became a formidable block to comprehensive planning. Local political officials, developers, bankers, and real estate investors concentrated their energies on using the zoning and subdivision ordinances to protect and enhance the land values of property owners, rather than on supporting the development and implementation of a city master plan.

The local planning commissions, however, offered more hope to comprehensive planning. Municipal officials were to appoint to the commissions citizens with relevant expertise. Ideally these were not to be political patronage appointments. The independent commission reflected the Progressive reformers' mistrust of electoral politics and their respect for the powers of municipal government. Reformers hoped the independent commissions would use the expertise of their members to compose and review plans for local government jurisdictions—mainly municipalities and counties. The planning commission device institutionalized planning expertise within local government, independent of partisan electoral politics. However, it also institutionalized moral and ideological splits between elected officials and professional experts.

During the economic boom of the 1920s, the independent planning consultants and planning commissioners with their Progressive era confidence in the master plan and zoning played well. The reforms that planners advanced enjoyed support as the links between the popular Progressive political movement and the profession legitimized the spread of practical expertise about how to organize the geographic and physical form of city development. Other design professionals studied the proposed master plans to understand how to order and arrange the flow and distribution of future urban development. The professionals were bound together by a reform movement based on a shared concern for the future provision of the city and a body of knowledge accumulated through conferences and research bureaus. The integrity of planning seemed ensured. Only the independent planning expert could compose a master plan, based on the latest scientific knowledge, to guide future physical development. The epitome was the creation of the *Regional Plan for New York*. Experienced architects, landscape architects, and engineers, working under the guidance of engineer Thomas Adams, spent years preparing a multivolume plan designed to promote, channel, and accommodate the seemingly endless waves of urban development rippling outward from the nation's mightiest metropolis (Adams 1927; Mumford 1932).

PROFESSIONAL PLANNING AS A GOVERNMENT FUNCTION

In the early decades of the twentieth century, planning for settlements had expanded primarily as an activity to coordinate and order the physical arrangement of growing places. With the deep economic decline of the Depression, the instruments of the growth-oriented city planning movement—the master plan, zoning, and subdivision regulations—were not so much ineffective as irrelevant.

During the New Deal years a new thrust in planning emerged among the expert advisers of the newly elected President Roosevelt. His brain trust's leadership in developing government housing and resource conservation programs signified a direct intervention into what had been the exclusive domain of corporations and private investors. In the crisis setting of the Depression, planning as independent expertise was usurped

by planning as the product of political advisers drawn from among public employees and professional experts. Planning activity became an extension of executive authority—a staff activity that focused on policy
and institutional design, rather than a line activity organized to implement established goals. Planning as a federal government activity gained
not only power, but scope. Through the purposeful allocation of resources
to alleviate economic and social distress, federal planners began to challenge the authority and direct the activities of market institutions, which
in the past had been rarely touched by local planning commissions. Federal planners proposed and developed housing, redevelopment, and new
town schemes that required government deployment of eminent domain
to take private property for public purposes. The design, construction,
and management of projects became centered within government.

Ironically, as Charles Abrams (1967) observed, local chambers of commerce, city and county officials, and Southern senators who had been
champions of states' rights in more prosperous times came to the defense of federally funded and managed projects. Unable to cope with the
economic distress of the Depression, former opponents of an active federal government became its champions. Federal land condemnation,
however, was challenged by property owners. The lower courts ruled
that federal condemnation was an intrusion on state authority. In many
cases the Supreme Court upheld these decisions, which further limited
direct federal involvement despite the support of hard-pressed state and
local officials. The federal government eventually withdrew from direct
involvement in the building of new towns and in the redevelopment of
slums (Abrams 1967).

Blocked by court order from using federal authority to design and develop housing and new town projects, Roosevelt's appointed planning
officials found ways to work with state authority. For example, New York
State passed enabling legislation creating the New York City Housing
Authority, which served as the conduit for federal funds to produce low-
cost housing. As a state agency, the housing authority successfully faced
legal challenges to its use of eminent domain. In 1937 Congress passed
legislation forming the United States Housing Authority, which allowed
the federal government to play the roll of underwriter, while local authorities acquired land and built projects (Abrams 1967, 245–46).

The impact of the New Deal federal policies continued after World War
II. They channeled the enormous postwar growth in the U.S. economy
through policies that indirectly subsidized the decentralization of cities

and the renewal of older central cities and directly subsidized planning. The unprecedented federal investment in professional planning generated an enormous increase in the number of people engaged in planning and in the scope and intensity of their activities. The spread of planning as a legitimate government function did not, however, guarantee its adoption, as in the Depression years at the federal level, as a form of local executive authority.

THE GROWTH OF LOCAL GOVERNMENTS AND PLANNING

Professional city planning as a government activity grew only slightly during the 1930s and 1940s. With the federal government's metropolitan investment after World War II, municipal officials once again began to plan. The federal government used funds to subsidize state and local development of new infrastructure and housing on the periphery of metropolitan regions. This distant, but generous federal government fostered the rapid geographic expansion of urban development (Scott 1969, 452–67; ULI 1940).

The federal government's court-enforced abdication of involvement in the acquisition and development of public housing and new towns in the early years of the New Deal left to local governments the location, design, and construction of federally subsidized urban infrastructure and housing. Efforts to plan coherently and comprehensively these federally sponsored public works, especially within metropolitan regions, were seriously compromised as each local government pursued its own purposes without serious regard for its neighbors' plans. The federal government could threaten negative sanctions, but congressional representatives were keenly interested in maintaining the flow of federal funds to their local constituencies.

Federal subsidies and agency policies inadvertently stimulated the expansion of local government. Developers, farmers, industrialists, chambers of commerce, and others with land interests pressured, manipulated, and even formed local governments to acquire municipal services and to protect their property investments. In many cases, federal and state growth subsidies reduced the costs of forming new governments and provided unexpected windfalls as well. Newly incorporated suburban municipalities competed with their older neighbors to annex territory made valuable by the same subsidized infrastructure improvements that made living in and commuting from the suburbs an attractive alternative. Local land use regulations made possible the exclusion of undesirable industrial, commercial, and residential development, such as polluting industry and housing that might attract lower class or minority tenants. Municipalities offered local elites taxation and police authority, which they used to compete with one another to attract economic growth and exclude socially undesirable residents (Danielson 1976; Woods 1961).

Between 1950 and 1970, of the 1,881 newly incorporated municipalities in the United States, the vast majority were suburbs. This rate of incorporation was five times greater than between 1930 and 1950. Central cities in the South and West mobilized aggressive annexation campaigns, but suburban municipalities did the same. A comparison of annexation activity by large suburbs (50,000 or more residents) and central cities for all 260 Standard Metropolitan Statistical Areas between 1950 and 1970 shows that suburban municipalities were winning the battle for territory. The large suburbs increased their area by 74 percent and their populations by 174 percent, while the territory of central cities grew only 18 percent with a population increase of 105 percent (Forstall 1976). Large suburbs, however, were not the only municipalities that annexed territory. In 1970, 1,471 suburban municipalities with populations greater than 2,500 reported making 4,496 annexations in the United States, adding 672 square miles of new territory (Forstall 1975). Politicians and officials from these growing suburban municipalities mobilized local demands for more and better public services. In many cases, the push for expanded municipal services meant a larger role for planning.

The fiscal disparity between the aging central cities of the Northeast and Midwest and their growing suburbs was accelerated by the geographic distribution of intergovernmental grants-in-aid from federal and state sources.[2] For instance, large portions of federal urban renewal and public housing funds went to the older central cities, while federal funds for highway, water, and sewer construction subsidized the growth of new suburban communities. State and federal aid to cities grew from $491 million in 1942 to $11.4 billion in 1972. Municipalities, especially older central cities, came to rely on intergovernmental transfers, doubling their reliance on such revenue from 15 percent in 1942 to 33 percent by 1972 (Pettergill and Uppal 1974, 118).

Federal and state government policies successfully accelerated what Mark Gottdeiner (1985) calls the deconcentration of urban growth and the redevelopment of select pockets of desirable central city real estate. The numerous local governments in decentralizing metropolitan regions created a competitive and complex political environment for capturing the territorial benefits of the expanding federal grants economy. This competition increased the number and intensity of fiscal disparities and land use disputes among local governments, especially between the central city and the suburbs. In effect, the New Deal planning innovations and compromises had inadvertently fostered a public grants economy that legitimized and enhanced local government power. Planning analysts and reformers in the late 1950s and early 1960s criticized the arrangement and its consequences, which they referred to as "the metropolitan problem." They urged greater federal oversight and authority. Many offered and supported the formation of metropolitan regional governments with authority to overrule local municipalities on land use issues in the region.

Planning analyst Charles Abrams called for federal authority over urban and suburban development projects. He did not expect that federal control would prove more efficient than local government control, but

> it would have had more comprehensive jurisdiction over the nation's regions and would have been free of the petty jurisdictional limitations they prescribed. It would have made or influenced better plans for the millions of acres now sprawling throughout suburbia. By offering each jurisdiction the right to build or not to build but asserting the right to do so itself if the jurisdiction refused, it would have retained concurrent authority over the national environment and been better posed to foster its proper development, either through public or private mechanisms. It would have been able to fill the gaps where housing and new cities were needed and where it did so, dispose of it to the states or local governments. The possession of the power would, in fact, have brought better cooperation and made its exercise essential only in few cases (1967, 248).

Federal Support of Regional Planning

The failure to secure federal direction of the organization of metropolitan growth deeply concerned planning analysts during the period of rapid suburbanization in the 1950s and 1960s. The local disposition of federal funds often betrayed the purposes for which the funds had been allocated. Federal officials perceived that local governments were generating political conflicts and inefficiencies in their piecemeal division of regional opportunities. Planning seemed to offer a promising and relatively inexpensive means of rationalizing the unprecedented growth of metropolitan regions.

Significant federal support for planning came in the form of Section 701 of the 1954 Housing Act, which authorized the Comprehensive Planning Assistance Grant Program. The program subsidized one-half the state's planning costs for cities with fewer than 25,000 people. (Eligibility expanded greatly over the next twenty years.) The program targeted the rapidly growing suburban cities on the metropolitan fringe, complementing the planning support that was going to big city urban renewal efforts as authorized by the Housing Act of 1949. The program proved extremely popular and a boon to the planning profession. By 1959, the federal government was providing one hundred new grants each year, giving a $2 million subsidy to local government–sponsored planning. That amount increased more than twentyfold by 1968, with 1,287 grants totaling $42,945 million (U.S. Department of Housing and Urban Development 1978).

This funding pattern had a tremendous impact on planning employment. In 1949 there were 640 members of the American Institute of Planners (AIP). By 1959 these numbers had more than doubled to 1,771, with enrollment accelerating during the 1960s to reach 4,880 members in 1967 (AIP 1967). Figures on planning employment in local government indicate a similar pattern of rapid growth. The census bureau started counting planners in 1960. Planning analyst Robert Beauregard's study of the census counts shows an even greater increase for the 1960s. Urban and regional planners, who numbered 861 in 1960, had increased almost twelvefold to 9,589 during the decade. This growth was accompanied by a significant shift in occupational composition as the proportion of planners working for government increased from 64 percent to 79 percent (Beauregard 1985). Changes also occurred in the organization of planning activity within and between local governments. "Planning became a legitimate (if ancillary) function of local government deserving ongoing support" (Hoch 1985, 82).

These changes brought conflict. The federal emphasis on planning as a rationalizing and organizing staff function challenged the authority of local officials and threatened the institutional loci of planning in the independent commission. By the 1950s it became obvious that the subordinate institutional location of planning and the highly fragmented nature of local government left planners with little authority to develop and implement comprehensive plans that could prevent or reduce the numerous land use, infrastructure, and fiscal conflicts among local governments within metropolitan regions. Federal officials, concerned with the inefficiency and inequity of fragmented local development, were anxious to rationalize the rapidly expanding grants economy. Planning analysts were more than willing to help out.

The pursuit of comprehensiveness in the production and implementation of plans took center stage in debates about the identity of professional planning among planning educators and analysts in the 1950s and 1960s. Planning theorists offered up a rational model to serve as a scientific guide to both predict and justify professional planning actions within the fragmented, but otherwise benign government institutions of the growing welfare state.

Analysts designed programs that would use the powers of the national government to tame or subvert local government. One such effort was the design of new regional governments to conduct comprehensive planning. These schemes drew on the planning tradition instituted during the New Deal (Walker 1941). Historian Sam Bass Warner expressed little confidence in the ability or willingness of local governments to carry out rational plans:

> The early large scale relief projects struggled against the inherent weakness of America's municipal and state civil service, and much of the confusion of the 1933-1935 New Deal programs came from the lack of sufficient local bureaucracy to carry them out.
>
> Over the years the New Deal put into practice on a national level most of the earlier experiments of local and state government, but because of constitutional limitations the New Dealers had to finance their programs by grants-in-aid to the state, and to administer them by federal supervision of state and local civil servants. The result has been to immerse the federal government in local government and to draw its domestic programs down into the marsh of state and local civil service (1966, 52).

Warner argued that although local governments contribute important innovations, they cannot adequately implement them on a regional or national level. Like many other planners in the late 1950s and early 1960s Warner believed in the importance and efficacy of federally initiated domestic urban development programs. He voiced few doubts about the desirability of planning, but serious concerns about the competence and coherence of local government:

> Since the beginning of the grants-in-aid program for highways in 1916 the federal government has imposed planning and administrative organization upon the cities and states of the nation. It is currently trying to impose land

use, development, and transportation planning upon metropolitan regions. This planning and its planning agencies, however, cannot become effective until they are connected to strong political units. Only the conflicts and partial resolutions of the political process can produce effective plans (1966, 56).

For Warner, effective plans required authorities sufficiently competent and powerful to weather all opposition. Hence, he wanted to make the granting of federal government services and funds dependent on the formation of a metropolitan-wide governing institution with strong taxation and police powers (1966, 53).

Historian Mel Scott expressed little optimism over regional reforms:

> [M]ost professional planners were by temperament or training incapable of fashioning or helping to fashion the regional political forums or legal entities needed to lift regional planning above the level of an academic exercise (1969, 580–81).

Reviewing the formation of regional planning efforts in the Philadelphia, San Francisco, and Minneapolis–St. Paul areas, Scott documents how political squabbles between the growing suburbs and the stagnating central cities undermined the formation of areawide governing authorities with significant planning authority.

In spite of the weakness in regional authority, federal support for regional planning continued to grow. The federal government fostered the creation of regional planning agencies, or councils of government (COGs), to coordinate and regulate the huge number of categorical grants between federal agencies and local governments in metropolitan areas. These agencies were governed by boards composed of local elected officials. Membership and participation were voluntary. Local governments retained their land use powers and could easily defect if regional plans did not reflect their interests. Local and state governments helped fund these agencies, but most of the budget came from federal funds.[3]

The growth of COGs was fueled by the expansion of Section 701 housing eligibility criteria in 1965 to include regional planning agencies. As Scott asserts, federal support for comprehensive planning was widespread:

> Throughout the Kennedy and Johnson administrations much of the pressure upon state and local governments to cooperate in metropolitan planning and to experiment with new metropolitan political mechanisms came from the federal establishment—directly from the Congress and the executive branch

and indirectly from the Supreme Court and lower federal courts. For example, the Congress included in the Federal Aid Highway Act of 1962 a provision that after July 1, 1965, the Secretary of Commerce must not approve aid to highway programs in any urban area of more than 50,000 population unless projects were based on a continuing comprehensive transportation process carried on cooperatively by state and local governments. The effect of this requirement was to precipitate a headlong rush into areawide transportation and land use planning, either under the auspices of agencies with statewide planning authority or new metropolitan or county planning agencies (1969, 585).

The number of COGs engaged in regional planning leaped from 35 to 352 between 1965 and 1972 (ACIR 1974, I, 74). By 1972, these planning agencies averaged fourteen professional employees (ACIR 1974, I, 94–95), almost twice the average of eight professional planners in each municipal planning department for the same year (Harman 1972). In 1965 only 6 percent of professional planners reported working for a regional agency (AIP 1967). By 1977 more than 15 percent reported doing so (Longhini 1980).

Supporters of regional planning authorities believed that the connections between large infrastructure improvements (utilities, transportation routes and facilities, and water and sewer lines) and land development required comprehensive, rationalized control. Local political officials astutely grasped the connection between infrastructure improvements and enhanced land values: Capturing the increase in land value was the prize all hoped to win. They viewed the notion that local suburban municipalities should together provide services for a territorial cluster of residents as the pipe dream of economists and planners. The politics of infrastructure development and municipal formation provoked acrimonious conflict among contestants whose financial, real estate, land development, and political interests made voluntary appeals to territorial unity and comprehensive cooperation ludicrous and efforts at regional reform a serious economic threat. The regional planning efforts of the newly formed COGs exercised only the most minimal regulatory authority. The voluntary nature of most COGs meant that the land use disputes and fiscal mismatches between different local governments could not be addressed without one or more parties defecting.

The astute and experienced analyst Harvey Perloff failed to recognize the blow planning took when efforts at regional government failed. Like many others whose experience and hopes for planning had been shaped by federal programs, Perloff underestimated the impact of planning's subordinate position in local government and overestimated the depth and persistence of federal government support for planning. As late as 1975, when the Nixon Administration had instituted policies to consolidate (and eventually shrink) the federal grants economy while increasing the discretion of local (especially suburban) governments, Perloff could still write about the efficacy and promise of comprehensive planning on a regional scale. He believed that local officials would eventually recognize their interdependence and the costs of pursuing local interests without concern for regional consequences. He believed that planners merely had to make a greater effort to foster this recognition to succeed in strengthening planning within local government (Perloff 1974). How could the hopes of Perloff and many other planning advocates have been so misplaced?

THE PROMISE OF RATIONAL PLANNING

During the 1950s and 1960s, the hope of Progressive reformers that planning function as a part of government became an institutional reality, as federal government program requirements resulted in the formation of thousands of suburban planning departments. Between 1960 and 1970, 20 percent of U.S. municipalities with more than 10,000 residents abandoned exclusive reliance on independent planning commissions and created planning departments (Harman 1972, 55–56). These planning departments were established as line agencies within local county and municipal governments, institutionalizing planning as a functional service like fire, police, and sanitation. Professional planners found legitimacy in the exercise of local government authority over the development of land and the management of decentralized urban growth. Planners used their specialized knowledge to design and justify plans and programs rationalizing the use of government powers to tame the excesses of rapid growth. They worked mainly as public bureaucrats for local governments for whom the application of comprehensive rational plans promised to remove unnecessary conflict, foster consensus, and occasionally garner federal funds.

Briefly during the late 1950s and early 1960s, analysts celebrated the functional integration of planning. For example, Norman Beckman described the dutiful planner bureaucrat, who could be both a rational planning professional and public servant without experiencing any conflict (1964). Powerful planners and an empowered profession could overcome the ineffectiveness imposed by unnecessary but pervasive political obstacles to fair and efficient urban development and growth. The gap between politics and the public good could be bridged (Webber 1973).

Confidence in the efficacy of rational intervention had long been part of the reform tradition that developed earlier in the century and was institutionalized by the federal administration as part of Roosevelt's New Deal. The new development of the 1950s and 1960s was a rationale justifying state-sponsored planning reform: The rational planning model claimed to link professional expertise and bureaucratic authority in the service of a democratically determined public interest. In the context of rapid growth and strong federal support for government planning, the rational model became the premiere rationale for professional planning practice.

Professional planning, however, did not become more powerful. As a government staff function, planning does not provide a direct service to citizens, but rather develops information and advice for the city manager, mayor, and governing board. Such advice shares the same standing as that from other government departments. Planners find that instead of coordinating the multiple functions of government to meet citywide development objectives, their expertise is relegated to its own organizational niche, competing for attention with the priorities and plans of other department heads. City managers and mayors are under little institutional pressure to rely on planners and their plans to coordinate the work of city departments. Although planning departments officially claim to serve a municipal staff function, specialized line functions tend to define their practical sphere of authority (Dalton 1985; Spencer 1979).

The activities professional planners could conduct with some discretion were the zoning and subdivision of land, which most older municipalities had administered for years without a planning department or professional planners. More complex development standards and proposals and escalating public expectations outstripped the capacity of independent commissions to respond to these demands and of professional planners to meet the challenge. Employed in a line department in local government, planners perceived themselves to be insufficiently empowered to prepare the comprehensive plans that would meet federal and state mandates for municipal and regional coordination and control. George Hemmens states:

> [T]he federal mandates for comprehensiveness through the 701 programs for small towns, urban renewal and model cities in the big cities, and metro-

politan wide land use and transportation planning were all impossible under this structure. Local governments expected planners to staff the independent planning commission, but hired them in regulatory and administrative line positions. Planners expected to move up to a staff role on the inside and continue working from the outside through the planning commission. A mess! (Personal communication 1991).

The rational model of planning joined in theory what remained separated in practice: private interest and public good. Whereas Perloff (1974) was arguing forcefully that local governments should use planning in both staff and line departments, planning was developing almost exclusively into a regulatory line function of local government.

The growing ranks of liberal public planners generously tolerated the few dissenting voices. The old guard patrician planners who had worked as consultants celebrated the commitment to comprehensive rational planning, but warned about its institutionalization in local government. Ladislaus Segoe, speaking at the 1964 American Society of Planning Officials (ASPO) convention, praised the widespread adoption of planning, but complained that government employment of planners

> introduced or induced certain attitudes and practices—incident to the rules, procedures and their administration in some states—which are at variance with recognized professional-client relationships and which are also tending to erode our professional status (1964, 103).

Segoe felt that government rules and policies undermined the autonomy and discretion of the professional planner and frustrated the deployment of the expert knowledge needed to meet community needs. Effective community-serving expertise required detachment from the political interests that shaped the organization of government.

Advocate planners criticized their liberal colleagues, but for different reasons. The advocates claimed that government planners honored bureaucratic commitments that served the interests of the powerful and ignored the needs of the powerless. The left-wing critics argued that planning's primary thrust must be the implementation of egalitarian values. Planners should take their liberalism seriously and use comprehensive rational planning to identify and meet the needs of the poor and disenfranchised (Davidoff 1965). To the advocate planners comprehensive planning referred to social as well as geographic inclusiveness.

The proponents and critics of rational planning by government agencies actually shared a sense of confidence in its efficacy. This confidence faltered in the 1970s when the growth of the profession slowed and planning came under ideological attack from conservatives at the national level. Debates among liberals, traditionalists, and advocates over organizational and political choices for planning practitioners would continue, but they would no longer use the language of institutional reform. Rational planning became the subject of abstract theoretical debate among planning theorists and analysts seeking to make sense of an increasingly frustrated practice (Hall 1988).

THE DECLINE OF PLANNING IN THE U.S.

The successful expansion of rational comprehensive planning among all government agencies in the 1960s was tied closely to administrative and fiscal support for planning at the federal level. With the energy and economic crises of the 1970s and 1980s planning proved vulnerable to cutbacks, especially at the regional level. The growing consolidation and power of global corporate enterprises further undermined the strength of the federal government, which for decades the public had come to expect would deliver more and better public goods at a cheaper price.

Republican-initiated reforms in the federal grants system consolidated numerous programs into a revenue sharing scheme that reduced the need for regional coordination. The consolidation resulted in cutbacks in many grants programs that had supported planning. Funding for Section 701 declined in the late 1970s and was eventually eliminated by the Reagan Administration in 1981. The proportion of planners who reported working for regional agencies dropped to 8.5 percent by 1981 and to 6 percent by 1989 (Hecimovich 1983; 1989). During the 1980s federal policy discouraged and actively rejected many of the ideas and policies long associated with comprehensive rational planning, which reduced government employment opportunities for professional planners. Whereas 72 percent of professional planners reported working for government in 1977, only 64 percent reported doing so in 1981 (Hecimovich 1983). The drop was not permanent. The real estate boom of the 1980s returned the share of public sector planners to the 1977 level by 1991 (Morris 1992).

Enrollments in planning schools peaked in 1975 and then dropped off (Krueckeberg 1984), reducing growth in the number of graduates and professional planners. Throughout the 1960s and 1970s newcomers to the profession had kept the proportion of inexperienced planners rela-

Table 2.1—Percentage Distribution of Years of Professional Planning Experience

Number of Years	1965	1977	1981	1989	1991
Less than 5	37%	33%	27%	19%	16%
5 to 10 Years	30	35	38	28	23
More than 10	33	32	35	53	60

Source: AIP 1967; Hecimovich 1983; 1989; Morris 1992.

tively high, but during the 1980s this figure dropped precipitously (see Table 2.1). Survey reports from graduates of planning programs suggest that the proportion working in the public sector may be much lower for newcomers to the job market than for veteran planners. Only 53 percent of the new graduates reported working in the public sector (Glasmier and Kahn 1989). If, as seems likely, public sector planners are more likely to join the American Planning Association (APA) than planners working in the nonprofit and for-profit sectors, APA's membership list of planners working in the public sector may overstate the actual share. The decline in the proportion of newcomers in APA ranks may reflect a tendency among planning graduates to work in sectors for which membership in the public sector–oriented APA offers few benefits.

DISENCHANTMENT WITH THE LIBERAL WELFARE STATE

The election of conservative Republican regimes in the 1980s indicated a revival of classical liberal ideology and the discrediting of the interest group liberalism that had propelled the growth of the welfare state and planning. The proliferation of specialized bureaucracies and programs at all levels of government to meet the needs and interests of different clienteles had greatly increased the size of the public sector and its budgets. Social protests for civil rights, the alleviation of poverty, and the removal of environmental pollutants had wrung concessions from liberal regimes (both Democratic and Republican), which had implicitly promised to alleviate the injustices of capitalist society. These same regimes remained, however, deeply tied to the growth of the capitalist economy and fostered programs to support and subsidize the economic growth of entire industries.

Welfarists shared with marketeers a commitment to the priority of economic growth. The welfare state cannot accumulate the revenues it needs to redress the adverse effects of private enterprise unless the private system provides it with a large tax dividend; and the tax dividend depends on the success of economic expansion in the private sector. The welfare state is thus deeply dependent on the system it seeks to regulate; it must subsidize and nourish the private economy while it strives to tame and regulate it (Connoly 1987, 19).

With the lags in economic growth in the 1970s and the resulting fiscal crisis, many middle- and working-class taxpayers began to doubt the legitimacy of government initiatives. They no longer saw federal initiatives as reforms designed to rectify injustices, but as political payoffs to organized special interests. Americans expected the federal government to ensure their economic security, but at the same time they resisted the burden of increased taxes. Their resentment over cutbacks in programs from which they benefited caused them to question the legitimacy of the entire enterprise. Government officials responded by making cuts in public budgets. Planning was hit hard.

> In 1983, the open positions in planning were so few that the APA stopped listing them in their regular publications—both for economic and psychological reasons. There was a virtual crisis at the 1983 National Conference of the American Planning Association, because the traditional Job Market, which occurs annually to match prospective employers with available planners, had only one job opening. After a tumultuous effort, the Job Market was held after a national search turned up an additional 23 employers. Unfortunately, 1,000 planners crowded the room to talk with these very popular people (Catanese 1984, 21–22).

Planning consultants, adapting to the new ideology, began to put together and sell packages of planning policies and programs in the growing marketplace of local governments. No longer needed to prepare federally subsidized comprehensive plans, planners conducted fiscal analyses of annexation proposals or proposed development impact fees. The public interest and the bottom line converged. In-house staff planners sought conservative justifications for their existence. The roles of cop and broker, rather than advocate and technician, merited approval. Liberal talk was out and business talk was in. Planners were to implement local regulations to help police the local land market against extreme forms of speculative and environmental abuse and to resolve not-in-my-backyard (NIMBY) controversies. Planners began to market the qualities of the local municipality, district, or county so as to attract business and residential wealth and to obtain valuable development to improve the area's fiscal health through increased revenues and enhanced land values. Liberal planners and the liberal profession felt the squeeze. How could they respond effectively?

Diversification

The specialization of planning activities in the 1960s and 1970s in response to changing government legislative programs had increased the diversity of occupations for planners, but had diminished the impact of professional socialization. By the mid-1970s, professional planners were specializing in land use planning, community development, regional planning, comprehensive planning, environmental planning, social planning, transportation planning, housing, human services planning, and urban design. A survey of 1982 to 1986 graduates of planning schools found an even greater degree of diversification with additional specialties including economic development planning, health planning, financial analysis, and real estate research (Glasmier and Kahn 1989, 9).

The innovation within and expansion of planning provoked frequent complaints about professional dilution and distraction. Critics charged that these mercurial changes in professional practice in response to legislative initiatives and ideological shifts signified a lack of integrity and strength. They charged that members were busy expanding the scope of activities under the professional umbrella, rather than reproducing the tradition of good practice. Furthermore, the diversity enabled those schooled and socialized outside the profession to engage in the activities that critics felt should be the exclusive domain of the profession. Geographers, lawyers, administrators, and social scientists were beginning to get planning jobs (Levin 1979). Still, in the retrenchment of the 1980s, diversity proved an important asset to planners, as job opportunities were available in both the nonprofit and private sectors.

Accommodation

Declining federal support also changed the structure of local planning activity. The active promotion of comprehensive planning gave way to increased attention to the administrative and regulatory functions of planning. Competing with other line departments for funding in an era of fiscal retrenchment, planning directors scrambled to raise revenue through the regulatory processes they controlled. Linda Dalton's mid-1980s survey of California planners (a state with a strong tradition of government-mandated planning) found that planning departments spent most of their time on regulatory matters and not plans (1989b). This shift partly reflects the reality of small staffs burdened with large work loads. It also illustrates how the institutional location of planning as a line function of local government holds the profession hostage to cycles of growth. Planning departments funded through development fees are robust when times are good and frail when times are bad.

Diversification and accommodation appear to betray the liberal hopes at the core of the profession. Comprehensive planning had for several decades been legitimized by government authority. Conducting rational planning activities without institutional support and in an atmosphere of penetrating criticisms from both the right and the left seems neither desirable nor feasible. The hope of the staff planner to obtain official standing evaporated with the conservative shift in federal priorities and the open celebration of competitive self-interest as the foundation for public service. Planners began to give precedence to the fiscal prosperity and economic standing of their local employers over long-range comprehensive planning.

A VULNERABLE PROFESSION

The failure to institutionalize professional planning as a function of executive authority at any level of government has left planners vulnerable in tough economic times to political attack by enemies with greater authority. The political vulnerability and cultural marginality of professional planning, however, does not mean that planning activities are not useful and important. Planning gets done, but usually without a commitment to comprehensiveness and the public good. The list of urban problems remains as long today as it was thirty years ago.

The conservative enemies of the profession try to strip planning activities of the moral reform elements that make the field attractive as an aspect of democratic governance. Conservatives characterize planners as bureaucrats who frustrate efficient and desirable development. They portray planners as elites trying to impose their designs on an unwitting and vulnerable public. During the era of postwar urban growth, planners could turn to federal officials for support in the face of attacks from conservative local officials, citizens, and developers. As confidence in the liberal welfare state faltered, however, conservatives managed to capture federal power by attacking the planning ideas that led to the creation of the agencies that the new leaders were now putting to private use. The conservative call for privatization was not a return to some pristine state of laissez-faire competition, but an excuse to use broad public powers to shore up private investments.

The successful institutionalization of planning as a government occupation cut planners off from both the strong professional culture that Segoe advocated, as well as from the political movement of Progressive reform. Planning became a frantically paced bureaucratic function, but planners had very little power. There was some truth to the conservative attack on planners as inefficient and meddlesome bureaucrats. Most planners *were* bureaucrats. The conservative argument assumed, however, that planners had political power. This was much less evident. Some did; most did not. The cultural marginality of planning, the institutional vulnerability of government planners, and the pervasive political prejudice against serious planning did not make for a strong defense of the profession. These institutional liabilities also made it impossible for planners to establish a powerful democratic planning practice.

The increase in government employment and in political marginality encouraged planners to embrace professionalization as a source of legitimacy. Planners codified the rational model, despite its incompatibility with institutional reality, into an array of methods, principles, and customs to form a rational protocol. What is this protocol and how does it work?

NOTES

1. The first three chapters in Mel Scott's *American City Planning Since 1890* (1969) offer detailed stories about the contributions of the landscape architects, architects, and engineers who prepared park plans, housing schemes, and comprehensive plans as independent planning consultants. A more recent and lively account of these efforts, including comparative treatment of British planning efforts, can be found in Peter Hall's *Cities of Tomorrow* (1988).

2. In the early twentieth century, American local government experienced a brief revival. Before World War I the core municipalities of the fifty-one metropolises of the United States flourished, and so did their problems. Because large portions of middle-class Americans worked or lived in the core cities and these municipalities were relatively rich, the problems generated imaginative and effective reforms and experiments. Since the 1920s, how-

ever, accelerated residential and industrial suburbanization has drained tax wealth and middle-class voters from the municipalities. The combined loss of economic resources and balanced electorates has proved a heavy blow to municipal management, both in the new suburbs and the old core cities (Warner 1966, 49).

3. According to a 1972 Advisory Commission on Intergovernmental Relations (ACIR) survey of 300 COGs, two-thirds got 50 percent or more of their revenue from federal sources (ACIR 1974, I, 89).

3

The Rational Protocol and Political Conflict

PLANNING EDUCATION: FROM STUDIO TO UNIVERSITY

Theory plays an awkward role in an applied profession. Professionals can learn to act in useful and effective ways without knowing why their actions work. The founders of city planning made practical proposals and vivid plans. They did not write theories. The craft of planning, such as it was, was taught on the job. The first planners learned their craft in the studio and the office. Most, schooled as architects, engineers, or landscape architects, treated the city as an object of practical design.

As planning became a government function, occupational criteria and official policy revised and expanded the standards of the design craft. The widespread legal adoption of zoning regulations, planning commissions, and master planning by municipalities in the late 1920s set the trend. During the Depression, new federal programs used planning to organize regional development, public housing, new towns, and other large public works projects across the nation. The federal government sponsored large-scale local planning research that drew on methods from the new social science disciplines of sociology, economics, and public administration. The studies of regional and community problems, which ranged from soil erosion to slums, examined these difficulties in terms of theoretical models and possible government remedies.

Reformers, convinced of the efficacy of government-sponsored planning, sought ways to build local support for these federal initiatives. Professionals formed the American Society of Planning Officials (ASPO) in 1934 with the intention of educating local planning officials to plan on the vast and detailed scale required by large public projects. Historian Mel Scott describes the problems planning and housing reformers faced in educating local commissioners, planners, and officials about the function of comprehensive planning:

> First of all, city planners and housing officials had to make sure that they themselves fully comprehended the integral importance of housing in urban planning and development. For years the planners had touched upon the matter, but only since the advent of the PWA [Public Works Administration] low-rent projects [in 1934] had they really faced some of the larger issues associated with housing, such as the formulation of municipal land policies, the relation of social and economic planning to so-called physical planning, the need for future land use plans distinct from zoning maps and ordinances, the renewal not merely of the worst residential areas but of the more extensive blighted districts of which slums were often but segments, and the development of governmental machinery for preventing and arresting urban decay (1969, 331–32).

These issues required comprehensive plans:

> Preparing such a plan required foreseeing as clearly as possible the major technological, economic, social, and political changes likely to affect the area, as well as some of the ways in which various kinds of change might manifest themselves. Had city planners the knowledge and prescience to undertake so formidable a task? (1969, 332).

The conventional design-oriented planning practice of the 1920s did not address the problems associated with fitting population to place nor were practitioners trained to use government police powers and revenues. The functional procedures of government bureaucracy favored the uniform over the unique. This shift from the physical plan to the comprehensive plan represented not just a broadening of scope, but a change in the kind of knowledge needed to do planning. The social sciences offered methods for analyzing problems of inefficiency, disorder, and inequality. Planners collected and analyzed abstract measures, guided by socioeconomic theories and political objectives blended together to meet the demands of government agencies.

The rational model of comprehensive planning, popularized in the 1950s (Meyerson and Banfield 1955), offered a refined synthesis of various applications of the scientific method to government planning. The model was a distillation of theoretical efforts to justify the scientific coherence and validity of the comprehensive planning process for contemporary governments. Planning reformers had urged the adoption of comprehensive planning throughout the 1920s and 1930s, but the formulation and testing of the rational model came from the growing ranks of university faculty.

PLANNING EDUCATION IN THE UNIVERSITY

The rapid growth in employment opportunities for planners in the 1950s and 1960s stimulated the formation and expansion of graduate schools of planning. The conferral of graduate planning degrees increased from 100 a year in 1955 to almost 1,500 a year in 1975 (Krueckeberg 1984, 79). The impact on the education of practicing professionals was twofold. First, university graduate education virtually replaced (and discredited) apprenticeship as a prerequisite for professional acceptability. The old guard resisted, but the rapid growth in demand overwhelmed conventional on-the-job training methods. Second, the share of planning professionals from the design disciplines of architecture, landscape architecture, and engineering declined. In the early 1950s, virtually all professional planners had been trained or held undergraduate degrees in these disciplines. Few had graduate education. In the late 1950s, the graduate planning degree was still relatively rare, but the proportion of planners drawn from fields other than design, especially the social sciences, was increasing. By 1959 only 40 percent of professionals had undergraduate degrees in architecture and landscape architecture, while 16 percent had degrees in social sciences. The share of designers had declined to 33 percent by 1967 and to 25 percent in 1974. Meanwhile, planners with bachelor's degrees in the social sciences increased their share in 1967 to about one-third. The proportion held steady until 1974. The proportion of professional planners with graduate degrees in planning increased from 7 percent in 1959 to 49.2 percent in 1974 (AIP 1967; Vasu 1979, 208–9).

The newly formed university-based planning schools emphasized the production and dissemination of knowledge rather than the acquisition of practical skills. Faculty and research analysts in the schools adopted forms of inquiry and expectations for professional practice shaped by the theories and methods of social science research. The scope of planning expanded to include a wide array of social and economic problems.

Preparing students to work as government employees rather than as independent consultants required knowledge about organizations. This emphasis on the study of institutional behavior and relationships pushed questions of physical design toward the margins.

Harvey Perloff (1957) laid out a planning curriculum that combined social science and institutional knowledge. According to Hemmens:

> Perloff argued that planning's claim to professional status could not be realized without a research and theory base for the field.... He looked to social science for the research orientation of planning. At the same time developments in government and in the social sciences concerned with government called for a change in planning process. The rational planning model attempted to provide a framework for both the planner's social scientist role as a generator of knowledge and staff role as an administrator. This very inventive combination of the knowledge base and process issues made the rational planning model very appealing, and it was subsequently widely adopted (1988, 87).

Ironically, efforts to legitimize the new planning faculties and schools elevated theoretical and methodological activity above practical and applied activity. Faculty were drawn together from diverse disciplines, mainly the social sciences. Although the planning schools offered an applied professional degree, few new faculty had professional experience as planners. The faculty shared instead a commitment to the protocol of scientific inquiry and to the norms that safeguard its proper use.

Perloff built his curriculum around a core of general planning courses from which students would select a social science specialization. He expected faculty would use the social sciences to advance new planning theories based on research rather than on design principles. Planning graduates would then have the knowledge to provide rational guidance to powerful government decision makers.

The model, intended to produce the generalist with a specialty, had unexpected results. The core, similar to the undergraduate liberal arts curriculum, offered generic survey and skill development courses that prepared students for participation in a number of different specializations. The specializations, however, did not supplement the planning knowledge students acquired in the core curriculum. Rather, the specializations tended to frame the students' occupational choices. For instance, students learned that scientific knowledge about economic development, housing, environmental impact assessment, community development, transportation, or other functional specializations was more important than practical knowledge obtained through supervised studio or internship experiences. Planning schools began to drop from their core curriculum courses in design and practical modes of inquiry and replace them with courses centered on theories of rational scientific inquiry and methods of scientific investigation—those modes of inquiry that the faculty shared and found important. The widespread adoption of the rational model and social science research methods made scientific knowledge the primary source of reliable and valid understanding about planning.

Social science analysts studied policy rather than master plans. The artistry and craft used to design physical plans lost value. Designers judged a plan for the beauty and utility of its visual image of a city's future physical form. Analysts treated planning as a process of ongoing inquiry made tangible in occasional written policy reports. They claimed the designers had not grasped the complexity of cities, unlike the social scientists, who could develop and test theories to identify and classify the cause-and-effect relationships that shape the modern metropolis. The social scientists held that such knowledge was crucial in preparing and justifying the comprehensive plans for social, economic, and administrative reform that were being supported by federal funding and implemented by local or, even better, regional government.

Faculty proponents of the skeptical scientific approach avoided making commitments to particular planning reforms. Value neutrality gained pride of place as analysts worried that moral commitments would undermine the integrity of their research and analysis. Planning reformers from the Progressive and New Deal eras had assumed that science was on their side. They now faced a growing group of university-based analysts whose critical skepticism not only separated scientific inquiry from practical reform, but elevated scientific knowledge above professional experience.

SCIENCE AND REFORM

An important common assumption of the social science ideal and the administrative process ideal was belief in the efficacy of information. Right information in the right place was expected to be a powerful force in democratic process and contribute to the quality of public decision making (Hemmens 1988, 87).

Hemmens argues that the rejection of the design tradition in planning was an overreaction that unwisely promoted a preoccupation with the objective integrity of analysis and with the pursuit of abstract procedural theories to integrate the increasingly fragmented analytic specializations. The proliferation of scientific research also reflected and fostered functional specialization within planning practice. Not only did governments adopt a wider variety of programs generating demand for specialists, but the universities hired faculty with backgrounds in these specialties to meet this demand (Krueckeberg 1984).

During the decades of growth in the planning profession after World War II, the bureaucratization and specialization of planning occupations increased the range and complexity of everyday practice. The knowledge and protocols of the design consultant proved inadequate and inappropriate for coping with the regulatory, financial, and organizational problems government planners faced. In 1963, Melvin Webber asserted that the reform spirit that had provided the moral justification for planning activity in the first half of the twentieth century had been replaced by the pursuit of professional values that accompanied the rapid growth of government planners during the 1950s:

> The natural course of professionalization has taken its toll, by turning would-be missionaries into security-conscious bureaucrats. But, potentially more important than that, the processes of professionalization are also establishing the channels through which the findings of the social sciences are being fed into practice settings. One result of the expanding flow of knowledge is the transformation of many do-gooders into good-doers, as Meyerson once phrased it (Webber 1973, 96).

Webber and many of his academic colleagues were wary of the frequently irrational and dogmatic approach of reformers whose do-good tendencies blinded them to the necessity of scientific inquiry. The social sciences permitted planners "to simulate what would happen if given policies were adopted, and thus to pretest the relative effectiveness of alternative courses of action in accomplishing shared ends" (Webber 1973, 103). Professional planners could offer effective alternatives because they know how to apply scientific methods skillfully. To Webber, the real danger to planning was not reliance on scientific methods, but bureaucratization. John Dykman also expressed this concern:

> Once messianic, the planner has become bureaucratic and conservative. Not politically powerful in most cases, the planner takes his reward in profes-

sional prestige, for respect for his profession grows even as its threat to established forms diminishes (1973, 248).

As an antidote to the perverse consequences of specialization and bureaucratization, Dykman proposed the virtues of the scientist: humility, tentativeness, self-criticism, and doubt. He warned: "There is no need for planning to reduce all observation to calculation and to oppose reason to imagination: science itself is no longer so naive" (1973, 249). Contemporary planning analysts with the benefit of hindsight would probably find Dykman's critical liberalism quite up-to-date. However, Webber's notion of an applied science in the service of liberal pluralism better represents what was to become the guiding norm—the rational planning model.

FROM RATIONAL MODEL TO RATIONAL PROTOCOL

The rational model is rooted in scientific practice. As a prototype for professional practice, the rational model offered an ideal image that practitioners could use to make sense of their work. The model allowed planners to assess the efficacy of their expertise by classifying their actions and comparing them to the criteria of a rational prototype. Similar to research analysts, who use the prototype to develop hypotheses and guide scientific tests, practitioners could use the rational prototype to uncover public purposes, analyze problems, and formulate alternatives. With this in mind, the profession adopted the rational model as the proper protocol for practice.

The rational protocol advances the image of the public-serving, autonomous professional as the ideal standard. This image reduces the range of responses professional planners might adopt by presuming that planning and politics are antagonistic. Unfortunately, the protocol simultaneously overstates the amount of power available to planners by virtue of their particular expertise and pretends that those powers that planners do enjoy are simply matters of technique. The professional protocol, in drawing on the presuppositions of the rational planning model, either banishes the politics of uncertainty entirely or translates these political relationships into methodological presuppositions and procedures. These abstractions are useful in the conduct of specialized scientific inquiry, but impose serious impediments in practical matters. Planners who adopt the model as a guide blind themselves to the political relationships that shape their work. The model often promotes a blind faith in science and a naive failure to perceive how the political manipulation of scientific and technical knowledge can contribute to social and environmental risks and can open up new domains for the exercise of power.

Many contemporary analysts of planning practice (Baum 1983a; 1987; Dalton 1986; Marris 1982b; Throgmorton 1990; 1992) have found that planners use the rational, scientific model more as an excuse than as a guide. Practitioners adopt the rational model as a rhetorical device to legitimize their professional persona as an expert. The rational model serves less as a prototype of planning thought than as a protocol of planning expertise that fits a wide variety of institutional settings. The protocol helps planners bridge the gap between politics and vision through their individual acts of expertise.

The rational protocol advances the image of the public servant and relies on the authority of bureaucratic power. Those few planners who work for bureaucracies with broad authority and wide discretion can use the protocol as a sword and shield in adversarial battles with private interests and other agencies. For those many planners with little institutional power, however, the protocol functions as cumbersome armor, which inhibits more than it protects.

THE RATIONAL PROTOCOL IN PRACTICE

A protocol presents a set of rules or procedures guiding how people with social standing, position, authority, or power are to act toward others in different institutional settings. Practitioners have taken the abstract theory of rational planning and added qualities of moral character and professional craft to fashion an image of the ideal planner. The image relies heavily on conventions of rational expertise drawn from older professions (e.g., law and medicine), combined with the practice of scientific research.

The professional-client dyad remains at the center of the protocol. Planners, like many other middle-class professionals, pursue a sense of achievement and moral virtue in their modest organizational positions by emphasizing competence and integrity. Seymour Mandelbaum observes that the professional protocol

> survives despite the threat of a great many experiences which do not fit easily within its frame because it allows professionals to justify themselves and to command resources. The image has been maintained by absorbing criticisms of the narrowness of the technical conceptions of advice-giving, allowing some planners to think of themselves within the dyadic relation-

ship as political experts (Baum 1982; Vasu 1979). In landscapes without clients, planners have sustained the image by creating clients in their minds and (occasionally) in the streets—soliciting and inventing briefs where none exist (1985, 3).

University-trained planners learn to think about planning problems in terms of the social sciences. Good professional analysis means conducting objective, scientific analysis. Good professional planners classify and order urban problems, not through practical deliberation and understanding, but by using the social scientist's modes of explanation and prediction.

By contrast, planners on the job learn about their daily tasks in ways that do not require, much less inspire, reflection on the professional protocol. The technical requirements of the job and the complex political intrigues of the employing organization offer planners a rich arena in which to learn, gain experience, and advance their careers. In the work place, fidelity to scientific rationality does not often appear to play a defining role. Professional planners usually work with other planners. The formal rules and informal customs of the planning department and its parent organization impose obligations and expectations on planners. Their daily conduct is determined more by the routine rhythms of organizational procedures and the pressure of exceptional political demands than by their own initiative and technical prowess. Professional skills get tamed and shaped by the purposes and power of those with more authority.

As specialized participants in the business of public governance planners spend much time making, analyzing, and distributing information; giving advice about the meaning and intent of regulations; judging the value of routine and exceptional proposals; and offering praise and encouragement or warnings and remedies. The moral, emotional, and political relationships within the department and with employees in other departments complicate the routine activities. Unfortunately, the rational protocol takes little account of such crucial and yet routine relationships. The planner defined solely by the protocol is like a ship captain who concentrates solely on the craft of steering and the mechanics of charting a course and pays little attention to currents, waves, and weather. Nevertheless, when planners justify their advice, they tend to use concepts that isolate their technical expertise from the political context. They appeal solely to the rational conventions and procedures that compose their protocol of expertise.

For example, the professional protocol encourages practitioners to interpret power in an instrumental and cynical way. It encourages them to describe power as a mechanical force that pushes and pulls them independently of their intentions and actions. They may characterize their acts of power as immoral violations of the professional code of conduct. Depending on a planner's disposition, these violations will either be threatening or tempting. In either case, power remains outside the responsibility and control of the good professional. On the job, however, planners respond frequently to power relationships by drawing on rhetorical moral and political beliefs to describe, promote, and justify their proposals to others. The more successful professional planners prove to be at lobbying and pressuring, the less they appear to be guided by the protocol. Entering the political fray violates the norms of detached, objective expertise.

Those who honor the distinction between technical and political roles seem to believe in the professional protocol as a guide to professional development and identity. Others use the guide simply as a rhetorical strategy. Tim and Fred, introduced in chapter 1, exemplify these different approaches.

Tim, the urban design consultant pursuing his vision of the proper and beautiful city, finds the opinions, desires, and compromises of public officials to be a corruption and distortion of good planning. Fred, the city planning director, packages and promotes his development idea as a public project that will foster community benefits and pride. Fred sees his development plan primarily as a social activity, not as his professional design. He uses argument and persuasion to build political consensus among diverse groups for a set of downtown development policies.

Both planners use what they consider to be their professional knowledge to extend and infuse the power of the plan at hand. Tim works hard to get approval of a design that reflects his image of proper streetscapes. Fred struggles to evoke among residents an attachment to the local community and to link this attachment to support for his policies for downtown development. In both cases, the two planners base their judgments, advice, and arguments on their personal beliefs and attachments and their perception of the local context. Both sincerely believe they are working as objective, unbiased professionals. If challenged, Tim would point out his fidelity to design standards and Fred would claim his work serves the public interest.

Each adapts the professional protocol to justify what he does, but both would have difficulty justifying the other's activities. Their differences could be described as ones of style or role: Tim chooses to act as a designer technician; Fred works as an organizer advocate. This dualistic classification, however, simply translates the liberal paradox of expertise and political choice into discrete categories. The ambiguity runs deeper than this.

Many planners, like Tim, who identify closely with the protocol feel ambivalence and discomfort when they encounter, much less engage in, the conventional liberal politics of persuasion, lobbying, and organizing on the job. They use the rational protocol to protect them from the heat generated when they rub up against the institutional and moral boundaries that organizational communities establish to settle matters of justice. If these planners take the political initiative, they not only face the ensuing risks, but also serious doubts about the professional integrity of their efforts. Even should their political persuasion work and former adversaries take their advice, these professionals still harbor doubts about the legitimacy of their efforts. Did I succeed because of good reasons or political influence? If political persuasion was the crucial factor, then what is the value of my professional knowledge?

For planners like Fred, the professional protocol offers a shield of legitimacy for the pursuit of the political objectives they hold dear. For Fred, meaningful planning entails the use of his specialized knowledge to persuade skeptical or uninformed citizens about the value of policies designed to enhance the growth and prosperity of the city. Planning's role is to mediate between citizen desires and particular improvement schemes (such as, the downtown plan) to show residents how they might benefit and to encourage them to interpret the project as a symbol of community identity. When he speaks to the elderly, Fred evokes memories of downtown in more prosperous times, while to children he speaks of challenging opportunities for civic improvement. Fred is a booster for his old industrial hometown, seeking ways to stem its decline.

When enemies of the plan attack Fred, however, he quickly dons the veneer of professionalism. He describes procedures. He tallies the results of studies. He answers questions in the language of facts. However, given his commitment to the future prosperity of his hometown, he cannot legitimately claim the detachment of professional understanding as a guide. Norman Krumholz (1990), in the book he coauthored with John Forester on planning in Cleveland, rejects the professional protocol as a guide for practice, but embraces it as a useful rhetorical device. In story after story, he tells how he and his staff developed and used their organizational reputation as experts to pursue political objectives and policies that would benefit the city's poor. Krumholz asserts that the value of his technical analysis and judgment rests in the practical consequences that follow when this advice is shared with political actors whose cooperation and support are crucial. The planner's legitimacy goes beyond claims of expertise. For Fred and for Krumholz, the professional protocol is merely a political tool. For many planners, however, the protocol and its close affinity to the rational model shape their identity and the meaning of their work. They may not be as deeply attached to the protocol as Tim is, but these planners cannot drop the protocol as simply as they might shed a costume after a masquerade ball.

I will describe how two planners—Tom and Martin—use the protocol to bind together public good and political interests in their planning conduct. Both face difficult conflicts that challenge the integrity and value of their professional advice. Tom puts the protocol into practice confidently, expecting to persuade skeptics and opponents to adopt a professional planning outlook. Martin uses the conventions of the protocol to develop and organize his plans, but hesitates to use the protocol to engage in the adversarial political relationships that would be necessary to challenge and defeat his opponents.

Tom: Man with a Mission

Tom is handsome with short blonde hair and soft blue eyes. He stands over six feet tall. His movements are gentle and determined; neither slow nor fast. I envy his stature. His posture is what my mother always pleaded me to adopt as I slouched my way through adolescence. Tom makes standing straight look easy. His nose and lips possess a canny symmetry. Balance and grace surround him. His desk and office show no signs of carelessness or sloppy paperwork. As he speaks, his words are even and well ordered; his tone soft; his resonance deep. His stories, however, are neither cold nor rigid. He speaks with feeling.

When I first spoke with Tom he had been working as a planning director for the suburban village of Fern for about seven months. He liked his job and showed every indication of a long and successful tenure. He spoke of his working style and commitment to professional planning.

> I am very process oriented. It's been a philosophy I've developed from my
> experience. It's always better to meet and discuss proposed changes in de-

velopment plans with developers before the plans reach the hearing stage. So when I meet with developers I ask them about their intentions and the way they plan to use the site. In this way I can grasp the potential impacts of the development on others. I try to understand the design objectives and identify them clearly. This enables me to conceive of alternatives that the developers can practically consider.

Tom has adopted a demanding version of the professional protocol. Tom identifies strongly with the profession of planning as an activity that he has learned in school and on the job and which his employer, the Village of Fern, pays him to practice. He interprets the interests of his employer and his clients from within this framework. For example, in describing his relationship with members of the appointed planning commission, he emphasizes his role as an educator and role model. He also acknowledges that the commissioners can engage in certain political activities from which he is prohibited by his professional protocol.

> I think the planning commission can play a potentially useful and productive role. These people are close to the property owning residents and the trustees. Getting them involved in the planning process will enhance the prospects of local planning efforts. If the commissioners do planning, then citizens are more likely to pay attention to plans. I seek to remove barriers to participation in planning.
>
> The present group of commissioners is relatively new (about half), but they intuitively know what's going on. The problem is that they've never been trained or oriented to the planning process. Every time I prepare reports I try to teach them about how to understand plans and regulations. I lead them through the process. I think they appreciate it.
>
> In the suburban city I worked with before, I started out with a planning commission whose chair would call the mayor before the meeting to find out how to vote. Virtually no one spoke at the meetings. But after six years, when I left, the commission was able to make useful and reasonable land use decisions. I helped them learn to do planning.

For Tom, the planning commission members must learn how to follow the tradition of rational expertise—the professional planning process—in conducting deliberations. Tom recognizes that his expertise, as a quality of professional practice, separates and distinguishes him from others. On the one hand, this exclusive expertise represents an important accomplishment as well as the basis for professional development. On the other hand, it is the source of separation between Tom and the village's many "amateur" commissioners, politicians, and citizens. Tom tries to teach these participants the rudimentary principles of the planning process and how to use them when judging particular plans and projects.

> The owners of a local factory that builds electrical components sold worldwide wanted to build a 30,000 square foot expansion here in Fern. I did a concept review of the sketch plan.
>
> The proposed expansion was larger than the zoning code allowed. The proposed building was too large for the lot and left insufficient setbacks. Now, instead of just going to the planning commission and pointing this out at the hearing, I set up a meeting with the company's lawyer, engineer, architect, and management representative. I flagged this conflict for them and pointed out that they had done the design without paying attention to the ordinance.
>
> I discussed options with them. I showed them ways they could get the same square footage using two smaller buildings, or how they could buy some vacant land next door to acquire sufficient land to meet the standards. I even discussed the possibility of a two-story structure. My purpose wasn't to do the design, but to facilitate the design process with respect to the code. I asked them to think about the options I suggested and prepare a new sketch.
>
> They decided to buy a twenty-foot strip of land from the owner of the abutting property. In addition, they reshaped the proposed addition, relocating some loading docks to meet lot coverage standards. After I received the second sketch plan I conducted a detailed code review.
>
> Here I showed how they needed to change some parking and move a loading door that would disrupt the on-site traffic circulation. The sketch met the space standards, but they were going to have to meet severe performance standards to get a special use permit.
>
> There was resistance. The company submitted a written statement of the standards they expected to meet in the use of the site...and that was that. In our next meeting, the company people came with an attitude. The company architect did most of the talking and challenged everything. He was defensive and antagonistic. I started to point out the rules and offer the reasons for the regs.
>
> They had met previously with my predecessor who had emphasized enforcement, so they perceived me as an antagonist, despite my earlier efforts to help. By the end of the meeting they had changed. I pointed out why a ten-foot driving lane for trucks is too narrow and why a loading dock facing residential homes is not allowed. The reasons showed them the purpose of the regs.

I probed for reasons why the architect and company officials had changed their minds. Tom admitted that his powers of reasonable persuasion were enhanced by the potential threat of regulatory enforcement.

It was not simply the quality of his argument about the merits of different design alternatives or the likelihood of undesirable land use conflicts that got the attention of the owner's representatives. Rather, Tom,
much like the flagman who alerts motorists to upcoming dangers, waved
a warning, which persuaded the representatives to attend the meeting.
Tom mentions the prospect of regulatory adversity to nudge developers
into meaningful negotiations. Tom raises uncertainty over the outcome
of a regulatory proceeding should the owner proceed unilaterally and
without his support. To reduce this risk of failure, the representatives
must engage in conversation about modifications to the proposal.

> Every planner has leverage because the developer is afraid of not getting
> approval. I use this. I say, "If you do this, you will likely get approval from
> the board." It's an informal sort of power.
>
> But since I'm new here I don't have enough of a track record to make it
> stick, although so far, every regulatory recommendation I have made has
> been approved. I do point this out to developers. It gives me leverage. I also
> know how to figure out the board's intentions.

Tom does not threaten enforcement because he wants to play cop.
Rather, his intent is to encourage private developers to consider other
alternatives that will meet code and still fulfill their purposes. Tom does
not appear to execute overzealously his limited powers, but rather he
puts them to use in service to his broader educational efforts. He uses
the proposal and project reviews to discover the developer's interests
and then applies his knowledge and skill to compose alternative designs
that will both satisfy the owner's interests and better serve the orderly
and efficient development of the village. Drawing on his interpretation
of the principles and techniques of professional planning, Tom engaged
the representatives in deliberations about the consequences of the proposal for the entire community. His first interest was not rule enforcement for its own sake, but changing the representatives' understanding
of the project. He wanted to educate, not police.

Tom does not calculate, but rather anticipates (see Forester 1987a; 1987b;
1989). Tom justifies his actions by referring to what he calls the principles of good professional planning. In describing his actions, however,
the principles disappear and practical reasoning and argument take center stage. When he reviewed the original sketch plan, Tom anticipated
the code violations this design would produce. He then proposed alternative development schemes that would both fit the code and meet the

space needs of the manufacturer. The representatives took his advice and adopted one of his alternatives, only to learn that there were additional performance standards they were supposed to meet. When the owners resisted making additional changes, Tom did not threaten them with enforcement, but described how the violations would create land use conflicts. He explained how modifying the location of loading docks or widening driving lanes would avoid these conflicts. Once again, the representatives listened and learned.

At each point, Tom uses his authority and knowledge to make judgments and compose arguments, which together shape the form and content of the deliberations with the representatives. Tom tells the story as an example of good professional planning. Unlike his predecessor, who Tom suggests was too much of an enforcer, Tom describes himself as an educator who uses practical arguments to persuade developers and owners to understand and embrace the intentions of the town regulations. He believes in the planning process and his story offers a successful example of putting the process to work.

I saw Tom eighteen months later. He had been fired a month earlier and was looking for work. He spoke in the same even and balanced manner, only now he expressed anger. The surprise and betrayal he felt over his dismissal brought him pain. In his story, he reconstructed and adjusted the professional protocol, which he had relied on to guide his judgment and which had failed him. He reaffirmed the integrity of the professional protocol and the planning process, but he also raised serious doubts about the efficacy of good argument and fair-minded professional judgments when these conflicted with powerful political affiliations and interests.

> I had gotten excellent evaluations for two years before I was fired, but for the last three to four months it was obvious something was changing. I had reviewed several development proposals during the previous six months, about a half-dozen. I reviewed them with respect to whether or not they conformed to town ordinances and met basic principles of good planning. I was advising a variety of owners: a development company proposing a car wash/gas station, an owner subdividing a five-acre lot, an industry putting up an office warehouse for distribution of their product, and another small builder. None of these people, it turns out, liked my advice.
>
> My downfall was a classic case. The town didn't have much room to expand. There were twenty acres vacant at the one and only exchange for the new expressway. This was the last chance to take advantage of this prime

location in the village. Even though the expressway had been planned for thirty years, this vacant land was still cheap, only about two dollars per square foot. A company came in and bought four acres outright. They wanted to build a car wash and gas station.

A year earlier the trustees had adopted a land use plan for the area, which called for a high intensity commercial land use. This included standards to discourage strip development, limit curb cuts, and unify design. This proposal was the antithesis of the policies in the plan. This company had done only auto-commercial projects in the central city. I explained the land use plan policies to the developers and the difficulty they would face in conforming to the plan. After the second meeting they started asking me what they could do to get around the plan. I gave them standard stuff. Do a market study and compare your use with the use proposed in the plan—the typical planning rationale for this kind of case. They did conduct a study. The results proved my point and disproved theirs. But, they used it anyway.

At the planning commission hearing, I pointed out how the car wash project didn't conform to the plan the trustees had adopted. It would not only not be the best and highest use of this prime commercial property, but would have a negative impact on hopes for future high value commercial development. I had refrained from conducting a site plan review and mainly emphasized the land use conflicts. The planning commissioners went along. One member, a realtor, understood how the land values would be negatively affected.

A reporter from the regional newspaper of business and commerce came out and did an interview with me about the plans for the interchange. I told how we expected the development to be substantial and high value. Everyone who read the article and spoke to me agreed with my comments, even the trustees. It seemed that there was support for the plan and not the car wash. Well, the planning commission agreed unanimously to deny approval, but the trustees disagreed and sent the project back to the planning commission. Eventually, the trustees voted four to three to approve the car wash project. I was surprised.

By "classic," Tom refers to the conflict between private development and a public plan. The trustees have adopted a land use plan for the vacant land that strictly prohibits commercial development like the proposed car wash, but when the developer arrives with a specific proposal, a majority of the trustees ignores the plan and embraces the development proposal. How could this be?

It happened that the car wash developer told some trustees that I had refused to meet with them. This after I had spent over twelve hours meeting with them! They claimed I was unreasonable when I insisted their proposal did not follow the plan. A few trustees saw through the lie, but others agreed and didn't bother to consult me and check out my side of the story.

I got my first formal warning of trouble when my new boss, the acting manager, told me that the trustees said a developer had complained to them about me. This manager was new, an assistant to the former manager who had been fired about six months earlier. Instead of helping me, she just reported the facts. She was the one who would later ask for my resignation. Having come up through the ranks of the local bureaucracy, her loyalty to the trustees was evident.

I tried to find out the nature of the developer complaints. The manager would not say. Later, near the end of my stay, I pressed the manager and trustees for specifics, but they refused to say anything because the town legal counsel had warned them of their liability and possible lawsuits.

After the manager made the accusations public, I thought there had simply been a misunderstanding and so contacted each of the seven trustees either on the phone or at city hall. Five were very noncommittal about my status. Two had their minds made up. One trustee did make an attempt to explain. He started out trying to speak impartially. He gave examples of things he claimed I had done wrong.

For instance, in one case the trustee mentioned, a potential buyer had called my office to check out a developer's claims. I gave the buyer the facts. "Yes, there are wetlands on the site," I responded when he asked. "No, the development has not received final approval." The buyer decided not to buy the building and cited the facts I gave as reasons. The developer complained to the trustees that I had wrecked the deal, but all I had done was give the facts.

The trustee said I shouldn't have given the information out. The developer and the trustee felt I was giving my opinion, but I told the trustee that I was giving facts. The trustee countered by saying I couldn't prove it. I knew then I was being victimized unfairly. I felt vulnerable and foolish. Since my advice was rational and right I had felt safe, but as he spoke I realized I had not adequately documented my advice-giving. As it turned out, I wasn't safe at all. None of the other trustees would give me a straight answer when I asked them why they were firing me. They were unanimous in the decision to ask me to resign.

I knew that my methods were professionally sound and above reproach, but that was based on my sense of ethics and my fourteen years of experience as a suburban planner. I think what they wanted was a development cheerleader. Whatever proposal came along, they wanted me to find a way to make it happen.

Ironically, Tom's actions, which derived from his dedication and commitment to the professional protocol of good planning, undermined his legitimacy in the eyes of the town trustees. It also misled Tom into believing things were going better than they were. In the first story, Tom enforces plans by ensuring that regulations are followed properly and fairly. His professional judgments are based on his experience and competence to advise the trustee about how to best organize growth in the town. He pays attention to the economic and political interests of owners, petitioners, and developers to ensure that his advice is objective. In the second story, developers went behind his back to avoid deliberations and compromises that would reduce their discretion and possibly their profits.

One of the trustees tried to explain to Tom why the majority no longer trusted his advice. Tom knew that the trustees were anxious to attract new development, but he did not share their sense of urgency and willingness to approve any investment. Tom's knowledge and expertise told him that the rejection of poorly designed or inappropriate development would benefit the community in the long run. The trustees, however, wanted their planner to make development proposals work, even if that involved violating professional principles of good planning—principles they clearly did not hold.

When the trustee told Tom he should not have given a buyer information about a proposed development parcel that reduced its attractiveness, he was showing Tom what mattered to the trustees. Tom, in his embrace of the professional protocol, missed the point. He assumed the criticism represented an effort by the trustees to compromise his moral integrity. To defend himself against the trustee's accusation that he had offered an opinion, Tom insisted that he had simply told the facts. This response further infuriated the trustee.

Tom was stuck. He could not answer the trustee in a way that would keep his sense of professional integrity intact. If the dispute were simply a matter of fact, then providing evidence might settle it, but the trustee was not really asking for evidence. The trustee and his colleagues did not trust Tom's presumption of professional objectivity. Tom's independent judgments, arguments, and recommendations had, over time, convinced the trustees that he did not serve the interests of growth, but his own interests as a professional expert. It is in this sense that the trustee claimed that Tom offered opinion rather than facts.

Tom did not believe he was taking sides in a political struggle between the community of professional planners and the local political community represented by the board of trustees. He interpreted the claims of the trustees as illegitimate infringements on his professional integrity.

His regrets at being fired did not center on his performance or the political activity, but on his failure to document his actions in sufficient detail to be able to sue his employer.

I asked Tom why he had been caught so unawares. He reviewed his history and identified the signs of distrust and resistance that he had overlooked at the time. He had, it seems, relied on the advice and aid of the long-time city manager in making his decision to take the job.

> I had done research before taking the job to see how the trustees had treated planners and the town record on past hiring and firings. I talked to many people. The trustees in my interview said they would support me, but it's difficult to get a read on the political environment of a municipality until after you get hired. One person I relied on was the town manager who had been there for twelve years. It turns out that the trustees were plotting to get rid of him at the same time as I was hired. He didn't see it coming either. He was fired about a year ago.
>
> It made me uneasy when the manager got fired. If they fire the manager without cause and without perceivable evidence, then they can fire anyone without cause. They replaced him with the assistant manager who was a patsy. She went along with whatever the trustees wanted.
>
> I knew there was a distrust of experts among the trustees. That was clear from my first town board meeting. One of the trustees was a libertarian who questioned the validity of any planning. Although the most extreme, he wasn't alone. There were three members who resisted various types of routine government regulation. I learned to anticipate the sorts of questions they would ask and addressed these in my reports.
>
> I wasn't too concerned about these differences initially because the trustees went out of their way to solicit my professional opinions. I felt reassured. When there were split votes I avoided pandering to one or another faction. But the town was not growing. Many trustees believed that some development was better than no development. Gaining a tax base outweighed all other considerations. I was aware of this and made plans to increase densities and upzone areas, but these approaches still meant following the adopted rules and plans. I was a good professional. But in the end I had a false sense of security. I think the trustees kept a mental score card and the disappointed developers in the last six months tipped the scale too far.

With benefit of hindsight, Tom explains the trustees' politics and priorities, which did not fit well with his own concept of good planning. Still, Tom believed that he could advise them, even though he did not support the growth agenda and did not express political loyalty in ways the trustees would recognize and value. He had trusted in the efficacy of avoiding pandering to any particular interest and of offering rational alternatives. This tack proved insufficient. Tom felt victimized and betrayed.

Tom directed his anger at the trustees and their patsy manager, but it may be that the real target for his feelings should have been the professional protocol he relied on to define the meaning of his work. Tom wanted to believe that his professional judgment was objective, that is, unbiased and dispassionate, but adopting the expert's protocol did not really insulate him from political interests and passions. Even if he had documented every detail of his work and used it in court to successfully sue his former employer, he would not have escaped the anger and disappointment he felt on learning he had been fired. Tom cared deeply about his work and its consequences for the town. Tom's desire for vengeance and sense of injustice flowed from his emotional political involvements, which the language and form of the professional protocol cannot address.

I suspect Tom overlooked the signs of mistrust and animosity early in his tenure precisely because he was not dispassionate and unbiased in his evaluation of the trustees and the developers. His mission to educate city officials and developers about the values and benefits of the planning process may have blinded him to the growing distrust of the trustees. His sense of mission may also explain why he did not busy himself documenting his decisions. Doing so would have required that he either stick to the protocol without hope of promoting local planning or adopt a more overtly political strategy that would break the boundaries of the professional protocol he relied on to define his identity.

Most planners recognize their own institutional weakness when threats are made by powerful antagonists, but do not acknowledge that they share this vulnerability with other planners, both in the organization and in the broader community, because they remain attached to the professional protocol of individual expertise. Hence, they adopt their own strategies of political and emotional defense, which isolate them from others. Their isolation increases their weakness and intensifies their belief in professional autonomy. As Baum has argued so convincingly, this defense process is flawed, burdening planners with doubt, ambivalence, and shame (1987).

Martin: The Dangling Practitioner

Martin is employed in a large nonprofit corporation in a central city. At the time of the interview he worked as the principal planner responsible for developing and coordinating plans for the physical expansion of his institution. His soft-spoken and mildly self-deprecating manner belies the intense feelings that animate his judgments. Trained as a psychologist and transportation planner, Martin simultaneously expresses deep commitment to the proper protocols of analytical research and ironic skepticism about the efficacy of this approach in the institutional and political context of his job. Martin truly believes in the efficacy of a properly applied scientific rationality in planning and winces when he describes the all-too-common instances of distortion and deceit. He speaks quickly. He spins out short sentences. He is both the narrator and critic of his stories.

Martin begins by talking about his efforts to develop a plan for the physical expansion of the agency onto the site of an aging and dilapidated retail district.

The agency has wanted for more than twenty years to expand onto the land occupied by the district. Others want to see the district go as well. A local lawyer and long-time resident of the nearby neighborhood, Willie Loomis, who was known to have been involved in illegal and unethical practices, has lobbied the agency to take action.

When I was given this assignment, my first inclination was not to save the retail district. It's a sinkhole. Eventually, I changed my mind. There are many people who want it to stay. Most of the markets and shoppers are poor. I was persuaded by the evidence of my own research and especially what I learned from others that there might be some way that the spatial expansion of the institution and the district might coexist. The guy who really convinced me was a planner for the city, Tom Potts, who pointed out the district's unique value. Loomis hates Potts and thinks the planner has risen above his working-class roots. Potts wanted to take this unique, but drab district and turn it into something much better. I decided to work with him and for about a year we engaged in frequent discussions about plans for the area.

One faction of park advocates, named Friends of the District, was organized by a guy whose wife sells art work in the district on weekends. This group wants to keep the area just like it is. This guy seems motivated more by self-interest than by genuine concern for the district. He wasn't an effective organizer, and was seen as more of a symbolic than a real threat. Besides, keeping the status quo in the midst of the agency and city expansion plans won't work. [Not to mention that Martin thinks the place is a cesspool as is.]

So Potts and I worked together on plans that would offer an image of what a revitalized retail district bordering the planned physical facility expansion could look like. We solicited help from the architectural faculty of a local university to use a studio class to develop pictures and plans that would attract the eye of the agency board and city council. In addition, Potts and other city planning staff prepared an even more ambitious scheme that laid out site plan features, traffic flows, landscaping. Our intent was to persuade the president of my agency and the city planning director that coexistence was a good policy and to make a public statement supporting some development guidelines to carry it out.

When the work was near completion I drafted a letter of agreement between my agency and the city. It laid out the boundaries, basic design features, and time phasing for acquisition of the land. It also assigned the separate and mutual responsibilities for both the city and the agency. I liked the plan. It allowed for anywhere between three and six blocks of expansion for my own agency, basically meeting more than its present and anticipated spatial needs called for, while allowing for coexistence with a greatly improved district.

I sat down with my boss [Thompson], who is the vice president responsible for the capital development programs of the agency, to discuss the letter. He tells me that Loomis and the mayor don't want this. When I point out that the work by my colleague Potts at city hall suggests there is support, he tells me that Potts is either misinformed or uninformed. It's not what Loomis and the mayor want.

As he spoke, I start having second thoughts about my relationship with Loomis. Just after I took my present job several years ago, Loomis asked me out for a cup of coffee. Given his reputation, I felt that associating with him could only lead to trouble. Tactically it was a mistake. The guy is a close personal friend of the mayor and, therefore, has a lot of influence. So now, when I make recommendations he doesn't like, he just goes around me.

Still, I was able to persuade Thompson to meet with the president to discuss the options that had been developed. I still thought that the agency could get the parcels it needed for its expansion without destroying the district. The president read my letter and we discussed two options. Option A produced a down-sized retail area in a temporary location during the phasing in of the new development. It was a death sentence for the retail district. Option B, which was the one I wanted, required only one relocation and provided adequate space for a critical mass of retail activity.

During the meeting, discussion focused on the issue of demolition. Thompson insisted that the buildings in the area were in bad shape and had to be demolished. However, he pointed out that such large-scale destruction would raise serious protest and cause some trouble for the new president. Most troubling was the agency president's suggestion that Loomis take the letter with him to speak with the planning director about Option A. I was really distressed.

A year earlier, when I first drafted an agenda for a meeting on the future development for the area, the issue had come up about who speaks for the agency. Loomis had been a friend of the agency since it was first located in the neighborhood. His interests in the neighborhood and property development coincided with agency interests, but he was not an employee or official representative. This proved to be a problem in the agency relationship with the city, and especially the planning department. Potts could not figure out who represented the agency—me or Loomis.

A veteran city planner speculated that Loomis wanted to have my agency demolish the buildings in and around the district so that he could come in and do some profitable real estate development. So I knew all along that there were deep political ties involved in the project, but I still tried to come up with a reasonable compromise. So far, the planning director has not agreed with the choice of option A, although Thompson has assured me that he will. I'm not sure.

The mayor faces other pressures than those from the local developers like Loomis. The city hall folks know that the letter they got was the product of disagreement within our agency. So they also know that the letter delivered by Loomis was not official. It was not on letterhead or signed by the president. Our agency director wants to avoid taking responsibility for a project with the potential for raising considerable public protest. He wants the city to take responsibility for the project, but the city hall officials and bureaucrats are not foolish. There's still a chance they can do it right.

At least we should have the public hearings about the transfer of land before the buildings are demolished. It can be done quietly. Line up the votes on the commission. Do the notification properly and officially before phasing in the development.

I could have had coffee with Loomis and been included in the inner circle of political actors...and maybe even ended up with a secretary and my own limo [sarcasm here]. I dared to question Loomis and the result was getting sidetracked.

Martin's unwillingness to engage in what he considered unseemly and unethical political activity was not the only factor in undermining a compromise. He also faced some serious organizational impediments.

It was Thompson's job to ask questions about where the institution was going. But he was not my only boss! I also reported to the vice president responsible for managing the physical plant, Jeb Salmon. This guy was a wheeler dealer who knew all the details of managing the organization. He was very bright and didn't much care for me or my work.

It was Thompson who had authorized my study of development options for the land surrounding the district, but at the meeting with the president, Salmon paid little attention to my advice and simply said that we should do what Loomis wants. At this critical moment Thompson said nothing. He simply clarified the choices and made no effort to persuade the president. My proposals went nowhere.

Thompson is responsible for a lot of organizational activities. This was just one of many. Besides, his job is to make sure the agency makes decisions consciously [raising questions, offering alternatives] and not the decisions he wants. So I took the same tack. I had no commitments from either boss. I was tired and discouraged by the political maneuvering. I wasn't about to go down in a blaze of glory [with so little hope of victory].

Martin creates plans with the aid of a city planner and support of his own boss. He makes it clear, however, that he has failed to gain the support of a local political actor who has strong ties to the mayor and the ear of the president of Martin's agency. Here is rational comprehensive planning in action. Martin proceeds in hopes of winning the support of his supervisor and convincing the president. He wants to build a reasonable plan that will attract the support of his superiors. Yet all along, his political intuition sets off alarms. Martin knew early on that he would have to make plans and political commitments with the power broker Loomis, but he feared him and held him in contempt. Martin's attachment to the values of his professional craft and his hopes for serious deliberations with his superiors kept him from following his intuition about the importance of pleasing the powerful Loomis.

Martin showed a good deal of ambivalence. He wanted to contribute a useful plan that would minimally disrupt the merchants, but he was cynically detached from the entire enterprise. He produced a fine product by the standards of rational land planning. He offered useful alternatives for saving the retail district, which catered to low-income customers, and for satisfying the agency's expansion plans. His plans, however, fell on deaf ears and suspicious minds. His collaborator, Potts, lost faith in the joint enterprise as Loomis used his ties to the mayor to sidetrack the planning efforts. Even Martin's immediate boss could not muster sufficient political will to support the plan. Martin was unwilling to engage in the adversarial politics of the local neighborhood and of his own agency. His proposals were ignored.

Martin did not appear angry or resentful. He spoke with wistful reverie and cynical detachment. The interview was clearly a favor to me. Martin reminded me of the comedian who can tell a tragic tale and set his audience laughing. Although his advice was ignored and his moral sensibility rubbed the wrong way, Martin still managed to make institutional maneuvers often unavailable to less well-positioned planners.

Planners who encounter threatening political conflicts, especially those who lose, usually experience a shameful vulnerability that contrasts sharply with their expectations of professional practice. The story of Tom represents such a case. Planners like Tom constitute a promising audience for challenges to the masterful professional as a model for effective practice, since they are living with the burden the model imposes on those who fail to measure up.

Martin exemplifies the practitioner left dangling between the powers of craft and the powers of coercion. His self-mockery betrays his ambivalence about abandoning the professional protocol to obtain the political support for a good plan. Unlike Tom, he did not believe that he could educate or persuade people like Loomis to adopt the plan. He did hope to receive support from within the administrative hierarchy, but he underestimated the influence of Loomis and the city officials on his boss's judgment. In retrospect he admits that building relationships with these other political actors was important, but he did not want to abandon his standards of professional integrity. Martin did not want to engage in adversarial politics, although he recognized the crucial impact of these political relationships on the fate of his plan.

POWER, PLANNING, AND THE POLITICS OF UNCERTAINTY

Planners compose and offer advice on preparing for an uncertain future. Planners expect their advice to be heard and followed and to reap the intended results. Planners expect to act in powerful ways. As they work to identify and reduce collective uncertainty, planners participate in power relationships based on craft, coercion, and consent. Planners do not act as apolitical technicians or nontechnical politicians. Their actions necessarily draw on both political experience and technical knowledge.

What purposes do planners pursue and how successful are their efforts to achieve those purposes? Laboring in the middle-management ranks of government, planners can use their professional expertise to enhance their institutional authority and individual discretion or they might try to improve the prospects of various clients by enhancing the predictability of organizational and community life. At one end of the continuum, the planner is a power broker; at the other, a public servant. Most planners assume a combined role. Regardless of their choice, planners usually rationalize their actions in terms of professional competence and the protocol of professional expertise.

The Power of Craft

When planners point to the power inherent in their profession, they draw on their everyday work. In this sense, power refers to efforts to transform the world. Power flows from the talented and experienced worker's hands-on manipulations. The carpenter frames a cabinet. The engineer draws plans for a bridge. The computer scientist simulates urban design alternatives.

We want to take a journey into unfamiliar territory, but ignorance of the local geography makes us uncertain about what route to take. The solution? Make a plan. Explore the unknown terrain, survey its dimensions, and then plot a course. Good travel planners match their knowledge of our destination with a particular means and route of travel. The good plan is a powerful plan because it works. It helps us reach our destination.

The rational planning model relied on and promoted instrumental manipulation as a guide for powerful, effective planning. If planners follow the proper rational methods, their advice will prove both persuasive and useful. In truth, however, planners must deal with diverse communities with competing interests and moral orientations. They all require and demand recognition. Abstract and instrumental rationality does not answer the question: When there are competing purposes, whose interest will win the competition?

The Power of Coercion

In the world of public affairs, power usually refers to command, rather than to craft. The powerful possess the authority to demand obedience based on the threat of force. The captain commands the corporal. The boss controls the employee. The jailer handcuffs the prisoner. Similar to the pursuit of a rational optimum, the pursuit of complete domination proves unworkable. The more inclusive and extensive the net of coercion, the more expensive and complex it becomes. Once citizen resistance is eliminated, the ruler faces the uncertainty caused by bureaucratic maneuvering among the agencies of control and surveillance. The ruler ends up exchanging the threat of revolts with the threat of coups. The use of force is best disguised.

Planners can blur the distinction between coercion and craft in their exercise of physical control. Powerful planners appear to exercise control over people and their environments just as engineers do over the physical environment. Robert Moses offers the best twentieth-century example of a power broker planner (Caro 1974). Even practitioners at the zoning desk, under the guise of expertise, can use their institutional authority to threaten and cajole petitioners into submission (Schon 1982). People, however, are rarely passive, and frequently resist the imposition of coercion. Coercion requires disguise precisely because it is so unpopular. Power in liberal settings flows more from consent to authority, than from submission to the threats of coercion.

The Power of Consent

Power also refers to authority within social relationships. Someone we trust warns us about a possible danger. We follow their advice. Our parents ask us to stop teasing a younger sibling and we obey. We join a religious denomination and faithfully follow the advice of its minister. Innumerable relations of trust and authority compose the fabric of social order. What counts here is less the instrumental outcome of a social bond than the quality of moral consent. The predictability of our lives relies on the stability of the social order. If the order we know and live by becomes uncertain and the familiar network of relationships gets torn apart, we can lose our way. Most of us can handle the small rips of everyday life, but when we face more disruptive changes we often turn to others for help and advice.

> Our adaptability depends on being able to treat social relationships as orderly and reliable without submitting our own responses, inflexibly, to the constraints of that order. The management of uncertainty, therefore, is inherently biased against reciprocity.... The exercise of social power is directed constantly towards securing the most favorable balance between autonomy and constraints. The powerful can exact commitments which they do not have to reciprocate (Marris 1982a, 10).

In bureaucracies we go along with our superior's desires not only for fear of sanction (You're fired!), but also because we assent in some way (She's right!) or lack good reason and motivation to resist. (It's a job.) If our boss acts like a tyrant, we lose trust in her. We find reason to disobey her commands and perhaps even join with others in efforts to resist. We base our resistance on liberal values of mutual respect and reciprocity. We are willing to risk resistance because the domination threatens our integrity. Of course, we might also choose to comply, offering ourselves and others justifications for our deference: "I'll never get a job this good elsewhere." "She's right, I'm no good. This is the best I can expect."

Efforts to obtain moral stature and fulfillment through free choice require predictability. Any uncertainty generated by others erodes this predictability and undermines the pursuit of our goals. If the uncertainty becomes too great, then social collapse may occur. Demoralization frequently accompanies large-scale disasters. Survivors of a tornado, flood, hurricane, or fire often wander about aimlessly, unable to perform even the simplest routines. The rapid and dramatic loss of home, possessions, loved ones, and familiar landscapes can provoke an uncertainty so profound that even the simplest goals appear overwhelming (Erickson 1976).[1]

Planners' distinct, yet overlapping, powers inherent in their craft and embedded in acts of coercion and consensus get separately channeled by the institutions and customs of their working lives. Similarly, planning lore ignores the complex and frequently interdependent relationships among these forms of power and rigidly classifies them as either technical or political. The conventional professional protocol keeps this dualism alive, portraying the planner as an expert applying technical skills to solve public problems independent of the coercion of political influence and interests. (Imagine an independent planning consultant offering advice to the city council with the support of a wealthy and altruistic patron.) The protocol elevates craft as a virtue and coercive power as a vice. Furthermore, it takes relationships of consensus for granted in its glib images of the common good. Consensus proves more difficult to achieve than the professional planning literature generally allows. Researchers have understood this for decades, as they explored how adversarial politics made a mockery of comprehensive planning efforts. These accounts inadvertently promote a cynical understanding of planning practice: What planners do is determined by forces outside their control; planners are largely powerless, but they do not realize it; planners get results not through their expertise and deliberations, but because of their skills at adversarial politics.

Planners work in an organizational world in which coercion, craft, and consent operate concurrently in complex ways. The bureaucratic chain of command puts tight limits on the exercise of craft. The uncertainty of political competition among city elected officials and among department heads fragments public consensus. New knowledge about environmental risks or growth management introduces innovations in professional craft that erode existing conventions and public expectations. Historically, the powers of bureaucratic coercion and adversarial consensus-making have had the upper hand. The authority of planning craft has usually played a minor role in setting priorities.

Many professionals, like Martin, seek to adapt the powers inherent to their craft to fit the demands of administrative authority and adversarial politics. Martin hoped to win the director's approval for his plan and thereby neutralize the influence of the special interests represented by Loomis. Others, like Tom, have tried to elevate the planning craft above power relationships. In Tom's situation the rational protocol, as a guide for professional behavior, is a product of misplaced idealism; in Martin's, a failure of political strategy. The protocol not only fails to distinguish among the different kinds of power relations that planners experience, but also discourages them from adopting political strategies.

The culture and institutions of the United States do not favor planning or planners dedicated to rational deliberation about public goods. Bureaucrats and public officials often use planning expertise and argument as rhetorical cover for advancing their special interests above those of others. Despite such impediments, professional planners carry on, developing schemes to reduce the uncertainties generated by the politics of adversity and the economics of competitive self-interest. Often professional planners adopt a protocol that hampers these efforts, as the stories of Tom and Martin show. There are other professionals, however, who take a more complex and robust approach toward their professional activity and succeed in retaining their jobs and getting things done.

NOTE

1. Most changes create more modest uncertainty than do disasters. People not only take actions to resist, assimilate, and accommodate the uncertainties others impose, but seek ways to shift these burdens onto others. In liberal democratic societies, the distribution of such uncertainty frequently (although not exclusively) occurs unevenly, based on differences in wealth, political authority, legal standing, and social status. The rich obtain useful knowledge at their leisure that the poor can acquire only at great sacrifice. White men escape the police scrutiny that black men must endure. Citizens make plans that remain only wishes for illegal aliens. This poses a serious problem of justice. When planners imagine and compose schemes to anticipate, identify, and evaluate the uncertainty and risk that communities face in the pursuit of collective or joint purposes, they encounter this uneven distribution.

4

Research and Rationality

The activity of the research analyst exemplifies the closest fit between the professional protocol and actual practice. When planners engage in research they tap into their acquired supply of scientific and technical knowledge and put it to practical use. Planners occasionally have the opportunity to impose the "good" methods of analysis they learned in school in the context of competing institutional demands. When clients, superiors, and colleagues need answers to questions of fact, independent of their convictions and powers of control, then the planner's expertise comes into its own.

In adversarial settings, however, various sides often recruit the planner's expertise to defend preestablished views and attack those of the opponent. Methodological squabbles become politically charged, as each set of experts attempts to discredit the opponent's research. For instance, in the courtroom, the jury knows that the two parties in the dispute have hired experts to testify on their behalf. The crucial test of expertise hinges on the independence of the analysis.

Imagine a courtroom proceeding in which expert witnesses are testifying about the impact of a proposed group home on neighboring residential property values. The expert for the plaintiffs, a representative of Neighbors United for Justice, takes the stand and gives testimony:

> I am in the employ of the plaintiffs. I answered the questions they asked about the effect of group homes on neighboring residential property values. The results of my research offer evidence of fact that support their beliefs. Property values did fall by x percent over y years in the z cases we analyzed. I did not

fudge or otherwise tamper with the method of inquiry. Anyone else following our procedures would get similar results for this inquiry 95 percent of the time.

The defense attorney cross-examines the witness, raising questions about method. What assumptions did you make about the definition of a group home? How did you select your sample? How many homes did you include in assessing property value change? Did you control for changes in property value in other similar places without such homes? These sorts of questions test and challenge the reliability and validity of the method. If the defendant's attorney can uncover instances where the analyst exercised judgments favoring the sponsor's case or made errors that benefited the plaintiff, then the jury will have cause to doubt the testimony of the expert.

SENSITIVE OBJECTIVITY

Good scientific research uses objective methods to test the evidence supporting various policy-relevant judgments. Good analysis avoids bias. Doctoring or fudging evidence to favor a partisan position undermines the legitimacy of the research. Valid research inquiry asks questions for which reliable answers do not yet exist. By contrast, politically biased research frames the problem and method of analysis to keep the range of outcomes within the bounds of partisan expectations. The community of analysts—the keepers of the scientific method—refine and enforce a critical skepticism to monitor such expectations.

Planners, however, are not scientists. It is difficult to make the case that planners function as objective analysts among institutional partisans. Planners are on the payroll. They formulate questions and collect information in particular institutional settings in response to the expectations of others. Usually planners address routine issues, but occasionally they must deal with contradictory expectations with high political stakes. Planners are sometimes called on to offer testimony in an adversarial proceeding in a courtroom, a public hearing, or a crucial development meeting.

How do planners conduct research inquiry in these institutional settings? How do planners go about reshaping institutional expectations to secure the freedom to gather the information that best answers the pressing research questions? Do planners do their research as partisan advocates for their sponsors or as fair-minded skeptics? And if, as I suspect is the case, they try to do both, how do they avoid sacrificing the independence that makes their expert judgment credible?

Norma: Trustworthy Research

Norma works for an old industrial suburb on the periphery of a central city. An African-American woman with a no-nonsense style, a gift for gab, and a knack for computers, she talks about her research like a carpenter talks about tools. I interview her after she has been at her job about a year.

I'm always looking at the job market for opportunities. I saw the ad for a planner in Burgess and sent in an application with a copy of my resume. I had studied with the planning director, Fred, while in grad school. Fred did not remember me when he read my resume, but selected me for an interview based on my qualifications. But when I saw him on the day of the interview it was no contest. He came up to me and said I was hired. The importance of our shared experience as students was the key. We had studied statistics together and I helped him figure the stuff out. He knew I was competent and we trusted each other.

I've been put in a situation here that is challenging. It tests me. For instance, Fred wanted me to develop the computer inventory for land parcels in the city. The purpose of the project is to provide an integrated database system that uses common parcel IDs across departments. The first big test was finding the best method. How could I figure out what the city departments that would use the system needed and wanted?

The county assessor offered an excellent data source and a good place to begin, but there was a longstanding dispute between the assessor and the planning department. My strategy was to take the chief assessor data clerk to lunch and talk. The planning data guy warned me not to do it. He wanted to resolve the dispute in a more formal fashion. I felt that someone new might help break the logjam, but he insisted. So I backed off. I decided to start with the water data instead.

I go out of my way to share information that we collect in the planning department. This is no big deal anyway since the amount of duplication among different city departments is enormous. That's why data integration would have such a big impact, but there is resistance to this notion of sharing. Departments guard their data and turf.

So I go to the water department. This elderly female employee for the department wouldn't even look me in the eye when I talked with her. I got stuff from her, but I wanted to establish a relationship. I couldn't get anywhere at first. One day she visited our department and requested a parcel ID number for an address. She didn't approach me, but first contacted my white intern. As she asked the intern for help, I simply typed the address she had requested into the computer and gave her the information she had requested in about ten seconds. She was amazed. She thanked me. Now we talk and she looks at me. Look, white people seem to have this innate fear of black people. I work hard to overcome these groundless fears.

Anyway, I got to work putting together an integrated, computerized information system. Before I came, the city staff could never get a unified data system together. As the new kid on the block, I was able to get access to the different information systems in the city and start setting up an integrated inventory system using data from planning, permits, assessor.... Furthermore, I made it clear that I wanted to develop a system that was built in and not dependent on me. This tended to reduce the turf tensions. Furthermore, when problems did come up, the fact that I had taught Fred all about the computer stuff when we were in classes together helped a lot. He supported my efforts to build links when they ran into bureaucratic snags.

I have been able to show the value of this sort of information system for meeting the information needs of our own department, as well as others. Fred is pleased. He takes me with him to speak with the city manager. He even hired an intern and data entry person to work for me and help speed up the project.

Norma understood how creating a computerized database across different municipal departments would increase efficiency in answering routine requests and in conducting more detailed analyses at less expense. Norma, however, is not simply a skilled technician. She developed credibility in the research technology by fostering reciprocal relationships that countered conventional expectations. Norma enjoyed and used her relationship of trust with her boss. This relationship gave her the freedom to move across department boundaries without fear of sanctions from her boss. She sensed that he would protect her from any resistance and protest from employees and their directors in the other units.

As the new computer expert, Norma did not parade the technical tools in her toolkit. Rather, she concentrated on establishing relationships with employees—not necessarily her peers—in other departments. She anticipated racial discrimination, as well as institutional resistance. She worked to persuade the clerks that the integrated information system would not diminish their authority, but enhance their capacity to organize the information at their disposal. The visit episode represented a crucial event. Norma was able to overcome the visitor's racial and institutional fears through her act of competent and gracious data retrieval, which illustrated her capacity to manage data efficiently without using any of her institutional power.

Norma, the local computer expert, does not adopt the role of the detached and objective analyst. The image of the outside expert would have increased already exaggerated levels of suspicion. She adopted the role of a friend and colleague, hoping to persuade other workers to do the same. A friend or colleague does not introduce changes in the work place that provide personal benefit at others' expense. Norma's act of competent generosity inspired trust in the suspicious coworker. The woman could now accept the legitimacy of the computer information. The innovation made the woman's job easier without diminishing her discretion. In the process, Norma's advice came to be perceived as trustworthy and valid.

PERSUASIVE OBJECTIVITY

The isolation of scientific investigation from the dogmatic imposition of religious beliefs and from the popular infiltration of fantasy, desire, and magic constitutes a long tradition of skeptical inquiry. Essential to our contemporary commonsense understanding of objectivity is the skeptical, detached outlook. Skepticism, however, does not reassure concerned and burdened officials, colleagues, and citizens. They want to know that planners who are conducting studies to relieve the burdens of uncertainty understand their fears and hopes.

This does not necessarily mean that the fears and doubts people harbor when they experience uncertainty should lead them to see only what they want to see. Nor does it mean that planners must shape data to fit the desired outcomes of their clients. Rather, this tension between the scientific method and human fears and concerns suggests that planners design their methods of inquiry to take into account these feelings. Good objective research does not solely seek skeptical detachment, but fair-minded attention to the purposes of others.

James Throgmorton has studied how the rhetoric of research and the rhetoric of public persuasion overlap in the public planning arena. He compares how the proponents and opponents organized their arguments concerning the expansion of nuclear power plants in Illinois (1990; 1992). Throgmorton argues that research is most persuasive when it incorporates the elements of a good narrative: a plot that lays out the differences among policy choices in a coherent sequence, characters whom the readers recognize as believable and relevant actors, settings that mark and clarify the relationships between the characters and channel how the characters enact the plot, and, finally, tropes (e.g., metaphor, irony) that shape the reader's feelings toward the characters and the plot. He contends that persuasive planning analysts do more than collect information, conduct tests, and present results. They write and speak about their research in ways that make their work appear valuable, useful, and relevant to specific audiences in particular situations. Throgmorton's detailed analysis of the Illinois Commonwealth Edison rate case illustrates how the powerful utility failed to provide a believable narrative to the public, the courts, and the state utility board:

> Edison's planners and managers failed to persuade consumer groups and the ICC because the company's story was weak in plot development, was written from an unbelievable point of view, and characterized consumer groups in a way those groups could not identify with (1992, 29).

The following stories in this chapter explore how various planners seek to maintain a balance between research that offers persuasive argument and their faithfulness to the conventions and craft of expertise. Peter Marris (1990) uses three analogies to describe how research analysts bridge the domains of inquiry and of practice: as engineers, witnesses, and storytellers. These are not mutually exclusive activities, but distinct styles guiding how analysts present their research in applied policy settings. Engineers concentrate on problem solving and adopt an instrumental approach in their inquiry, while witnesses focus on evidence that will stand up to critical examination. In both cases, detached review remains a crucial test of validity. Storytelling, however, depends on the authority of the author to craft a convincing narrative framework.

The three planners below combine aspects of each approach. Nancy and Esteban tend to emphasize the organization of evidence, while Kathleen stresses problem solving. None, however, resembles the self-centered analyst classifying the subjects of inquiry according to the rigid rules of the pure scientific method. These analysts understand that there are multiple methods for assessing each subject and diverse interpretations of the results. These three researchers have made commitments about what method to use, how to deploy it, and for what purposes. As they talk about their work and the merits of their research approach, they offer reasons to support the efficacy of their choice. Nancy and Esteban, especially, construct stories that put their choice of research method and organization in the context of a larger narrative. These stories tie their choices to larger, more inclusive efforts for social change and reform.

Nancy: Civic Responsibility

Nancy has carved out a career in government fiscal affairs, evaluating taxes, fees, and budgets. Her account of applied research bears witness to her opposition to the squandering of public funds on huge development projects. She is a storyteller with a strong sense of narrative and dramatic timing. More than most of the planners I interviewed, she possesses a carefully built moral framework for traversing the ambiguities between evidence and belief. The crafting of her research to offer useful and persuasive stories parallels the lucid story of her work that she recounts in our interview.

Nancy is the director of research at a small regional nonprofit agency. Her research focuses on fiscal issues. She spends much of her time using statistical and other analytical procedures to prepare fiscal studies and reports.

> What I do here at this nonprofit watchdog organization is conduct research on a variety of public fiscal issues, many of which prove controversial—especially budgets. I like it because we give the same information to all parties. Of course, if a candidate for local office comes to us and sort of runs a proposal by us and asks for our opinion of its feasibility, we will give our advice and not necessarily share it with others, unless the opponent asks, in which case we will give what they request.
>
> Our mission is to make government fiscal policies and their impacts clear to the general public. For instance, one of the important things we do is show how the property tax multiplier assessment and rate are organized in relation to different local government levies. This stuff is complicated, but of great interest to taxpayers. So we provide useful, educational information and present it to the media for public consumption.

Nancy does not waste a moment. She packs each one with rapid surges of words. Her spartan dress and professional posture belie the energetic zeal of her conversation. She takes obvious pleasure in the production of useful research. She distinguishes between, but does not separate, technical acumen and political savvy. Her intense and urbane talk is tempered by her provincial, even conservative, demeanor and dress. We sit in a corner office of an older downtown highrise, but I have a sense of relaxed comfort, as if I were listening to neighborhood gossip on the back porch of an aging urban bungalow.

> I come from a community organizing background. I was the head of a community school in another big city before I came here. It was there that I learned how to do organizing and programming. I know how to conduct public relations.
>
> When I first moved here I got a job as an executive director of a community organization, but the experience proved disappointing, if challenging. The organization was old and well established. The board consisted mainly

of home owners who wanted to protect their property values and avoid taking up the concerns and needs of local renters.

I developed my political sense there. I learned how to evaluate the different players on the board and in the community and assess what sorts of proposals were feasible. I figured out what was possible and how to do it. This political knowledge has proven useful in doing research.

What I have done is not classic planning. You know, the comprehensive planning stuff—researching and then developing alternatives for decision makers. I saw lots of that when I worked in a county assessor's office for several years on the coast.

I'm a historian by training. I can appreciate what planners do. Planners are like historians. The good ones learn about an issue (for example, housing), researching what they need to analyze the problem and formulate clear options for decision makers. Planners are good learners, able to move from issue to issue. Ironically, this flexibility often means that planners are not considered real experts, since real experts only have one special area of expertise.

Being an expert is an important professional asset. I learned this by accident. I got into tax issues working as a research assistant for a faculty member who happened to be doing property tax research. I developed this interest and eventually developed it enough to form the basis for my Ph.D. I have consistently worked on tax related issues now for over twelve years. The work I do today is possible because of the expertise I have built up over all these years.

Learning about the tax system eventually got me into other areas, for instance, my concerns for social justice and social policy. I learned how the tax stuff provided me with an expert role I could use to pursue social policies. For instance, I learned early on that tax information is politically important and that I could come under political attack when I used it. I had to depend on the quality of my ideas as a defense. Despite the pressures, I do not shape the data to fit political expectations. When hired as a consultant, you are not hired to please, but to inform and advise.

For Nancy, conventional planners engage in competent and even clever analysis, but they lack authority. By comparison, the research specialist has greater standing, not only for reasons of technical competence, but because political officials must rely on their expertise. The effective specialist uses her expertise in the context of political interests and debate. Ironically, specialized expertise offers both entry as a political player and insulation from the heat generated in political contexts. How do researchers mix politics and analysis without discrediting the legitimacy of the investigation?

Disinterested Sponsorship

The most dramatic case I can recall was a large downtown hotel development project in Central City. The mayor initially supported a tax abatement because of the political attractiveness of fostering a new big development project. It was a difficult struggle to get the city administration to realize the dangers and stop.

A colleague and I eventually worked together as pro bono consultants to a coalition of citywide and neighborhood organizations that came together to oppose the hotel project. But before making a commitment to conduct research for the coalition, we had conducted our own preliminary analysis. It was not a close call. The wasteful and ineffective effects of the project were likely to be large. So I felt fine taking sides against the city administration, which was pushing for a subsidized project without adequate justification. Besides, my work was not funded by any self-interested sponsor or government. I did the work on my own while living off my stipend as a research assistant at the university.

Nancy and her research colleague play the role of planning analyst advocates. Nancy, however, takes sides carefully, only after she is convinced that her professional expertise would not lose its critical edge. Still, her insistence that she was not on an interested party's payroll sounds a bit defensive. Hers was an act of public service that enabled her to apply and develop her analytical skills as a graduate student.

Exhaustive Research

This project was the first major tax abatement proposal of its kind offered by the city administration. The city officials were amazingly ignorant of the economics of the deal. They did not realize that a major abatement in an area with enormous property values would reduce the efficiency of the revenue engine that drives a city budget—especially in recessionary times. Property tax abatements in high-value areas handicap a municipal government's ability to deliver needed services.

Tax abatement can be a useful tool, but only when those who propose it understand the long-term fiscal effects on the entire taxing jurisdiction. In the downtown abatement case, the subsidized hotel would not only have robbed the city of revenue from that site, but also produced thousands of new hotel units in an already crowded market. Other hotels were likely to close, leading to a decline of tax revenues from those sites as well.

Basically my research used data on abatement projects from other downtowns to show that the abatement was neither necessary to ensure project feasibility [profitability], nor efficient. Property tax abatement wasn't cost-effective because the city administration was planning to give one dollar for each half dollar saved through the abatement by the developers. Worse yet, the project didn't need the subsidy. The developers could have made money without the subsidy, just not as much as they could with it. The city should use abatements for marginally unprofitable developments in needy areas of the city, not on valuable land in the heart of downtown.

Nancy, the analyst, produces research studies that challenge the claims of the city administration that the hotel project will offer great public benefits. She does her homework, gathering evidence that the proponents carelessly overlook. She enhances the persuasive power of her findings by emphasizing the perverse impact of the project. Not only will the city fail to get the benefits it claims, but the project will cost the city. The projected development project would actually contribute to the further decay of the city's tax base. She does not stop, however, with the report.

Astute Politics

I learned early on that the mayor and the independently elected tax assessor were political enemies. The mayor wanted the abatement, but the assessor could slow the whole thing down. The assessor first learned of my research analysis evaluating the negative effects of the abatement when I spoke at a downtown meeting of interested businessmen and public officials. He showed his approval of the ideas (despite the fact that a local public official had used a research study I had produced documenting racial inequality in the existing tax assessment procedures to embarrass the assessor).

Our strategy was to use our research to give arguments for the assessor to slow down the administration's push for the abatement. The assessor never liked the abatement idea. I found the assessor to be a competent guy. His office was usually methodical and careful in its research. They spent a lot of time evaluating proposals and produced good quality work. So he resisted the considerable pressure from the Central City administration and the hotel developers and conducted his own evaluation. The more time it took to get needed approval from the assessor, the more time the coalition of organizers had to mobilize protest and resistance.

Nancy simultaneously worked with community organizations and used her research to get the attention of a public official with enough clout to stall the mayor's plans. She exploited a longstanding political antagonism and offered her research as a resource the assessor could use to frustrate the mayor's plans. Getting the assessor to subject the project to further study proved a useful maneuver, since it gave the opposition more time to circulate doubts about the viability of the project.

Informed Rhetoric

The claims of the project advocates from the city administration were exaggerated and mystifying. So instead of taking the role of technical experts, we took a lot of time explaining the economic and fiscal effects of the abatement in a variety of public meetings. We made our work accessible. We wanted the interested citizens and activists to make informed judgments about the political positions they took and to put our findings to use in their own words.

I do not want to be a rabble rouser, using rhetoric instead of truth. I do not lie. I tell the truth persuasively. Since the project got lots of media attention, I was especially concerned to ensure the integrity of my research against the kind of media rhetoric that exaggerates.

My colleague and I disagreed about the relationship between politics, rhetoric, and analysis. For instance, he prepared a report that translated the fiscal effect of the hotel project costs on the tax bill of the individual homeowner. He made a lot of misleading assumptions to create a patently partisan piece of research. I opposed his use of a statistic that appeared more clear-cut than was actually the case. He had calculated the amount an individual homeowner's tax might go down if the revenue generated by the hotel development without the abatement were translated into a tax savings. I found this misleading because it was highly unlikely that all or even most additional tax revenues from this project would be returned to taxpayers in the form of a tax cut. I showed instead the amount of tax dollars that would be lost to the city and what these dollars could otherwise buy in the way of city services, like schools and streets.

Nancy's tale of advocacy research shows the complex ways in which an effective analyst can use political relationships and rhetoric to shape meaningful and practical research. Nancy claims that her desires and moral purposes do not distort her analysis. She criticizes her colleague for using individual tax savings as an evaluation measure because his analysis ignored how municipal governments usually allocate revenues. He violated standards of good research to fulfill the expectations of community activists. She does not tamper with the evidence to fit her expectations. Purpose and prejudice frame the questions, not the answers. Good research relies not on purpose and position, but on a fair-minded analysis of the evidence. Even as an adversarial researcher, Nancy rightfully belongs to the community of analysts whose work must meet certain minimum standards of reliability and validity if it is to count.

Nancy's institutional setting—a watchdog nonprofit organization—supported the kind of flexibility she needed to be able to shuttle back and forth between serving political purpose and conducting objective inquiry. Can research analysts with less institutional freedom conduct their scientific investigations and still provide politically relevant and useful knowledge?

Esteban: Procedural Review

Esteban is director of research for the Central City planning department. He is Mexican, middle-aged, and dedicated to expanding the representation and involvement of Hispanics in the political control of the city. He speaks with few movements or gestures. Rather than appearing stiff, he seems firm, like a rock having weathered many storms. His feelings emerge at the edges—a crinkle of the lips, a twitch of the eye, a fixed and angry stare. At the time of my interview, he was busy compiling information that would protest the expected undercount in the 1990 census of Central City's population.

Monitoring the Census

We've been focusing recently on ensuring that the census data for the city will be accurate. We are preparing to provide feedback to challenge the preliminary census estimates down to the block level. The census has provided us with estimates of housing units (not people or households) per block. If we find blocks where our own estimates vary significantly from those provided by the census, the census will return and check about 2 percent. Of course, we want them to check more.

I have a personal interest in making sure that minorities are fairly represented in the census. In 1986, the Latino think tank I worked for published a report I had prepared on the empowerment of the Latino electorate. The basic idea was that the Latinos have enough eligible voters who, if they were registered and voted for their own representatives, would possess substantially greater political influence over local government. But fear, ignorance, and negligence combine to keep Latinos not only from joining the electorate, but even participating in the census. I showed how the failure to participate hindered the social and economic development of Latinos and other minorities in Central City.

Minority communities possess fewer officially recognized members and so get less representation. A lot of local marketing decisions are demographically based. The undercount of minorities leads to failures to identify accurately the actual geographic concentrations of people. This discourages the creation of new businesses and leads to fewer community retail and service establishments. Similarly, the distribution of nonprofit and public social services is usually tied to population levels. When the population figures for minorities are too low, the existing populations suffer from too few services.

I used census data in my report as well as additional data sources to illustrate the large undercount in the Latino community. I called for a strong program to encourage greater participation in the 1990 census. So here I am. I got hired over a year ago because I had a lot of experience manipulating and analyzing census data. I had learned how the census data are organized and the value and limits of their use.

The decennial census represents a primary source of information on population and housing characteristics. Planning analysts seldom reflect on the omissions and errors in census data. These mistakes matter little when the data are summarized for the entire nation or states. However, the census is often used to describe characteristics at much smaller scales that often justify the location of new facilities and the distribution of public services and other goods. If the undercounts are increasingly concentrated in certain geographic areas, as studies indicate has been the case in poor, minority inner city neighborhoods, the distributional consequences can be substantial.

So, for the past month we [the research personnel in the planning department] have gathered information from a variety of data sources. No one file is comprehensive, so we have to use multiple sources to create an accurate estimate. The Harris file contains property information on parcels and housing conditions, while a file kept by the building department includes similar information on the physical structure by parcel. In addition, we got information from three different utility companies: electric, water, and gas. In addition to our aggregate file, we selected a sample of fifty census tracts, which we canvassed in depth. We used the results of the field survey to test the validity of our computer estimates. For the most part, our estimates appear sound.

Having completed the integration of the data sets, we were able to generate different estimates depending on the particular combination of sources we used. We plan to adopt the highest figures from the different source estimates because we believe this is the most conservative. That is, we would be less likely to miss counting someone this way. Of course, this also will help us pressure the census bureau to review its own estimates and hopefully increase the size of its count for the city. The bureau will not pay any attention to our protests without the sort of hard evidence we have gathered.

All the data sources we used have problems. They are not frequently updated to capture the new construction, conversion, and demolition that goes on all the time. The gas company data are probably the least reliable since so many structures with multiple dwellings have only one meter. The electric company data are better because individual dwellings tend to get metered more frequently. Of course, there are exceptions, like the housing authority units, which have only a single meter per building. So in cases like that we went to the owner and found out the number of dwellings.

Esteban and his staff have collected data from multiple sources to substantiate the undercount in the poor minority neighborhoods of Central City. Years of research have uncovered plenty of evidence. The real difficulty is persuading census officials and local politicians to take serious actions to remedy the problem. The researchers encounter a painful paradox. Their demonstration of the social and political inequalities in the administration of the census mainly elicits promises to administer the established procedures with greater attention and quality control. Esteban's basic complaint, however, is not with administrative malfeasance, but with the procedures. He wants the census officials to adopt special methods in select areas to improve the accuracy of the count.

We also have staff monitoring the census bureau operations to see that the proper procedures are being followed in the field. We have planted individuals in the district offices to flag administrative and operational problems in conducting the surveys.

The case written up in the newspaper was partly our doing. [Esteban is referring to an exposé article that compared the manufactured findings of an incompetent census taker with those obtained by reporters visiting the same addresses. The reporters found more than double the number of people than were recorded by the census taker.] Several census-taker crew leaders from this area came to the assistant director of planning and told her that they thought the census was being improperly conducted. They felt the directions they received were inadequate and ambiguous and that some crew directors were forging questionnaire answers.

The [honest] crew directors contacted the newspaper reporters and blew the whistle. Presently the city law department is suing the census over some of these administrative improprieties.

The deputy director of the census came to speak with us at the department of planning about the problems. We suggested several measures that field office staff could adopt when they conduct their field work. One especially crucial issue was the classification of housing units as occupied or vacant. The present census procedures allow census takers to classify a unit as vacant if the census taker can not find or otherwise determine the presence or number of occupants. We wanted them to change the procedure to conduct a follow up. The deputy director opposed the change (not because our suggestion was not good), because he claimed the census had to follow the same procedures everywhere (even if that meant misclassifying occupied dwellings as vacant). Planning staff in other older big cities have raised similar protests as ours, but to little avail.

We also met with regional census staff who had done the follow up in the neighborhood where the reporters had found forgery and undercounts. The staff told us that after resurveying the area they found about 2,500 more people. They felt this was not a significant problem given the large population size of the area. We argued that the figure was significant if one assumed the problem was not exceptional, but common. The staff vehemently insisted the undercounting was an exception. They claimed they resurveyed some 60 percent of the households, but we figure they didn't really do it.

Esteban points out two kinds of problems: The census takers do not follow their rules in the field, and the rules they follow do not work. The use of planning staff to police the census takers improves the quality of existing procedures. That is important, but Esteban cares more about changing the procedures. To serve that goal, he has had the staff build a demographic case against the procedures. Esteban's moderate proposal, however, actually challenges the image of the census as detached and evenhanded. If census officials make exceptions in Central City, then they will likely face similar requests by cities in other regions. The multiplicity of locally tailored procedures would raise questions about the reliability of the survey and greatly increase its cost. Therefore, although most demographers would agree that the evidence Esteban's staff has collected offers valid evidence of an undercount, the census administrators will not authorize procedural changes to rectify the problem. The more extensive the undercounts based on specific characteristics of race, ethnicity, and location, the more reluctant census officials are to remedy the problem. Therefore, Esteban pushed to increase public awareness of the census to expand participation in areas where undercounts were likely.

Promoting Minority Participation

Well over a year before the actual census my unit was given responsibility for promoting participation in the census by all citizens of the city. We developed an educational and advertising campaign. I helped form a network of organizations that could disseminate the information on the census and encourage participation.

We created the Complete Count Committee with a board composed of corporate and foundation representatives. Their primary task was to help us raise money for the campaign. We also formed another committee called 1990

Counts with a racially and ethnically diverse board. The basic message was that the city receives state and federal revenue based on population formulas, so an uncounted household costs the city future revenue. However, we also pointed out how the distribution of funds within the city is frequently tied to the population size of communities. A bigger community gets more services. Finally, many agencies deliver services and funds on the basis of the proportionate share of certain income or racial groups. So different minorities, especially the organizations, had an incentive to ensure that their respective populations were accurately counted.

We produced a rough estimate of the amount of future revenue the city would lose for each person not counted. The amount was four hundred dollars. This helped us quantify in dollars and cents what an undercount of the population might mean for the city's future.

I did a lot of the promotional stuff myself, especially in the Latino communities. I am bilingual and so I could approach all the Hispanic media and get air time. We used a lot of electronic media and my personal interest was focused there.

We also tried to mobilize the churches to involve their congregations. We had some large meetings. I remember one meeting with five hundred people from three hundred community organizations who were there to learn how to get the word out. We thought the churches would be the best contact with people. Community groups don't have large memberships like the churches do. Furthermore, the pastors see their members a lot more.

One of the good things about working on the census participation project is that nobody disagrees with the purpose. Everyone agrees that participating is a good idea. This helped us avoid a lot of potential antagonisms. Morale among my staff was quite high. (I have eight full time and three part-time interns as well as a media consultant.) The problems were not with the community, but with the bureaucracies of the city.

We had lots of opportunities to get press attention about the census undercount issue, but the mayor's press office didn't allow us to release most of our innovative stuff. They just decided it wasn't important. Some just didn't give a damn and others were ignorant. Most of the bureaucratic obstacles came from departments within the city for whom the census was not a priority. We couldn't even get the office of special events to let us set up booths to distribute census materials at different city sponsored and supported activities. "People come to play and eat," they said, "not to read about the census."

We had more success recruiting participation from other agencies (school districts, city colleges, human service agencies, transportation authorities) who had a stake in an accurate census count. We received support and aid from the staff of these agencies. They helped us get the word out and promote participation.

Esteban's public relations campaign did not reflect detached expertise, but rather his deep political commitment to rectifying a serious injustice. He set aside scrupulous attention to fieldwork and data analysis. The planners sought sponsors from a wide range of community organizations. They wrote advertising copy and gave speeches to dramatize the benefits of participation and the injustice of the undercounts. Key city personnel, however, followed the lead of the administration and the mayor, who had never championed the concerns of minorities. The staff could carry out their census participation campaign, but they did so without crucial political support. Other campaign participants, however, especially those allied to the mayor's opponents, were not above using the promotion to pursue their own political agendas.

The Politics of Race and Ethnicity

At the Urban League, the agency run by and for the interests of Afro-Americans, the director of human relations was a woman who supported the efforts and plans of my division. She was very receptive to the promotional plans. She understood that all minorities face the problem of the undercount together. She was willing to work with the Latino groups to go to local foundations for the funds needed to support the promotional campaign. If we all went together rather than separately, the likelihood of getting funds was greater and their use more efficient. But she resigned soon after the project got underway and her replacement was an official in the previous political administration—the administration of an Afro-American mayor.

In the initial agreement there was a division of labor between the community organizations and the city. The planning department was to do things that would be of use to all the community groups. So we agreed to the printing and production of promotional media spots. This would be the most efficient approach, but the new human relations guy at the Urban League was suspicious and claimed that I was going to use the planning department resources to help the Latino community at the expense of Afro-Americans. Since he didn't trust the new administration (with a white mayor), he didn't trust me.

One especially nasty episode was a meeting with a major private donor. I was there representing the city along with representatives of the community organizations including this guy from the league. I was discussing our promotional plans when he started yelling that the city wanted to use the funds for purposes other than promoting participation in the census. He complained that the white administration was not supportive of minorities. I told him that this outburst was out of order and that we had no hidden agenda. We were following policies that had been discussed and agreed on by the participants.

When we got down to allocating the funds we had obtained from donors to conduct the promotional campaign, this guy openly turned against the Latino organizations. The Urban League human relations guy wanted the funds distributed on the basis of the 1980 undercount correction study that had been done in the early 1980s. This study was dated and weighted the count in favor of Afro-Americans. The Latino Institute representative objected and said that the distribution of funds should be done proportionately, based on the 1988 estimates of minority populations that had been produced using corrections from the earlier 1980 correction study. I stood by the latter figures, as these were the ones provided by the city and represented the best estimate.

So the Urban League guy accused me of being biased. No matter what I said, he wanted to politicize the process to show that the city administration was not sensitive to the Afro-American population. He hoped to develop an issue that could be used in the upcoming election campaign.

A unified coalition of participants had launched the public relations campaign. The racial/ethnic conflict proved especially divisive because it ruptured the trust central to the viability of the largely voluntary campaign. The new African-American public relations officer had no previous relationship with Esteban or with the process of building the campaign. The entire effort must have appeared to him to be merely a public relations campaign for the white mayor. Hence, he lobbied for the early census study, because it favored African-Americans. He believed that the technical arguments about the superior accuracy of the latter study were merely rhetorical devices in support of the Latino over the African-American population. In neither of his roles as analyst or consensus builder could Esteban bridge this racial divide.

Unlike Nancy, Esteban is not interested in advocacy research. Nancy spends most of her time in the archives, at the computer, and on the streets. She confronts powerful organizations with challenging information, while Esteban struggles to make organizations collect and use information in more responsible ways. Esteban expends much effort in trying to modify institutional relationships. He has political purposes. He wants to include Latinos as citizens who count, but he does not assign them status as an interest group entitled to special attention and treatment. He perceived the census participation project to be an opportunity for organizational collaborators to share a basic consensus about inclusion. The conflict with the Urban League representative was especially disturbing because the African-American opponent was substituting exclusion for inclusion and engaging in adversarial politics. Esteban did not celebrate his victory over his adversary, but rather felt frustrated that the consensus he had relied on was gone.

The next story tells of a planner who acts as the patron of a planning grant. Here is a case of a planner using her authority and influence to encourage regional planning research with a focus on implementation.

Kathleen: Implementing Results

Kathleen is the consummate professional in her tastefully understated high-quality suit, scant jewelry, and only a whisper of artifice. Her graceful poise and formality project confidence and authority. She has found a way to make the professional uniform charming without diminishing its power. Her voice similarly offers a gentle decisiveness. During our interview she explained to me why she turned from a promising career as a talented seamstress in the fashion industry to planning:

> I had a calling to become a planner. It seemed the logical occupation to make an impact. I didn't see myself in a corporate setting marketing clothes. I wanted to do more than that. I asked myself, "What kind of value do I want to add?" Clearly, government was a way to do that—solving problems, changing the world. But I was not a product of the 1960s. I was only in junior high school in the late 1960s, although in the early 1970s I did get exposed to the possibility that I could change things and that doing so was alright. I can remember reading in the newspaper about what was going on in city hall. Only I was not interested in the political intrigue, but the projects and proposals for public improvement. What were the public problems and what was going on to solve them? That's what interested me. My image of the good public-serving professional was someone who blended the no-nonsense business emphasis on financial feasibility with a strong sense of public responsibility.

Kathleen has worked in a historic preservation office, for the public finance division of a large bank, as a staff member of a state development finance department, and now as a state transportation planner.

> Public finance was also a kind of calling. When I was an undergrad, I had researched the fiscal crisis of New York City and written several papers about the source of its troubles and what was done to prevent bankruptcy. I found it shocking that this could actually happen to the largest city in the U.S. This research fueled my interest in public finance and especially the financing of infrastructure.

What I like about private business is the necessity of having to meet the bottom line. I find that a lot of public agencies do not prioritize because they don't face this sort of economic pressure of profitability. In addition, there is greater opportunity for creativity in the private and quasi-private agencies I worked for. Public [municipal] agencies are more restricted by political pressures, while the agencies I have worked for have all been removed from political conflicts from the outside. Finally, the time I spent working as a financial analyst in the private sector gave me skills unavailable in the public sector—especially the skill of assessing the economic viability and feasibility of capital improvement projects.

The planning process should start with a variety of ideas. You start with many ideas, but in deciding on which ones to pursue you must select which ones to spend money on. Since money is scarce and valuable, we should try to pursue those schemes that offer the greatest likelihood of financial success. This not only minimizes waste of scarce resources, but also helps set priorities and establish order in the creation of public improvements.

Kathleen is not interested in planning analysis in the abstract, but rather in research backed by the government and fiscal powers needed to carry out the resulting plans. Her instrumental and strategic approach helps her pay attention to issues of implementation from the very outset. She strongly supports actions for the public good, but expresses distaste for the adversarial politics so common within and between local governments.

A meeting has been scheduled by the regional planning agency for the metropolitan area to discuss how to implement a grant received from the state department of transportation. Kathleen attends as representative of the state agency. She monitors the grant, which is funding an effort by the regional planning agency to focus the attention of local municipal officials and planners on the importance of developing regional transportation centers to counter suburban traffic congestion. The assumption is that the creation of diversified regional centers would reduce automobile reliance. The state transportation agency hopes to increase ridership on trains and buses. The task at hand is to find ways to encourage the automobile-oriented suburbs to accept such a view and put it into practice.

The meeting is attended by a working group, which is a subcommittee of a larger standing committee of the regional agency that focuses on local development policy. The coordinator for the group circulated before the meeting a memo that defines the diversified regional centers (DRC) and proposes three charettes to design mature, emerging, and potential centers. In the charettes, the professionals are to brainstorm alternative solutions to specific design problems.

The participants are to address four questions:

- What changes in land use intensity and location within a regional center would reduce automobile reliance?
- What changes in the roadway, pedestrian, bikeway, and public transit networks would promote greater access to a center?
- What is the optimal service area for a center and the critical linkage corridors that would tie it to other centers?
- What shifts in proportion and amounts of housing and employment are recommended for testing transportation impacts on urban development?

The memo also asks the committee to take the following planning steps:

1. Evaluate current conditions, existing plans, and regulations within the context of the regional center goals:
   a. Increased land utilization and intensity
   b. Diversification of land use and transport mode
   c. Improved integration of transport systems
   d. Reduced travel time and shorter distances between land uses
2. Develop design schemes for the prototype DRC
3. Translate design schemes into components useful for evaluating costs and functional benefits
4. Identify possible implementation strategies.

Finally, attached to the memo is a matrix serving as a model worksheet for the charette. On the matrix is a list of topics organized under functional headings. For each topic, the participants are to consider existing conditions, current plans, the DRC plan, and implementation strategies.

The Meeting

The memo is an excellent example of the rational planning model in practice. Its authors believe in the functional efficacy of DRCs and prepare a formal scheme for discussion and analysis that presumes others will follow the logical order they propose. The meeting begins with the chair briefly summarizing the memo, but Kathleen interrupts.

Kathleen: Can we introduce people here? I don't know everyone. [Introductions ensue. There are fourteen in attendance, including me.]

Bob [chair and staff member of the regional planning agency]: Referring to the memo, I want to make a comparative analysis of the different components of the DRC. For instance, I envision a series of maps for each of the centers with measures of success to enable us to make analytic comparisons among the different kinds of communities (mature, potential, and emerging)—such things as physical condition, quality of urban services, amount of activity (for example, office vacancies), and such transportation factors as ease of access from each center to its hinterland. Assessing scores on these measures would give a good sense of the positive and negative qualities of each type of center [relative to the others]. There may be patterns that will help us point out what sorts of transportation policies might work [to enhance the positive and reduce the negative qualities].

So, in the charettes we need to present some of these basic facts in comparative fashion before we open it up to discussion. I anticipate people would have a lot to say about the indices, drawing on their own understanding and experience of their locale to focus in on the meaning of the comparisons.

Dick [staff member of the regional agency in charge of implementing the charettes): To what extent is it possible to generalize from one regional center to another? There are plenty of unique factors.

Bob: Well, I guess we could end up saying each area is unique, but hopefully this is not really true.

Kathleen: How do you identify features [of a DRC] that make the center work well?

Kathleen's question indicates her concern with the focus of the regional planners' research. She wants an applied focus.

Bob: If you compare the relevant components, you can pinpoint the positive and negative attributes of the DRC. For policy purposes we want to focus on the positive. If we can agree these sorts of centers are good, what can we do to encourage their survival?

Dick: [Seeking to offer an example] What if you compare areas dedicated to parking? If the problem is a lot of vacant land dedicated to parking, then what strategies can we propose to reduce this use?

Bob: Another measure of success may be the commitment of local political leaders to take action on the DRC issue.

The staff have adopted a rational research design: uncover the causes, evaluate consequences, and engineer alternatives that fit. The participants, however, begin to chafe under the pressure of the presuppositions.

Paul [planner from an older industrial suburb]: We may need to go beyond the classification of mature, emerging, and potential as types of DRCs. The real question is what are the commonalities among DRCs. Are they all tied to the same basic processes of change? How are they the same or different in response to these processes?

Paul's view is that if the three kinds of DRCs are the product of a common process, the committee should focus on the process or cause, rather than on the effects. Paul does not necessarily agree with the staff framework.

Bob: [Holding onto the classification] The components [that make a DRC] may be generically the same, but with a difference in emphasis.

Ken [transportation planner from Central City]: Do you anticipate a clear definition among the three types for the DRC?

Paul: Yeah. If we have a DRC, then here are the components...the common characteristics?

Ken: [Speaking to Paul] I thought you meant there was some sort of ceiling. Once you become a mature DRC, that's it. You no longer expand.

Paul: No.

Bob: No, I don't see that. They're on a continuum. The mature DRC simply has a shift in emphasis.

Dick: [Joking] All are buffeted by the winds of change and they, too, will change.

Paul: What constitutes a center may be more important than local differences.

Norma [planner from an aging industrial suburb]: I think in the case of mature centers [referring to her own suburb of Burgess] the issue is how do they remain centers. Do they go back to rail? How do emerging centers sustain effective transportation?

Paul: Some communities are not regional centers!

Paul raises the political issue: Classification schemes involve exclusion. If every place is a center, then the concept loses all meaning. So which areas will be defined as centers?

Dick: Identifying which [suburban] communities are centers will be difficult.

The politics of classification comes clearly into the open. Selecting the centers is difficult, not only because the transportation and land use relations are complex, but because officials from most suburban municipalities will resist a classification that reduces their chances of being a center. Dick's comment reflects the political worry that is at the heart of Paul's, and now Norma's, questions.

Paul: Do DRCs rise and fall? Once a DRC, always a DRC?

Bob: Not sure our agency would want to support a policy that mature DRCs be allowed to fade.

The classification scheme with its strong notions of hierarchy and centrality appears to give way here.

Paul: If an older area wants to become or remain a DRC we [the local planners and officials] need to determine what they need to do.

Paul wants to shift the emphasis away from the analysis and classification of DRCs by regional planners to giving officials and staff of local municipalities the opportunity to decide what sort of DRC they are or hope to be.

Bob: That's what we hope will come out of the charettes. Is this what others here see as the outcome?

Kathleen: I'm paying attention to how this works and am interested in how development occurs around transit stations near train stations. What makes a center work is density and diversity. We do agree that generally it is these conditions that make for a successful DRC. The problem in the region is getting different localities to make a commitment to these successful centers.

I envision the charettes as an activity in which participants will envision centers with greater density and diversity, taking into account local context. I sense that we [planners] have a hard time getting policies accepted that would make DRC centers possible. Will the charettes take us any further in getting support for these policies and getting them implemented?

Kathleen speaks with authority and some impatience. Previous speakers had focused on research issues concerning the origins and characteristics of the DRC. She considers the issue of definition settled: We know what DRCs are and what makes them work. How do we get the local planners and officials to accept and implement these ideas? How can we use the charettes to gather information and compose scenarios for implementing DRCs? Kathleen wants the research to focus on consequences, not causes; implementation, not analysis.

Dick: [Chastened somewhat, he shifts emphasis to include Kathleen's concerns.] I guess we could ask that each charette result in recommendations that include not only the general criteria, but also lay out how they could be implemented in a specific locale. I think we have to create relevant proposals [proposals acceptable to the local governments in the region, suggesting to Kathleen that the group can't presume consensus].

Bob: [Speaking to Kathleen] Your question is significant. I read the proposal [and the charettes] as being more of a way of focusing information about the conditions of a local area to assess whether or not the community is a successful DRC. You're going beyond this, saying we know what makes a successful DRC already and that we use the charette to get it accepted and working [showing some modest disapproval]. Does everyone agree density and diversity [as criteria for identifying a successful center] are enough [information to move ahead with implementation]?

Dick: They are important.

Ken [Central City planner]: That's a foundation, but each DRC is different. I wouldn't be willing to go into the charette with the thought that density and diversity are the only criteria. Put it out there, yes, but we want the participants to draw on their own experience and other local factors to assess the strengths and weaknesses of their locale as a DRC.

Ken returns to the political issue raised by Paul that municipalities and not the regional planners should assign the proper classification.

Bob: [Still speaking to Kathleen] I gather you want people to get more committed to making DRCs work. You don't want us to spend time collecting and analyzing more information?

Kathleen: [Shaking head in agreement] My preference is to move us to the next step.

Dick: [Appearing worried and concerned, he wants to salvage the planning scheme he laid out in the memo.] Can we dispense with describing conditions? Can't we lay out the existing conditions first and then turn to the policy issues?

Kathleen: [Leaving room for analysis, but not if it does not lead to implementable projects] The charette would have two parts. In the first session you focus on what's there. Maybe use some sort of democratic brainstorming process to get the ideas and information out. We absolutely need this, but then we must focus on what tasks are necessary to make an improved DRC happen. In the charettes I've participated in, it is good for participants to come away with something new and useful.

Bob: [Adapting to the comments of those representing the funding agency and seeking compromise] Well, using Dick's idea we would have two parts in each charette. A presentation of information about the DRC, followed by efforts to focus on what to do to solve its problems.

Ken: I'm unclear, Paul. Are we going to have one definition of DRC? You suggested there's a continuum from potential to mature. How do we respond to the need for three different kinds. Someone will ask, "What is the definition of a mature DRC?" But I find it hard to differentiate.

Ken's comment reflects the unwillingness of local officials to accept a definition of their community as marginal or deficient. Ken pinpoints the confusion between scientific and political assessments. Scientific analysis suggests causal inevitability, but political evaluation opens the door to subjective decisions about local improvements.

Paul: Maybe.

Kathleen: [Unwilling to leave the issue fuzzy, she wants the regional planning staff to take a stand.] I think we should say one thing: that the goal of this agency is to try to foster a set of DRCs able to meet the transportation needs of a decentralizing and complex region.

Kathleen emphasizes regional hierarchy and authority. In her view, local places should not define the DRC hierarchy. Local jurisdictions cannot adequately organize a functional form of regional urbanization. These local government officials and planners do not create the centers. Kathleen has already decided which local places are DRCs. How can the planners get the municipalities to adopt programs and policies that will strengthen rather than impede their roles as centers?

Bob: I don't see the three types as stages. The places in the region emerged at different times. The emerging DRC of the future will be different than the emerging DRC of the present. Not all are heading in the same direction.

The notion of a hierarchical and developmental theory of regional centers does not fit Bob's scheme. The hierarchical, developmental notion is too deterministic, not to mention politically risky.

> Paul: I see different policies for different types of centers: one set geared for the older center where walking and trains were the base of the center and another [set of policies] for newer auto-dependent commercial centers. These different transportation characteristics require different policies. The outcome is likely to be different policies for different places. The charette case studies will lead to contradictory results if we stick to a single definition.

> Kathleen: We could have a follow-up meeting to assess this sort of issue.

Kathleen disagrees with Paul. She has a clear commitment to a single, basic notion of a DRC. Her regional approach is hierarchical, not pluralistic. In contrast, Paul the local advocate wants to use multiple definitions to ensure a plurality of acceptable policies geared to the functional needs and political purposes of different places. Kathleen, however, is not as tolerant as Paul of an auto-centered commercial DRC: no train or transit, no DRC.

> Dick: We've wanted to come out of this with an attractive report that is exciting. So conceptual graphics and pictures are important.

> Jane [staff member from the state planning agency and Kathleen's colleague]: These communities ought to do these things. We know they don't get it. The report should lay out what should be done. It will help local officials understand what they need to get or become to achieve the status of a DRC.

Jane, like Kathleen, wants the group to provide criteria for the good center. The criteria will exclude some places and encourage others to embrace this status. Local officials should not define what counts as a center. Rather, their role is to determine whether their locality qualifies as a center and what they might do to improve their standing. Jane's position is that the group already knows what counts; the locals do not.

> Paul: [Still hoping to leave room for greater discretion by local participants] I'm sure we [planners] will not have identified all the places with the potential for being DRCs. They could use this report to put forth their own ideas about becoming a DRC.

Jane: [Quickly pushing this concept aside] We [the regional planners] need to lay out the threshold a community needs to meet before being a DRC.

Paul: So you specify clearly what makes a DRC?

Jane: Yes, then each locale can determine where it stands relative to the definition and what it would have to do to reach it.

Bob: What is the final product?

Dick: A report.

Ken: Descriptive or how to?

Dick: Some description, but mainly a guidebook, a framework for future action.

Jane: You will have an implementation plan?

Dick: [A bit defensive] Yes, the report will include actions. But the regional agency itself doesn't implement. We would like to orchestrate actions taken by local jurisdictions.

Jane: [Pushing for something with implementation] The outcome should be practical. You need to end up with some sort of program.

Kathleen: [Coming to Dick's rescue] I think the final product may be difficult to predict right now. The emphasis will change after we go through the charettes.

Dick: [Grateful] The charettes are designed to take place sequentially so that we can learn from our efforts on the first one.

Norma: [Speaking with an edge in her voice] I have a question. The communities listed in the memo [referring to the regional agency staff's initial classification of places into the three categories], are these the ones targeted?

Dick: Yes.

Norma: What about the ones that want to participate, but don't manage to present information? They won't be included?

Dick: Right.

Norma: [Facetiously] Might that not leave the whole process a bit skewed?

Kathleen: I think we have to structure what we want. We need to involve people willing and able to help structure the content of the charette. This will help target the needs, keeping the discussion short and to the point. A good facilitator is crucial. The event should be educational as well as participatory.

Norma: [Skeptical] Yeah, but is all this going to happen now or after the charettes?

Dick: The charettes are just a beginning. You can only push this sort of method so far. The process will raise important questions and suggest some work items for the different participants.

Kathleen: This phase [charettes and report] should synthesize what we learn and get the attention of local entities. We want to make sure that what we find out and write up will be used to develop local policy.

Norma: I'm still hung up. Is it our purpose to set goals? If so, the making and setting of goals takes time.

Dick: The purpose of the charettes is to involve local people in the process and I will be soliciting this participation ahead of time.

Norma: But is this really possible?

Kathleen: The goal is to set up a participatory process.

Norma: We need to have some goal that we share before we go into it [the process] or we'll end up like this [meeting].

Dick: We hope the charettes will give us ideas about potential actions that might be taken to achieve improved regional centers.

Fred [planning director for the industrial suburb of Burgess and Norma's boss]: But not everybody [locale] should be a regional center. Places come and go on the basis of transportation policy. I am interested in learning how older centers like Burgess can sustain themselves as such centers. I want to see action proposals that focus on keeping older centers viable.

Norma: If you don't have goals ahead of time, then there's no efficient way to narrow people's interests so they can all fit through the bottleneck.

Kathleen: If the charettes are properly structured with good moderation, you're focused on the issues at hand. If you work with Dick to structure and focus the case study, then you can avoid this risk.

Fred perceives that the group does not seem to want to give equal time to mature, established, and emerging centers. He believes that the emphasis should be on the mature centers, because they already have rail networks. Norma believes that if you are going to set regional policy that will justify the allocation of transportation resources, then you need to agree up front about whose interests will be served. Postponing these political decisions generates inefficient conflicts. She thinks the emphasis should be on the older centers like Burgess.

Political Rationality

The regional planning staff had adopted a research method that avoided the political problems that emerge with implementation. Kathleen and Jane, the two grant monitors, would have no part of this. They made it clear that implementation research would be the more proper focus. Kathleen and Jane did not want to see the charettes used to legitimize the fast-growing, auto-dependent municipalities. They wanted to revive train and transit centers. Bob and Dick backed away from their initial proposal during the meeting. In the process, they reconsidered the initial purpose of the charettes as instruments of basic research and redefined them as educational devices to create practical schemes for improving existing DRCs.

The adversarial rumblings of Paul, Fred, and Norma suggest that the charettes will not simply focus on how-to projects, but provide arenas for debates among participants about purpose, classification, and just deserts. The participants from older, declining suburbs with train infrastructure will likely disagree with the participants from the new auto-dominated edge cities. Kathleen, Bob, and Dick finesse the difficult prospect of disagreement and competition by suggesting that a facilitator be brought in to mediate the potential disputes. While hardly a panacea, this proposal satisfies the more skeptical participants, who seize on the participatory fuzziness of the charettes to make plans for their own political maneuvering. Representatives of several older suburbs with aging rail infrastructure—obvious candidates for DRC status—offer their cities as case studies in the charettes.

In this meeting, issues of power and analysis overlap and interweave as the representatives of the funding agencies push for commitments to action and the regional planners carefully recast their original plan. The participants engage in a theoretical debate about the origin and structure of DRCs, with implications for determining what sorts of places qualify as centers. The meeting would have been considerably more contentious had there been more planners from the fast-growing suburban edge cities in the region. The older suburban centers and Central City were well represented in these discussions, precisely because their centrality was being or had already been eclipsed. The charettes offer the opportunity to explore the revival of earlier centers and to challenge the inevitability of suburban growth centers. The broad and friendly consensus of the deliberations reflected the relative powerlessness of the regional agency sponsoring the charettes.

FOR THE SAKE OF ARGUMENT

We often imagine research, as the word implies, to be a kind of search or exploration. What we want and need to know is covered over and hidden. This commonsense perception, however, does not adequately capture what planners do when conducting research. Planners do not uncover facts like geologists do, but rather, like lawyers, they organize facts as evidence within different arguments. The planners in this chapter do not work in the protected world of the laboratory, but within institutional and political settings that make skeptical, experimental inquiry impossible. They carry out research in applied settings that require them to make commitments, change assumptions, and adjust procedures in ways that violate the norms of scientific investigation. Still, they manage to produce reliable, useful, and valid knowledge—practical knowledge.

Research usually receives a great deal of attention in school, but less so in practice. In the practical world of competing priorities, pressing needs, and limited resources, research appears to be a troublesome prelude to more important activities. Occasionally, politicians and powerful patrons want the legitimacy of rational inquiry without the research costs or the risk of unfavorable results. Quick and dirty research becomes a rhetorical device. Research is used to fabricate evidence, which is not sincerely or honestly tested, but which supports the political goals of the powerful. The planners in this chapter did not succumb to this temptation, although their research enterprises are much more open and pluralistic than most skeptics might allow and more flexible and political than purists would like.

Once the researcher has properly framed a line of inquiry, issues of technical competence come into play. The analyst cannot change the rules of research to favor a predetermined outcome. Determining worthy subjects of investigation depends on the analyst's political acuity, but the conduct of the inquiry must follow the rules. However, deciding when the rules are broken and the research is compromised is not easy. Esteban's challenge of census procedures offers an excellent example of this problem.

Frequently, political patrons, and even planners, consider research unnecessary. The right option appears clear; the consequences obvious. Why squander valuable resources evaluating options, when it is better to get plans underway and take stock as we go along? Dick and Bob might have characterized Kathleen's comments and requests in this fashion. They had proposed an ambitious research design based squarely on the rational model embedded in the professional protocol: We need to learn more about transportation centers to classify them accurately and to develop policies supporting them. Kathleen understood their research objectives, but did not share their worries. Midway through the meeting, Bob and Dick reluctantly went along with Kathleen's suggestions. Their lack of enthusiasm was based on their understanding that Kathleen's proposals would generate some political heat for the relatively powerless regional agency. Participatory research with local politicians, officials, and planners would expose the staff to political controversy in ways that the more conventional research design would not. The research Kathleen proposed was not less valid, but more risky.

In effect, the analysts in this chapter all engage in persuasive rational argument. However, their arguments are not abstract and detached, but focused and attached to valued objectives. Norma works to overcome racial- and turf-related suspicions to create a community of data users that crosses departmental boundaries. Attachment to social justice inspires Nancy to rigorous analysis and Esteban to thorough documentation of the underrepresented and uncounted. Kathleen wants research that will inspire local commitments and direct practical action to strengthening train and transit centers. In each case, the analysts possess a conception of the public interest that includes some interests and excludes others. However, their efforts to conduct and direct research are not self-serving enterprises or shallow masquerades for the pursuit of personal or institutional self-interest. Pursuing their various modes of inquiry, they organize relationships of trust designed to persuade others of the merits of certain plans. They summon up evidence and argument to support their positions. Nancy embraces an adversarial approach, while Esteban and Kathleen seek consensus. All three carefully adapt principles of inquiry and moral purposes to the circumstances and contingencies of their practice. Their research anticipates and makes way for plans.

Planning research frames problems and organizes information into useful and persuasive arguments. These acts of inquiry, analysis, and assessment anticipate future consequences of current practice. Even in the most analytical and technical aspect of planning—research—moral and political judgments shape the purpose and form of inquiry. What practical alternatives do planners offer as solutions to the problems they define? How do planners make plans?

5

Making Plans

Planners make plans. They draw pictures of future landscapes. They study problems and write up alternative solutions. In school they learn how to conduct research, write reports, develop objectives, prepare maps, compose alternatives, evaluate options, and propose implementation schemes. The prototypical comprehensive plan is a six-step rational model: The planner must outline the purpose of the plan and the problem being addressed and provide analysis, alternatives, evaluation, and recommendations, and an implementation scheme. The memo that regional planners Bob and Dick prepared, as presented in chapter 4, offers a classic example of rational planning. Students of city planning have for more than thirty years learned variations of these steps from textbooks by Kent (1964), Chapin (1965), and Chapin and Kaiser (1979) and from the Green Book, *Principles of Planning* (Goodman and Freund 1968; So et al. 1979; So and Getzels 1988). Planners apply the model to a wide array of policy areas of central concern to local governments, including land use, transportation, housing, economic development, safety, public facilities, environmental quality, and design.

Unlike plans for individuals or organizations, comprehensive plans take up the purposes and problems of groups, neighborhoods, communities, municipalities, and regions. Individuals and organizations can pursue their plans with vigor and determination in competitive as well as supportive political environments. An individual may not possess sufficient power to win a battle or competition, but this deficiency does not discredit the person's effort to make and pursue plans, as much as it offers feedback on how to revise and improve the plans. The person may need to take a different tack or pursue a less aggressive policy. Comprehensive plans, however, typically seek to draw on and serve the purposes of many different social, economic, and political groups. Therefore, when purposes conflict and interests diverge among those groups, the various parties tend to suspend their commitment to the plan and raise questions about its relevance and legitimacy. Comprehensive plans only work when the participants are collaborators, not adversaries.

Planning reformers have worked hard throughout this century to propose and support federal, state, and local legislative initiatives mandating comprehensive planning. The rapid growth of the profession in the 1950s and 1960s was tied to the expansive, if temporary, planning requirements that accompanied the assignment of federal infrastructure, transportation, and community development grants to regional agencies (see chapter 2). The opponents of planning, however, managed to avoid these requirements, which, in effect, separated the symbolic or rhetorical power of subsidized plans from the political authority necessary to carry them out.

If comprehensive plans offer vision and guidance, then they should be referred to constantly by those who adopt them. Comprehensive plans and policies, however, rarely evoke much interest, inspiration, or guidance. Plan making may be a crucial aspect of the prototype of professional planning, but this activity gets pushed to the margins of the institutional life of most practitioners. Planners often prepare plans less as a source of vision, than as a rhetorical weapon they can deploy in adversarial development battles. In many communities, even getting the discussion of a plan on the local legislative agenda represents a major victory for local planning advocates. Then, even when plans are made and approved by local officials and citizens, the policies and programs may get watered down or left out altogether. The plan may be made so abstract that no one opposes it. Of course, no one can follow it either. Even plans that offer detailed policies can still be ignored, if those charged with carrying them out do not want to go along. Without political will, resources, and widespread commitment, plans languish.

THE CULTURAL CONTEXT

Comprehensive plans that challenge the goals of developers, investors, buyers, and other parties actively seeking private profit and advantage in the local land market do not fare well. In a society that values individual initiative, property, and investment, the preparation of comprehensive community plans is of marginal cultural importance. Therefore, public comprehensive plans seem to work best in thriving communities. Like their national and state counterparts, local governments generously respond to environmental and even modest social objectives when profits, interest returns, and rents translate into healthy tax revenues. (Even in sound economic times, however, most local governments do not engage in redistributive policies, but distributive ones [Peterson 1981].) The various competing groups find less reason to oppose a comprehensive plan when it provides some of the services, activities, and capital improvements they each want. When local growth declines, so too does interest in public objectives that must favor, because of financial restraints, some neighborhoods, facilities, and groups over others. There are exceptions. Some wealthy municipalities are insulated from all but the most devastating recessions and will pursue plans for public open space, design amenities, and commercial renewal with little regard for economic downturns. Others may champion the cause of planning to police and protect the social character of threatened communities even at significant economic cost. In both such cases, the opponents of planning are likely to be a relatively weak minority (Fishman 1978, 5.1–5.31).

Although most local municipalities produce a comprehensive plan, the document is more a list of New Year's resolutions than a set of binding agreements. Some planners treat the plan as a serious covenant and work hard to ensure that each element includes proper design standards and high-quality analysis. Tim, the planner introduced in chapter 1, is representative of this group. These planners urge legislators, officials, and citizens to learn how to develop the right plan and then adopt and follow it. Other planners place less emphasis on the document and seek support for policies and procedures that include planning as a regular, routine activity. Fred (also in chapter 1) used the planning document as a symbolic tool to inspire interest in and care for the community. He used the plan not as a covenant, but as a general scheme that different members of the city could use to project their hopes. Drawing on his rhetorical skill, he tied together the images portrayed in the comprehensive plan into a persuasive picture of downtown development.

PLAN AS WEAPON, TOOL, OR STORY

In an adversarial setting, plans offer competitors strategies for achieving their own purposes. The competitors use the plans to justify their exercise of discretion and control over others. Plans also lay out the enemy's strategies, giving the other side an opportunity to anticipate and counter them. The metaphor of war aptly captures the meaning of plans forged in the heat of political conflict. However, plans that are developed in an adversarial setting and serve mainly as means in the struggle at hand reinforce differences and overlook opportunities for mutual gain. Critics of planning in the United States point to examples of overpolitized planning, which subordinates planners and plans to political ends. This kind of planning is cynical, since schemes are not expected to persuade opponents to find a common ground, but to pressure them to concede. When planners treat plans solely as weapons of political warfare, they lose faith in the power of ideas and images.

Planning as a design activity uses knowledge to compose forms that will reduce a constellation of uncertainties. This kind of planning works best in settings where political interests are relatively balanced or in which one political interest holds unilateral authority. Planning serves as a tool for translating political purposes into specific policies, programs, and projects, rather than as a weapon to vanquish opponents.

Most planners want to make plans that do more than fight or finesse the purposes of the powerful. They hope to refine the purposes of the powerful by composing plans that will meet the needs and solve the problems of many different groups of citizens; some powerful, some not. In this light, appeals to comprehensive planning do not reflect a desire to impose a scientific order based on elite theory, but a hope of persuading others to attend to the interdependencies and uncertainties that crosscut political interests, boundaries, and factions. Authors of such plans use rhetorical and practical knowledge to encourage deliberation among the representatives of different and even antagonistic political domains. Recall Tom and Martin's unsuccessful efforts in chapter 3 to persuade skeptical and indifferent superiors. How do planners create plans that persuade political antagonists to recognize similar purposes and to support mutually beneficial policies?

The first story here is of a suburban planning director trying to launch a renewal plan in an adversarial political environment. What political strategies does he use to get planning on the agenda in the face of the reluctance among several village-elected officials to accept the legitimacy of planning? The story offers insights into how adversarial political relationships can undermine even clever and careful efforts at consensus building.

George: The Struggle to Put Planning on the Political Agenda

George is director of a small, suburban planning department with three planners and one full-time and one half-time secretary. George greets me with a warm handshake. Tall, thin, and crowned with a fine shock of well-managed, wavy hair, he appears flawless. No lint graces his dark suit jacket and zesty tie. His glasses lend authority and distinction to his soft, almost dreamy gaze. My academic uniform of wrinkled slacks, corduroy jacket (with patches), and athletic walking shoes seems rather tawdry by comparison. He does not seem to care, however. He speaks in a calm voice. His words flow evenly, undisturbed by the ups and downs of his tale. He offers no sidebars or kibitzing; no playful or cynical commentary. He expresses his enthusiasms and hopes with a detachment that seems less a psychological defense and more a product of careful composition. George projects a fitting image of professional authority. He briefs me on his efforts to persuade the town council to prepare a redevelopment plan for the aging downtown. Following is my interview with George and excerpts from the town meeting that occurred immediately afterwards.

> I came to this suburban municipality about two years ago with hopes of doing some downtown redevelopment. The town is old and the downtown a mix of disorganized uses [a commuter bedroom suburb with a passenger train stop]. I want the municipality to purchase some strategically located parcels, which, when added to the considerable acreage the city possesses from its recently vacated public works site within the area, would allow for some substantial new construction of an integrated retail commercial center. Most of the owners downtown are not interested in redevelopment on such a scale. A large [electric store] wholesaler is looking to expand business onto land that I think should be prime retail space. Another landowner, with a franchise grocery store tenant who is leaving, wants to do a commercial redevelopment project on the large parcel of land he owns, but his plans are piecemeal and rather mediocre. If we allow such improvements, it will foreclose redevelopment that would be more beneficial for the town in the long-run.
>
> The electric store has a showroom, but really serves as an outlet for contractors and builders and not local consumers. The owner wants the municipality to purchase and demolish an old theater building and existing body shop to provide room for the expansion. But the high costs of such removal would not be offset by any projected tax increases based on such wholesale use.
>
> I've been holding hands with the owners. I want them to expand to the

west instead of to the north so as not to disrupt the need for east-west road access behind the proposed retail development planned a half-block south. Talking to the patriarchal electric store owner is difficult. I feel like I'm pouring sand down a rat hole. He just keeps talking about the details of his business needs and will never settle down or make a firm decision. I want the town board to tell the staff that the electric store expansion should go west and not north along Main Street. The mayor knows the difficulty of dealing with this guy.

Farther west on the site is the large commercial building whose supermarket tenant is leaving. The owner is considering buying two and one-half acres of land adjacent to his property that formerly served as a public service yard for the town. I'm not excited about this because his purchase would foreclose the opportunity for larger scale redevelopment for the entire downtown. The site was considered as one of the alternative locations for a new combined police and fire station. I wanted to use the old public works site as redevelopment land rather than put in the fire/police facility. I hired a consultant to raise planning issues and lay out the long-term redevelopment opportunities and fiscal benefits to the town. The consultant could speak more frankly than the staff. Eventually, the council voted to keep the fire/police station where it has always been, even though it cost a million dollars more than the downtown site. The public works site will serve as a temporary location until the new facility is built. I invited the consultant to come tonight.

I have spoken with some large commercial developers in this region about the downtown site. All have emphasized that the town would need to acquire and consolidate land using its condemnation powers. I have worked up some figures on expected property values to estimate potential increments, should the entire site be included in the tax increment district [or a TIF, which is a tax increment finance scheme. Part of the small downtown has been included in an area designated as blighted. This area is eligible for redevelopment using borrowed funds to be repaid by property taxes on the increased value of the newly constructed improvements]. I want the town board to include the whole area. However, the town board recently promised the local school district that they would not expand the TIF boundaries. So there will be resistance.

My allies in this effort are some members of the Downtown Commission who want to do something more ambitious than piecemeal redevelopment. [The commission includes local business people appointed by the mayor.] I expect the town board will want to go with the short-term investment opportunity offered by the local owner. The board two years ago expressed reservations about redevelopment planning.

There is a low-rise mentality in the village, which limits the density of the downtown and reduces its attractiveness. People could benefit from a viable downtown, but higher densities are crucial. I want to see higher densities to lower the land costs and make it possible for the development of something other than $200,000 town houses.

George has a coherent and comprehensive scheme for redeveloping the small suburban downtown. He recognizes the town council's general opposition to planning, but he figures he must act now or risk losing the opportunity altogether. George gave me a brief rundown of the meeting participants and his views about each:

- The mayor favors the downtown plan.
- Tim, a new board member, takes shots at the town manager and will favor short-term private redevelopment.
- Leo, an older gruff, heavy-set teddy bear, on the board for fifteen years, wants to see something happen.
- Philip, an accountant who takes an analytical approach to board issues, will measure the fiscal and economic costs of the development scenarios most closely.
- Mark, another new trustee and young, is likely to follow rather than lead discussion.
- Ralph, another older, long-time trustee, resists change. He will favor the plans of the local commercial owner.
- The town manager will probably not say much, since he does not seem to have a clear position on the redevelopment scheme.
- Hal, the chair of the Downtown Commission, favors large-scale redevelopment.
- Ervana, who is on the commission and ran unsuccessfully against the mayor in the last election, has indicated her support for development.
- Paul is on the Downtown Commission, but his position is unclear.
I ask George what he hoped for.

I would like the board to tell the staff to work with the electric company to expand to the west and to begin negotiations with owners regarding acquisition of land for redevelopment.

George has helped organize and orchestrate an informal meeting involving most of the town's key elected officials. George's objective for the meeting is clear: to win support for initiating a redevelopment plan for the aging downtown. The availability of the public works land and the pending vacancy of the large commercial space offer an opportunity to consolidate a large parcel of land to attract innovative development proposals.

George knows, however, that some of the officials will oppose this idea. Consequently, he has invited a consultant (Jack) to help facilitate discussion. Jack previously advised the same officials on the construction of the combined fire and police facility. George has also invited the Downtown Commission members who favor a redevelopment plan.

The meeting starts slowly. After a brief wait for Jack, who does not appear, the mayor calls the meeting to order and lays out the agenda.

> Mayor: I want us to come to some sort of decision tonight. Otherwise I threaten to hold evening meetings like this every other week until we do. [Laughter.] I want us to develop a project for the downtown that benefits the town as a whole. I want us to come to some consensus on the downtown redevelopment plans and I hope we can avoid the TIF issue.
>
> I think we selected the best site for the new police and fire facility, but I'm not sure we all agree. I want the staff to prepare the proposal to go before the voters in a November referendum.
>
> As regards the downtown, do we want to propose full-scale development or simply allow smaller scale piecemeal development sponsored by private owners? Full-scale redevelopment will require some acquisition to allow land consolidation. [The mayor looks to the town manager and George.] Can you bring us up to date on recent developer interest?
>
> Manager: The auto dealership owner has expressed some interest in the entire [former public works] site and so has the owner of the commercial building with the supermarket. Other developers want to purchase only a piece. I have seen a number of sketches [by the developer] and some have taken in the entire two blocks.
>
> George: I met with the commercial owner and reviewed his plans. The supermarket is moving and the land owner has proposed plans for a 32,000 square foot retail building with thirty-six units of residential development on the site as well. The plan has some advantages. The owner would purchase the public works site and we would get the sales tax and property tax revenues from the new developments. However, the down side of the development is considerable. The design cuts access from the site to Main Street and forecloses the redevelopment of the adjacent areas. Selling the land to the owner would also foreclose using the public facility site as a temporary location for the fire and police forces while redevelopment of the existing facilities takes place. The owner is anxious to meet with the board and make his plans known.
>
> Manager: The proposal was not well configured. The densities were not high enough.

Ralph: This sketch means nothing to me. Are we going to level it [the public works building] or sell it with the building intact?

As George predicted, Ralph moves quickly to focus on the local development proposal, ignoring the opening remarks about a larger redevelopment plan. George's assistant, Ken, tries to get the discussion back on the planning track.

Ken: The developer's interest is tied to what the board approves the staff to do. The local developer plans are here because he is nearby. The town could, if it consolidated some of the private parcels with the public site land, attract some large-scale developers to come and prepare more ambitious plans.

Ken's aggressive and assertive proposal leads the manager to sense conflict and to seek a middle ground. He reminds the board members that he (and the staff under his authority) knows the decision remains in their hands. He also offers evidence supporting the piecemeal approach.

Manager: It is really up to the town to consolidate the land, but the commercial building housing the supermarket is quite expensive, at least several million dollars. This makes piecemeal development appear more attractive.

Hal [head of the Downtown Commission, quickly responding]: We have to develop the downtown piece by piece, but we shouldn't develop one site without taking into account what's going to happen on the others. Right now we don't have any sort of model that helps us move from the large picture of the whole to the small-scale decisions. We need a global scheme for assessing case by case the revenue-generating prospects of the different redevelopment proposals.

George: [Now that a proposal for planning is on the table] It is difficult to make assumptions about the mix of uses without having some sort of plan. What sort of retail do we want? Do we want apartments or town house development? The lack of such policies makes any sort of fiscal impact modeling impossible. What direction does the board want to take?

Ken: We don't even know yet what parcels to include in the redevelopment area.

George: Once we know the boundaries of the area and some basic sense of direction, we [the staff] can determine acquisition costs and payback estimates. Since most of the area is not in the tax increment finance district we will get little in the way of payback for residential development. As for retail, you get an average of about $1.50 a square foot. So, a 32,000 square foot retail center should generate about $50,000 in tax revenue per year. Acquiring property does increase the costs and reduce the revenue cash flow from taxes.

George and Ken speak with enthusiasm, providing argument and evidence for planning. The elected officials do not respond in kind. The mayor expresses reservations.

Mayor: A step-by-step redevelopment is preferable, but any changes should include retail, office, and residential uses. I have my doubts about office space and wonder if a lot more retail would be enough to make for a successful redevelopment. I'm not sure how much residential we could accommodate either.

Ralph: Remember that we're putting the fire and police in the old public works facilities for several years, so keep that property out of the picture for two or three years.

The mayor's opening remark about dissension on the recent public works decision gets confirmed. Ralph, who had opposed the public works decision, threatens to renew a political battle that others had hoped was settled. The mayor ignores Ralph's ploy and moves discussion back to the redevelopment plan. However, the battle lines are drawn.

Mayor: Part of the attractiveness of downtown development is to get a good price from prospective developers.

Paul: There could be developer interest here.

George, sensing the mayor's support for planning, introduces the politically sensitive topic of local government land condemnation and acquisition. He tells the assembled officials that the staff are looking at an expansion proposal by a commercial establishment, which, if approved, will eliminate crucial east-west access to the public works site. Without a plan for the downtown, the staff has little basis for rejecting the proposed expansion.

George: I want to discuss the "untouchables" [a local code word for the use of town police powers to condemn and acquire land from private owners]. The proposed expansion of the TIF was to include the electric wholesale company and accommodate their expansion plans. The architect for the electric company produced three alternate schemes. First, a proposal in which the town acquired the old theater and body shop properties so that the electric store could expand along Main Street. This option would isolate any redevelopment undertaken to the west and use up all the potential retail street facing on Main.

The next alternative leaves a small parcel, but still requires acquisition of the gas station, which cuts the other businesses off from Main Street. The staff wants an alternative that sees the electric company expanding toward the west in a way that allows room for access from Main Street to the public works site, but we need direction from you before we can proceed with this alternative. Do you want us to make plans for such a westward expansion and prevent the move to the north?

Manager: [Speaking now with obvious caution] You'll [the board] have to explore the possibility of condemnation.

Anticipating the board's disfavor with the necessary land acquisition, George lays out a scheme for avoiding massive condemnation.

George: The town could do a land swap in addition to some condemnation. The town could swap land to ease the westward expansion plans of the electric company.

Ervana: Regarding the staff option, what if the electric company wants to move to a different location? They must really want to stay where they are to go through all this. But you never know. Would they move their business to a new warehouse outside the town?

George: Well, it's already a single-purpose building.

Ken: It's the same kind of building as the public works building. Both used to be auto dealerships.

George: One option is to approach the electric company and offer to purchase the land to the west together.

Hal: Why do they want to go north?

George: They want to improve their visibility on Main. Most of their trade, though, is with contractors [implying that enhanced visibility is not really necessary to get additional customers]. The design would involve a shorter distance from their proposed storage facility to the showroom.

Paul: Expand retail use?

George: Yes, they want to expand their retail.

Paul: Seems strange to have a warehouse building expanding downtown.

Ralph: I don't like warehousing on Main Street, but the owner of the building is likely to resist condemnation.

Ken: I talked with the owner about different land swap possibilities in the downtown triangle. If we did a swap with the old bowling alley and games store, he showed interest, but really we can't carry on such talks until the board is willing to look at a different mix of uses for the area and settle on a plan. Then we can take up the issue of the untouchables and consider acquisition.

Tim: [Referring to Ken's discussion about land swap] Any response?

Ken: He didn't say no. Would consider whatever we brought to the table. He seems open to options.

Manager: [Again questioning Ken's judgment and undermining his credibility] The owner of the bowling alley wouldn't even speak with an appraiser. He's presently renting space to a printer.

Ken: [Proceeds now with diminished enthusiasm] But all such negotiations are premature without some commitment from the board. The electric company expansion plans are going to require zoning approval and there are problems here, especially with respect to parking. [In effect, he is suggesting that the board has the power to pressure for serious negotiations with the owner.]

Hal: Well, we've always had plans to assemble the parking for downtown.

George: If we acquired the body shop/gas station and the theater we could undertake that sort of assembly, but it's difficult to continue talking without some commitment [from the board].

Jack finally arrives, explaining that he was in court all day. He apologizes. He stands well over six feet tall and sports a beard with wisps of grey.

Jack: I want to help you come to some decision rather than give you facts or knowledge. I'm relieved of that responsibility. [Contradicting himself now] Perhaps I can help you learn from what other suburban communities are doing [with respect to redevelopment]. The difficulties suburban cities face are quite common. I am hoping the group tonight can work together as well as the group did that met last Saturday [to decide about the location of the police/fire station]. Basically, I think we should try to look for the criteria you need to define the decision [about whether or not to proceed with a redevelopment plan]. We need to get beyond particular details and explore some of the larger principles affecting change in your downtown.

Jack starts out talking like a facilitator and then quickly assumes the role of teacher. He draws a map of downtown on a flip chart. He tries to implement George's agenda right from the start. The planning pitch gets under way. After his quick miniclinic in small town redevelopment planning, Jack asks the board for a commitment to plan. He steps forward and leans toward the assembled group sitting around the large conference table.

Jack: Is there a consensus about how to proceed? [Silence.] Could we identify the key issues? [Silence. Jack steps back and straightens up.] OK, I'd like to write down the basic objectives and the kinds of benefits and costs for each. We might end up discussing some possible solutions. This sort of redevelopment usually means that some people will be displeased, but the worst thing is to keep people in the dark. It is uncertainty that drives local business owners crazy. [He writes a list.] Do these make sense [pointing to the list]? Have we limited our thinking about redevelopment by focusing on constraints?

Though Jack missed the first part of the meeting, he has been well briefed. He has identified correctly the main areas of conflict:
• The temporary location for the police/fire station
• Carte blanche for the electric company
• Property condemnation
• Identification of the TIF areas
• Density limitations.
  A few members agree that they may be limiting their options, but most are silent.

Jack: What about the electric company issue? Is your intent to help the firm or expand commercial development in the downtown?

Ken: [Impatient] How far does the town want to allow the electric company to expand without frustrating future redevelopment plans?

Tim: Our effort is to bring the electric company along with our plan. We want the owner to be a part of the plan, but not if he opposes the redevelopment.

Hal: The expansion north was never part of the plan.

Ralph: [Changing the subject again] I don't like the way the TIF was gerrymandered.

Mayor: It's never been our attempt to only help the electric company, but to simply assist commercial expansion downtown.

Jack: [Probes here, seeking to make disagreements public] In effect, then, the town [board] is not that committed to helping the electric company [with its present plans and its interest in TIF funds to help finance its expansion].

George: Existing TIF boundaries limit the electric company to only a one-block portion of the downtown [where it is currently located].

Ervana: The TIF is another subject.

Jack: Is George's suggestion OK? Are people comfortable with that?

Mayor: That's a fact of life [referring to the electric company's plans]. They will do what they want to do.

As the meeting continues, Ken uses the consultant's observations to push for a commitment from the board members. He wants the board to use its authority to get the electric company owners to negotiate. The electric company's effort to use TIF to fund their expansion plans illustrates to Ken the sort of injustice and inefficiency a redevelopment plan would prevent. Ralph, however, resists. He portrays the electric company as a major contributor to the town, with every right to do what it wants.

Ralph: We're handcuffed. They [the electric company owners] want to expand on their present site.

Paul: But what about the other businesses nearby?

Ralph: [Raising his voice] The electric company is the biggest sales tax payer in town.

Leo: [Showing anger, disgust, and support for Ralph's critical commentary] I don't see how you can take one of your most successful businesses and get them to leave. Maybe they don't fit, but this is impractical. "You're doing well," we say. "Why don't you leave?"

Mark: Don't touch the electric company [alluding to the untouchables].

Philip: Look, this is a contract wholesale use in a retail business area. It should not be there. It's not an appropriate use.

Leo: There's a lot of home remodeling going on and business there is booming.

Ken: [Still emphasizing the power of the municipality to pressure the electric company to negotiate] The bakery left downtown and went somewhere else to expand its wholesale business. The present zoning doesn't allow for the expansion of the electric company. The retail portion of the business is compatible and could stay, but the wholesale should be moved elsewhere.

Hal: The owner said he has the potential for a home improvement center. This would actually be a kind of commercial center.

Paul: You don't want a white elephant building in your new redevelopment.

Jack: [Pointing to the map and pushing for a commitment to plan, he tells a horror story.] The retail along Main Street appears survivable now, but if the expansion of the electric company takes more of the street front space, the area may become a dog. Most important is opening up more leasable retail space fronting on the streets. The wholesale activity should be pushed back off the streets. You can make it possible for the company to stay, but minimize its impact on retail improvements.

The supporters of redevelopment planning counter Ralph and Leo's resistance. Discussion meanders around how a variety of different parcels might be acquired and developed.

Ervana: I don't think that if the right price were offered with the right developer that the property owner would not sell.

Philip: Some properties will resist. Others will not. So we find out and then determine if we can pull the parcels together [into a redevelopment area].

Jack: Where [city or village] boards balk is over just this part. Yes, the board is willing to condemn, but when there is pressure and you get questions from your constituency, it gets tough. It's an important decision to use condemnation. You hire consultants, waltz with developers, and then the investment requires condemnation that will arouse some opposition. But...there are no untouchables.

Mark: [Hearty agreement] Everything is for sale. [Looking at other board members] In two years there's another election. [Laughter.]

Jack: (Buoyed by the show of support, he pushes for the commitment to plan.] At any time there needs to be a public policy to guide the board and justify condemnation efforts.

Philip: [Balking] We don't have enough money to purchase these parcels.

Ken: [Impatient] I want to know if what I am going to tell the owners about redevelopment is true. Is it policy?

Ralph: [Angrily] We can't set policy tonight. I am unwilling to set policy.

Jack: [Retreating a bit] Does the board want to talk about the untouchables idea?

Mayor: [No longer offering support, since talk of condemnation appears to have gone too far] Well, it depends on the parcel. We have no real proposal. What makes condemnation worthwhile?

Jack: Whenever you proceed, you can negotiate or reject. There are lots of options, but you need to give a set of ground rules.

Mayor: I'm not willing to acquire properties.

With the mayor's retreat, Ralph goes on the offensive. He pits the board against the planners, cutting them off from their support from among the elected officials. By pushing for a decision, Ken gave Ralph the opportunity to draw the planners into his conflict with the mayor and the downtown commissioners.

Ralph: You [planners] tell us that developers want to have land consolidated before proceeding, but the developer needs to come forward first.

Tim: We [the board] will not say that we will acquire land as a blanket policy.

Not everyone goes along, however. The plan proponents rally.

Hal: Ken wants to know if the board will use negotiations to acquire land. We don't want to condemn. That's the worst thing that can happen.

Ken: [Taking heart and pressing for a commitment] But friendly condemnation is a possible negotiating issue.

Jack: [Addressing the increasing anger and tension] There are language problems here. Strong language here. You don't need to condemn all the parcels, but probably some. In most cases you will negotiate a purchase price.

Hal: Condemnation is a last ditch effort.

Unfortunately for Ken and Jack, the mayor abandons the objective of the meeting and turns instead to the proposal by the local developer to purchase the old public works site.

Mayor: We haven't decided the issue of increments versus the whole. Should we sell the city public works site to the neighboring owner?

Sensing that getting a commitment to planning is fading fast, Jack speaks with a sense of urgency and authority. He implicitly reminds the board that their inability to commit to planning in the past has fostered their present confusion.

Jack: Determine a realistic redevelopment area and then frame the development proposals within it. Does this proposal help focus your decision about a redevelopment area? You [the board] have been working on this for years.

Ralph ignores Jack's interpretation, responding sarcastically to the mayor's retreat from the plan. The premier adversary of planning, he has captured the initiative. He mocks the mayor.

Ralph: [Sarcasm] Thought that's why we were here, Mayor?

The proponents make another effort to revive the planning agenda.

Jack: First, you've got to have a plan: Lay out the criteria you want to organize the logical use of the properties.

Hal: We could use city-owned property to prime the pump.

Jack: Sure, that's OK.

Hal: We own this property [the public works site]. What can we do with it? Lay the uses out. Can we organize the uses to do something we want? The plan would show the acquisition costs and constraints.

Jack: You can't focus on an ideal solution. There are many clever solutions that people can come up with. You are still struggling here to give the outside world [developers] something to address. This doesn't commit you. The town of Oakdale just got six different development proposals in response to its redevelopment plans.

Hal: You can't go to a developer without ground rules.

Jack: Your job is to create certainty in the land marketplace. Your position downtown is stronger than zoning control because you own key properties. I hope this is reassuring. Can we define the boundaries of the redevelopment area, perhaps take a different tack? Show of hands? [There is a slim majority to continue. The mayor does not vote.]

Jack pulled out all the stops. First, he warns: If you do not plan, your retail area will fail. Second, he chastises: You are missing opportunities that other more prosperous suburbs are taking. Third, he appeals: You own enough property to shape rather than react to development. His appeals, however, do not work. The split vote strengthens Ralph's resolve to derail the meeting. He responds in kind to Jack's testimonial. Ken, still hoping to win the debate, does not realize that the opponents have already achieved victory.

Ralph: It's impractical. Nothing's going to happen because the area is too large. [Speaking with contempt] Look at that Swallow Hills development [a relatively high-density redevelopment that included multifamily residential uses].

Ken: [Angrily] I don't think it's a fair comparison, Ralph.

Ralph: I don't care if it is fair.

Ken: [With passionate urgency] That redevelopment put in place a density not appropriate for this town. If we limit our focus to just a few blocks we will be making a mistake.

Ralph: We [the municipality] and one developer own this block. We should develop this. Also, we have the owners of the electric company willing to work with us. Why worry about all the others? Process will not accomplish anything. You got a gold mine here. A guy owns half the block; we own the other!

Ken: [Standing up and speaking with intense feeling] Vision! Vision! Vision! It's not just in college.

Ralph: [With contempt and derision] Planners build little models to get their jollies.

Ken: The guy who built the Bellwether Mall [a commonly acknowledged boondoggle in a nearby municipality] thought it made sense. The plan was lousy [because it was the product of a single-minded developer]. The plan sucked.

Ralph: [Smiling with obvious pleasure and speaking in a calm voice in intentional contrast with Ken's outburst] Planners talk like that.

Ken sits and is silent. The meeting drifts to an indecisive conclusion.

Planning Held Hostage

George's assessment of the board's feelings about redevelopment planning was accurate. At best, the mayor and the other proponents of planning would support an overall redevelopment scheme, but their unwillingness to approve the inevitable use of condemnation undermined any meaningful discussion. The interests of the property owners and the initiatives of the local developers dominated. Ralph, the rogue opponent, played on board members' fears, especially the mayor's, that condemnation would bring political protest.

The meeting went through cycles of argument and protest, culminating in Ken's dramatic and impassioned appeal for planning. Ralph cynically and effectively discredited Ken's appeal by characterizing planners as intellectual experts out of touch with reality. George, Ken, and Jack all appealed to the town board to embrace comprehensive planning for the downtown. They defended the notion of developing a plan that would consolidate land and attract an outside developer. They argued that the destiny of each site should be tied to the destiny of adjacent sites in a predictable and orderly manner.

Although George accurately identified the supporters of planning, he misjudged the town board's hostility to the use of public powers to make that planning effective. The opponents' refusal to engage in deliberations reflected their ideology that local government should be run like a small business. When you get a customer, you make the sale. Don't wait around for another customer, who may never show up. Although planning supporters outnumbered opponents, they did not possess the same confidence and conviction. In part, old political battles held the planning agenda hostage.

George understood better than Ken the political dynamics of the meeting. Ken carried on as if the officials had an open mind toward planning. He presumed that ignorance and inattention were the reasons why the officials resisted the idea of developing a plan. His passionate appeal for comprehensive planning as a superior source of vision and insight backfired. Instead of changing minds and inspiring confident support, his appeal strengthened the opponents' belief that planners do not understand the politicians' audience. Ken's approach ignored and dismissed the elected politicians' worry about the political costs of condemning private commercial property. George offered schemes for minimizing the political damage. Ken, however, wanted the officials to adopt the plan to pressure the owners to negotiate a sale under threat of condemnation. Ralph identified with the local owners and respected their accomplishments. The more Ken embraced the tenets of rational planning and the protocol of expertise, the more Ralph was able to discredit his testimony. When Ken vents his frustration by claiming that the development boondoggle approved by the elected officials in a nearby suburb "sucks," he slips completely out of character. The mask of professional detachment and expertise slips off. Ralph, a clever, if unhappy, politician, takes that moment to point out the contrast. Planners are not really the detached intellectuals they want others to believe they are. Planners are not good guys, but bad guys.

All of this occurred in just one meeting about a redevelopment plan for a few acres of old commercial land in an aging bedroom suburb. The tale illustrates the formidable sources of resistance to even the most modest land use planning ideas. Imagine the difficulties George and Ken would encounter getting the town board to consider multifamily housing, not to mention a group home or public housing? George worked hard to build a framework for consensus, but adversarial politics carried the day.

MOVING FROM ADVERSARIAL TO CONSENSUAL POLITICS

Making plans in adversarial settings is difficult. For opponents to be able to plan together, they must at least have a tolerant and respectful willingness to deliberate. The factionalism and individualism of local politics, however, are a formidable obstacle. The professional protocol can be a serious impediment to planners. Anthony Catanese holds out few hopes for deliberative democracy. Convinced of the necessity and virtue of adversarial politics, he urges planners to build loyal relationships with local politicians by taking a stance in controversial issues.

> Loyalty is hard to come by, but it is best exemplified by a true political commitment. The true political commitment is most obviously seen in working for a politician's election. That is the essence of the elective system, and it is the hallmark of representative democracy. For planners to pretend that they are professionals who should not be involved in realpolitik is stifling, although it can work sometimes for extraordinarily gifted technicians of the apolitical-technical character (1984, 207).

Many professional planners who adopt the professional protocol also engage in activities associated with electoral politics.[1] Furthermore, most undertake such activity as liberal partisans, or left-leaning independents. In this respect, Republican cutbacks that targeted planning institutions and programs in the 1980s were well aimed. The political affiliations of planners may also explain why many local elected officials with Republican sympathies might consider planners to be untrustworthy advisers and appointees (Catanese 1984, 209).

Planners' participation in electoral politics that might affect their work environment poses moral questions and political risks. In some localities, civil service rules, designed to undermine patronage practices, prohibit planners from actively participating in electoral politics. In older, big cities, structural and civil service reforms have loosened up restrictions on political participation. Planners may engage in electoral politics, expecting that their help organizing and working on a campaign will translate into future employment if their candidate wins.

Participating in adversarial politics, however, does not complement the politics of deliberation, which planners use to persuade others about what problems to consider and what solutions to try. Winning political contests and successfully building cooperative agreements usually require different skills, relationships, and beliefs. How does a professional planner use arguments advocating for a particular policy or candidate in one context, and then propose evenhanded arguments that can reconcile differences among policies in another context? Consider Annette's story.

Annette: Disillusioned Campaigner

Annette speaks in a Midwestern style of provincial informality. She speaks fast and earnestly. She occasionally pauses, offering an open and engaging smile. Her professional dress and formal posture are subtly and charmingly softened by generous and slightly nervous laughter. She works in her father's architecture firm and has yet to earn her voice as a partner. The duties of daughter and employee appear to chafe. She has returned to school to earn an architecture degree and prepare for a leadership role in the firm. The office, located on the edge of a central city downtown, has many architects busy at work. Annette leads me to a vacant desk. In her mid-twenties, she walks confidently and gracefully. I ask about planning, doing good, and politics. She responds easily and quickly, looking me full in the face and speaking with a gentle intensity.

> Politics is a way of life in this city. When I left graduate school, I worked on a couple of election campaigns (one gubernatorial and one mayoral). In this work I learned what it means to develop contacts. For instance, although my campaign work in the governor's race was city based, I soon learned that talking with suburban campaigners was practically important. We would trade notes and come up with press coverage strategies. I developed a rapport with these campaign workers, these political groupies—basically professional campaign organizers. However, I didn't become like them.
>
> The groupies rely on stationary professionals for substantive information. Although city administrators are not supposed to get involved in election campaigns, they frequently do so. These administrators and professionals often get their jobs because of their campaign efforts. So my campaign work tied me not only to the groupies, but to those who got settled in policymaking roles. The campaign work ultimately put me in contact with government officials possessing useful information and authority.
>
> Of course, I was not doing the campaign organizing work so as to build future professional contacts. I did it because I enjoyed the pace and excitement of the campaign. I cared about the candidates I worked for and I possessed a certain naiveté about the process. What I learned from this work was how important information was to power.

The campaign organization had two parts: the day-to-day organizers and the kitchen-cabinet (or transition team). The day-to-day people kept the schedule moving, but the real power rested with the kitchen cabinet. The staff who gained status and promotion throughout the campaign were those who offered information to cabinet advisers who used it to enhance positive media coverage for the candidate or negative coverage for the opponent. I watched how people manipulated information to ensure that they would get credit for its use. I even learned to do it myself. I even lied so as to protect my claim to exclusive knowledge and thereby improve my position within the campaign organization. I hated it.

I did use my planning knowledge and writing skill to prepare agenda items and issue papers. These were sometimes important, but political manipulation was pervasive. I helped a local candidate for city council by giving him a copy of my thesis [a neighborhood improvement scheme within his district]. He published the plan as his own and did not give me any credit for the work. I was outraged, but for the sake of our firm's future business relations with the city I did not take any public action against him. I couldn't even stand to call him and complain.

Sometime later he called me and asked if I would let him appoint me to a city commission position. I didn't want any part of this manipulation. He would just want me to represent his ideas.

I have learned from such [painful] experiences that there are serious limits to political relations. The tit for tat kind of politics that is organized around manipulation is not what I want to do. This is the way things operate politically in this town, I know. And I do believe that the only way to change things is to get involved, but I am not going to get involved in another election again until I really like and trust the candidate. You rarely get rewarded for political work unless you manipulate and use knowledge to promote yourself or the candidate.

Annette found the aggressive and self-serving qualities of many of the campaign participants too demoralizing. She hopes, however, to be able to tap the professional contacts she developed doing political work to shape the projects she cares about and to carry on her work as a consultant. These political relationships, however, do not exactly represent reciprocal interests. Annette's first-hand experience in electoral politics taught her how competitive exchange based on interests and influence diminishes the sense of solidarity and meaningfulness that originally attracted her to political campaign work. Despite her intellectual commitment to political activities based on shared collaboration and rational deliberation, in the campaign work she found herself aggressively hoarding important information, offering it to superiors in intervals and amounts that ensured her personal credit and honor.

Annette did not reject adversarial politics entirely. She qualified her condemnation by explaining how the next time she decided to help campaign, she would make sure that she trusted the candidate and that she was harboring little desire for personal political power. Her search for the qualities of unitary politics—solidarity, shared purpose, and equal respect—was not fulfilled by the antagonistic and self-serving qualities of adversarial politics. In her story, Annette describes a political arena in which she practices both forms of political activity. She tries to establish through her network of friendships a political community that serves as both a moral reference point and a source of information and support. This community, however, remains outside conventional occupational and political settings.

Ethical Advocacy: Making Way for Deliberations

In this story, Annette describes her work on a large inner city neighborhood site plan. She has no difficulty in convincing her sponsors of the importance of planning. They believe in planning. Rather, her problem has to do with setting the purposes and priorities of the plan. As a consultant, what are her responsibilities to her sponsor and to the community? What should she do when they conflict?

> For this project, when I came on board the data had been collected. I organized all the information into a geographic form using both census tracts (which were much too general and dated) and individual parcels. The crucial step was the use of parcel data. I visited each parcel in the eighteen-block area to assess occupancy and demolitions in an inner city neighborhood that has undergone extensive disinvestment. The parcel analysis enabled us to develop housing design prototypes for different types of lot configurations.
>
> We had conducted a community survey that told us that existing residents liked the neighborhood and didn't think it was too bad. However, the middle-class developers and agency officials [of a large nonprofit agency just to the north of the neighborhood] described the area either as a wasteland fit only for demolition or as an opportunity for potential redevelopment. The project developer held the latter position. The development company staff had together with the nonprofit agency officials conducted a survey of clerical and maintenance staff. They determined that there was a demand for housing near the office complex. The project we were helping plan for this neighborhood was to offer a supply of affordable housing for these employees.

So we knew the population to whom our client wanted to sell the housing—workers at the nonprofit agency. Our client also wanted to minimize displacement. This was a reasonable proposal for this area, since there were so many vacant lots and abandoned structures. But we also figured that the residents of the neighborhood would resist, since the units were not being constructed for them. We prepared for their criticism.

When we met with our clients, including staff from the nonprofit agency and the nonprofit developer, we initially focused on each type of land use. For instance, we might concentrate on the problems with commercial uses in the area and offer proposals for solving these, but we finally gave this approach up and ended up dealing with all the uses at the same time. The meetings were organized around major problems or design issues that cut across the different functional areas.

The area has very little commercial use. The old commercial uses had run along a strip on the southern border of the area, but most shops were closed. There was one grocery store on the southwest corner of the development, but with virtually no other stores toward the east. A problem emerged as it became evident that our clients wanted to promote such retail uses as dry cleaners, restaurants, and clothing stores, while discouraging fast food places, liquor stores, and currency exchanges. The latter uses were already prominent in the inner city and our clients wanted to provide commercial activities that would serve the more prosperous residents they hoped to attract.

I knew, however, that a competing community organization wanted to allow any kind of commercial use in the area. This organization was more militant and represented working and lower class residents. I thought there was merit to their concerns, but my client disagreed. I felt that my role was to represent the interests of both organizations, and yet I found myself adopting the position of my client, doing what I had thought I would not.

The right thing to do would have been to take into consideration both points of view. I knew there was political conflict. I warned my clients, but they simply wanted to proceed with their own plans. I went along and felt bad.

I think it's important to consider all the sides fairly before deciding on a scheme or plan. I resent when developers or clients can have their way without taking into account the interests of others who are not part of the decision-making process, but who have to bear the consequences. I feel that in this case I did not live up to what I believe in. I didn't persist in representing the values of others who would be influenced by the decisions, but who didn't have any say.

It upset me that the clients had their minds made up from the very beginning. The representative for the nonprofit development company was especially annoying. He told me that I was not to speak about the development with anyone, including planners for the city, local residents, or community organizations. It seemed to me that such talk was important for conducting a fair planning process. Furthermore, it would help anticipate, circumvent, and prepare for community resistance, which this sort of large-scale development would likely provoke.

I did talk to some of my friends in city hall to check out if the city had undertaken any improvements in the development area. Also, I asked if they had heard of any community organization initiatives that might be planned for the area. These planners were personal friends. I asked them not to tell anyone that I had called. They agreed. We do this sort of thing all the time. When they ask me questions that are risky, I respect their confidence. Sometimes we do more than just share information. We try out different scenarios to get advice, for example: What do you think might happen if...?

Annette faced a conflict. Going along with her client violated the fairness principle in which she believes, but as a consultant under contract she felt obligated to respect her client's wishes. She decided to remain loyal to her employer, as is the common practice among planners in this situation. Annette, however, did not see any serious moral conflict when she used her social ties for information, violating the loyalty and obedience expected of her by her client. In Annette's moral hierarchy, the demands based on loyalty were not binding because they violated a more important norm—conducting a fair planning process.

Annette is part of a network of professional friends with ties of collegial reciprocity. The network is an important source of technical and political information. It also comprises a community to which Annette and her colleagues can turn to examine the moral quality of their judgments and to solicit advice on various scenarios. However, this network did not provide the political support that Annette needed to help her stand up for fair planning in opposition to her client's interests. Thus, she kept her divided loyalties a secret. In this case, making plans fostered divided loyalties. The next scenario illustrates plan making that avoids adversity and fosters deliberations.

Donald: Planning for a LULU (Locally Unwanted Land Use)

Donald talks with his hands. His curly red hair is swept back. A small bald spot peeks through on top. His office is packed with paper, file drawers, reports, boxes, strange looking tools, several pairs of muddy work boots, and abandoned coffee cups. His round cheeks and soft eyes convey whimsy. His generous smiles and confident air put me at ease. The office has the feel of a lived-in workshop. He is the landfill planner for a rapidly suburbanizing county and is called on to check out illegal dumps.

He was hired to help plan the siting of a new county landfill. He had three years. When we speak, he is midway through the process. Preliminary plans have been completed and potential sites have been located and assessed. He briefs me on the site location discussion and process.

> We started a year and a half ago with the advisory meetings. The consultant drafted some criteria for siting. We revised their draft and sent it as a draft to the technical and policy committees. It took four months of meetings to develop and select the criteria. We achieved a consensus, but without taking a vote. We simply kept working until all objections had been settled. The basic trust was there. If we apply these criteria faithfully, it will lead to a good site.

Donald frequently uses the first person plural, when, in fact, in most of the events he describes, he was the primary organizer. His unselfconscious use of "we" reflects his tacit commitment to the participatory process he has worked hard to implement. Participation, however, is no substitute for expertise.

> There are basically two ways to assess sites: the geological and the sociological. We used the sociological, focusing on proximity to population centers, sources of potable water, and potential impacts on humans and on the fauna and flora. Once we found a set of basically acceptable sites on this basis, then we applied the geological criteria.
>
> The county board approved the criteria discussed by the committees and copies were distributed to the press. The approval took place about a year ago. We used the criteria to develop a series of overlay maps for the county using a CAD [computer-assisted design] system developed by the state. We quickly eliminated some 60 percent of the county. We were searching for three hundred-acre rectangular sites at least five hundred feet from any residence. Eventually we found about one hundred potential sites.
>
> The consultants scored each of the sites using the criteria originally selected. I reviewed their calculations for each site. I modified the scores. In some cases, I thought the natural topography could be used as a buffer for a site. I gave these sites a higher score, and so a greater preference. I would try to minimize stream impact and so lowered the preference score for sites near streams. I applied and qualified the criteria in ways that we could not have recognized before we conducted the selection.
>
> I especially wasn't satisfied with the way the consultants scored the zoning and land use regulations affecting a site. Their scoring scheme was too restrictive and ended up making all the sites seem basically the same with

respect to land use regulations. They found differences, but their scheme did not treat these differences as big ones. For instance, their interpretation distinguished between residential and agricultural zoning based on the proportion of the area zoned for each use. If an area had only 10 percent zoned residential, then it was marginally more desirable than an area with 40 percent of the area zoned residential. This had the effect of making the differences among sites appear small. But I wanted these land use differences to stand out. So I changed the scoring. If a site had any portion of its area zoned residential, then we scored it as having 100 percent of the area zoned residential. This had the result of increasing the size of the differences between sites. [Instead of using an interval measure, Donald used a less precise nominal measure.]

Donald had no reservations about modifying the preestablished evaluation method to ensure that sites with residential land uses would not be selected. Knowing that opposition in such cases would make any siting efforts extremely difficult, he introduced a political feasibility criterion to the consultant's report.

We eventually identified the top sites and picked one. We have not as yet publicly announced that we have a list of sites arranged by a preference hierarchy. This avoids discussion about the alternatives and the competition and pressure from operators who are anxious to get the list to try to acquire and build a facility in the next best site (while lobbying to have our original site rejected). We want to avoid this kind of battle. We really don't want to move to the next best site if we end up in a bidding war with private vendors. So we act like there is one and only one site.

Donald organizes the preference hierarchy of feasible sites to serve as a rhetorical and political strategy for public persuasion. Donald does not treat the operators as citizens, but as political competitors whose plans he must anticipate and counter. He blends together the political and the technical requirements of his task.

In the meeting with the county executive today, we need to talk about the political steps necessary to get the number one site. I hope we can walk out of the meeting with a series of tasks that will include finding out the availability of the site. Since the site [an abandoned arsenal] is located on federal land, this will require contacts with several federal agencies and federal representatives.

The site is located on federal property controlled by the army. I think it's best to talk with some of the bureaucrats at the army and especially the federal reps for the area. I know where to start with the bureaucratic staff, but I'm not sure about the elected officials.

I did tell the local county board member in whose district the site is located. I didn't offer the information, but he came up and asked me the other day. I said, "Yes." He said, "Thanks for telling me. You know, I'm going to oppose it tooth and nail." I replied, "Yeah, I wouldn't expect any different. I won't take it personally."

A legislator can be against a LULU like this, or *really* against it. I'm hoping his opposition will be rhetorical. I trust the guy. I've gotten to know him and felt telling him ahead of the official announcement would help him and avoid nasty opposition. I have also been working to get a bunch of local municipalities to pass ordinances in support of the site. This will help us make the case for the site as good, sound policy. If we can get the municipalities coming out in public saying they support the site and will use it, well, this helps sell it at the county level.

Donald has worked hard to build a series of political relationships among the local governments who will need the site. He has included local government representatives on the various working committees that have developed the criteria and policies guiding the site selection, design, and operation procedures. Interestingly, he avoids votes because they tend to set up adversarial relations. He pushes for consensus by negotiating compromises, offering concessions, and scheduling additional meetings. All this is possible because he has had a considerable amount of time. He knows that once a site is announced, the neighboring landowners will fight the decision, and political conflict will ensue. Therefore, he seeks to build a consensus each step of the way strong enough to sustain the inevitable political heat.

Today, he has his first meeting with the county executive since he has ranked the sites and picked number one. He has sent the executive a memorandum listing the sites by location and rank. I have been given permission to observe the meeting, but I am sworn to secrecy as to the site selection. No one is to know the site until the details of acquisition and soil testing have been completed. Donald seems more excited than nervous. Jimmy, a planning consultant who works for Donald and the county and is scheduled to join Donald for the meeting, arrives a few minutes before the county executive. Slender, clean-shaven, and in his late thirties, he seems a bit harried. With many years experience analyzing and testing landfill sites, he knows this meeting represents an important step in the site selection process.

Donald: How are you doing up in Burdett?

Jimmy: The decision being made [to select a new suburban landfill in a northern county] has nothing to do with its technical merits. The officials can't stay focused on the substantive issues or even the project.

Donald: A lot of this work entails working with government and private agencies. I was dealing with a large waste management corporation and it was phenomenal seeing what they know about a dumping site.

Jimmy: They are the largest landowner in the state. Eco Corp owns them. They've got lots of money and clout, but there are problems. The other day I got a call from a guy at Eco Corp. I answered his technical question using information that I had received from a different department of his company. And they call government a bureaucracy!

   The Eco Corp guys showed up at a public hearing for a fill where I was working for the jurisdiction as a consultant. They bring six people. They are all dressed impeccably. Each gets up and tells what a great job they're going to do to meet the "expected" shortfall in capacity.

   I simply pointed out how their estimates were off and that there was already plenty of capacity. Furthermore, I cited instances where Eco Corp was in trouble for not doing the good job they claimed. Still, they looked and sounded great.

Donald: Using spit and polish.

Jimmy: They do a good selling job.

Donald and Jimmy have developed a close working relationship over the past year. Donald easily empathizes with Jimmy, the hero of a modern David and Goliath environmental saga. Jimmy is a civil engineer with a populist streak, struggling to find good places for all the garbage and impressed with the power of his opponents.

The county executive enters the room accompanied by the county attorney. The executive moves swiftly and with a sense of urgency. The grey hair, dark blue suit, ruddy complexion, and portly build are all of one piece. No fidgeting, excess movement, or doubt; just decisive action. Like a ship cutting a wake in the sea, he enters the room. The attorney follows, bobbing along in his wake. A few quick hellos and Donald gets right to business.

Donald: We have decided on the top site. The agenda I gave you lists the tasks I think need to be taken to act on securing the site and getting it approved. I've started to do some of the things on the list of tasks from the meeting agenda. [He discusses the relevant political actors he has contacted to determine potential support and opposition to the site.] The arsenal committee had no opposition. We want municipalities to pass resolutions supporting the fill, but they needn't commit yet as they need the price to do that, and we can't give them a price until we've done more analysis on the operating and development costs of the site.

Executive: What if a municipality doesn't support it? [Raising the serious issue of political conflict and resistance at the outset. This player does not finesse.]

Donald: [Slowly] Well, we will have to leave them out. The idea is to get as many as possible on board as soon as possible.

Executive: The federal arsenal would be the site?

Donald: Well, the idea is to see if we can get approval from the army. I think we should talk with the federal [congressional] reps and run it by them as well.

Executive: The arsenal site is not going to hurt people. The local representative might want it because it means three hundred fewer acres for the planned airport he opposes.

Donald: It's in Franklin's district [speaker of the state House of Representatives]. Would this site offend him?

Executive: Send a letter to both and set up a meeting with both of them and myself. I want to be sure both are at same meeting. That's the protocol.

Donald: OK, I'll send a letter out.

Executive: Find out when they're in the area. Make it convenient for them.

Donald: What about the state reps? Should we talk with them now about the site? It's in Silva's district. He's on the house environment committee.

Jimmy: I think you should only tell the state reps after you're sure you've got control of the site.

Executive: The pecking order is federal reps, army, and then state reps. Don't we have condemnation rights here?

Attorney: Not on federal land.

Jimmy: You'll need a congressman to promote the idea. The army will not want to give it up. What about state senators?

Donald: We should decide about senators.

Executive: In the meeting with the congressman, we can ask whom we should speak to.

Donald: I don't know about the township executive. Who's the executive out there?

Executive: He's OK. I was on the zoning board with him years ago.

Attorney: You've got to involve the local officials and not just the feds.

Donald: I'm holding off.

Executive: You're doing it right. We have to hold off until we get a yes from the army.

Donald: From a legal standpoint, they [the locals] don't get involved until local siting is approved and you need to secure a permit.

Jimmy: But they can mess you up. It's easy to fight against that.

Donald: Let's hold off until we get army approval. If this site doesn't work out, we will have to turn to private property and it will get tougher. [Talking to the executive] I haven't briefed the county board about this. When should we do it?

Attorney: Do it soon. You don't want them being angry at having been left out of the process. Sit down with the chair.

Jimmy: Once you start telling people, you've got to be prepared to work quickly [to anticipate and avoid opposition].

Executive: You want the meeting to be confidential. Tell Glenn [the county board chair] and ask him not to tell the others. We inform him, but keep word from leaking out.... I hope this site works out.

Donald: Anything else?

Executive: This is the way to go. We've got to go forward. Can't stop now. We've got the snowball rolling down the hill. This site has the least negative impact and you can prove to the public that you did a good job.

Jimmy: The siting process has been thorough and fair.

Executive: You've done a good job here. No one's going to want it [the land-fill], but you've done it [the siting] above board.... We could meet with the chair after the next board meeting.

Donald: Can I count on you for that [meeting]?

Executive: Yeah.

Jimmy: Building consensus is crucial. Conceptually you want to keep the momentum rolling. If you take too long, you lose credibility. We need to lay out all the tasks from A to Z. First, Donald and I need to work up an attractive agreement with the army. We can't just walk in with a request for three hundred acres.

Donald: First, the army has to find that the land is surplus. This determination is a long process. We need to get an option on the site so that we can get onto the property and conduct our tests for suitability. This will take some bureaucratic work.

Attorney: The army can't give us an option.

Jimmy: OK, we'll get a right of entry.

Donald: I think they're going to negotiate, but they're going to go by the book.

Executive: Goodbye [leaves with lawyer].

The short meeting was packed with decisions about mobilizing political support for the site. Here was an excellent choice for the site. If the army cooperates, the risk of political conflict will be greatly reduced. The site is politically attractive for the executive, because it promises minimal conflict among the multitude of local governments and citizen groups involved in the selection and use of the landfill. However, Donald has no illusions about the military bureaucracy. He clearly wants and needs the county executive's support. Getting agreements will take time.

Maintaining secrecy will be extremely difficult as more elected officials and bureaucrats learn of the site. The need to build political support for the site and obtain military permission poses a serious challenge for Donald, who recognizes that he will be vulnerable should the process unravel.

Working on such a controversial project could have transformed Donald into a pariah on the periphery of local politics. He has worked hard during the past year, however, to make it clear to all the involved parties that state mandates and the pressures of urban growth place heavy burdens on all local governments. Localities everywhere must provide better means of waste management and disposal. Coming together in the face of a shared vulnerability does not happen automatically. Donald has fostered a sense among the various players of mutual collaboration that recognizes local self-interest, shared risks, and a public commitment to improving environmental quality. The executive respects Donald's work and obviously trusts him. He does not tell him how to do the political work, but simply helps clarify priorities.

Donald and Jimmy discuss the meeting and their respective roles in laying out tentative plans for implementing the site plan.

Donald: You think we're going to have to do a whole dog and pony show with the department of defense?

Jimmy: You have to go in with a done deal.

Donald: Yeah, but how much do we need done?

Jimmy: First, you have to have exhibits prepared with the congressmen's approval. Give them the whole deal. Important to go in with political backing.

Donald: Neither of these guys [legislators] is stupid. When Franklin comes to a meeting he always brings an expert aide whom he trusts.

Jimmy: Look, we can get the congressmen on board and then spend five months trying to get on the site. It won't work. We have to keep at least six weeks ahead of the opposition. When we slow down or stop, everyone against us can catch up. The worst is people asking questions you can't answer in front of the press. This really stirs up the conflict.

Donald: But we don't have all the answers. We still are only going to do two or three borings.

Jimmy: What if they ask you about the number of trucks the fill will generate?

Donald: I'd have to look it up.

Jimmy: We have to have those answers now.

Donald: Well, with this site we figure at least two transfer stations. Only about a third of the county could ship their waste direct. For the preliminary analysis of the site we're going to do two or three borings.... We can't say we have all the answers.

Jimmy: We've got a guy on our consulting staff who knows the army. You're going to need a lot of help in this. You've also got to be sure you've got enough budget. Right now there's only about $10,000 left.

Donald: I think we can find some more money without too great a problem.

Jimmy: Developing an implementation schedule is important.

Donald: Right. Getting the tasks listed and set up is important, but there are still a lot of uncertainties that make early commitments to some things a waste of time.

Jimmy: What do you plan to do if they [the army] says no?

Donald: I don't know, but it depends on their reasons. If they have other plans for the land, that's one thing, versus just giving us the runaround.

Jimmy: You need to identify other consultants. You need to put together your implementation team. Identify some guys at Eco Corp you'd like to hire away.

Donald: Eco Corp is already ahead of us and has put some people together [as a possible site team management firm]. There are other guys around. I will run an ad asking for qualified underwriters.

Jimmy: It's going to take a lot of your effort to keep the political infrastructure together. You won't have time to do much of the technical work.

Donald: Yeah, I understand that. As for the potential land use team, I don't know whom to pick, but there's a lot I don't know.

The discussion shifts and both begin to talk about the relationship between private waste management firms and government environmental regulators.

Jimmy: There are rumors that permit reviewers for your county are going to get hired by Eco Corp.

Donald: I watched in a recent meeting how the permit staff distanced themselves from county policy and listened to the well-dressed and slick Eco Corp rep's ideas.

Jimmy: I was interviewing some young students for potential jobs and it's clear many have been snowed by Eco Corp's TV ads. They think the company is great. Then there are the granola heads. They think all the Eco Corp guys are gangsters.

Donald: Well, there's this one employee in the county health department who's spending a lot of time obsessing about Eco Corp's facilities, telling me how great they are. It's clear she's making the move.

Jimmy: In the industry that's the way it works. We hire from the state and they hire our people. You try to get the best people.

Donald: Well, more power to them, but I'm concerned that public employees who work for the county are selling themselves to private agencies even before they leave. There's too many of them. That woman's attachment is keeping her from doing other important work. It's frustrating to me.

They return to business.

Jimmy: So what do we do?

Donald: I'm going to meet with the executive and the board chair. We want to keep them informed and committed. Next, we set up meetings with congressmen. The county executive and Silva are old friends.

Jimmy: There's little we [the consultants] can do [technically] until you take the site.

Donald: We'll need help influencing the army.

Jimmy: I can help you find a contact up the chain of command in the army.

Donald: OK, someone outside the area. And we'll also try to get right of entry.... People have been saying informally for some time that the arsenal is the site. I just let it slide. These are speculations. It's not until we officially substantiate the site that the talk will matter. Do you think the executive seems wishy-washy?

Jimmy: I don't think he's read the report.

Donald: What concerns me is that he keeps calling this my project. I'm concerned that he'll change his mind and back out.... Well, I'm not going to stay long anyway. I want to go back to Colorado.

Jimmy: What are you going to do out there?

Donald: I don't know. I want to go back to land use planning. [Pauses] If the executive walks away from the site, then we're in trouble, but, some of the new Democrats are interested in this and they will work with the executive, who's a solid old-line Democrat. The board is mainly Republican, though, and I don't want the Republicans to butt heads with the executive on this.

Donald and Jimmy trust each other. Jimmy lists his worried advice, which is based on his widespread consulting experience throughout the state. His comments are ironic and tinged with cynicism. He chants a litany of must-do actions, only to be met by Donald's laconic admission of his limits. Jimmy is compulsive; Donald is not. Although Jimmy wants to keep his contract alive and help out with implementation, he seems less motivated by self-interest and more by an urgent concern and a sympathetic desire to see Donald and the county avoid wasteful conflict.

Jimmy's professional and instrumental focus contrasts with Donald's careful and measured concern about the proper conduct of inquiry and with his own limits. Donald cares deeply about procedure, not simply as a protective device, but as a source of morality, pragmatic results, and meaning. He did not go to all those meetings and work with all those officials just for self-protection. He believes that a consensus can be forged to provide practical, political support for the plan.

Donald had modified the landfill site selection criteria to reduce the likelihood of selecting a site with inhabitants. Since one of the objectives of the site selection process was to avoid population centers, his modifications made sense. They also reduced the risk of political protest, enhancing the political acceptability of a proposed site. Political feasibility is crucial to the siting of a LULU, but this criterion was not included in the original research design. Did Donald go too far?

A strict interpretation of the professional protocol would suggest that Donald is violating the limits of expertise. It could be construed that by changing the site selection criteria after they have been put to use, he is undermining the claim that the evaluation is detached and objective.

Donald, however, makes a practical distinction between environmental and social selection criteria. He faithfully complies with the environmental criteria to select and rank the physical viability of potential sites. This listing yields a top cluster of acceptable sites. He then manipulates the land use criteria to justify selecting a final site that he believes local officials, activists, and residents will find unobjectionable.

Donald's use of the first person plural expresses his sense of his work as a kind of public-serving collaboration. He confides in Jimmy that he questions the sincerity of the county executive. The executive does not say "we," but rather assigns responsibility to Donald. Donald has his own plans to return eventually to Colorado and has a generous severance provision in his contract should he be made a scapegoat. He does not trust the adversarial arena. Jimmy is the warrior anxious to get on with the battle, while Donald believes that public deliberation can work if given a fair chance.

Donald's public-mindedness becomes especially evident in his complaint about the county worker being lured away by the large and lucrative waste disposal company, Eco Corp. Donald perceives that she is no longer applying regulations fairly and with a sense of public concern. He does not resent her interest in private employment, but rather her misuse of her position to curry favor. The more cynical Jimmy is attracted to power and prestige, but by the end of the meeting his ambivalence toward public service seems less pressing than at the beginning. Perhaps Donald's calm and confident purposefulness rekindles Jimmy's hopes of offering good and useful service. Donald can confide his worry about the executive once Jimmy stops scheming and starts listening.

Years of hard work have yielded a promising landfill site attractive to Donald's superiors. The complex planning process, which has involved hundreds of meetings and volumes of reports, has worked. Ironically, everything must remain a secret. Donald receives only the most modest of thanks from the executive, who, Jimmy claims, has not even read the report. Furthermore, the implementation effort remains vulnerable to a host of political and administrative agreements, over only a handful of which Donald can exert direct control. Jimmy wants to outrace the opposition, but Donald understands the limits they face.

DESIGNING POLITICAL CONSENSUS

Making plans involves a great deal more than drawing up blueprints or plotting a course. Producing plans requires that the author recognize, acknowledge, and develop relationships with the participants, patrons, and consumers of the plan. Through these relationships, the planner learns that meaningful policy addresses the interests and concerns of the various members of the community and that many skills are required to obtain practical commitments to carry out the plan. None of the above planners operated as narrow-minded obsessive technicians.

George had plans for downtown redevelopment, but he knew that it would be difficult to get the board to even put planning on the agenda. He had hoped to build support over time, but circumstances forced him to act. His attempt to use an informal meeting packed with supporters failed to win approval for his plan, but not for lack of preparation. Even overlooking Ken's headstrong enthusiasm, the deep-rooted ideological opposition of local elected officials gave George little room to maneuver. Appeals to the owners' property rights heightened fears of condemnation proceedings among George's supporters, including the mayor. Ralph cleverly used the threat of adversity to undermine the consensus needed to approve a redevelopment plan.

Annette started her professional career expecting to realize her planning ideals through participation in electoral campaigns. Her experience with adversarial competition, however, convinced her to practice her professional craft in the context of deliberations rather than political contests. Working as a consultant for a large developer, Annette finds herself facing a very different sort of conflict. In her case, all parties were committed to a plan, but disagreed about whom should be included and what purposes should be met. Annette found her loyalties divided between her employers and the local residents. She does her client's bidding, but has doubts. To share her doubts and seek advice, Annette tells her planning colleagues about her dilemma, violating her client's desire for secrecy. Annette trusts her confidants, who give her not only useful information about local plans in the study area, but also an opportunity to test her beliefs about her role and responsibility. She does not violate the trust of her employer for personal gain or ideological advantage, but to discover how best to balance her competing loyalties to her family, firm, profession, friends, and residents. The planning counselor seeks advice.

Donald's story of planning for a landfill illustrates how the elements of the rational planning process do not follow in linear fashion. The textbooks say analyze the problem first and implement the plan last. Donald, however, tells how from the outset he has nurtured relationships with local officials, environmental groups, and private waste management firms. He understands how practical political concerns shape expectations and fears about landfill sites. He sets out to anticipate and address these fears. He enjoys the support of the county administrative and elected officials, who are likely to bear the nasty political consequences of a rancorous site selection process. Donald plays an open and public role, which means that the politicians can easily lay the burden of blame on his shoulders, should the site selection plan fail. This risk, however, also gives him the opportunity to draw on the authority and support of county officials for his plans. The successful meeting with the county executive was no accident.

Donald believes in building consensus among each group of actors involved with selecting a site. Each step of the way, he works to keep the relevant parties informed and involved. The antagonists appear, but at the margins. He seeks to build support for democratic deliberations about the best site, thus, avoiding unnecessary adversity. The largest test still remains. Once the site is announced and the commitment made, the previous agreements might fall apart. The obvious political value of the military site Donald has proposed is that it minimizes the potential for adversarial fallout. As the animated banter between Donald and Jimmy makes clear, many things can go wrong. Jimmy not only fears the cynical self-interest of waste management firms and local advocacy groups, but his own self doubts. Donald offers a more hopeful approach: He tries to ensure that his actions communicate a fair-minded and responsible plan. He knows his efforts are precarious and vulnerable to political disruption, but he accepts that as part of the fragmented and divisive political system within which planning occurs.

NOTE

1. In his national study of planners and politics in the mid-1970s, Michael Vasu found that most planners were far more likely to participate in conventional political activities of every sort as compared to either the general population or to people of similar socioeconomic status. Professional planners are neither apathetic nor passive technocrats. Vasu also found that only about 12 percent of the planners identified themselves as Republicans; the rest were evenly split between Democrats and Independents. Detailed analysis of the Independents found more than 60 percent leaning toward the Democratic party. Controlling for socioeconomic status, the study found that planners had much stronger ties to the Democratic party than did their peers in the population at large.

Vasu's assessment of political ideology among planners showed that they were much less likely (9.2 percent) to adopt conservative principles than members of the public at large with the same socioeconomic status (36 percent) and far more likely (50.2 percent) to adopt liberal views than their class peers (43.4 percent). Most significant were Vasu's findings on political activity. Compared with members of the same social class in the general public, professional planners were four times as likely to work for political parties or attend political meetings (Vasu 1979, 127–34).

CHAPTER

6

Planning Regulation

As employees of local government, usually municipalities, planners put plans into action by designing, adapting, and deploying the police powers delegated by the state. The zoning ordinance plays perhaps the most prominent role, but housing codes, building codes, and various environmental ordinances can also be part of the regulatory arsenal. These regulations usually lay down relatively precise guidelines and standards for the location, density, scale, design, quality, and use of the built environment within the jurisdiction of the local government. Planners enjoy considerable discretion in interpreting the application of the regulations to proposed plans for individual projects. In effect, layers of regulatory standards that have been established incrementally and independently over several decades, combined with a tradition of precedent-setting decisions, have produced a complex set of relationships that planners must consider in judging the merits of a development proposal and formulating useful and desirable modifications and recommendations (Solnit 1988).

As local government civil servants, professional planners are not officially authorized to grant or deny approval of specific projects. The professional protocol has planners propose, not dispose. In practice, however, local government planners tap the authority of local governing boards, executives, committees, lawyers, and, occasionally, of national and state officials. Some planners may enjoy a generous and others a stingy share of political authority and regulatory discretion. The complexity of the regulatory landscape, however, requires that someone be able to make informed judgments within the bounds of local, state, and federal laws about the application of regulations.

The complexity and uncertainty surrounding the regulation of development give the local governing boards some discretion. City council or planning commission members may take advantage of the loose fit between regulations and specific proposals to pursue purposes and interests that are ancillary or even antagonistic to the original intent of the regulations, and, if one exists, the comprehensive plan the regulations are supposed to enforce. Consider the alderman who wants to repay a political favor to a campaign contributor and so urges lax enforcement of a density regulation, which will enhance the profitability of the contributor's development proposal. Consider the council member who wants to punish an enemy and imposes an unnecessarily strict interpretation of a regulation on the opponent's development proposal. Reformers have long proposed regulations that mandate uniform compliance (Adler 1990). These reform efforts usually founder, however, because they tend to produce wildly unpredictable outcomes. For example, the use of fixed development caps in early growth control efforts fostered a rigid and undesirable escalation of local housing prices in the 1970s (Frieden 1979).

Most zoning regulations enforce standards rather than the desired outcomes of those standards. Planners regularly debate the modification and removal of fixed standards that serve no particular planning goal, but they find few local supporters of their reform efforts. Most local planning commissions and city councils treat zoning regulations as ends, not means. Performance zoning (the regulation of land use based on measurable impacts of activity, rather than type of use), for instance, only can work when city officials adopt specific policies and plans that they expect the zoning regulations to follow and complete (Kendig 1980).

At the core of the urban planning tradition is the understanding that planners do more than just apply the laws. Rather, they should be executing a comprehensive plan. Zoning and other development regulations should follow the adoption of a plan: First plan, then regulate. Most members of the profession agree that imposing a regulatory decision and then making up a plan to justify that decision is rather tawdry. However, the institutional boundaries between regulation and planning receive little political respect in the United States.

As the narrow master plan gave way to the more inclusive policies plan of the 1960s, the distinction became blurred between the master template for development and the means for achieving it. Many criticized the spirit of physical determinism that infused the master plan designs of the early twentieth century, but these documents offered vivid images of future development independent of the means of implementation (Hubbard and Hubbard 1929). As comprehensive plans became the subject of government policy, they lost their independent moral authority. As both planning and regulating became government functions, the sequential relationship that planners held dear—first plan, then regulate—was compromised. Outside the planning tradition, local government officials could easily adopt policies in any order they wished. Usually this meant first zone, then plan. Even more frequently this meant first develop, then zone, no plan.

Planning lobbyists frequently advance legislative initiatives to impose the proper sequence of activity. For example, they have proposed state legislation to require local governments to make their zoning regulations conform to a comprehensive plan. Local officials, however, are reluctant to place authority in a plan. They would rather keep hold of the regulatory reins. In 1939, Rexford Tugwell proposed that planning become a fourth power of government. Checked by the powers of a parallel planning authority, elected officials would have to face the political necessity of creating and following plans for public benefits that extend beyond the next development proposal or the next election. There is merit to Tugwell's extreme suggestion in light of the profession's failure to persuade local government officials to create and follow plans. Of course, the organization of local democratic authority precludes this sort of arrangement.

In the 1980s, the primacy of planning faced great obstacles. Regulating seized the helm. Many fast-growing, prosperous municipalities adopted growth management regulations to preserve the attractiveness of their communities. Meanwhile, local governments with large and diverse populations, pressured by tax payer revolts, reductions in state and federal subsidies, and increasing economic uncertainty, sought to develop new sources of revenue to meet growing service demands. Planners developed a variety of regulatory fees that proved popular, especially for those local governments experiencing rapid growth. Linda Dalton found in California that planners spent most of their time preparing for, conducting, and evaluating the merits of development proposals in light of local regulations (1989b). She asserts that these activities seriously compromised comprehensive planning.

Today's planners may share with their professional forebears a deep caring for comprehensive planning, but may doubt its efficacy. They no longer expect plans to be official documents that speak with authority to governing boards and employers. The creation of an authoritative planning document in the domain of local government requires considerable time, effort, and skill. There is no guarantee that it will prove relevant or useful. Often, a particular plan will remain viable only during the tenure of the particular regime or cadre of elected officials that supported it.[1]

So how do planners plan if there is no official plan? What makes planners who spend most of their time as regulators and administrators for local development more than just land cops? How do planners regulate in the face of political resistance or indifference on the part of local elected officials?

POLITICAL SETTING: FROM STAFF
MEETING TO PUBLIC HEARING

What happens as planners move from the informal domain of unitary politics in their staff meetings to the risky adversarial arena of a public hearing? What changes do the planners make in their stories in talking to those outside their community, especially to those who question their judgment? The following tales describe a planning staff meeting and a public hearing on the same day. The central focus is the argument of the zoning administrator for an aging industrial suburban municipality. The small planning department consists of only three planners and a secretary. Their offices are located in the basement of the fire department, several blocks from city hall.

In the staff meeting, the planners discuss a subdivision proposal that they agree will probably dominate that evening's planning commission and zoning board of appeals meeting, for which they are preparing. The case under discussion is a request by an industrial property owner to subdivide his lot into two parcels. The zoning code setback requirements will not allow him to build a large warehouse structure on his lot as it is currently configured. His letter of request is ambiguous about his intent. The letter suggests that he is interested in building the warehouse, but he is also looking forward to relocating his business in several years and wants to enhance the salability of his property.

The zoning administrator, Andrew, has prepared a memorandum describing the petitioner's intent, background, and nearby properties. Andrew relates that Mr. Trimble, the owner, requested permission to subdivide several years ago, but was denied. The owner has renewed his petition.

Andrew: Mr. Trimble now hopes to obtain this new subdivision and variances so he can construct an industrial building to the west of his present plant. At the time of my discussions with Mr. Trimble, I was under the impression that his intention was to use this new building as a warehouse serving his present plant building. The letter that Mr. Trimble submitted with his application for the hearing, however, says that he wishes to build in order to relocate his business. I have not yet seen building plans, a site plan, or drawings for the new structure.

The village policy is not to approve subdivisions done solely or primarily for the purpose of enhancing the sale value of the parcel. Andrew's memorandum raises the question of the owner's intent.

Pat [junior planner]: Are we in favor of the Trimble subdivision?

Andrew: I can see pros and cons. The new lot he is cutting off is only marginally smaller than the code allows, ninety-four versus one hundred feet.

Pat: But compared to the rest of the neighboring uses, is it going to be out of scale?

Andrew: I think we want to promote the location of more small- and moderate-sized industry in town. If Trimble is sincere about using the subdivision to build a new warehouse, then this effort doesn't make sense. He could just add on to the existing structure and request a variance to get approvals.

Michael [planning director]: He's been clear about his interest in selling the property down the road.

Pat: Do you know what kind of warehousing Trimble's talking about?

Michael: No, but I think he's going to sell the property. I feel he already has someone in mind.

Pat: There's no time restriction after subdivision approval. So if he gets the approval, he's going to do it fast.

Michael: He pulled the permit early on another project that he did earlier.

Pat: What else can you do with the site?

Andrew: This is an economic question. What's good for the village? What if the two hundred foot lot had one large versus two small buildings? Would that make a difference?

Pat: [Wistfully] Would that we knew the trends.

Michael: [Shifting the focus of the discussion and speaking to Andrew] Did you do a report on this?

Andrew: [Hands the two-page report to Michael] Yes.

Michael: What about the mechanics of the plat? Are things moving? He filed this only two days ago?

Pat: Still not following the rules [by filing late], is he?

Michael: Yeah, he's not following the ordinance.

Andrew: [Looking at a copy of the ordinance and studying the materials] He needs topographical information and he needs to indicate the location of easements.

Pat: He does sort of have a topo. The land is very flat. How picky do you want to get?

Michael: [Firmly] We're not going to get picky at all.

Andrew: We don't have all the certifications signed off yet on the plat, but that can be added later.

Michael: Let's talk with them before the meeting starts and give a bye [waiver].

Pat: This is a preliminary plat, so he doesn't need certifications.

Michael: I think we're fine.

Andrew: I still have a background question on the subdivision request. We end up with a property platted into two lots with a single owner. Does that not remain a single zoning issue? I think he's going to build the new building and then sell both.

Michael: What are you stuck on, Andrew?

Pat: You have me confused, too.

Andrew: If he builds the warehouse and uses it himself as one zoned lot and then seeks to sell it off, he will need to subdivide it again. For instance, imagine two lots platted some eighty years ago that were substandard. Today, one lot is vacant and the other has a house and both are owned by the same person. The owner decides to sell the vacant lot, but finds he can't because it is substandard. No one can build on it and meet code. The same thing applies in this industrial case.

The key may be in the subdivision ordinance. I want to make sure that if he subdivides first [before getting a zoning variance], that we can still control approval of occupancy. He shouldn't be allowed to subdivide if he's just going to sell the lots and speculate. He should only get this approval if he's going to use the building for his business.

Michael: You think he's creating a hardship for himself?

Andrew: Yes, because he could build the building so as not to need setback variances. Meeting the zoning ordinance would not be a hardship, but that's true of at least 50 percent of the variance requests we review. If the lot were five feet wider, then he wouldn't need a side yard.

Pat: He's doing this to make some money?

Andrew: This subdivision request flies in the face of another standard. You're not supposed to be allowed to do a subdivision for purely speculative purposes. He's not doing this to increase the city tax base. [Speaking cynically now] Look, everybody creates their hardship and we have to dance around that.

Andrew judges the proposal in light of his view of the public good, particularly the community's economic welfare. Approval to subdivide would enhance the value of the industrial land. It would not guarantee, however, any increased revenues to the town. The subdivision would have no necessary impact on the quality or quantity of the owner's manufactured goods. Andrew wants the owner to obtain a zoning variance, which would encourage expansion of the existing plant and discourage speculative development. Andrew looks to the authority of the municipal regulations to justify constraining the discretion of the owner. Andrew rehearses his argument in the trusting informal setting of the staff meeting. His colleagues understand and sympathize. However, the director, Michael, reminding Andrew of the legal limits defining the request, sets parameters on the evening performance: "We're not going to get picky." He gives Andrew permission, however, to raise the important question.

The formal hearing occurs at city hall. The planning staff, dressed in full professional garb, whisper among themselves. George, the director of the planning commission, speaks with each of the members quietly. When the petitioner arrives with his lawyer, George meets briefly with them to make sure that the petitioner has not altered his subdivision request. Only the petitioners, the commissioners, the staff, and I are in attendance. The meeting opens on time with an official call to order by the chair. The Trimble case is first on the agenda.

After introducing himself, Trimble's lawyer (J. P.) briefly describes the subdivision request. The petitioner wants approval to divide his 194 foot wide by 230 foot deep lot into two parcels, 100 by 230 feet and 94 by 230 feet. He is also requesting a variance from the 100-foot width standard for the second lot.

> J. P.: The purpose of the subdivision is to get additional warehouse space for the owner's business. The owner has been at this site for two and a half years. He purchased the land to conduct his business and because it offered room for expansion.

The owner moves forward to a chair facing the planning commissioners.

> J. P.: Mr. Trimble, please explain why you want to subdivide your property.

> Trimble: We are crowded in the present building. Presently, I need to expand into another building with at least five thousand square feet, but building such a small structure is not advisable. So I want to build a separate building with ten thousand square feet.

> J. P.: If the subdivision request is not approved, the existing space will not be buildable. Unless the new subdivision is approved under the zoning ordinance, the newly subdivided vacant lot is not valuable [because it will not be saleable]. We want to make it buildable and saleable.

> Chair: Why didn't it stay the lot of record?

> Trimble: When we originally proposed a subdivision, the town board had not approved an occupancy permit. There was a problem between the builder and the village. The two lots were consolidated. So now we have to unjoin them to make the now vacant portion buildable as a separate lot.

> J. P.: My client wants to ensure that it is easier to sell the buildings later on, but it's not his intention to build a building just to resell. He wants to build

the structure to meet his present needs, but which also will be attractive to future buyers.

Chair: This is a warehouse?

J. P.: The way his business is going, my client needs to know he can leave this space and sell it quickly. If he were to add on to the present building to create an eighteen thousand square foot structure he would have difficulty finding a buyer. Two structures of ten thousand square feet on separate lots would be much easier to sell.

The lawyer turned the hearing into a court room. Although he did not administer an oath to his client, he placed him in a chair at the center of the room and examined him, as if he were an expert witness in a trial. This enhanced the credibility of the petitioner's testimony. Furthermore, the lawyer posed the very question that Andrew had raised with his colleagues earlier in the day. The attorney's preemptive strike undermines Andrew's authority as a planner. He becomes an attorney cross-examining the witness.

Andrew: You couldn't put up an addition [on the subdivided lot] without getting a zoning variance, but you could put up a building on the space by simply requesting a zoning variance. If you just want to build usable space, you only need to get a zoning variance. Why ask for both a subdivision change and a zoning change? What's the reason for creating a subdivision at this time?

Trimble: If I add on to the existing building, I will pay almost as much as I would for a new one. Better for me to invest in a new building, which I can more easily sell, than improving my present building and creating a larger structure, which will be hard to sell. Furthermore, the elevation needed for storage requires sixteen-foot ceilings, a height that greatly increases the cost of a build-on.

J. P.: From the village's point of view, you end up with better spacing and a more aesthetic looking building [with subdivision]. There is a reciprocal benefit here.

Trimble: [Turning to face the board with a look of anguish] We're just jammed.

Chair: [Asking the big question] Are you planning to build this building to resell it soon?

J. P.: [Answering quickly and firmly for his client] Categorically no!

Trimble: If I did [sell it], I'd have to move.

Andrew: [Persisting although the commissioners have given informal gestures of satisfaction] Why aren't you just getting zoning variances now without the subdivision? You only need to get the subdivision when you want to sell.

Trimble: Well, what if the village denies the subdivision later on? Then I'm in big trouble.

The owner realizes that the town board is more inclined to approve his subdivision request now, when he is hiring residents and contributing tax revenue, than in the future when his request would be coupled with his intention to leave town. He expects the public body to support his economic discretion, but feels no responsibility for the public welfare beyond the payment of his tax bill.

J. P.: [Jumping into the conversation] My client deserves the right to protect his discretion to meet his business needs.

The chair calls for a vote and all approve the subdivision request. The owner and lawyer get their way.

In the hearing, the lawyer and his client were able to shape the rhetorical frame of reference. The lawyer portrays his client as the dutiful and prosperous businessman seeking, first, to expand his business and only secondarily to ensure the future salability of his land. He is petitioning the town to remove a longstanding impediment to his expansion plans. By framing the terms of the debate before Andrew had the opportunity to raise questions about public responsibility and nonspeculative economic investment, the lawyer was able to make Andrew appear to be meddling with the rights of the owner. The courtroom ritual precluded the prospect of deliberation. The commission members did not challenge the lawyer's frame. His adversarial rhetorical structure kept the staff from playing an influential planning role.

At the staff meeting, Michael, the planning director, anticipating the owner's legal response, indicated his unwillingness to fight him. At the hearing, he went with the flow. For Andrew, however, deliberations still mattered. He believed that the commission could be persuaded by argument. Michael knew they respected good arguments, but that they also listened to their friends, followed their interests, and feared lawsuits. The more experienced of the two, Michael decided early on not to push the staff's industrial policy with regulatory sticks.

The sense of solidarity, humor, and informality that marked the earlier staff meeting played no part in the formal hearing. Andrew did as he promised in a difficult setting. The commission proceedings were cordial, but adversarial, while the staff meeting had been intimate and cooperative. The petitioner was a witness, but also a defendant—innocent until proven guilty. In his opening narrative, the lawyer told the story of an enterprising and efficient businessman whose future prosperity required that the village support his discretion in the disposal of his own land. The commissioners were the powerful actors; the businessman, a vulnerable and needy petitioner.

Andrew narrated a different story in the staff meeting. He told of a successful and ambitious businessman who was benefiting from his location and now wanted the town to improve his chances of making even more money by enabling the sale of his industrial real estate. Andrew reminded his audience that the town policy prohibited subdivisions for the purpose of resale and warned that resale would be the owner's eventual goal. Andrew did not want the town to accept on faith the owner's promise that he would not speculate. Andrew wanted the town to retain its regulatory discretion to review any future lot sales through the subdivision review process. He also wanted the town to ensure that private owners would respect the policy regulating speculation by limiting the landowner's discretion in the resale of subdivided land.

At the first meeting, the staff used humor to bridge the distance between their policy priorities and the interests of the town's officials and landowners. In the staff meeting, Andrew could use rational argument to persuade his colleagues because they shared his concern for the public good over the property interests. They were not idealists, however. Andrew knew, as did his colleagues, that his argument was pushing the envelope of institutional legitimacy. His cynical self-commentary served to remind them what they were up against.

The public hearing did not allow for humor or commentary. The role of dutiful zoning expert precluded Andrew from shaping consideration of the case. His performance was limited by the protocol of public servant and expert and even more by the courtroom rhetoric. He could ask questions and testify as to the fit between request and regulations, but the framework of the hearing did not allow him an opportunity to speculate about the consequences of undesirable petitioner behavior. He could police, but not plan.

The small staff meeting allowed the planners to engage in unitary and cooperative politics. The planning director did not impose his authority on the staff, but used it to guide their deliberations. In contrast, the zoning hearing was an adversarial proceeding. Its formal structure precluded deliberations about the planning implications of the case. The case held little significance in the larger scale of local planning issues. As with most regulatory zoning decisions, undesirable cumulative effects did not get much play.

Adversarial politics tend to leave little room for the kind of deliberation that planning students learn to embrace. In such settings, the planner as political advocate is a ludicrous image to most practitioners, who are only too familiar with the tight institutional boundaries of their work. Planners enjoy the most discretion in the institutional settings that precede, parallel, or preempt the adversarial proceedings. Here they have greater freedom to deploy the politics of vision and deliberation. In the staff meeting, the planners both challenged and conformed to the contours set by custom and by the expectations of those possessing greater authority and status. Despite the constraints in the wider community, many planners persist in challenging local customs, in framing the problems with project proposals, and in persuading local officials and citizens to consider alternatives.

THE BATTLE OF THE SETBACKS

The next two regulatory stories show how planners can become quickly embroiled in risky political conflicts through the smallest mistakes. Two planning directors for large suburban municipalities must deal with an error in a zoning setback case. One director, emphasizing craft at the expense of strategy, embraces a version of the professional protocol. The other emphasizes rhetorical strategy at the expense of craft. Neither planner simply lays down the law, but rather formulates a working plan as a guide in evaluating and coping with the development problem at hand. In their judgments, they combine technical, legal, political, and moral concerns. They fall back on the professional protocol to reinforce their sense of identity and interpret the complex political relationships inherent to their work.

George: Defending Regulatory Integrity

George, who appeared in chapter 5, is the suburban planning director who tried unsuccessfully to get town council members to prepare a downtown redevelopment plan. He describes a regulatory error made by his staff.

People always come in expecting red tape. I help them through the process. A lot of times I have to say no, but I always want people to have a sense that they were well served. I also make every effort to ensure they understand the rules—the reasons why I make a positive or negative recommendation.

This story involves a parcel in an older part of town. The owner submitted a permit for a new single-family dwelling on a fifty foot wide lot. The zoning administrator approved the plans and did not notice that a proposed bathroom on the side of the dwelling would create an eighteen-inch encroachment into the side yard setback area. The owner went ahead and had the contractors pour the foundation. It was only after the inspector came in with the new drawings based on the actual foundations that the planning staff member realized that the structure violated the code.

The mistake was complicated by the fact that the owner's neighbor had called the building inspectors and asked that they come out and check for the encroachment she saw, based on the location of the frames the builders had laid to hold the cement for the foundation. The inspectors did not respond to the neighbor's warning and so didn't discover the nonconforming encroachment until after the foundation had been poured.

The inspectors contacted the architect for the project and told him that the construction would have to be halted until a proper variance had been obtained. Understandably, the architect was angry and protested that he had received approval from the inspectors early on.

I knew my staff member had made a mistake, but it was still important to ensure that a variance was obtained. I offered to streamline the hearing for the owner from the usual twelve weeks to only three. The staff and I looked at similar encroachment cases recently reviewed. We wanted to find precedents for this sort of encroachment. We found three, including one instance in which the setback was as small as three feet. [George wanted to ensure that the planning commission would approve the variance, not only to reduce the impacts of the staff mistake, but to reduce the city's liability.]

I met with the city manager and legal counsel soon after I discovered the mistake and raised the pertinent issues. If we allowed the owner to continue building, we would increase the liability of the city, but at least the owner would avoid losing money and be less likely to sue. However, we did face the prospect of the planning commission and village officials deciding to follow the rules in the face of neighborhood protest. I wanted to avoid the risk of liability, but the manager and legal counsel wanted to avoid placing a greater economic burden on the owner.

The neighbor who had tried to warn the inspection staff, when informed of the public hearing requesting a zoning variance, wrote a long critical letter. The letter was distributed to the members of the zoning board of appeals. The neighbor claimed in the letter that the addition would "look like a gangway in nearby Central City," while "blocking the sunlight on her own house." But most significant was her detailed account of the inadequate response of city staff to her warnings. Her fears about the physical impact of the building were exaggerated. For instance, the new structure would not block the sun, as it was located on the north side of the neighbor's lot. Unfortunately, none of the board members thought to send me a copy of the letter, so the first time I read it was during the hearing when the woman got up to speak.

At the zoning hearing, the board spent a great deal of time discussing the neighbor's complaints about the staff. I was upset that they were not focusing on the merits of the case. When they asked me to speak I told them that they should base their decision on the merits of the case and not engage in discussions of personnel matters, which were outside their jurisdiction. The board members got really mad and kept asking, "How could this happen?" They rejected the variance and the case then went before the village council.

During the two weeks between hearings, one of the zoning board of appeals members took the initiative to meet with the neighbor and served as a facilitator between her and the owner seeking a variance. The owner agreed to do some grading and landscaping in return for keeping the nonconforming encroachment. She agreed to this settlement. So the substantive matter was basically solved.

However, when the variance was brought before the city council, the neighbor showed up again and asked in no uncertain terms that the staff be punished or fired for their mistake. Three zoning board of appeal members came and testified on her behalf. They said that had they been properly notified of the proposed development early on, they would not have approved it.

The village trustees approved the variance, but decided to appoint a committee to look into the issue of staff negligence. I was upset because I did not think the staff was negligent. I was upset that the city manager let the trustees do this. I think he should have told them that no investigation was necessary. He's a weak manager, unwilling to stand up to the trustees for his own staff.

I expected the committee to report that the staff had made a mistake and that the manager had unnecessarily exposed the city to risk by allowing the owner to continue building after the violation was discovered, but the committee eventually found fault with no one and simply acknowledged that a mistake had been made.

George closely identifies with the professional protocol, which places expertise in the service of the local administrative hierarchy. He believes professional planners should honor the integrity of the split between politics and expertise. He is especially interested in maintaining the rules and seeing that they are enforced with propriety and fair-minded flexibility. He is troubled by the zoning mistake because it represents a lapse in the kind of rule enforcement that attends to both the ordinance and the feelings of the citizens. However, he does not berate the planner who made the mistake. He does not serve him up as a scapegoat.

George adopted a principled strategic posture to defend the integrity of his craft against what he considered to be the illegitimate political attacks of an irate citizen. He feared that an open admission of failure would provide a political lever for others to use to undermine both the legitimacy of the planning department's regulatory discretion and the city's general authority. He identified closely with the municipality and hoped to protect it from liability. He was also worried about the reputation of his own department. He did not want to set a precedent of suspending zoning rules in the wake of staff errors.

A faithful municipal employee, George felt betrayed when his superior failed to defend the integrity of the regulatory planning domain against the encroaching city council investigation. George saw the manager as weak, because he chose not to uphold the planners' position against the negative accounts of the protestor and the sympathetic zoning commissioners. George also considered the manager to be reckless for leaving the municipality open to a lawsuit. The protestor questioned the integrity of the local planning craft and with great rhetorical skill transformed a trivial mistake into a purposeful and routine act of incompetence.

Bruce: A Consummate Strategist

Bruce loves to talk. He seems hungry for challenges and a bit of glory. He directs the planning department of an old industrial suburb on the economic rebound after a long, but not devastating, decline. His high cheek bones and full eyebrows make his eyes appear recessed. His gaze is intense and penetrating. As he speaks, he paces across his well-kept office, gesticulating vigorously to make his points. He is the teacher; I am the student.

> Every planning situation is unique. Rules are written for the convenience of those enforcing them. For instance, the city presently has a bizarre set of procedures in regulating the construction of roads. They are overly restrictive, adding enormous and unnecessary costs to development.
>
> I don't mind getting into fights about these things. One developer said I have a coercive personality, but this does not bother me. I get high on comments from others who complain that I tell it the way it is in public. I lay out

the ground rules. No surprises! Then I stick to an agreement. Even if we make a mistake, there's no going back. I make it clear to my staff that we take responsibility for our mistakes.

As a planning director friend said to me, "It's the stoplights that will get you fired." In my case, recently a downtown bank (and its stubborn president who thinks urban renewal requires destroying and then rebuilding the downtown) was planning to demolish the oldest building in the city and the building department failed to realize its historical significance and initially OK'd its destruction. However, the city manager learned of the proposed demolition and warned the bank president that the demolition was illegal. We did manage to save the building, but the bank also created a parking lot nearby. This lot created a serious problem for me.

The proposed lot had only a six-inch setback between the building and the curb. We proposed a three-foot compromise setback in negotiations with the architect. However, one of the planning commissioners, when the proposal came before them, insisted on a six-foot setback. The commission went along with him because he was bureau chief for the design department of the state department of transportation. I met with the mayor and described the problem. He said that the six-foot setback seemed reasonable and necessary. Unfortunately, I mentioned this in a meeting with the bank's architect, who passed the information on to his client, the bank president. I soon learned that the bank president had blown up when he got word of the mayor's OK. I knew then that the city council meeting in which the setback would be discussed would prove risky.

I called some friends who had previously contacted me with an attractive job offer and asked if the offer was still good. After I got this reassurance, I was prepared to say my piece before the council, including the mayor, basically defending the planning commission recommendation. I expected to be the one speaking and taking the heat for the planning commission decision (and my own indiscretion of telling the architect about the mayor's involvement).

But when I got to the meeting, I learned that the mayor was so angry with me that he didn't want me to speak at all. The meeting went on for an hour and a half. The setback was approved. Afterwards, the mayor called me an idiot. I took the abuse at the time, figuring I would talk with him about the mistreatment later, after he'd cooled down. The other city department heads were quite supportive and told the mayor he was out of line for speaking with such disrespect.

So, I dodged this bullet.

From the outset, Bruce was aware of the conflicting interests that eventually undermined his efforts to negotiate a consensus. His use of insider information to leverage an agreement backfired. He did not treat this mistake as a professional identity crisis, but as a risky goof-up. Instead of staking out a professional position that escalated the conflict, as did George, Bruce took precautions to ensure his future employment and deliberately (if, resentfully) played out his role as the dutiful public servant at the council meeting. Bruce's strategic maneuver proved volatile because it violated the mayor's expectation that the planning director be a loyal public servant and objective expert behind the scenes as well as on the public stage.

Bruce identified with a vision of proper land use order and adapted the rules of regulation and participation to enforce that order. Because he did not want to sacrifice good land use plans to the political needs of the mayor, he violated the professional protocol by passing on the mayor's judgment about the setback to the architect to convince him to persuade his client, the banker, to conform with the compromise setback requirement. Tripped up by his strategic maneuver, Bruce first protects his professional survival, before enacting the protocol of regulatory expertise at the public hearing. A consummate strategist, he has developed the rigorous discipline of the public warrior who enters battle in service to the order of the whole. He has mastered relations of power in several domains and willingly enters into conflicts. In the setback skirmish, he describes how he dodged the bullet.

Learning from Mistakes

Both planners faced regulatory mistakes in which questions of technical expertise were marginal since the rules were clear. The mistake George inherited was due to carelessness, while Bruce's flowed from his own political maneuvering. Both, however, adopted the protocol of professional expertise to cope with the consequences of these mistakes.

Which response was more effective? This question has no simple instrumental answer. Neither planning director had his way. The professional protocol tells us to applaud George's loyal defense of the planning process and criticize Bruce's political maneuvering. If we acknowledge the unavoidable political involvements of professionals, however, we are likely to find Bruce's efforts more attractive. In both cases, the directors got into serious conflicts over trivial matters because they sought to use authority that their superiors had no intention of sharing. Both directors remained attached to planning principles as a guide for regulations and engaged in risky conflict to defend the legitimacy of their enterprise.

Planning directors do not simply pursue personal and departmental goals. They try to shape and change the moral and political order in which they work (Forester 1993b). Despite differences in their outlook and strategy, both George and Bruce believe in the authority of planning norms and their importance in improving the future development of their municipalities. Furthermore, they both believe in taking action to obtain and exercise this authority. They both exercise moral initiative as a response to actions that threaten the integrity and legitimacy of local planning. However, the escalation of small mistakes into risky conflicts underlines the considerable organizational vulnerability that local planning directors face.

Bruce and George are both interested in power, but they want far more than the power to police through the exercise of regulations. They want the power to establish institutional respect and authority for the planning activity through each act of regulatory discretion. Planners with weak institutional powers are in too risky a position, however, to change the organization and distribution of political power and authority, whether within the bureaucracy or, more broadly, through individual action.

REGULATORY EXCLUSION

In the setback scenarios, the planners got into political hot water simply trying to administer zoning regulations. The controversies arose because the rules set limits on the individual freedom of property owners and land users. Even more troubling are those situations in which municipal officials use the regulatory power of zoning laws to maintain racial, social, or ethnic homogeneity. In these cases, the planner's discretion is swamped by the town officials' scrupulous application of rules whose importance stems not from their immediate effects, but from their secondary consequences. A municipality adopts large lot zoning not simply to minimize traffic and protect broad vistas, but to keep out low-rent housing that might attract low-income minority residents. How do planners cope with the unjust and irresponsible use of zoning regulations?

Bill: The Tight Squeeze

Bill takes me into an office crammed with papers. I feel right at home, watching him maneuver among the precarious piles of books, binders, files, and office paraphernalia. Hailing from New York City, he has retained his accent and charming directness. Words come out in surges, bunched together by the speed of his delivery and punctuated by long draws on a cigarette. He possesses a ruddy Irish complexion, which transmits changes in feeling like a traffic signal. He is working for a small, middle-class bedroom suburb.

I used to work as an economic development planner for both public and nonprofit agencies in older large industrial cities. I found the internal conflicts and bickering among the nonprofit developer crowd demoralizing. I was stymied by dogmatic classifications that pigeon-holed me and reduced the effectiveness of my work. After I completed my master's work, I took a job for an economic development agency that received support from a conservative, big city council member. I had spent considerable time working with other economic nonprofit agencies that enjoyed the political support of liberals and progressives. When my colleagues learned of my new position they treated me as a traitor.

But the problem was deeper than that. I had worked for the liberal nonprofits and found that they didn't treat me with much respect. I had years of experience in industrial park development, but the boss of one local development corporation treated me as a quisling. I got fed up with this sort of treatment and wanted to spend my time doing things that were effective and that would be appreciated. That's what I like about working here.

The staff is small and the atmosphere friendly and supportive. We definitely share the values of good government. There is a town manager and five department heads: fire, police, public works, finance, and planning. I have no staff and work alone.

I report directly to the manager on most development issues that involve any expenditure of tax funds or involve the extension of public facilities and services to private parcels. The manager is definitely the one who makes the big decisions, although as zoning administrator I have the authority to deny applications I find nonconforming.

When someone calls to complain or ask about a petition, you've got to have a third ear. You've got to listen well to what they say. I look for spite matches or social agendas—people using the zoning hearing as a way of settling other disputes. I talk with village employees who are long-time residents. I'll say, "I'm confused. This guy seems to be getting very upset about a minor setback variance or fence location. Could something else be going on?" One of the employees might respond, "Oh, his son ran off with the petitioner's daughter ten years ago and he's never forgiven the neighbor."

The down side of this kind of evaluation is the risk I take of forming a fixed prejudgment of the protestors and complainers. I may end up making a mistake. In cases where I am uncertain, I talk with my boss. I'm really cautious about being some kind of bureaucrat; you know, exercising my limited power to say, "I know better than you." I want to take their complaint and grasp it in terms that respect the meaning of the petitioner's proposal.

Two forces pull at me. On the one hand, we have elected officials who want developers and citizens to go away from hearings feeling good and that their problems have been dealt with fairly and efficiently. On the other hand, there are officials who want to take time looking at the details of each case and want to make sure the rules are followed in ways that promote high-quality growth and development. These officials are frequently unsympathetic to developer or citizen arguments about the costs of delays or meeting strict design standards.

I work hard and prepare detailed memos on each case. The officials and village staff checked my work out early on. They know I'm competent, but since they now consider me trustworthy, they don't really read what I write. Only occasionally do I get good positive feedback.

When I make recommendations I try always to offer the down side and up side. I'm not like a loyal planner whose whole experience has been in planning. One of the things that serves me well in this job (with its contradictory demands) is the street smarts I picked up growing up in New York City, which tempers good will with a touch of paranoia and distrust. I can tell when someone is bullshitting me. My military experience helps me out as well.

Bill holds a rather complex sense of fair-minded zoning regulation. He does not approach rules as an enforcer, but as an interpreter. He considers protests and requests for zoning variances in terms of their inherent merits, but he also investigates the motivation and character of the petitioners. Through public deliberation he tries to construct schemes for balancing the long-term needs of the community with the immediate needs of individual owners. What happens when these two conflict?

In June 1990, fifteen residents complained to me about the presence of portable toilets in one of the local parks used by the Little League baseball teams. Since the baseball season for the children ended in early July, I initially tried to procrastinate because I thought the complaints foolish. The residents persisted and their claims were true. The portables did not conform with the village code, but I did not want to enforce the rules. I went to the city manager and explained the problem. A former zoning administrator, she understood the problem. She and I agreed that we had to comply. I called the Little League team organizers and told them they would have to remove the portables and apply for a conditional use permit. They were not pleased.

Shortly after I gave the bad news, the village fire chief, with whom I did not get along at the time, stormed into my office and started chewing me out for "pulling out the kids' toilets." He screamed that I was crazy and that my decision was unfair. Why did we pull the portables only from the one park and not elsewhere throughout the city? He kept ranting and wouldn't stop. He had three kids in Little League.

Finally, I managed to take him with me to the manager's office. She mediated between us as I tried to explain the municipal policy. The manager explained the history of the decision and that I had consulted with her before enforcing the rules at her insistence. The fire chief finally listened, but left angry. As I was leaving, the manager said she wished I could avoid antagonizing the guy.

I was caught in a kind of Catch-22. I was enforcing a policy I did not like or believe in. If I didn't enforce it, I was violating village law, but when I did enforce it, I was violating my own common sense and alienating coworkers and others. This happens a lot in this job.

Bill found himself squeezed between the law, his conscience, and the expectations of important colleagues. The zoning law, which prohibited land uses that were not explicitly allowed, enabled a few local residents to disrupt the Little League program. The law protected the interests of a few owners over and against the desires of numerous families. The fire chief, unfamiliar with the law, presumed that Bill was exercising excessive and unreasonable authority. Even the city manager's explanations could not relieve the fire chief's anger.

Bill cannot simply ignore the law. He sets out to convince the planning commission to amend the zoning ordinance and to work with the Little League organizers to ensure a timely outcome that will meet with the approval of all the participants. He assumes several roles. As a faithful employee, he takes seriously the potential threat of litigation on the part of the complaining property owners. This threat haunts every step he takes. Bill must respect the exclusionary power of the zoning ordinance and yet find ways to deflect it.

As an organizer, Bill addresses the practical and immediate needs of the Little League leaders, by first convincing them of the necessity of complying with the law and then recruiting them to help change it. The fire chief was not the only angry parent. Bill spoke with the Little League organizers to express his sympathy and inform them of the law. He also explored with them ways to change the law. Finally, as a planner, Bill gathered information about the concerns of the complaining residents, the Little League organizers, the park district, and the planning commission and presented alternatives to the planning commission.

He left the planning commission with the task of developing an amend-ment to the zoning ordinance that would include portable toilets as an allowed use in the parks. He helped the commissioners develop a list of the neighbors' concerns that the ordinance should address. Bill sched-uled a meeting with the head of the local Little League to explain the regulatory response and to build support for amending the zoning ordi-nance. I attended the meeting.

The Meeting

We meet in a small conference room. Fred, the Little League represen-tative, is tall with dark hair, modestly combed back. Well groomed, clean shaven, and tucked neatly into a pressed suit, he is all business. Bill, by contrast, wears his suit like a bathrobe. His white shirt, wrinkled and bunched at the waist, hangs over the edge of his belt, which squeezes in a resentful paunch.

> Bill: I ran the questions [getting portable toilets for the Little League that meet the revised code that Bill has prepared] we spoke about by the plan-ning commission to see if there was any resistance and to see what concerns they might have. Six of the seven members were present. All agreed that the toilets were necessary, but they want to take some actions to mitigate the appearance of the toilets.

> Fred: There wouldn't be a problem at the big park. The toilets would be set well back from the street.

> Bill: But we're trying to come up with some new standards that apply for all parks in the village. Do you think there is any interest on the part of other sports leagues to use these toilets, who also use park district property?

> Fred: No.

> Bill: OK. Now as far as setbacks go, the only concern is that the toilets not be placed as a hazard to traffic. The police did not want them placed near those turns in the road at Willow Park, but we can't do fixed standards here. The parks are too diverse. The problem you've got at Willow is that when it rains hard, the field areas will flood. The toilets need to be placed above the flood plain and near a road where they can be serviced easily.
>
> I spoke with our attorney about including a comment that they be placed in as aesthetically pleasing location as possible. This is difficult. Maybe at some point before the hearing we could visit the sites and pick some loca-tions for each park. A map with the select spots could be attached as part of

the amendment. The commission members are sensitive to the issue of access. They do not want the portables too far from the roadway, creating problems for servicing.

As for screening [the portables from view], the commission did not expect to spend much money. We may be able to get the park commission to put in a few evergreen trees to screen the portables from the nearest residential units. Others suggested that we use some sort of temporary fencing to screen the portables.

Fred: Don't think the park district would do that.

Bill: We've got the hearing scheduled for the nineteenth. My gut feeling is that I think we should invite the residents who complained to the hearing. Normally, when we do amendments, we don't send out notices to property owners. We usually do so only for legal variations. Since amendments affect everyone, we don't invite just a select few.

In this case, though, since we had so many calls, I think we should invite them. Otherwise they will still raise the same protest again next summer. The commission members are sympathetic toward the needs of the Little League, but still want to address the concerns of the residents who complained. So I think we should invite the neighboring residents to voice their complaints—the complaints we are anticipating here.

Fred: [Showing little enthusiasm, but not resisting] How do we go about getting permission [to use the portables]?

Bill: [Opening a map outlining city parks] These are the public use districts. The amendment will apply the same in each area. But you need to get the permission of each public owner, the park district, and the schools. I would also suggest you invite your supporters to attend the meeting on the nineteenth, since we plan to invite the residents who complained.

Fred: [Showing some enthusiasm] You can bet on it! So all I need to do is check with the portable toilet company on the markings?

Bill: Yup, that's it. Just have your troops ready on the nineteenth. I don't think there will be any trouble from the board.

Bill was well focused on the main issues. Fred obviously did not want to go through all the necessary procedures just to get approval for the toilets that they had been using for years. This was a defensive battle, however, and Fred realized that without the approval of the municipality, the league would be in jeopardy. Clearly Bill was on Fred's side, seeking to ensure that the commission would approve the code amendments allowing the portable toilets in city parks.

Although Bill has little sympathy for the complaining residents, he creates a threatening image of them, which he uses to set limits on the options to be considered. For example, when Fred proposes changes to the amendment that would extend use of the parks to August, Bill warns Fred to avoid any "padding," lest the neighbors see this as evidence of bad faith. The items Fred and Bill discuss represent concessions to a third party that neither likes, but whose power they must anticipate and respect. Exclusionary inertia persists even without a voice.

Bill addressed this issue not as a technical legal problem, but as a practical planning problem. He developed a proposal that would remove the rational and legal grounds for the neighbors' complaints and would simultaneously allow the Little League to place the portables in the parks. However, to meet the objections and goals of both parties he had to reduce their uncertainty by applying the amendment to all parks in the municipality. Bill explores aloud the advantage of establishing an abstract standard that could be applied to all park locations. He advises that including all park sports activities would make the amendment more comprehensive, which would foster greater political support and legitimacy. Crafting a good ordinance, that is, one that will sustain legal challenge and also encourage park use, involves rhetorical and political judgments about whom to include in the process and why. Bill reminds Fred to bring many supporters to the hearing to put political pressure on the commissioners.

Bill moves back and forth among different roles, respecting the legitimacy of zoning, while composing a rational amendment and building strong political support for it. He does not agree with the judgments of the complaining neighbors, but he cannot refuse them a hearing without undermining the legitimacy of zoning, which is the bedrock of the town planning process.

The Zoning Hearing

The fifteen or so people in the audience include five planning commission members, the city attorney, and Bill. The portable toilet case is first on the agenda. After the opening rituals, the chair asks Bill to introduce the case. Bill briefly recounts the complaints and the ensuing conflict over the portables and reminds the commission that he has been asked to prepare an amendment to the zoning ordinance that would include the portables as an acceptable use. He reads the new provisions he has drafted, which recommend that the siting of the portables be allowed under special use permits, rather than a zoning amendment. He informs the commission of his recent discussion about the portables with the director of the park district.

Chair: [Turning to the audience] Fred, did you see this ordinance? [Fred approaches the podium and nods his head yes.]

Bill: Basically, Fred, this translates into legal language what we talked about in our meeting.

Fred: We don't want to get a special use permit. That's ludicrous, having to come back every year to ask for the portables for seven hundred kids.

Bill: [Explaining why he changed his recommendations] The zoning amendment would invite the resident owners adjoining all the city parks the chance to voice their views. I considered sending letters to these owners, but when I finished tallying the parcels it amounted to 480 owners. Given the difficulty of making a decision with lots of angry complaining citizens, I thought it would be better to only invite residents around each park.

Chair: I do not see why we want to repeat this process each year.

Board member: I feel compelled to grant this request even with protests.

Chair: [Complaining] The park district isn't doing their job. They let the user group come in here and beg. I don't think we can get the park district staff to come here and I don't want to make [the sports organizers] keep coming here.

Legal counsel: I recommend a first-time special use permit request without requiring rehearings.

Commissioner: Automatic renewal, unless there is reason to change.

Chair: The city council, Fred, wants you to come to their meeting to explain what you're going to do and request a permit. We do this to make it look nice. The council does not want a staff guy making the decision.

The planning commission voiced unanimous support for allowing the portables for the Little League as a special use. However, they also defended the legitimacy of the zoning ordinance, and, thus, required the

Little League organizers to collaborate with the municipality in locating and disguising the portable toilets.

Between his meeting with Fred and the hearing, Bill had decided that there was much greater political risk in amending the ordinance than in employing special use permits. When Fred complains about the burden of annual requests, zoning commission members and their legal counsel scramble to find a way to amend the permitting process to make it automatic after the first issuance. They are reluctant, however, to empower Bill to make the permitting decision. The city attorney and the chair both argue that zoning decisions appear more legitimate to opponents when they issue from the city council, rather than from the planning staff.

None of the participants in this regulatory episode wanted to deny the children the availability of portable toilets, but the sweeping exclusionary standards of the zoning code placed Bill and the commissioners in a bind. Bill, together with the city attorney and an imaginative board member, managed to find a device that would offer the Little League organizers relief, while still protecting the legitimacy of the city's zoning powers. Adapting and rationalizing the zoning regulations in the trivial matter of temporary portable toilets was so important because the process established a precedent for the city council and city attorney to use in more controversial cases, such as in the exclusion of multifamily housing. Bill's authority in these matters is clearly circumscribed. He can offer plans for zoning relief, but not for zoning reforms. What happens when the stakes are higher? What happens when a suburban planner tries to persuade a local government to change its regulations and allow affordable housing?

Tom: Regulating the Fast-Growing Exclusive Suburb

Remember Tom, the planning director in chapter 3 who lost his job? He told me the following story about his efforts to plan for affordable housing when he worked for a prosperous and fast-growing suburban municipality. Tom is the consummate professional. Although he has liberal values, he would not consider himself an advocate planner. He avoids conflict and searches for consensus. His tale illustrates the difficulty of even discussing, much less changing, municipal policies that exclude affordable housing for low-income, predominantly minority populations.

> This was when I worked in Parkville. I continually raised the issue of affordable housing in this growing suburb, not by singing its praises, but by playing on the fears of the council members. I pointed out how the regional hous-

ing advocacy council, which monitored suburban municipalities for housing discrimination, had filed suit against a neighboring suburban city. The city was also in danger of losing federal funds if it didn't pass a fair housing ordinance.

I kept urging the council to take some action. I found an ally in the mayor. He had a daughter who had gotten married, but couldn't afford to live in the city. I found other citizens who told similar tales—human interest stories that brought the affordability problem home. I did a survey of city employees. First, I asked, "Would you live in the city if you could afford to?" Most said yes. Second, I calculated what affordable housing for the employees would cost and compared it to the prices of the housing that was being built. The difference was enormous. The survey results got the attention of some commissioners and council members who now began to consider getting some affordable housing, but affordable housing without "undesirable" minorities.

There was support. The local Chamber of Commerce representatives were complaining of the difficulty of getting clerical help for their businesses. Many of their employees commuted fifteen miles or more to work. The city council members wanted to promote economic development that would create a more diverse city and move away from the bedroom community development of the past. At one point, they tried to lure a semipro hockey team.

I was writing memos and having frequent conversations, but what it came down to was a proposal to change the comprehensive plan's housing policy. The change was innocuous enough, but I knew if I could get the policy approved, then I would have the justification I needed to develop implementation schemes for mixed-use developments that included affordable housing.

At the same time, I had started meeting with a group of developers to propose a series of changes in local subdivision and zoning regs that would reduce construction costs without lowering the quality of the developments. I created a forum for their complaints and pulled these together into formal recommendations for the planning commission and council to consider. My intent was to get the city to call for the development of some affordable rental units as part of larger developments.

I composed different development scenarios showing how [at that time] different versions of Section 8 funds could be applied in mixed-use developments. The key was limiting the proportion of units in any one building to prevent the concentration of low-income tenants. I called it the melting pot scheme.

I kept pushing the notion. I enlisted the help of a local school principal, who acknowledged the importance and value of diversity. I spoke with Chamber of Commerce members, school district officials, developers, citizen clubs, and whoever else would listen. I did this for about three years. My boss, the planning director, was agreeable, but was not willing to take any initiative.

Finally, I got the plan recommendation on the agenda of the city council, but it was tabled. I was to reach the same stage six more times, but with the same result. The proposal would be tabled.

When the city applied to the state to become a certified city [a good government award that enhanced access to economic development funds] the city council finally paid attention to my efforts. As part of the certification, the city was supposed to set up a housing commission, but the council set up a paper commission. Still, I appointed myself as staff to the housing commission and began to use this group as a vehicle to promote affordable housing. In fact, I tried to use the same commission to conduct a needs assessment justifying a recommendation to get a nursing home within the city. The study did get underway, but I left before it was complete. My efforts to use the commission alarmed the city council, which began to send a representative to the meetings. I still kept at it until the end.

So here I was trying to do some advocacy within the planning office and not being too successful. I sometimes wonder if I should have taken a more confrontational approach, but on second thought, it probably would have been counterproductive.

Tom's story illustrates the limitations municipal officials impose on efforts to pursue planning objectives that might increase socioeconomic diversity or foster the redistribution of municipal funds. Tom used his professional skills to make rational arguments for the value of affordable housing. Beyond making plans, he tried to build support for his ideas. In his pursuit of affordable housing, he was engaged in a good deal of political activity that pushed him well beyond the business of crafting good arguments.

The liberal planning profession with which Tom identifies defends zoning laws, which give planners access to government authority. However, the profession also condemns exclusionary zoning. This generates a paradox. Evidence of the widespread use of zoning for exclusionary purposes strongly suggests that this practice is not an exceptional abuse, but the rule. Planners like Tom and Bill, despite their fair-minded liberalism and sensitive political actions, cannot remedy the abuse. Openly opposing, on moral and professional grounds, the exclusionary use of zoning would simply get them fired. Challenging such practices means challenging an important legal power that elected officials use to protect the social, economic, and cultural identity of the municipality.

In overlooking this paradox, the profession fosters ambivalence among those who closely identify with its norms. Tom is a frustrated, though faithful reformer, who remains detached from the exclusionary values of his suburban employers and seeks to implement professional planning principles. By contrast, Bill possesses much weaker ties to the profession. His loyalty to the municipality and his colleagues shapes his judgments. He expresses little moral ambivalence about exclusionary issues, accepting the division of political authority as the given institutional landscape that he must learn to traverse rather than redevelop. Planners can play a role in bulldozing the exclusionary landscape, but usually they need the assistance of political pressure from outside the municipality.

Fred: The Annexation

During the 1950s and 1960s, newly incorporated suburban municipalities annexed land aggressively (see chapter 2). The problems and costs of annexation, however, did not become apparent until the 1970s. Economic and environmental decline and fiscal retrenchment encouraged municipal officials to examine the economic impacts of future annexations. Fiscal impact analysis became a new activity for planning staffs and consultants as part of the effort to assess the long-term merit of infrastructure expansion and new subdivision development.

Annexations can be politically contentious. The procedures vary among states, but usually they require the approval of the landowners and a majority of the residents in the annexation area. The following story tells of annexation competition between the old industrial suburb of Burgess and several of its newer suburban neighbors. The protagonist and storyteller is Fred, the planning director of chapter 1, who identifies deeply with his hometown. His civic booster spirit easily trumps the moral claims of his professional persona. Yet, Fred's lack of concern with his professional authority does not undermine his enthusiasm for planning.

> Mostly we react to things that come up, rather than getting to plan for them. For instance, take the recent case of an annexation dispute between our city and some neighboring suburban municipalities. Several suburban municipalities on the outskirts of Burgess have long engaged in annexation efforts, seeking new development at the city's expense. The officials of these towns constantly complain about our city and call it a bad place. They regularly and falsely claim that Burgess is actively expanding its subsidized housing. They want to stir up racial fears among their largely white, middle-class residents.

The conflict emerged when we found out that a neighboring suburban municipality was planning to file a seven thousand acre annexation proposal that would basically have surrounded Burgess, precluding any future geographic expansion. Luckily, a surveyor hired to prepare the boundaries informed one of our staff members of the suburban plan. We had about three days (including a weekend) to prepare an annexation proposal that would overlap the one proposed by the suburb. We needed to file before the suburban officials did. Many of the city staff, including me, worked considerable overtime that weekend to prepare a small, three-parcel annexation proposal. The attorney who directs our legal department spent the night in the county courthouse to be the first one in line to file the proposal with the clerk. It worked. Our teamwork paid off. Our annexation preempted theirs.

The suburban officials were furious. These were the same officials who claimed that annexing to our city would create lower property values because we have a substantial population of blacks. They had proposed large lot zoning for their annexed areas and played on racial fears to get support for their plans.

For thirty years or so, Burgess did not grow outward because of the prosperity of its industrial base. But by 1980, the decline in the manufacturing sector had left the city in serious fiscal trouble. Annexing land and preparing it for new development has become an important way of capturing a new tax base, especially large commercial centers.

We do not use [small] involuntary annexations, like these other suburbs. When we undertake annexations we go out and persuade the landowners of the value of participating. This means changing the misleading perception of the city and pointing out the obvious economic advantages. Our long-term purpose is to provide the infrastructure and services for high-value residential and commercial developments on the periphery to help fund our downtown improvement plans. We met with the farmers and other landowners and showed them how the provision of streets and sewers would enhance their land value.

When I work with others to prepare an annexation plan, I go out of my way to meet with owners and residents to not only provide evidence of the benefits, but also to share the feeling of being a part of the city. I want them to be part of the plan. So to build a constituency for the plan, I spend my time persuading people of its value.

We put together land use plans for the annexed areas. We used the plans to offer development opportunities different than the ones proposed by the suburbs and supported by the regional planning agency. In one large, two thousand acre voluntary annexation that we recently got approved, suburban officials challenged it as inappropriate on planning grounds. These were the same officials whose annexation proposal that we defeated had included huge areas zoned as five-acre lots to serve as buffers against city encroachment. Our annexation proposal offered more diverse land use plans and met all the procedural rules that have developed around annexations in the state. When we went to court, the judge upheld our annexation.

We worked together as city staff, officials, and citizens to stop the large suburban annexation. We worked with the same sort of feeling a football team has when it plays a conference championship. We sacrificed and struggled together. The city was threatened and we all came together to help protect its future. This was an important planning effort.

Unlike Tom, whose sense of professional identity flows from the principles of the planning profession, Fred ties his planning efforts closely to the purposes of his employer, the city of Burgess. Fred has deep attachments to the people and place for whom he works. In his youth, Burgess was a thriving industrial city. During his lifetime, it has become a bedroom suburb, which has retained a substantial working class and minority population. This socioeconomic legacy has encouraged the nearby suburbs to develop annexation schemes to prevent the growth of Burgess.

Fred expressed a sense of civic solidarity with his fellow employees as they outsmarted their suburban opponents. Their blocking maneuver and successful annexation application helped ensure the future expansion of Burgess. Fred's development plans contrast greatly with those of the surrounding bedroom suburbs, which advance large lot zoning to foster land speculation and exclude moderate-income residents. Fred works to encourage a diversity of suburban developments. He builds consensus for the annexations by offering land use plans that promise to organize and channel growth. His liberal community-building orientation finds support among colleagues and officials worried about increasing social problems and a declining tax base.

Fred and Tom share similar values about fairness and good planning. Fred, however, is able to express openly his views with his colleagues and public officials because of his enthusiastic membership in the local community. Also to his advantage is the diversity that already characterizes Burgess and renders exclusionary zoning pointless. Do these regulatory tales suggest that Fred is a more effective planner than Tom?

Parkville's exclusionary policies made Tom's campaign to get affordable housing on the public agenda much harder and riskier than Fred's annexation efforts. Fred worked for a city that already had affordable housing. Tom's opponents were politicians on the inside; Fred's were politicians on the outside. Tom labored for a new municipality on the upswing; Fred for an aging municipality trying to slow its decline. Furthermore, the two planners were engaged in vastly different activities. Fred was promoting the local growth agenda, facilitating the development of new subdivisions within the city's boundaries to improve its tax base and foster diversity. Tom was pursuing a redistributive housing policy that threatened his employers' perception of the community's social and racial identity.

Tom admits that his efforts to get affordable housing on the Parkville public agenda were unsuccessful. He does not, however, seem to take his failure too hard. He carefully tried different planning strategies, but each one met with resistance from the council. His closing remark indicates he had considered being a more openly aggressive advocate, but had concluded it would have made little difference in the face of such powerful institutional and ideological obstacles. Tom was faithful to the liberal planning principles that he associated with the profession. Had he identified closely with the values and purposes of his employers, he probably would never have pursued the housing affordability issue at all.

Unlike Tom, who uses the first person singular, Fred uses the first person plural. Fred knows the professional rules and standards, but treats them as mere techniques, rather than as a source of values. He explains how the land use plans for the annexation proposals reflected professional standards, but he reserves his greatest efforts for what he believes to be the more important task of building a consensus for the plans among city staff, politicians, and residents. Fred speaks to them not as a professional, but as a fellow citizen and friend who happens to possess useful professional skills and credentials. His annexation tale reconstructs a public, community event and celebrates the sacrifices of citizens for the public good. Solidarity of purpose and shared effort, not individual professional prowess, carry the day.

The implication here is not that Tom should act like Fred. If Tom had identified with the values of the city officials, he would never have tried to put housing policy on the public agenda. His moral commitment to fair housing inspired his persistent, if unsuccessful, efforts to develop a local housing plan. Imagine if Fred and Tom had switched places. I suspect that the Burgess annexation would have had the same ending, with Tom offering less political gusto and more technical finesse than Fred. In the Parkville case, however, Fred would engender serious political conflict if he conducted the kind of active promotional efforts he favors to mobilize and build support for affordable housing. Fred would probably lose patience with the locals and quit or escalate the conflict and be fired. Class and racial inequities, especially when they are sustained through the authority of municipal government, prove a powerful obstacle to the planning efforts of even the most clever professionals.

REGULATION FROM ON HIGH

The conservative Republican regimes that dominated national policymaking through the 1980s relished deregulation. The removal of red tape, especially in the form of burdensome federal requirements and the meddlesome bureaucrats who enforced them, was a constant theme. The federal agencies and programs that had expanded to offer funds and assistance to the poor inner cities and to enact urban improvements in the 1960s and 1970s lost funding and favor. The ideological abstraction of federal bureaucrats, however, is far removed from the reality of daily practice. Stereotypes mislead. Take the case of Alice.

Alice: The Advocate Bureaucrat

Alice works in a large, aging office building on the edge of downtown. She shares a desk in an open office area with twenty-five other employees. There are no partitions. She arranged for us to meet in a small conference room. She has an oval, well-tanned face and a slightly harried look. She speaks with warmth and feeling.

> I work for the regional office of a federal agency, but I advocate for the interests of Central City. I help local public and nonprofit agencies figure out how to properly and appropriately apply for federal funds. Over time, I have developed ties with the directors of agencies that have successfully used federal funds. I help them secure needed and useful funding and they in turn provide examples of "how to do it." They are willing to meet with others, both down the ladder and up, to show how funds can be used more effectively. We have built reciprocal ties based on mutual trust and advantage.
>
> [Answering the question: What kind of power do you use in these relations?] Let me give you an example. The director of a Central City umbrella organization with a lot of nonprofit community and industrial development organization members asked me how much of certain program funds had been received by Central City. He wanted to know the total to point out the large amount of UDAG loan repayments sitting in the bank waiting to be used. He wanted to use this information to put pressure on the city to allocate those funds that were not presently committed to local projects [versus going into the city's general fund].

The budget officials of the city were not excited about making this information public. However, I knew this nonprofit director and shared his views about the use of the funds. I also knew that the information he wanted was public knowledge to which he had a right as a citizen. So after he contacted me, I helped him get the information. But, I also called the city budget office to tell them what I had done and warn them about the potential political use to which the director hoped to put the information. They weren't happy about what I'd done, but grateful that I had called. "Look," I said, "I'm just doing my job."

Alice made it her business to keep both the nonprofit and the budget officials informed so that they would be equally prepared for the ensuing political battle. This approach allowed her to maintain the integrity of her social ties with both the public bureaucrats and the director of the nonprofit development corporation, even though the public bureaucrats would face more political uncertainty because of what she had done. Alice knew that many local nonprofit organizations were trying to secure additional funds to provide more services and investments. City officials, by taking UDAG loan repayments and channeling them into the general fund, were avoiding the requirement that the funds serve redistributive goals. Alice could have stonewalled the nonprofit advocate, but chose instead to provide the information that could be used to challenge the current practice. She defends her action to her bureaucratic colleagues in the city by reminding them that the information was public.

A couple of years ago I monitored one of Central City's departments responsible for using and distributing program funds to neighborhood nonprofit agencies. I found that the city department was not responding to our monitoring efforts. So I tallied every finding of misused or ineligibly used funds for the previous five years. It turned out that Central City owed about $40 million to the federal government.

I wrote a letter that laid out the problem and gave the amount. I wanted the Central City agency to change how it went about allocating and evaluating the use of funds. This got their attention. I knew the letter would pressure the department officials to make the monitoring of how they used federal funds a priority.

At the first meeting with Central City officials, I repeated the major findings of my investigation, but then explained that I thought that most of the findings against the city could probably be closed [reversed]. Most of the problems stemmed from the fact that the department had not given the management and monitoring of the federal grants sufficient priority. The funds were allocated incompetently and without care. In effect, to remedy the problem, the agency had to go back and document that the funds were used properly in eligible areas. I told them that this was likely to be a difficult task, but that I was more than willing to help them get things in order.

Instead of getting angry with me, many of the city officials were in agreement. They knew they had screwed up and faced serious trouble. Most were happy I was willing to help them rectify the situation. This response was also helped by the fact that I had already established ongoing relationships with many of these people over the years, providing technical assistance based on a sort of professional give and take. They knew I was not out to embarrass them or jeopardize the city.

[Answering the question: How did you help?] For instance, in some cases, city employees had justified the use of program funds for physical improvements in geographic areas that census tract information indicated were ineligible. Although funds had actually been allocated properly to provide improvements for a small geographic concentration of low- and moderate-income residents within the tract, the allocation appeared to be improper because the low-income residents were only a small portion of population in the entire census tract. On paper the allocation appeared ineligible because the census tract level data showed a population with income levels that exceeded the eligibility threshold. I suggested that they use block data instead of tract data to justify their allocation in such cases, and showed them how to find the data and make the case.

I would often travel with staff to sites that were marginally legitimate. I would spend time helping them develop adequate rationales. We would negotiate. It was always an issue of getting things done properly. The city staff were so busy doing the routine administrative stuff that they lost sight of their priorities. The major upshot of the letter and the one and a half year process was the establishment of a monitoring and compliance unit in the city agency, dedicated to ensuring the proper use of funds. My hope is that the city would stop its fragmented and inefficient allocation of funds to a Chamber of Commerce here, a facade rebate there, and some street improvements somewhere else. I keep urging them to adopt a more comprehensive spatial approach that coordinates and phases projects. They like the idea, but it never seems to get implemented.

At times I work as an ally to city staff. For instance, in one case, fourteen organizations in the more prosperous middle-class areas of Central City had been allocated program funds. The city department staff knew the organizations were located in ineligible areas, but felt compelled to include them because city council members had insisted. I wrote a letter that made it clear that ten of these organizations were ineligible. The issue was volatile. At first my supervisor would not let me send the letter for fear of the bad press for our agency, since it was a popular program. I pointed out, however, that the use was in violation and that the city staff were not really supportive. The director let the letter go. Acts like this let the city staff know I was willing to take some risks and some heat to help further their objectives, as well as my own.

Alice does not fit the stereotypical image of the federal bureaucrat nor of the objective public servant. She does not exercise her authority as if she were a grants cop intent on expanding her powers or opportunities for enforcement. Rather, she uses her enforcement powers to put pressure on the Central City bureaucracies and to create strategic uncertainty. Local staff can put this uncertainty to use to achieve the objectives of the federal program designed to remedy the social, physical, and economic ills of the aging metropolis. Alice's relationships with the local staff and her understanding of their political and organizational constraints inform her enforcement plan. She uses her powers to create arenas of uncertainty and then offers her expertise to help restore order and achieve the required program objectives.

Alice started her public career as a community activist and organizer. She had faced corporate and government bureaucracies from the outside, protesting and pressuring to be invited inside for negotiations and to obtain concessions. Now, ironically, she is empowered with top-down federal authority. She fashions enforcement encounters that enhance the opportunity for purposeful deliberation and organizational innovation within city bureaucracies constrained by entrenched routines and adversarial politics. Local staff who want to implement the redistributive program that Alice monitors are often frustrated by routine obligations and paralyzed by the fear of political risks. When Alice threatens enforcement from the outside, however, she shifts the organization's priorities to enable the staff to pursue objectives that had previously languished.

Central City's politicians had paid lip service to plans for redistribution and instead had allocated funds to meet the distributive needs of local developers, campaign contributors, politicians, special interests, and agency heads. Alice used her federal regulatory authority to challenge these practices and make room for planning deliberations and appropriate program implementation. Instead of planning and then regulating, she used regulations to make way for plans.

REGULATION IN A VACUUM

Regulatory enforcement seldom resembles the stereotype of bureaucratic nitpicking. The planners in this chapter developed and administered regulations with little sense of unilateral control or entitlement. They worked hard to convince and persuade others to follow rules. They did not hesitate to use the threat of enforcement to shift, in the interest of fairness, the burden of uncertainty onto the shoulders of owners and developers anxious to turn the public goods of location to private advantage. The planners, each in their different ways, try to tame the sense of individualism and entitlement that tends to accompany the disposal of private property in the United States.

The local municipal governments considered here failed, however, to include plan making in their police powers. Indeed, they often undermined the possibility of planning. Planners find themselves in a can't win situation. On the one hand, when owners, to avoid sharing a burden, protest the implementation of reasonable and lawful regulations, they attack planners as meddlesome bureaucrats. Furthermore, if planners make mistakes in such settings, they are susceptible to claims that they abused their bureaucratic discretion. On the other hand, private owners often use regulations to enhance their own security at the expense of others. The two-edged sword of regulation actually blunts planners' discretion in the public arena.

The plans that the actors in this chapter had in mind as they applied regulations were not the classic documents that the professional protocol holds dear. None of the planners referred to a comprehensive plan as guiding the regulatory episode. They offered principled rationales that combined elements of political feasibility, professional standards, moral argument, and legality. Most tried to build respect for planning by broadening and deepening the regulatory deliberations, yet their efforts were hampered by the adversarial settings of the episode.

As the regulatory authority of planners increases, so too does the probability of adversarial conflict. This makes collaborative planning especially difficult as antagonists seldom trust each other. Andrew, Bill, George, and Bruce take great care with relatively mundane zoning cases because they want to anticipate and diffuse needless political disputes. The adversarial quality of regulation, however, tends to undermine consensus building. Planners, therefore, frequently try to find other ways to encourage deliberation and consensus about local plans before regulations kick in. The next chapter discusses what some planners do to attract potential antagonists to the negotiating table.

NOTE

1. I cannot offer systematic evidence for this claim. In my introductory planning class, I require students to interview planning directors and collect comprehensive plans for hundreds of municipalities in the greater Chicago region. Few municipalities possess current or updated comprehensive plans. Most planners engaged in comprehensive plan making work as independent consultants, rather than as local government employees.

7

Negotiation and the Bottom Line

The notion of public-private partnerships gained widespread popularity in the 1980s and 1990s as conservative federal administrations undertook efforts to shift declining domestic revenues away from public development programs and toward efforts designed to attract and leverage private funds for the financing of public facilities. Local government programs had, in fact, always engaged in such partnerships for redevelopment, infrastructure improvement, and service provision. The conservative emphases on these partnerships represented an ideological and political shift characterized by less reliance on federal funds and complete rejection of redistributive programs. Conservative political leaders believed that the fiscal inequalities between central cities and suburbs were testimony to bureaucratic waste and misguided federal largesse. They believed that the big cities and large aging suburbs had squandered their fiscal resources and were seeking to make up for their inefficiencies by obtaining federal funds.

Conservatives successfully attacked the liberal endorsement of the efficacy of an active federal government and discredited the legitimacy of a public vision. They characterized comprehensive planning, especially as it had been tied to federal programs, as a cynical bureaucratic exercise in the manufacture of false hopes and red tape. They believed that the public good could be better served by relying on the calculus of consent.

Privatization and competition promised efficiencies in the public marketplace with the added benefit of protecting individual freedoms. The liberal emphasis on the inherent differences in the public and private domains gave way to the conservative emphasis on the primacy of the private and the inherent danger of the public.

Planners, in an effort to adapt to the conservative thrust, began to embrace competitive, adversarial programs and styles of organizational behavior. Planners working in the growth-supportive local planning departments of rapidly expanding suburbs could easily absorb the virtues of competition. They turned their regulatory departments into valuable revenue producers by charging for an increasing array of development and user fees. Riding the crest of the real estate boom, they found ways to obtain fees, services, and improvements from developers in return for the relaxation of zoning restrictions. Instead of controlling growth, planners sought to manage growth by negotiating regulatory deals that tapped a share of the development value for local government (Nicholas, Nelson, and Juergensmeyer 1991). McClendon and Quay (1988) could persuasively urge planners to view their work as a form of customer service, precisely because many were in the business of brokering development deals that generated significant revenues for their municipalities.

Planners in rural, urban, and older suburban communities, however, faced with environmental problems, an aging infrastructure, a shrinking tax base, and crippling evidence of inequalities, had little opportunity to purvey development deals. Strategic planning, privatization, salesmanship, entrepreneurship, and negotiation found fertile ground mainly in growing communities.

The image of the planner-entrepreneur tends to ignore the uncertain politics of planning. Planners do not produce clear and identifiable commodities to be marketed to an ever-expanding cadre of consumers. Brokering deals and negotiating incremental improvements does not ensure, and in fact, often undermines development with a plan that incorporates a vision and a sense of wholeness and of the public good.

FROM NEGOTIATION TO MEDIATION

Negotiation refers to discussions about possible agreements among people with conflicting interests. The word often describes acts of economic bargaining or of political exchange. Deals or settlements are negotiated. Negotiating is viewed positively in capitalist cultures. Those seen as good negotiators by their friends and colleagues should be pleased. It means they are able to shape useful agreements.

Negotiations in adversarial settings involve bargains, trade offs, and compromises to settle disputes among opponents. Political competition is translated into political exchange. For instance, the owner of a parcel that includes wetlands proposes a development that would cover a portion of the wetland. Local environmentalists opposing the plan file a lawsuit. The antagonists now face a long and expensive court battle with an uncertain outcome. Instead of continuing the contest, they decide to negotiate a settlement based on a variety of trade offs. The environmentalists might agree to a revised plan that provides for a buffer between the development and the wetlands. In return, they may agree not to oppose the construction of additional housing at a higher density. The parties do not achieve consensus, but rather settle for less desirable, but more predictable outcomes.

Efforts to negotiate political agreements may also focus on modifying the relationships and positions of the antagonists rather than on outcomes, especially in the case of long-standing disputes. Third party mediators play a crucial role here. They help antagonists recognize, acknowledge, and respect domains of shared interest upon which a negotiated agreement can be built. Fisher and Ury, in their guide to the art of negotiating (1983), advise negotiators to construct symbolic and emotional relationships that will evoke trust and reciprocity from others and improve the chances of obtaining an agreement. The approach acknowledges the futility of forcing opponent compliance.

Exchange-Oriented Bargaining

Exchange-oriented negotiating enjoys widespread popularity. Planners apply it when they work out with developers an exchange of public benefits and fees for the selective modification of regulations. Negotiations work best in the settlement of marginal or quantitative differences, for instance, negotiating an impact fee amount based on the size and value of a development. However, when qualitative trade offs are at stake, for example, negotiating ecological buffer zone boundaries for an endangered species, negotiations take on a chunky quality characterized by friction and the pressure to offer concessions. When individual identity and social solidarity are at stake, for example, in cases of racial antagonisms or ethnic rivalries, negotiation loses its attractiveness as a mutually beneficial activity (Kartez 1989, 452). Parties fear that negotiation may require a willingness to change. These conflicts cannot be negotiated unless the antagonists have indicated a need for relief.

Mediated Negotiations

Mediated negotiations are useful in resolving difficult disputes. Professional mediators encourage opponents to examine their positions and consider negotiating an agreement. Mediators motivate the opponents by pointing out the futility, expense, and waste of the conflict or by showing how particular agreements could actually help realize goals. Professional planners find this approach attractive, because the disputing parties grant legitimacy to the mediator as a neutral go-between. Parties involved in local land use conflicts rarely, however, call on planners to act as mediators and, hence, such legitimacy eludes them (Kaufman 1990).

John Forester (1992a), analyzing the rhetorical claims of dispute resolution consultants, observed that mediated negotiation is a form of political deliberation that seeks to extend and deepen participation in efforts to anticipate or resolve public conflicts. Instead of presuming that interests are private and fixed, this process presumes that participants will change their interests through deliberations. Crucial to this process are mediators who serve not as neutral go-betweens, but as sensitive and engaged advisers (or, according to Forester, "friends") who, while they possess no stake in the outcome of the deliberation, remain deeply committed to the integrity of the negotiations. Hence, the good mediator remains detached from the immediate concerns of the participants, while weaving and reweaving networks of understanding, opportunity, insight, need, and vulnerability to form a moral and political context for agreement that participants will recognize, try out, and eventually accept.

In the following story, Tim, a planning consultant, adopts an aggressive exchange-oriented negotiating strategy with a subcontractor named Jack. Instead of capitulating or escalating the antagonism Tim sets in motion, Jack shows that his work is compatible with the original contract agreement. Over the course of the conversation, negotiations shift from bargaining between differences to reconciling differences.

Tim: Subcontracting Negotiations

Tim, the planning consultant introduced in chapter 1 who works for a large architectural consulting firm, has allowed me to sit in on a meeting with another consultant whom he has hired. As part of a neighborhood design project for a commercial district near a new rail, bus, and auto transportation center, Tim has subcontracted a market survey report assessing the need for and viability of commercial development in the area. Tim has some questions about the consultant's draft report. He makes a point of telling me beforehand that he expected more and better work from the subcontractor. He appears determined and a bit righteous. He is worried, perhaps, that he may be getting suckered by a colleague.

> Tim: [Crisply and with effortful formality] I just want to go over a few points here. First, the organization of the report is lacking. I'm reading this from the point of view of the client and find it hard to follow at times.

> Jack: [Interested, but quizzical] Sure.

> Tim: Second, I think the report has some flaws. Presently, there are three sections. It needs a preface to pull these together.

> Jack: You want it to be a stand-alone document?

> Tim: No, this is part of a larger report.

> Jack: How does it fit?

> Tim: First, describe the neighborhood infrastructure. Second, describe the existing physical conditions of the area and the market analysis. Just need a paragraph or two introducing this.

> Jack: [Seems to be drawing inward] Yeah.

> Tim: Something of a short executive summary for the reader. I think the retail section is fine. I like it, but it's a bit short. You need to include a profile of the neighborhood giving its strengths and weaknesses, pointing out the potential.... You need to label the sections more appropriately. The report is too fragmented. You should adopt the same sort of format for the housing and cultural sections.

> Jack: [Puzzled and a bit resentful] You're aware this is a real limited budget. Only five thousand dollars.

> Tim: [Acknowledging Jack's comment with a nod, but with little sympathy] How much time?

> Jack: This [the draft report] is about a week of my time and some of our secretary's time.

Tim: Well, I think the revisions are a half-day's work. [A subtle shift here in rhetorical posture from contractor to colleague] I'm confused by the present draft and afraid the audience won't be able to use it.

Jack: [Looking less puzzled] OK.

Tim: In the retail section, what about the census tract data?

Jack: You gave it to me.

Tim: [Continuing to raise criticisms about the report] OK [pause] you've made certain assumptions. "Main Street doesn't lend itself to shopping because of the green space," you write. Why does a parkway discourage retail use? On page four you talk about underserved provision of full service restaurants. You emphasize how the area is overserved with fast food and take-out type restaurants. You make these claims [searching here for a rationale or justification for the judgments made by Jack].

Jack: That's the perception.

Tim: OK, then be sure and say it that way. It's *your* perception. Your contract is based on your professional opinion. Be sure and make it clear when you are giving your professional opinion and when you are using hard data.

Tim is hardly subtle in his criticism of the report. He finds omissions and errors. Jack goes along until Tim starts to chastise him for failing to distinguish between fact and personal opinion. Jack begins to resist.

Jack: [Getting a bit upset] You can't begin every sentence in the report saying this is fact and then this is interpretation. ·

Tim: OK, but write about the difference more clearly. The food unit concept on page five. Where has that worked? [The idea proposes multiple take-out food services sharing the same site and driveway.]

Jack: This is a new idea.

Tim: I had a hard time understanding how it would work on a street. How would you make a shared drive-through work?

Jack: [Draws a possible route on a base map] First, you go to a central box here and then go to different windows. The particular layout is a resolvable design issue.

Tim: [Questioning and skeptical] Well?

Jack: If you don't like it, then don't go with it.

Tim: I had reservations about the kiosks and food vendors along the street.

Jack: These proposals attempt to take successful retail strategies involving vendors and put them in this neighborhood. Some neighborhoods have lots of street vendors. You know, the guy with an armful of watches. Others don't. The idea is to encourage vendors in this area.

Tim: I find it hard to imagine how this would work in this space.

Jack: [Draws the vendor carts, showing their location to scale on a fifteen foot wide sidewalk] The vendors lend a festive air to the retail center. I saw a cart in a mall in Kensington with a computer system that fed the sales information to the main store keeping track of inventory and sales. [Jack's explanation anticipates any criticism by Tim that these retail activities might be seedy or marginal.] Maybe you don't want the vendors on the street corner. Perhaps near the train stop entrances. The vendor carts are good because they bring the goods to the people.

Tim: You talk in the report about transplanting retailers.

Jack: [Sidestepping the tough political issue of relocation] It's all just a master plan concept, a vision for the area. Elise [a neighborhood organizer] and her people down there can talk to the different owners and residents to persuade them to participate.

Tim: OK. There's a statement that the theaters don't lend themselves to multiplex use. That's odd. Some theaters have done just that. Why not consider that option for the existing theater?

Jack: Most [theaters] in fact don't [lend themselves to multiplex conversion]. There's the old Zayre's building on Main. The front could be used for retail and the large back portion converted into a multiplex theater. In South Boston and even here in town there are examples of successful multiplex conversions, but in both places the locations had a lot of foot traffic. In our study area, however, there's not much pedestrian traffic, so you have to provide a lot more parking, and there's just not enough space. I do know a second-string theater operator located in one of the older suburbs who might consider relocating to this location, but the market is not that strong.

Tim: With respect to the housing in the commercial area, you say most people won't want to live in the area, but right now there are some 250 residents living in existing housing.

Jack: Well, we mention that there are some residential uses for the elderly that would work, but families aren't going to want to live on a busy street like Main. I want them to consider rehabbing the large residential building.

Tim: I talked with Elise about that possibility, but she said the owners were set against it. The building could be saved and converted to artists' lofts, but the commercial developers want to tear it down so as to make a statement against the druggies who have used the building as a base. The owners agree with the developers.

Jack: You can still use our findings to make an argument for saving the building.

Tim: OK. Later on in the report you suggest that a multiplex theater would be a potentially good idea. This seems contradictory.

Jack: While we have limited expectations of success, there is some evidence supporting conversion.

Tim: [Shocked] But that's contradictory!

Jack: [Ignoring Tim's outrage and responding with hyperbole] I'm not God.

Tim: But you're the marketing consultant.

Jack: [Restating his case] Well, there is some potential for multiplex conversion, but we are not sure what they'll do. We can't predict.

Tim: [Sounding increasingly skeptical] What about the demographic data?

Jack: We used data to determine retail demand in the market area [referring to census data about ten years old]. As far as age and race data, I'm not sure there's anything to add.

Tim: But the population has been getting older.

Jack: Yeah, but the population is getting older everyplace. The real issue is the fact of neighborhood decline. Median income estimates show an increase, but the projections include an increase for inflation that is unrealistic for this population.

Tim: [Ignoring Jack's warning] That is a good increase [in income] based on the estimate. [Tim's defense of the projections reflects his desire that the design proposal be considered feasible. If income increases in the area, there will be more demand for the different retail and commercial shops proposed in the plan.] You mention several retail addresses in your analysis that don't appear on the map.

Jack: I included those stores to serve as examples of successful stores outside the study area, but in the central city. Of course, the examples aren't a good fit. The buildings for this plan are on a strip and I used examples from plazas. The existing plazas don't usually relate to the surrounding neighborhood. They use fences and parking to separate the commercial activities from the neighborhood. We don't want to do that here.

Tim: The fence doesn't seem so crucial a barrier. I don't want to see just strip commercial.

Jack: [Addressing Tim as a colleague] The overall long-term problem with the market area is the fact that half of what would be a normal trade area is lost because the area borders on the lake. This limits the area to neighborhood-serving uses.

Tim: [Ignoring this bad news and responding in an apologetic tone] That's all the changes I want you to make. I thought they would help make the report more readable.

Jack: [Responding now as a fellow professional] I wish we had more budget. This is the first job our firm has ever done for less than ten thousand dollars.

Tim: [Showing some sympathy now after finishing his list of complaints and criticisms] Yes, it doesn't make any sense.

Jack: A lot of the data we've got, the budget won't allow us to analyze.

Tim: [Speaking now with genuine curiosity] What else are you working on?

Jack: An amusement park proposal in Kansas City.

Tim: What's the turnaround time for your revisions?

Jack: A week from today.

Tim and Jack shake hands. I accompany Jack to the elevator to solicit his impressions of the meeting.

> I don't know why we took the project for only five thousand dollars. It is an interesting and exciting project—building a successful neighborhood commercial center near a new train station in an inner city neighborhood. Challenging, but terribly underfunded.
>
> Tim has high expectations. We were supposed to give just an opinion about the market feasibility of some proposed commercial improvements using existing data. However, there was little useful data, so we used up our budget gathering new data. As a result we could not conduct much of an analysis.
>
> All the format stuff Tim raised questions about in this meeting was never discussed at the beginning. The initial concept was for us to provide a memo. Now, he wants this report. I often work on similar projects. The more needy and challenging community projects spend less money and so get less useful studies.
>
> Tim will probably be disappointed with my revisions because he wants to get more from our firm than the contract allows for. I don't take this sort of thing personally. I agree with a lot of what Tim's trying to do. It's the limits imposed by the small size of the budget in the original contract [that bother me]. I guess one of the partners in my firm thought this small contract might offer a foot in the door in the future, but this is not likely to happen.

Tim's interaction with the economic consultant is pressured. Tim goes into the meeting feeling that the consultant has done a less than adequate job and wanting to squeeze more out of him. Tim shows some anger and a desire to impose his will. Tim starts out grilling the consultant, who refuses to play along. The consultant neither protests nor rationalizes his efforts and, thus, avoids giving Tim a justification for his criticism and prevents an escalation of the conflict. Tim is taken aback and begins to temper his righteous zeal as he ticks off the items on his prepared list of complaints. With each complaint, the urgency—the edge in his voice—gives way. What he first conveys as an imperative becomes by the end of the meeting a gentle inquiry.

Was Tim an effective negotiator? In the sense of getting his way, the answer is both yes and no. The consultant provided a foil for Tim's anger and frustration by giving reasonable and reassuring responses. However, the consultant never said, "Yes, I will do what you request in the way you suggested." The consultant agreed to improve the report, but in terms so vague that Tim could not know precisely what he intended to do.

The subcontracting consultant was the more effective party by virtue of his clearer grasp of the bottom line. Jack went into the meeting with the firm understanding that he had fulfilled his contractual obligations, the time was up, and he was not about to do any additional substantive work. He was willing to sacrifice the professional relationship. Tim, dependent on the consultant's work, was in a more vulnerable position. However, he had not considered the consultant's situation. Tim's large list of requests failed to convey their relative priority. Also, by taking such a strong position, Tim jeopardized his working relationship with the consultant. Ironically, Tim's fear and worry, which came from his deep involvement in the project, led him to overlook the obvious affinities he shared with the subcontractor. Tim approaches negotiating like a ratchet. With each issue he introduces, he sets a standard of performance and pushes responsibility for compliance onto the consultant.

The moral core of the story, however, rests beyond this interpretation. Both men seemed to possess unspoken hopes for the project. They both cared deeply about the importance of new investment and commercial revitalization in the poor inner city neighborhood. Tim became less attached to the issues he was raising as he realized that the consultant had not taken advantage of him and had actually devoted considerable effort to the project. Tim's closing questions about the consultant's other responsibilities reflected collegial solidarity not found at the outset of the meeting.

Sam: From Adversarial to Mediated Negotiations

Sam is a high octane kind of guy. His deep voice and quick, crisp sentences command attention and respect. His gestures offer measured reassurance. He carefully and gently attends to my feelings and mood, while his inquisitive energy presses for advantage. Sam actively promotes the planning profession by helping sponsor local events that highlight planners and their projects. He works as a principal planner in the finely appointed offices of a successful big city consulting firm. We talk over lunch. He seems uncomfortable and impatient with the interview. I try to reassure him as to my purpose. We begin with his discussion of a planning episode in which he offered advice in the face of difficult political obstacles.

> I was working for a large developer under contract to our firm. The developer was proposing an office park on a large parcel of vacant land on the edge of a suburban municipality with about sixty thousand people. We were

hired to put the master plan together and develop guidelines that would take the project through the development review and approval process. I was in charge. We had won the job on the basis of a conventional bidding process. The contract was $150,000 stretched over a year and a half.

Early on, we recommended to the developer that he and his staff meet with the different community interests. For instance, we suggested meeting with the municipal planning staff and such community groups as a neighboring homeowner association, several large long-term homeowner groups, an experienced environmental group with a successful local track record, and some parent groups from the local school district. We suggested an organized schedule of informal meetings with representatives from these different groups immediately after completion of the initial site analysis phase. It was important to us to get their feedback at an early stage of the development analysis without imposing preconceived notions. We wanted to ask them about potential conflicts and problems with the proposed use at the site. We wanted to identify potential conflicts and prepare for them early on in our plans.

Anyway, I made this pitch to the developer and about ten of his staff. Since I was the project plan leader, I laid out the proposed work program and schedule for completion. Here's what we're going to do and this is who is responsible for each task. Part of the process involves public participation, which includes meetings with community groups and municipal planning staff to discuss potential problems.

The developer and his staff balked at this. One of the staff said that he expected the project to be especially sensitive because of its size (about five million square feet of commercial space). Well, we all knew that there would be people who would not like this sort of high-density project. We also knew that traffic and density impacts would be the main sources of controversy. Furthermore, the site, although entirely within the municipality, was located right at the boundary of a suburban municipality. We expected neighbors in this municipality to resist the development.

The developer and his staff wanted to work around these people. I felt it was important to communicate with them, even those who would disagree early on, not only to get their input, but to gauge the depth and breadth of the resistance.

After I had finished, the developer and his attorney said it would be better to wait until the formal hearing to get the public involved. I disagreed and urged them to consider talking with local groups. They countered that the local residents were too emotional and had unrealistic expectations. Involving them early on would simply increase the risk of costly litigation. Better to leave them in the dark until the last minute.

"That's fine," I said, "but we're still going to get into heated conflicts with emotional people anyway. If we talk with them ahead of time, we can save both the time and money [it will take to deal with these conflicts at the hearing stage] by tailoring the process to anticipate and defuse public opposition. Sure, the hearing is the formal way of conducting such business, but it often just inflames the resistance of participants."

I went on to lay out the pros and cons of our position about participation. The number of meetings we scheduled was reasonable and organized to bring the key public actors into the process at each of the three phases. First, we would inform the community and solicit input on problems and later we would present them with design options that would address some of their concerns. We would sincerely try to incorporate the ideas of residents in the preparation of design alternatives. It was all for naught, however. The developer would not approve the participation.

This wasn't the first time [I'd experienced such a refusal]. I was disappointed, but not cowed. Here was a case where such participation was clearly the proper way to go. The project was so large and so obviously controversial that you needed to anticipate resistance and reach out to involve opponents and supporters early on, so as to ensure success.

[Responding to the question: Did other planning staff share your values?] Yes, they did. Of course the more technical types, the engineers doing traffic and environmental analysis, don't usually pay attention to such things, but this is changing. Planners are learning the importance of participation. We talked about our disappointment, but we decided we'd just put on our flak jackets and walk onto the battlefield. I still tried to gather as much information as I could, especially from the municipal planning staff, but we didn't have the benefit of ongoing discussion and review.

[To the question: Did you contact any of the citizen and environmental groups on your own?] No, no! I was hired to give advice. I gave good advice the best way I could, but the developer chose to ignore it. I did not feel any ethical conflict. I knew that at a minimum the development would go through a three-month review process. The size and scale of the project meant it would probably take much longer. Furthermore, I knew the planning commission for the suburban municipality had a good track record of development review. They did not just rubber stamp big development projects.

I also knew that I would play a role in negotiating with the planning staff, commission, and council over different development issues. So, I would raise some concerns I had at that time—concerns that could have been brought in much earlier.

As a private consulting firm, we sometimes tell a client upfront that a particular proposal won't fly legally or politically. If it's a really bad proposal, we can always walk away, but I'd say that 85 percent of the time clients listen to our advice. Developers who flagrantly violate good planning principles and development procedures, well, we don't serve them.

We are hired to bring the big picture to the attention of clients who have specific projects in mind. We understand the issues. That's our expertise. If they don't want to hear it at all, then we don't take the contract.

[Continuing the story] So the project gets underway and being the political and active planner that I am, I go out of my way to take public perceptions and needs into account. For instance, I noticed how a residential subdivision was going to have increased difficulty providing for pedestrian traffic and flagged this as a potential hot spot. So we anticipated this as a problem and prepared some sidewalk linkages, ideal road crossing points, and even a pedestrian bridge as potential design alternatives. At the hearing, when local school officials and parents raised this issue, we were quick to agree and just as quick to point out suggested solutions.

The hearing process dragged on for ten months. The project was discussed in twelve public hearings. Eventually the developer got so frustrated with the delays and changing requirements that he withdrew.

The attorney for the developer ran the meetings like a trial. He set an adversarial tone that kept the proceedings too formal. He interrogated the municipal staff about the details of the plan and regulations. He focused on details that obscured giving a sense of the big picture. The municipality with its attorneys and the community groups with their attorneys simply took turns fighting with each other. The end result was costly and wasteful.

I felt the city planning staff should have taken a more active role. They simply provided information. They never gave a report that compared different project alternatives. I think they lacked experience playing a facilitating role. I see the role of the planner as a facilitator who gets the experts together with the decision makers to identify problems, consider alternatives, and work toward closure. Too many municipal staff people are not aggressive enough at negotiating. The planning people should be the point people in getting projects reviewed and underway.

Sam clearly views negotiation and mediation as central planning activities. Planners should serve as active counselors, framing alternatives that reflect the purposes and circumstances of their clients. To Sam, participation is an ongoing act of involvement, not an afterthought. Furthermore, Sam is convinced that participation by those who will be affected by and are likely to resist a plan will contribute to more efficient planning in the long run. Early in the process, community participants can offer information and advice that planners can incorporate to head off future conflicts. Participation is a useful strategy for giving the plan legitimacy.

Sam understands the conflicts inherent to planning for new development, but seeks to minimize unnecessary adversarial relationships. For instance, since public hearings tend to exacerbate adversarial relation-ships, Sam tries to anticipate the conflicts that will emerge and involve the parties in nonadversarial discussions before the formal sessions take place. He complains that the developer's attorney makes his case in adversarial terms. Such an approach, by excluding the opposition, en-hances its legitimacy and encourages battles that need not be fought. Sam proposes an inclusive, comprehensive approach. The planner should get all the interests out in the open, but not take sides, to provide an opportunity for the development of relationships of compromise and adjustment.

Sam, however, does not have the authority to negotiate the terms of participation. He encourages the client to cooperate, but since the firm depends on getting contracts, he must not pressure the client excessively. The case is illustrative of the many developers who neither want nor expect to negotiate with those without economic stakes or legal stand-ing. Sam advances the efficiency, rather than the legitimacy, of engaging early in political negotiations with neighbors and residents. He advises his clients that they will save time and money down the road by avoid-ing conflict.

Sam promotes negotiation and participation squarely within the frame-work of the professional protocol. The good professional consultant care-fully selects a client and then remains faithful to this patron. Sam puts participation and negotiation to use as sophisticated elements of profes-sional craft to further the goals of his client. He felt no responsibility to organize citizen support unless his clients perceived that this action would serve their interests. He worked hard to include the interests of others, but only when such action did not diminish his client's goals. Sam's con-tract with his client and his professional integrity require him to keep his loyalty one-sided.

Jeff: When Good Negotiations Fall Short

Jeff works for a community-based nonprofit agency in a large central city. His work centers on economic development and housing projects. A tall, thin man with black curly hair and beard, he speaks in a soft voice. His understated, casual attire shows his rejection of a professional uni-form. His informal dress, however, does not imply casual or second-hand knowledge. Jeff has a keen wit.

> One of the things I'm facing right now is setting up a commercial employ-ment incubator in a vacant building in the neighborhood. We want retail on

the bottom floor and office uses on the floors above. Working on an eco-nomic development project like this has created confusion for me, since I find it difficult to figure out my role.

I am working with a partner who has a lot of for-profit experience. They seem quite competent. When we talk about the economic development project, I find myself at odds with them at times. For instance, the present contract arrangement would require those employers who rent space to agree to give preferred consideration to a list of low-income residents our agency would supply as potential employees. The central city government uses this sort of first source hiring agreement, which requires businesses that get city loans to take first employment referrals from the mayor's office of employ-ment and training. The for-profit developers agreed with the concept in prin-ciple, but were concerned that it would be more difficult to market the office and retail spaces to employers.

In my present role, I want to insist on the importance of hiring preference, so as to ensure that neighborhood residents get the benefit of this commer-cial project. I also know that the spaces must prove attractive to employers or we will have no jobs at the site at all. I find that my agency and I end up being "deal" driven.

In fact, I underwent special training sponsored by the staff of the non-profit Local Initiative Support Corporation, which showed how to get the deals made and implemented. I now spend about half my time working on the details of putting this real estate deal together.

For example, I wrote a proposal to acquire $250,000 of equity capital for our nonprofit organization to put into the commercial development project. I had to draw on a variety of funding sources and conduct a feasibility analy-sis for the project. But at what point am I willing to say that the deal may not generate sufficient benefits to neighborhoods to merit all the time, effort, and resources used by the nonprofit agency? When I have to make the num-bers work, it means ensuring that rental income is not only large enough to pay debt service and build a modest reserve, but also enough to make a profit for the development partners.

The neighborhood benefit is much tougher to assess. I want to get jobs for residents as well as provide business opportunities for local entrepreneurs who need space to expand. The idea is to recycle income within the commu-nity and the first source hiring is a device designed to help do that. In addi-tion, fixing up the building contributes to the community by enhancing the usefulness and economic value of a structure that can't leave.

Of course [speaking ironically], the more sophisticated developers prom-ise the same sorts of benefits that the nonprofit I work for is trying to create. The for-profit developers claim their projects will employ locals, create busi-ness opportunities, and enhance local incomes.

[To the question: Are they lying?] Well, not exactly. Their projects do provide some of these benefits, but the developers use the rhetoric of community development so as to enhance the legitimacy of their projects. They make it appear that they are mainly interested in providing a useful good for local residents, but they are mainly interested in making a profit. If producing the benefit won't make a profit, they won't produce the benefit. I think we should still try to provide these goods, even when they are not profitable.

Basically, what I am worrying about in this commercial development deal is that I am not creating enough social value. I may end up being a "player" in a traditional real estate deal, but fail to serve the needs of people in the local community.

Before this job, I worked in a local development corporation that rehabbed and constructed low-income units in the same inner city neighborhood where I presently work. I can recall reflecting on the end of a year's work in which we renovated twenty-four apartment units. I was pleased that we helped twenty-four poor households get decent affordable units in what had formerly been an abandoned building. It still gets to me after nine years to hear their story. Doing that sort of useful work sends chills down my spine. I felt happy because these poor people had shelter and stability. I got pleasure in helping provide real tangible benefits to the poor. The benefits were clear and obvious not only to me, but to the recipients in need. Housing security provides poor people with an important foundation to make it in a tough and unfair world.

In doing economic development work like I do now, the benefits are much less clear. For instance, my present agency used to run a job placement program for nursing homes. We supplied personnel for employers who needed largely unskilled or modestly skilled workers willing to service the elderly clients. After a year or so, a follow-up assessment of the placements revealed that most quit their jobs within six months. The work offered little in the way of advancement, wages were low, and the hours long. We asked ourselves what good were our efforts? We decided we were simply a conduit that the for-profit nursing home operators used to get and maintain a cheap supply of service workers. The residents got jobs through our efforts, but the work did not help them significantly improve their lives. The benefit of the jobs was much less clear to me than the benefit of a new subsidized housing unit.

At my present agency we started an answering service business to provide jobs for neighborhood residents and serve local businesses by offering a quality answering service. We optimistically figured this would be a money-making enterprise that would generate some funds for the agency as well. We discovered that this is a tough business with lots of competition that keeps wages and benefits low while demanding long hours. We started out paying five dollars an hour with a full benefit package for largely unskilled operators who had previously been unemployed.

Once underway, we discovered that the quality of performance was crucial. Initially we trained twelve employees and eventually selected four for full-time employment, but before a year was up two had quit and two were fired. To keep the business going we ended up hiring experienced operators from outside the neighborhood who could deliver quality service.

The unemployed residents who applied for these jobs were poorly educated and not prepared to record messages properly. They could not spell, left out crucial details in messages, and did not record the proper return number. The training was too short and incomplete to offer the basic literacy and interpersonal skills needed to do the job right.

With the new hires and a much more extensive training program, the business has expanded to serve some 150 businesses, but because the wage and benefit levels are high relative to other answering services, the agency has ended up having to subsidize the business. So, as a business, the enterprise is failing. Furthermore, local residents are not employed now. Although we are providing better working conditions and wages for operators who would otherwise be working in worse conditions, this seems like a questionable use of our resources. The payoff compared to subsidized housing units is more mixed and less tangible.

The organization eventually decided that the social benefits, which had diminished over time as labor costs escalated, were no longer significant enough to justify keeping the business afloat. After three years of effort, the answering service accounts were sold to a for-profit service and the business shut down.

I've got to see something happen as a result of my work. I want to have a positive impact on peoples' lives. The quality of the aid as a means of helping someone move from rags to prosperity is the key. Incremental impacts are OK, but less satisfying. It does help someone who just worked for us for awhile and then quit. Yes, they left, but for a time we gave them employment and encouragement. That's a positive impact.

Developers want to create economic value, but I want to create social value. The market is competitive and sets standards that pressure you to produce value at the expense of local community residents in poor neighborhoods. So, there ends up being trade offs. To keep working with our development partners we must respect the "bottom line," the threshold of their profitability. That takes precedence, but I worry that local nonprofit development corporations engaged in such deal making with private developers will trade away the social benefits of the projects.

OK, the community development corporations might respond that they are aware of the benefits, but in these tough economic times, you've got to be realistic. I suppose I agree. In my relationship with our private development partners, I assign them the role of ensuring financial feasibility, while I worry about community benefits. I am concerned that I don't make the case for these benefits strongly enough in the face of the economic constraints the developers are quick to mention.

For example, in our original memo of understanding, I had included a proposal that neighborhood businesses would receive discounted rents for the proposed spaces, but in preparing the final partnership agreement, this clause was negotiated away for economic reasons. The partners want to make sure rent revenues will be high. I went along with this sort of compromise because I was anxious to get the agreement signed. I allowed certain ambiguities of language to substitute for clear proposals that favored the interests of poor residents. I didn't insist on a first source hiring agreement for fear it would scare the developers away. The developers offered an impressive track record and valuable expertise and I sacrificed community benefits to get them to commit.

In negotiations, there must be give and take. I think this partnership deal was decent. It was certainly better for the local community than many other such deals I had seen put together elsewhere. I think we did well, even under the circumstances. Still, I think that the social benefits are more important than this sort of negotiation allows. I feel best now, not when I negotiate, but when I work in a shelter for the homeless as a volunteer. When I give this kind of aid, there is no difficulty for me in grasping the value of my work. I'm doing good.

In his negotiations, Jeff, unlike Tim and Sam, works hard to change the meaning of the relationship from one of instrumental bargaining and exchange to one of social reciprocity. Instead of simply negotiating a contract, Jeff tries to persuade the developers to become members of the community and share responsibility for the welfare of the residents. He realizes that this would impose additional burdens on the developers, who already have taken on significant opportunity costs by pursuing this project with sponsors with little business acumen. Jeff makes concessions to the developers, but only out of a grudging sense of necessity.

Tim and Sam conduct negotiations as part of their professional repertoire. Jeff expresses reservations about negotiating because he considers the real estate development game to be rigged. Jeff has reconciled himself to economic necessity, but without trusting the moral efficacy of real estate market transactions. He distributes incremental benefits to the developers and the community nonprofit, but he worries that the increments may not add up to much community benefit. Jeff ambiguously combines the roles of mediator and negotiator. He advocates social justice over economic profitability, but adopts a moderate position in the negotiations. He enters negotiations as a community delegate, but one whose knowledge of community need and market realities translates social policy objectives into the language of real estate economics. Despite his efforts, issues of profitability tend to displace concerns about social benefit. Jeff worries about the moral quality of the trade offs he helps craft, doubting his legitimacy as a representative of local community interests.

Mediated negotiations like these impose a moral burden on planners like Jeff, who take responsibility for reconciling social differences. As he seeks to balance community need and investor profit, Jeff builds reciprocal agreements among suspicious antagonists. He paves the way for others to adopt the double consciousness he exhibits, but in so doing, he jeopardizes his standing in the community. If the agreement fails, he will be the scapegoat for both sides. If the agreement succeeds, Jeff does not expect that his role as intermediary will be formalized nor that his power as an expert will be enhanced. He hopes the agreement will foster a democratization of negotiations for both sides and that community members and developers will learn to modify their expectations to accommodate each other's purposes, much as Jeff did at the outset. Jeff wants the members of the community to employ the expertise he brings to the negotiations, which would effectively forfeit any opportunity he would have to enhance his power.

THE FUTURE ROLE OF NEGOTIATIONS

Negotiation offers a way for planners to get beyond the often divisive, inefficient, and destructive adversarial relationships that plague new development. Practical guides give planners advice on how they might improve their negotiating skills by focusing on interests, not positions; the problem, not the people; and mutual, rather than unilateral, gains (Fisher and Ury 1983). Planning professionals, however, seldom enjoy a clear and legitimate authority to conduct negotiations. Furthermore, the disparities among competing interests in public planning disputes often cannot be fairly and efficiently represented in negotiations.

The stories in this chapter show the variety of negotiations in which planners must engage. The stories also touch on the importance of negotiations for harnessing public deliberation about important planning matters. Despite the formidable obstacles, the opportunities for negotiations are likely to increase as conventional institutions promote negotiation and mediation strategies. For example, Innes (1992) describes state-mandated growth management negotiations in Florida, New Jersey, and Vermont. Whether such institutionalization takes a narrow adversarial form, in which planners serve as brokers, or a broader deliberative one, in which planners serve as mediators, depends on how reforms get enacted. If planners hope to expand room for deliberations, they will likely have to organize themselves for change.

CHAPTER

8

Organizing for Change

In the previous chapter, the stories of negotiation described how planners tried to serve public ends using individual discretion in a variety of reciprocal agreements. The negotiations were not based on economic exchange, but relied on social and political relationships. Each planner was able to conduct negotiations because the various parties agreed to participate. In many cases, however, citizens, developers, and officials resist negotiations. The professional protocol urges planners to use their knowledge and expertise to persuade the various interests to collaborate, but this presumes that the parties have questions and want advice.

Professional planners have long sought government mandates to authorize their use of regulations to achieve community development goals. Clear mandates and strong rules, the proponents argue, would capture the attention of those who need approvals to proceed with their plans. The threat of regulation would motivate them to seek out and attend to planning expertise and advice. Conservatives never tire of cataloging the numerous risks and problems associated with the use of such power. However, since planners rarely possess a clear and powerful mandate to impose rules, the liberal hopes and conservative fears remain untested. How do planners convince others to collaborate in forming plans and putting them into practice?

Some planners try to increase their authority through political organizing. They stretch the boundaries of their professional position by engaging in political activities that will secure them allies during a conflict and the capacity to create consensus-building coalitions. Nancy in chapter 4 and Tom in chapter 6 used organizing tactics to frame research and build support for affordable housing, respectively. They organized attention, assigned priorities to problems, evaluated the opposition, and explored action strategies. Nancy and Tom might object to this characterization, however, since these activities were part of a much larger set of actions in which political organizing played only a bit part.

This chapter focuses on planners characterized by politically sensitive organizing at the center of their activity. They are not organizers by occupation, but they assign value and meaning to planning insofar as it is the product of political organizing. These planners are not engaged in creating organizations. Rather, their organizing mirrors the activities of labor unions and residential communities to mobilize support for greater social justice. These planners, however, are not partisan advocates, even though they may embrace adversarial politics and may build alliances to wage battle against their opponents. Rather, their advocacy is informed by their professional outlook. They push and perhaps exceed the limits of professional propriety, but they do not abandon their professional standing for a strictly political one. Some may redefine planning to include adversarial activities, rather than abandoning the profession. Others may hope to avoid adversity, but reluctantly engage in political struggle when less combative efforts have proven fruitless.

In his book with John Forester, Norman Krumholz offers some vivid examples of how, under his leadership as Cleveland's planning director, his staff focused more on organizing the community than on commanding an organization (1990). As an example, Krumholz describes how he purposely dresses like a conservative businessman, not because he cares about the image of power and prosperity this projects, but because it helps in his organizing work. Krumholz uses the dress-for-success uniform to improve prospects for communicating egalitarian ideas to an unsympathetic audience. He does not seek status, but an image that will reassure a suspicious audience whom he hopes to persuade to listen to radical ideas that they might ignore or be threatened by if the speaker were dressed in unconventional clothing. Since he dresses and acts as they do, Krumholz expects that they will presume shared values and listen to what he says. Furthermore, when speaking to a potentially hostile audience he uses concepts and examples familiar to them. Krumholz's masquerade frequently worked because many people found otherwise radical ideas compatible with their common sense. The Krumholz masquerade dulled the ideological censors that blocked appeals to solidarity across conventional social divides.

Krumholz's success emerged from his willingness to detach himself from the conventional trappings of power. He assumed a public identity that reflected both his modesty and broad social purpose. He played roles in the theater of politics, using the authority he possessed to introduce broad and potentially contentious issues of equity. He reduced the danger of ideological dispute, however, by translating redistributive issues into the language of the existing distributional system with its relationships of trust and track record of competence. He could not propose comprehensive redistribution schemes, however, for such grand proposals would raise serious questions about the legitimacy of the existing system and would focus political attention on the weak planning department. Instead, he organized modest redistributional projects in the interstices of the city's organizational structure.

Krumholz's approach to planning was neither suicidal nor crazy. He worked in a complex and uncertain political context. Responsibilities were not clearly assigned, which left gaps in the organization of municipal authority. Krumholz took advantage of these gaps by organizing planning schemes that revealed his commitment to a broad social purpose, regardless of their relevance to the advancement of his career. Instead of manipulating uncertainty to his own career advantage, Krumholz spread the benefits of reduced uncertainty widely among citizens, politicians, and department staff. Krumholz shared authority with his staff, encouraging and rewarding their initiatives. He attended to the political needs and interests of the mayor and city council members by framing policy options that addressed their concerns and offered opportunities for political gain. He assumed unclaimed responsibility and the accompanying risk of accountability. His strategy worked because of his committed staff and their shared commitment to greater social equity.

Also essential were the social relationships Krumholz and his staff formed with powerful bureaucratic neighbors and elected officials in their efforts to organize support for equity. Krumholz compensated for his institutional vulnerability by forfeiting any attachment to professional prestige and individual power. Instead of adopting the professional protocol, he put the protocol at risk through his organizing activities as he mobilized the powers of the weak. His efforts reflected his commitment to social justice and his firm belief in the efficacy of planning in the service of public redistribution.

ORGANIZING FOR COLLABORATION

The planners in this chapter organize in ways that resemble what Krumholz did in Cleveland. While they adopt political priorities other than equity, they all seek to build relationships with others for whom the promise of organized collaboration outweighs the risk of unilateral competition—even in adversarial settings.

Bruce: Lining up Support

In this first case, Bruce engages in organizing efforts to introduce more flexible subdivision regulations to help reduce development costs and increase affordable housing. The case illustrates how a planner can anticipate and deal with the powerful institutional forces arrayed against basic planning goals. Bruce represents a bridge case. He embraces negotiation as central to his practice. He turns to organizing only because without political support he can not implement important planning innovations.

Bruce is the clever planning director who managed to avoid getting fired over the setback fiasco in chapter 6. He does not go out of his way to avoid conflict and looks forward to engaging in negotiations with adversaries over planning issues. Bruce has arranged a lunch meeting with a local developer who is a former planner. He wants to discuss what can be done to reduce the infrastructure costs for new housing developments and to win support from local developers for possible changes in municipal subdivision standards. Bruce talks to me in the car on the way to the meeting.

> The mayor says he wants affordable housing, so I am looking for ways to lower infrastructure costs. The major obstacle is Jim, the city engineer. He wrote the present subdivision ordinance that has very costly fixed standards. I want to amend the ordinance to make it more flexible and more performance based.
>
> Jim and I don't get along. One of Larry's [the community development or CD director] main jobs is to mediate between Jim and me. Jim doesn't consider the cost of the subdivision improvements to the developer and how these get passed on to the consumer as higher housing prices. He also doesn't take into account future costs of street improvements. His value system is maintenance oriented. My values are ecological. I see the road network as an interconnected system. You don't need to use fixed standards for roads serving different needs. Where the volume of traffic is low, the roads can be narrow. Instead of putting all those dollars into the streets, you can put them into the housing.

Jim has engineer's disease. Although some good engineers look for alternative ways of doing things, he doesn't. He goes by the book. He serves the infrastructure, not the housing and its residents.

Jim has been around for decades. He is a formidable opponent. I see developers as partners. We want to reduce costs. The streetscape ought to reflect the scale and purpose of the development. The guidelines should enable us to vary the streetscape based on the scale and value of the development.

We arrive at the meeting. Hal meets us at the table with Betty, an associate from the sales division. Hal is short, balding, and middle-aged. He's the back office guy trying to make the numbers work. Betty has on a finely tailored suit, smart, but not too businesslike. From her perfectly permed hair to her high-heeled pumps she broadcasts a finely tuned balance of competent real estate analyst and trustworthy salesperson.

Bruce: We have a problem. Our subdivision ordinance basically says one size fits all. It sticks every subdivision with wide streets and barrier curbs.

Hal: It's maintenance oriented.

Bruce: The mayor wants us [the planners] to come up with plans to reduce the cost of housing in the city. He wants a city in which the employees can afford to live; a diverse city that can house the police and the CEOs. We have done some preliminary estimates of what the present ordinance costs the home buyer. We calculated that the high standards add anywhere from five thousand to seven thousand dollars to the cost of each house. Furthermore, every one thousand dollar increase in price, we figure, adds anywhere from eight to ten dollars on to the monthly mortgage payment. Reducing infrastructure costs can reduce housing costs to the consumer.

Betty: This impact is even greater on the first-time buyer.

Hal: Your calculations need to include the developer's profit margin. That one thousand dollars will also include a three hundred dollar profit margin. When you put $1,300 into your equation, the costs go up even more.

Bruce: So these costs have the greatest impact on the first-time buyer?

Betty: Unless buyers have at least twenty thousand dollars as a down payment, they must carry a half percent higher mortgage than those who do.

The first-time buyers are usually the ones with small down payments and so much greater debt burdens.

Bruce: The mayor wants us to come up with a definition of affordability.

Hal: Anything less than $100,000 is affordable.

Betty: We're not finding many dual income home buyers in our development. If we draw people from your town, we find we get households with a single employed person. They usually are upgrading from an $80,000 house to a $100,000 house.

Bruce: So we are attracting the low end of the upper income suburban market.

Hal: What's forcing people out of your town?

Betty: Taxes. Builder fees aren't a concern to buyers, except as these show up in the price of a house.

Bruce: One issue we've been talking about is lowering the long-term infrastructure cost of new developments. Another issue has to do with the quality and character of the residential community. The narrow streets, smaller lots, and minimal setbacks create a different feel.

Betty: Buyers don't pay much attention to streetscapes. They want the streets wide enough so they can back their cars out without trouble. That's about it.

Bruce: I am imagining that people want a tree-lined street. I'm wondering if this sort of design would make the houses easier to sell?

Betty: In custom-built housing that stuff matters, but in the production housing we do, people don't care about the street, they care about the size of the rooms.

Hal: If you can provide the same [service] for production housing by offering lower cost street improvements that translate into lower housing costs, that will impact the buyers.

Betty: The first-time buyer just wants a house. The third-time buyer wants more internal amenities. Most first-time buyers select production units from models and designs. They don't pay any attention to the lots and their location.

Bruce: What about lot size?

Betty: You don't want to have big lots next to little ones.

Bruce: [Surprised] But don't customers care about lot size?

Betty: Price is more important than lot size. The first-time buyers have few choices. There is little available they can afford. If we take $100,000 as the average price for first-time buyers, this means they must have an income of $40,000 to $45,000 a year to afford it.

Hal: The median household income in your town is only about $35,000.

Betty: Remember the restrictions on loans get greater for these first-time buyers as well, mainly those who put down less than twenty thousand dollars.

Hal: Street width is a function of traffic volume and the amount of off-street parking.

Bruce: We have increased off-street parking by requiring large garages and driveways.

Hal: The engineering solution is to solve the worst case problem everywhere, but street width does not really need to be applied the same everywhere.

Bruce: Sure. The police chief would like to have no overnight parking on the streets. This enables him to cruise areas more quickly.

Hal: Let's get back to costs. Say we shrink the street from thirty-one to twenty-nine feet. We can save money here. We seek ways to save money on anything we can. Marginal costs on a lot of infrastructure improvements will increase profits. The same is true for sidewalks.

Bruce: I think we have to keep the sidewalks. Kids play on them. We could make them narrower. Besides I want to keep some pedestrian orientation. Carriage walks work in many places, especially where there is not much on-street parking. These are cheaper to produce.

Hal: Look, we put the cost of the sidewalk into the house and not the overall development. The carriage walk idea would be OK insofar as it allowed us to get more buildable space. We think there's a direct ratio between lot size and housing price. People aren't buying a lot, but a house.

Bruce: Do you have some ratio between lot size and housing price? Is there some figure we could use to say so much increase in square feet of lot size would result in so many dollars of increased housing price?

Hal: If you allow smaller lots or build bigger housing on the same lots, the overall development costs go down, but not in a straight linear fashion. The larger the house, the smaller the cost per square foot, but usually the amenities increase as well. You can build really fine cluster projects with ten to twelve units, but some laymen sitting on the planning board only see greater density.

Bruce: Planning commissioners assume that the densities in new developments are the same as in older areas.

Hal: The more density in a development, the more affordable the housing. You do get more planning problems that deal with parking, fences, and landscaping. The development costs become a greater portion of the overall costs, but housing prices are still lower.

Bruce: We are going to write a report justifying changes in the subdivision ordinance that will bring costs down. Jim [the engineer] will fight. The CD director is the point man. He's going to take the report to the building developers committee for their input. We will need the support of the developers.

Hal: Yeah, that's my department. Among the developers there are some who don't like the city staff and its officials. They think it's a big useless bureaucracy.

Bruce: No, it's not useless, just rigid.

Betty: The former CD director was a power broker type who helped developers get their way.

Bruce: Yeah, he was formerly a city manager.

Hal: A lot of developers liked his style of leadership.

Bruce: Well, he was the mayor's company director and could overrule the engineer. Larry can't.

Bruce was pleased with the meeting, which showed that Hal shared his views concerning subdivision costs. Betty, however, reminded them that the efficiencies represented only marginal contributions to affordability. Betty the salesperson kept emphasizing what consumers wanted, while Hal and Bruce focused on schemes for reducing costs.

Hal and Betty seemed to enjoy the lunch conversation, but neither was enthusiastic about Bruce's plans. Both spoke longingly of the former community development director, who went out of his way to foster close working relationships with local developers. Hal had left planning to earn more money and avoid the frustrations of bureaucratic life. Neither he nor Betty appeared willing to spearhead a campaign to revise the local subdivision ordinance as championed by the planning director. Both were generous with their time and advice, but careful about making more substantial commitments. This did not deter Bruce's enthusiasm. He took me on a tour of a recently completed upscale subdivision of customized homes. The subdivision incorporated many of the reforms Bruce hoped to get the mayor to support.

Bruce observed:

> The former economic development director had made it clear that the strength of our town is its diversity. We've got low-end residential development, but what we need is the high-end stuff. So we solicited this particular development arrayed around a large golf course. The development got past the planning commission and was before the mayor. There were seven engineering related subdivision issues holding up final approval. The whole project was stalled, but then the real estate lawyer for the developer got the mayor, me, and Jim to agree to meet together in one room for one last meeting. He took off his watch and told the mayor, "It's 9 a.m. We will go over each issue. You decide, Mayor. We stop at noon. If decisions aren't made, the development is finished."
>
> We went issue by issue. The engineer would speak and then I. There would follow discussion and the lawyer would ask for the mayor's decision. We went through the whole list. The planning department won three of the seven, and the first high-value residential subdivision was approved. That was five years ago and since then we have developed two more high-end subdivisions.
>
> What this guy did was negotiate. I want to do more of this, but to make it happen I have to get enough pressure on Jim from other departments, as well as the developers, so that he will agree to negotiate. We have gotten victories over time—we use plastic sewer pipe instead of clay. I'm just as tenacious as he is, but without the pressure to negotiate, it won't work.

Bruce wants to build support for the planning reforms he hopes to get approved. The planning department does not enjoy as much political power as does the engineering department. Bruce works to organize constituencies to pressure the mayor to pressure the engineer to negotiate. However, engaging in adversarial political activity from within the bureaucracy has serious limits. The developers know that Bruce remains dependent on the community development director and the mayor for his authority. When the developers tell Bruce about the former CD director, they are implicitly informing him that they want someone who has the political clout to reduce the uncertainties of regulatory approval. They are reminding Bruce of his relative powerlessness. Bruce promises to deliver a better code, but the developers want a more sympathetic political ally able to reward their political support with generous regulatory approvals.

Bruce misses the irony of his negotiated success at the high-end development, which includes some of the cost-saving reforms he wants to implement throughout the municipality. The developers find it easier to comply with cookie cutter specs than to engage in risky negotiations that may realize only marginal cost savings. The upscale subdivision's developers could afford to negotiate up-front, since they could absorb the costs should negotiations fail. Developers engaged in "affordable" production housing are much less willing to take such risks. Not only does the engineer enjoy greater power than Bruce within the town bureaucracy, but the development process favors the sort of uniform standards that the engineer protects.

Although the successful negotiations set an important precedent, actually changing the code will require altering the relationships among municipal department heads, political officials, and developers, who rely on regulatory predictability. Bruce seeks to change these relationships by nurturing political alliances with developers and other city departments that can serve to enhance the developers' profits and also increase the authority of the planning and other community development departments relative to that of the engineering department. Bruce adopts an adversarial organizing approach as he strives to mobilize outside political support for his planning proposals. The next story focuses on organizing efforts within a new and innovative planning department, established as part of a larger effort to reform an aging big city social service bureaucracy.

Darlene: A Vocational Organizer

Unlike Bruce, who organizes with reluctance, Darlene embraces organizing activity as a vocation. Bruce worked for a large suburban municipality. Darlene works for Central City's public service bureaucracy. She uses organizing techniques to build morale among her staff and clients. Conscious of the lack of adequate funding and the seemingly endless needs of her poor clients, Darlene projects a passionate altruism. For her, organizing represents the end rather than the means. Organizing gives her community membership. She has entered the agency as an outsider and as a champion of reform, hired to help introduce innovation and efficiency in an aging bureaucracy. She wants to build a community of workers whose pay may come from the agency, but whose real reward comes through implementing reforms to improve the quantity and quality of clients' benefits and to enhance their dignity and authority. Many in the agency want no part of this agenda.

Darlene can barely contain her nervous energy. A thin, engaging, and articulate African-American woman, she worked in the Civil Rights movement and the corporate sector before getting a degree in planning and pursuing a service career in public agencies. She has recently been hired to head up the planning department in a corruption-riddled public bureaucracy. She served as staff to a blue ribbon committee that the mayor and other officials had relied on to propose reforms. Her small staff are crammed into dreary office cubicles in an aging downtown office building.

> I always believed that getting things done is what planning is about. However, people think planning just means writing up ideas and schemes. So when we proposed this department within the agency, I did not want it to be called a planning department and chose research and development (R & D) instead.
>
> I learned the significance of this sort of naming when I worked at the newly formed city development department several years ago. R & D was the institutional step we took to turn planning policies or concepts into real programs and actions. The key research activity was testing the ideas to assess whether they made sense—whether they would work. Further, we documented this testing so that we could learn from the results and change our proposed actions accordingly. We checked out each set of results with the appropriate bosses to ensure that our ideas fit with the larger institutional authority. That's planning.
>
> I believe that planning means always looking forward to change and obtaining the power necessary to make the change happen. For the R & D department here at the agency, this means getting support from the cabinet level at the top of the organization. With the protection of the highest authority, we can put forward risky proposals that push for changes that will require staff to do things differently than what they are accustomed to.

The agency as a public institution is in severe trouble. A crisis management team was formed at the request of the mayor to respond to a critical organizational study of the agency by a prestigious nonprofit agency. I worked on the crisis management team, and we spent a year studying the organizational problems that fostered institutional failure in the agency. We outlined what should be done to stabilize the organizational decay and begin steps to restructure the most destructive institutional relations. We treated the agency as an institution that was in need of complete restructuring—an organization that not only failed to fulfill its mission of providing decent and useful products for its low-income clients, but even worse, was incapable of learning from its failures. The R & D department is an institutional innovation put in place to help foster the sort of institutional learning that the agency no longer performs.

[To the question: Why not just focus on improving day-to-day operations?] Systemic change has to be planned for. Change of this sort is not organic. It doesn't happen naturally. The private sector understands that you need to plan for the future—especially in those industries that are failing. The private sector has learned the hard way through its organizational mistakes. The public sector is just starting.

The crisis management team came about as a result of an outside initiative. A new director took over as the executive director of the agency, just as Darlene came on board. The reformers are committed to the importance of planning. Agency oldtimers, however, do not share the commitment to or interest in reform. Darlene's team has tried to educate the employees about the value of the proposed changes and how to put them into daily practice. Implementation, however, has been constantly disrupted. In the face of problems, employees use old habits rather than new techniques. When there is uncertainty, people turn to the familiar, even if it is ineffective. Darlene observes:

> To anticipate and cope with the resistance to change, I want to plan with the people responsible for providing decent housing for the poor. This includes not only agency staff, but our clients as well. Both must be included and learn what it means to share responsibility in the delivery and maintenance of a decent product.
>
> A participatory approach, however, takes a great deal of time and therefore a lot of effort. Ideas do not go from the R & D department directly into the minds of these actors. All the proposals and procedures we recommend are discussed and negotiated. R & D has developed a model of client-based service delivery that is comprehensive and technically sound. Crucial to its success is ongoing client involvement.

To do this sort of work you have to be willing to face burnout. You have to believe in your ability to understand and propose a scheme that will work. You have to anticipate conflict and ensure that the plan is tight. [To do that] first, you secure your legitimacy from above, but also involve your potential enemies in the changes. Attempt to have them "help" you, so that they don't feel threatened. In older crisis-ridden agencies, the upper and middle management can feel pretty insecure. Participation, even when half-hearted, offers opportunities for education, while spreading accountability.

When a plan is tight, it means that those who will carry out the change understand the new incentives and new rules of accountability and have evidenced some willingness to try the changes. Involvement in formulating the rules and incentives provides the motivation for trying out the new ways. The involvement is encouraged by the realization that continuing the old ways in a changing organizational environment may pose greater risks.

Burnout emerges among R & D workers [planners] because we constantly try to think of ways to get changes implemented. The commitment to improving the lives of the clients means always taking your work with you. In addition, R & D staff are closely associated with the larger reform effort. Since so many people are interested in seeing how the changes will occur, we work in a fishbowl. Not only my supervisors and other agency staff watch what we do, but members of the public and agency clients as well. Enemies of reform also watch, hoping to pounce on examples of incompetence or unsuccessful planning to discredit the overall effort. Our performance does not just reflect on us, but the entire reform effort. This places pressure on the R & D staff to not only do more work than has been the tradition in this agency, but to do it better and more successfully. This is tough to do in a good situation and even tougher to do in the sort of crisis situation we face. I encourage the staff to share their commitment to the reforms as a source of hope in the midst of such pressure.

Whatever work we do, I take every measure to ensure that our actions are carefully documented. We want future organizational generations to learn from our successes and mistakes. Further, a good paper trail offers protection against attacks from enemies hoping to discredit our efforts.

I think I'm a good manager. I show people what to do, rather than tell them to do something. I use matrix management. This approach emphasizes team work among the staff, organized around tasks rather than divisions or specialties. Staff are encouraged to use each other as resources, rather than compete with one another for perks or choice assignments.

When we hire new staff we have the serious applicants come and spend a day on the job to understand that they are not just expected to do things, but to make a commitment as well. This is not a job in the usual sense [doing something to make money]. The product is more important than the employee. You need to care about getting results more than credit or pay. You need to believe in team work.

My role is that of final authority and resource person. I expect the staff to be competent enough to perform their job. I help negotiate problems that arise among staff or between the organization and other departments or tenants. If an employee needs daily supervision and constant guidance, they will not last here.

Part of the competence includes an ability to grasp the political implications of the work. I expect and encourage the staff to consider how other departments, agencies, and constituents would view their reports and proposals.

I back up my staff. I expect a lot, but I will go out on a limb to protect them from outside political pressure or public attack. Ultimately, the effectiveness of my defense hinges on the quality of my relationship with the executive director. The security I offer makes the incentives and burdens of a team-work approach viable in an otherwise traditional bureaucracy. I make sure we celebrate our victories and that all team members get praise and credit for their work. I appeal to the professional aspirations of the staff, encouraging them to use their talents as imaginatively and fully as they can to serve our mission. I think they can do this best in a supportive group process.

Darlene simultaneously appeals to the staff members' desire to develop their competencies and builds a sense of solidarity and shared responsibility among the staff for the projects they undertake. She offers professional challenge and support. The price of such support does not come cheap. Darlene expects a strong commitment to the agency's mission and a willingness to work hard and long to obtain it under risky, pressure-filled conditions:

I try to set the basic agenda, paying close attention to the crisis management report, but I use the staff to elaborate the priorities and propose how we should proceed. We presently focus on property management alternatives, economic development schemes, public policy issues like security, and architectural design alternatives. We also attempt to listen to and articulate ideas that come from residents, incorporating them into our priorities.

Darlene wants employees to treat their job as both a vocation of service and as a professional career. Darlene tends to gloss over the tensions between these two aims. A service vocation requires workers to put aside their own purposes to meet the needs of others, while a successful professional career is built on accomplishing self-determined purposes. Darlene tries to inspire and reward her employees as public service professionals by combining the organizational discretion of management reform with the dedicated solidarity of the Civil Rights movement. It sounds great in the abstract, but is difficult to deliver from within a fragmented and beleaguered bureaucracy. One R & D employee, who has a strong commitment to reform and a deep attachment to Darlene, finds it hard to reconcile the two.

Jean: Balancing Contradictions

Jean sports long, beautiful curly hair, which she lets tumble down in fashionable anarchy. She has strong ethnic and family ties to Central City, a passion for social justice, and artistic talent. Her pottery and paintings brighten her drab cubicle. She works as a research analyst and activist in the office with Darlene. She quickly gets at what is bothering her. As she describes her frustration with Darlene, she also conveys her fear of being disloyal.

> I spent some time over the past two weeks writing up a report that recommended Darlene for a national award. I read the report and for the most part felt she deserved the recognition. One thing was contradictory. I found myself balking when I wrote that she developed a great staff team. I like her and found myself rationalizing what I wrote by thinking, "Well, it isn't a management award."
>
> When I first started working, soon after Darlene was appointed head of the planning division of the housing agency, she did do teamwork stuff. She inspired incredible loyalty, but over time she has done things that make it hard for me to do a good job.
>
> She's especially inspirational when she speaks to us as a group, giving us a sense of mission, as she preaches about the injustices we are trying to overcome in our work. She does not want us to make planning documents, but to find ways to help the low-income clients learn to plan for themselves. I, too, believe in this sort of participation, and the staff really tries to act on it. We lend our skills to different groups of clients and listen to what they say.
>
> It's the way she talks. "I know you," she insists, "I have confidence in you. I need you." She makes me feel like we share the same mission. I felt worthy and filled with a sense of respect for her. "We're going to turn this agency around!" Her talk inspires confidence and affection.
>
> In the office I am the only white and probably the youngest. At first I was shy. Soon after I started working here, one of the guys came to me to ask how to rewrite something. "You want my advice?" I asked. "Yes," he said. I was pleased. There was a real openness to sharing and mutual learning initially. Many came to work at the agency because they wanted to work for Darlene.

Most have a strong sense of personal loyalty to her. For instance, the woman who coordinates her schedule is a long-time friend who used to work for the Girl Scouts. She and Darlene go way back.

The loyalty and teamwork get undermined, however, when Darlene tells us about our roles. "You're all going to get into management. That's why I brought you here. I made sure you get good salaries. I expect you to take your experience here and move up the career ladder." She says these things, but they seem to contradict the notion of team spirit.

Darlene does not delegate authority. She considers such delegation to be bad bureaucratic maneuvering. She wants to maintain a sort of collegiality that avoids hierarchy. Well, this is sort of contradictory. It is a bureaucratic agency and the magnitude of the work requires some sort of delegation to ensure that things get done. Of course, this indecision and delay is not all bad. It has given me a lot of discretion to do things I wanted and thought were important.

Last Monday, Darlene and I were scheduled to meet with the director of a nonprofit technical assistance agency to get his advice about the research method we were planning to use in a large client survey. She had already canceled the meeting twice and couldn't make it again. She told me to go and take my colleague, Judith, who was hired after I came to be what Darlene calls the research coordinator. We don't get along. I don't have much confidence in her ability. She uses all this technical jargon and often doesn't know what she's talking about.

So, I take Judith along reluctantly. When we get there, I introduce everyone without giving official titles, which might emphasize Judith's professional status. The director asks Judith for her title. She explains that she is Dr. Schwartz with a Ph.D. in organizational development and social psychology. Then she says she is the manager of the research unit. The director of the nonprofit organization asks her if Darlene works for her. Judith explains that no, she was in charge of just one division within the office, the research division, and that Darlene is in charge of them all. So much for collegiality.

I had briefed Judith about the purpose of the meeting on the trip down: "We want the director of the technical assistance agency to tell us that our decision to use a sampling method rather than conduct a complete census was the right decision. We want the director's support for our choice so that we can use his expertise to legitimize this choice to Darlene, who wants to include everyone. She is concerned that those who did not participate will be upset if they are not included."

I basically ran the meeting. The director eventually concurred with my desire to do the sample and not the census. He said he would call Darlene and let her know. So after the meeting, I am returning to the office with Judith and she asks, "Did you learn anything new at that meeting?"

I was aghast. She didn't understand what was going on. "No," I said, "I didn't expect to."

"But then why did we have the meeting?" she asked.

I repeated the reasons I had given earlier. "Look, we used the fact that Darlene didn't want to cancel this meeting for the third time to get support from the director for the research design we both favored. Get it?"

"Oh," she said.

I was exasperated to have someone like this with authority over me. She was using the R & D department as a step in her career ladder and had only the vaguest sense of what it meant to share responsibility.

Democratic practices encounter serious difficulties in bureaucratic settings and conventional professional hierarchies. Darlene tries to build a community defined by shared commitments and responsibilities. However, the specialized routines of bureaucracy and the workers' preoccupation with their professional advancement fragment the community. To overcome this splintering, Jean and her coworkers who have taken seriously Darlene's message about community must use their discretion to push forward the reforms, sometimes at the expense of their own careers. Jean is upset because Judith cares more about enhancing her institutional status and career than about the community. However, Jean also realizes that Judith is simply responding to Darlene's other message, which Jean questions, about advancing the staff's professional development.

Jean does not believe that you can have it both ways: an upwardly mobile professional career and mutual solidarity. Jean is annoyed by Judith's cavalier manner, because it testifies to the vulnerability and marginality of Darlene and Jean's efforts to institutionalize a democratic work community.

Krumholz, unlike Darlene, chose collegial democracy over bureaucratic power and professional career development. He believed that the bureaucracy would work for the weak and the poor only if they could bring political pressure to bear on the powerful and lobby for democratic participation. Darlene still believes in the efficacy of administrative reform. She understands adversarial politics and willingly enters the fray to pursue her ends. She believes that innovations in corporate management that encourage collegial participation can be adapted to public bureaucracies that provide services for the poor. However, if these innovations fail to extend to the powerless and simply shift power to a new chain of command, Darlene's hopes will founder.

Darlene's attachment to the conventional professional protocol undermines her efforts to democratize the administrative details of her department. However, her attachment makes sense. Her small department must constantly deal with the mediocrity, mendacity, and incompetence that characterize the agency's politicized bureaucracy. The image of the competent professional expert is compelling. The antidote to the self-serving and venal petty bureaucrat would seem to be the committed public servant who offers reliable and useful advice. As Jean's criticisms make clear, however, the professional protocol does not ensure competence, because it does not explicitly advance staff collaboration and teamwork, which are needed to succeed in this setting. The rewards for success would emerge from the democratic process. The protocol, however, offers planners respect by virtue of their individual professional status. Can planners engage in political activity without distorting or undermining the integrity of their technical judgment? Can they maintain their legitimacy while espousing egalitarian political values and strategies?

Stelian: Working the System

Stelian is the director of an urban economic development corporation, a community nonprofit organization dedicated to improving the number and quality of manufacturing and commercial jobs in an aging inner city industrial area. The nonprofit was created with the support of a local bank and some industrial owners and local politicians. The organization's modest offices contrast with the imposing classical facade of the parent bank a block away. The granite monument to an earlier era of local banking prowess is surrounded by colorfully decorated, but physically dilapidated retail stores, interspersed with dreary industrial and commercial buildings. Many are vacant.

Stelian does not go in for small talk. Direct and decisive, he speaks with a sense of hard-won authority. He sounds tough and earnest, yet a little unsure. He appears hard and judgmental, until he smiles. A swarthy, curly-haired, no-nonsense Greek, he talks shop. He includes in his stories justifications and reassurances, which seem to address his own doubts, rather than any skepticism on my part. Stelian has made deep commitments and formed passionate attachments to the people and projects in his work.

> I've been here for ten years. I got rooted after a while. I got good at raising my budget and bringing new people in. It's fun. What keeps me here is that there are probably no better jobs elsewhere. Government [municipal and

county] is reactive and maintenance oriented. It does not take the initiative. Working as director of this agency has enabled me to take the initiative and conduct a variety of activities and I am able to see the results. We have saved jobs and prevented the loss of valuable industries to this community.

All of my work here is a holding pattern in the face of larger forces, such as capital mobility and the lack of control from the top. Controlling national and international firms will require national and international authority. At the local level, the only practical response to capital flight is retention.

For instance, we helped initiate the walk home program. We showed businesses in our area how they could give equity loans to employees to help them purchase houses in the neighborhood. The idea was to ensure the availability of a work force, while improving the quality of life for employees, who were facing escalating housing prices. Unfortunately, the companies paid entry level wages so that, even with the subsidies, the younger workers could still not afford to buy homes. Instead of providing subsidies, we ended up giving counseling about home improvements to those who already had places, and directed them to sources of low interest funds to finance home improvements. We also offered counseling on family budgeting.

This mix of social and economic policy is central to community-based work. Whenever people throw free market ideology in my face, I argue that zoning to protect manufacturing is important and deserves special consideration. The lawyers who work for commercial developers frequently argue that the free market necessarily produces good results for all. I disagree. Untamed commercial speculation escalates land values, forcing up the taxes for industrialists, while making rents for new industrialists too high. The result is to discourage industrial employment. In an inner city neighborhood, this translates into a loss of decent jobs, most of which are replaced by lower paying service sector jobs.

The commercial investors enjoy the value that accrues to land due to the location of other neighboring uses for which the speculator has done nothing. The speculator profits from the efforts of others. Zoning for industrial land use simply attempts to even the odds. Using restrictive zoning preserves industrial, rather than commercial, land values. The outcome of any land use struggle occurs in a marketplace shaped by this political struggle. I believe—and so do most of the industrialists who are members of the board—that the key to neighborhood stability is a solid industrial manufacturing employment base.

It became clear to me early on that the real potential for economic development in this community of aging industrial sites was small manufacturing business investment. The shift from retail to industrial retention and investment made good sense. So I got busy writing a proposal for a foundation grant to fund a pilot industrial retention and expansion program.

This grant was an important beginning. The preparation of the proposal led me to articulate the important tie between neighborhood development and industrial advocacy, especially the importance of aggressive marketing for financial assistance. This initial project set the basic path the agency was to follow for the next eight years. We worked on a cooperative industrial security program and small business loans (using a city revenue bond program that offered low interest rates) for a small growing business that needed to make plant improvements that appeared too risky to conventional lenders.

The next year, I was able to get funding to do a neighborhood industrial retention program. We developed a system for tracking the availability of vacancies in the industrial real estate market in our area. Since many firms leave to find more and better space, we directed our efforts to finding desirable industrial space nearby. This is not as easy at it would seem. There are lots of vacant buildings in an inner city area like this, but few offer useful and efficient space. We provided an important community-oriented service that our members could put to good use in their location decisions. So things were going well.

Later that same year, we experienced betrayal by a member of our own board, the president of Acme, a local manufacturing plant, which had been bought by a conglomerate that gradually began to disinvest. The plant president, who was appointed by the parent conglomerate, sat on our board and mouthed the language of community industrial development.

Perhaps my most important accomplishment so far has been the Acme plant closing experience. The struggle to keep this manufacturing plant taught me both about the limits and strength of this sort of community-based organization.

In 1982, the Acme plant had received a million dollar revenue bond from the city to finance improvements. The plant had made all sorts of commitments to make jobs all the while planning the plant closure. The president gave no sign that the plant was to be closed. What sort of company would take a million dollar subsidy as part of an industrial retention effort and then shut down?

I was not only angry, but so were the other board members when the plant director announced the closure of the Acme plant. City councilman Faldo Contini, who sat on the board, ranted and raved against the closure. The president had lied and misrepresented Acme's future plans—an arrogant breach of trust. Contini and I pressured the city's economic development committee and the law department to bring suit against Acme to stop the shutdown.

Not all the board members were as outraged Contini and I were. Some felt it was the right of the plant owners to shut their plant down if they felt it was necessary. We had to make a convincing case. I argued to prevent the shutdown on two grounds. First, the Acme management had taken a public subsidy designed precisely to prevent shutdowns and used it without respecting its intended purpose. Here was a clear abuse of contract. Second, the members of the board had not only been misled, but lied to by the Acme president. He not only showed no respect for the purposes of the organization on whose board he sat, but he showed no respect for the other board members. The arguments worked and the board supported the use of staff time to prevent the Acme shutdown.

The campaign to prevent the shutdown had many ironies. Here was a community-based organization of industries seeking to limit the discretion of another large industrial firm. I was frequently in the middle, not only between my board and corporate interests, but also when meeting with workers and community members. For instance, our geographic constituency is heavily Hispanic, but our industrial management constituents are white and suburban. So, during some of the neighborhood organizing meetings around the Acme shutdown, I had a hard time establishing trust, but I did not take the side of industry, at least not if that meant exploiting workers.

We used interesting organizing tactics. For example, when the Acme personnel officer threatened to punish any employees who quit the company before the closing by cutting off any severance pay, I alerted all seven hundred members of our agency of the available labor force at Acme and urged them to call the personnel officer at Acme to find employees. This swamped the personnel director with calls offering hundreds of jobs. This undermined the officer's efforts to cow the workers into staying on the job. The result was that the personnel officer rescinded his threat of cutting severance pay and posted the available jobs. The overall organizing effort was so successful that the executives of the parent conglomerate contacted the chair of the Senate Banking Committee to ask our congressman to "call off the dogs," but he didn't go along.

Eventually, the plant closed, but the company kept 120 workers there for another year and repaid the bond. The struggle successfully increased public scrutiny of the use of public revenue bonds, a scrutiny that had been woefully lacking with the widespread use of IRBs to subsidize local industries in the early 1980s.

Stelian then offers, out of a sense of fairness, another example of his organizing work in the community:

Less successful was the case of Smart Printing Company. Its large building had been vacated and was proposed for major commercial redevelopment in an industrial corridor.

What had made the somewhat radical organizing activity in the Acme case possible was the arrogance and naked self-interest of the adversary. The members of my board could overlook the routine ethic of economic self-interest and take a strong community- and worker-oriented position because they felt so distant from the enemy. In the Smart case, some commercial speculator/investors were proposing a new development that would demolish an old industrial structure and replace it with a retail mall.

Councilman Contini was supportive of the zoning change for the commercial investors. Here was a prime industrial location that fit the retention criteria our organization had adopted. Although I tried to convince Contini, I soon realized that there was little hope in saving the site. While Contini could have taken a principled stand, I decided to rationalize its removal. The site was surrounded by residential users and despite efforts to find an industrial user for the site, the staff had been unable to find a taker. The commercial developers did claim that they would keep some of the area for industrial use, but this was a promise in which I placed little confidence.

The Smart property was simply not worth trying to save. The developer was using conventional financing for the project. The local residents were divided over the project. Some wanted it; some did not. The opponents did not provide any organized resistance other than testimony. Furthermore, Contini was firmly in favor and consequently the board was reluctant to support any staff initiative that crossed him. The organizational costs of trying to oppose it were simply too great, even though saving the building for industrial use was consistent with our mission.

[In response to a question about his relationship with the board and staff] Councilman Contini was the founder of our organization. He is a committed ward politician who legitimately cares about representing the interests of his constituents. He provides a service and exacts a fair price in return. During my interview with the board for the job of director, Contini asked me if I had done political work before. I had been involved in ward politics and responded affirmatively, telling Contini that I understood political reciprocity in the style of the ward politician.

For the first year or so, Contini, who had set the agenda of the organization from the beginning, tested me. He wanted to see if I would be loyal and competent. I formed close ties with other board members who eventually invited me to join the board as a member. Contini usually went along with what a majority of the board wanted. So I learned to first poll the other board members when considering a new proposal before speaking with Contini. Contini the politician had respect for majority votes, so I was careful to deliver them.

As the organization increased its achievements under my direction, Contini began to release his interest in setting the day-to-day agenda. I helped Contini accept the fact that he was not the central source of activity by ensuring that he got credit for successful projects. This was not only good politics, but also came from my own growing appreciation of and respect for him. I was eventually invited to social events by him and formed close personal ties with him and with his mission of maintaining community stability that was at the center of his vision for the organization. The testy relation at the beginning was replaced by a friendship in which Contini would confide in me, speaking frankly and receiving a respectful and frank response in return.

Stelian learned early on that to last as the executive director of this development corporation he would have to accommodate the interests of the board. What he did not bargain for was how much he would actually identify with the values and hopes of the organization's members. Stelian, like Darlene, cares deeply about alleviating social injustice, but he does not pursue his ideals using models of organizational reform. Rather, Stelian relies on his relationship with Contini and the other board members to realize his goals. He gained their trust by listening to their advice and holding off action until he had evidence of political support. Whereas Bruce and Darlene retained a strong sense of professional status and authority, Stelian submerged his professional interests to the local political community. Although he worked for a small nonprofit organization, Stelian tapped the authority he held as an adviser to the city councilman. As Stelian demonstrated his loyalty and competence, he obtained greater discretion in setting the organization's policy agenda.

Although Stelian holds liberal, if not left-leaning values, and the industrial businessmen tend to be conservative, he does not proselytize, but neither does he kowtow. In this era of corporate behemoths, he worked to promote public, nonprofit programs that would support small- and moderate-sized enterprises tied to the local market, suppliers, and labor force. Stelian works with these small firms to obtain infrastructure improvements, zoning amendments, environmental safeguards, educational improvements, and other place-based community benefits to reduce the costs of doing business and tame the externalities. Stelian does this not so much as a fan of accumulation but as a caretaker of community. These firms provide relatively high-waged manufacturing jobs to the working-class residents in the nearby neighborhoods. He wants to keep the big city neighborhoods alive by keeping their residents' incomes up through improving and protecting the viability of the local industrial firms.

Stelian relies less on his professional credentials and more on his social standing among the community leaders. In his description of the development of his relationship with Contini, Stelian tells of his initiation as a member and leader of the community organization and of the change he underwent from detached professional to community organizer. He did not lose his professional skills, but rather shed his persona of professional expertise. He framed ties of solidarity and reciprocity with community leaders. His relationship with the board reflected a mix of adversarial and deliberative democracy. Stelian first collaborates with the board members by listening, educating, and persuading, well before a formal vote takes place. By taking straw votes along the way, Stelian can determine the limits of compromise and negotiation with the board members. Stelian earned Contini's respect by carrying on the tradition of community democracy, bringing to it his egalitarian and professional values.

The Acme case was a fulfilling experience for Stelian. He could openly, aggressively, and imaginatively combine his egalitarian and professional values in the development of strategies and concessions. The more conservative board members remained silent in the face of the contemptuous lies of the cynical conglomerate representative. Here was a member who had betrayed the very purpose of the organization. He had not simply exercised unilateral power, but had belittled the other industrialists through his disrespectful actions. Stelian understood the exceptional quality of this case. When he tells about the Smart Printing Company, he points out the painful limits of his collaboration. His egalitarian hopes and professional craft run up against severe limits when he tries to curb the discretion of local owners. He can persuade and promote, and perhaps exact some concessions for community residents, but he cannot sanction. The organization is not empowered to police the economic policy of its members.

Alice: Organizational Roots

I first introduced Alice in chapter 6. She came to her position as a federal bureaucrat in a most unconventional way. She started her public life as a volunteer neighborhood organizer.

> I graduated from college in 1974 with my B.A. It took me twelve years to graduate. Initially I had refused to declare a major and was something of a professional student throughout the 1960s, both before and during my marriage. I had two children—one born in 1967, the other in 1969. At one point I dropped out of school and took a job as a clerk working for a large newspaper. I was treated like shit. Never again would I submit to such treatment. I reenrolled and ended up an English major. However, my real subject interest was sociology.

I got involved with neighborhood community groups in the early 1970s. I helped organize one of the earliest successful efforts to pressure a suburban S & L to stop redlining [the then common practice among financial institutions of refusing mortgage loans in neighborhoods considered a bad risk].

The organization I volunteered with was rooted in an old and relatively diverse suburban community and had adopted an Alinsky [a famous community organizer known for mounting grassroots confrontational protests against political officials] style. We all read his *Reveille for Radicals*. For example, we got a lot of people involved at public meetings in direct protest. In the S & L case, a local woman wanted to get a mortgage loan from the bank that had served her small Dutch community for decades. However, during the 1950s and 1960s, most of the Dutch population had moved out of the village, and the neighborhood in which the woman lived for so long had been redlined. When she applied for a loan, despite her sound financial condition and ethnic heritage, her application was denied. The bank officials said that only FHA loans were available in the village. We planned a protest that filled the lobby of the bank with irate residents whose chanting disrupted the bank's business. The bank president agreed to meet with a committee of about ten of us. Basically, he denied doing it [the redlining], but promised never to do it again.

I also helped get antiredlining legislation drafted and passed at the state level. All of this as a volunteer. I cared about the community where I lived. I learned that if you only allow FHA mortgages in a geographic area, this would encourage a concentration of low- and moderate-income home buyers. I was afraid that such a policy would destroy the social and economic mix of residents that had attracted me to the community in the first place. I grew up in a homogeneous middle-class Jewish neighborhood in the city and I wanted my kids to grow up with social diversity. But I guess I've become more conservative. I don't think you can solve large-scale social and economic discrimination by using community integration in only one community. The approach has to be regional.

I learned of a job opening in the planning department for a federal grants coordinator. This job was attractive to me. I had written grant proposals for the neighborhood organization, but the town hired me because of my knowledge of the community. I learned later that others, far more qualified than I, had been turned down. I was thirty-four and discovered that I was getting paid to do something I wanted to do. My neighborhood organizing friends joked that I had been coopted.

The planning director managed the department in a participatory, nonhierarchical way. For instance, he would solicit the views of the staff and listen to their advice. Although the final decision and authority were ultimately his, he would always include the dissenting opinions of staff in his reports to the planning commission and village trustees. Furthermore, he gave the staff a lot of freedom. We were given assignments and responsibilities, but he did not monitor our work all the time or try to control how we did things. I liked being able to take the initiative.

I kept my community organizing ties and put them to use. I was able to provide effective technical assistance in the preparation and administration of grants for local resident organizations. I was staff to a CDBG committee, which reviewed the applications for federal funds. Conflicts of interest were rare between my professional responsibilities and my organizational and community ties. For the most part, the two complemented each other. I can recall only one incident where there was a definite conflict. This was a case where local community organizations and I opposed a high-rise residential development that was supported by the planning director and many village officials. The planning director expected me to prepare a report supporting the development, which would have received a large HUD subsidy and contributed greatly to the village tax base. I prepared the report, but found myself in conflict with the community organizations opposed to the development.

I worked in most cases to help community groups achieve their purposes. My social ties and loyalty to these people were important. My other colleagues at work appreciated this and accepted it. For instance, the local school board proposed a parking lot that would asphalt over a large open green space in a village neighborhood. The neighbors protested the parking plan in true Alinsky fashion. They opposed the change as a terrible loss for the neighborhood. I knew that the community group was asking for 100 percent grass, while expecting to negotiate for something less than total coverage with paving.

Since the district was requesting village grant funds, their plan had to receive approval through our office. The school district staff was used to getting its way and they expected us to simply approve their proposal. We insisted, however, that the district come up with a plan acceptable to all parties. I knew that our requirements would eventually pressure the school district staff to negotiate.

I did support the neighbors' contention that the parking lot could be reconfigured to minimize the amount of asphalt and retain some of the grassy landscape. I also knew that keeping the area as grass was unrealistic. Both parties would have to make concessions. The neighbors understood this, but the bureaucrats had to find this out the hard way.

We ended up having a whole bunch of heated meetings between district staff and neighborhood residents. I loved the active participation of the citizens. With time and pressure, the district staff amended their plan. I had helped mediate the negotiations that made it happen.

The town has an active political culture. It is very parochial [as compared to the politics of neighboring Central City]. I found myself getting involved almost from the beginning. I kept track of all the local gossip, but tended to overlook the bigger political issues outside the local sphere. Now I have a job in a regional agency and find myself involved with larger political issues. I guess my political interests and attachments flow from the kind of job I have.

What job I am in and where I live shape my values and identity. So I guess when I worked to help community groups get what they needed, I was also caring for myself—meeting my own needs in my own community. Besides, in the school district parking lot case, the proposal was essentially stupid and deserved to be changed. It's not just that I care about the participation of neighbors in the design of neighborhood physical development, but also I believe there are elements of competent design that must be attended to.

Alice has built a successful professional and bureaucratic career without abandoning her roots in community organizing. Like Krumholz, she exercises her power with a detachment that enables her to move back and forth between her community ties and professional responsibilities. The stories of Bruce, Darlene, Jean, and Stelian tell of planners who persuade, negotiate, and organize, despite the opposition or indifference of their employing agency. Alice, however, worked for a planning director who shared her values. She found institutional support for using plans to empower local citizens.

Alice never seems to have cared much for rooting her legitimacy and power in professional expertise. From the very outset, she considers the action of planning professionals strictly in terms of their consequences for disadvantaged community groups and clients. Her sense of status comes not from her professional standing or bureaucratic position, but from the relationships she has formed through her political and social organizing. She adjusts and applies her technical knowledge in light of her political commitments, which are foremost in her work. Like Krumholz, she manipulates bureaucratic conventions in unexpected ways to shift the burden of uncertainty away from clients and toward bureaucrats and politicians.

Alice creates a professional identity by drawing on relationships that cut across the domains of expertise, bureaucracy, and friendship. Instead of identifying with the powers of her professional and bureaucratic standing, she embraces the principles of participation and uses them to fashion a vocation as a practical democrat. In the system, but not of it, Alice takes the values of her community of neighbors and liberal activists as a moral reference point. Like Krumholz, Alice avoids the quest for conventional professional status and bureaucratic power, which frees her to use the powers she possesses to pressure reluctant officials to adopt policies that improve bureaucratic fairness and increase social justice.

THE SELFLESS ORGANIZER

Organizing usually has an instrumental meaning. We organize others to get some desired outcome. This emphasis on consequences tends, however, to overlook the social roots of organizing and to promote a cynical functionalism that reduces organizing to a technical process for identifying and combining the interests of many individuals. This narrow view perceives that special interests get their way because they have effective organizations. This view shortchanges the power of social collaboration and consent.

Organizing draws its authority from the mutual consent of the participants. When individuals organize they become members of a group. In the process, their preferences, interests, and purposes mingle and change shape. Modern social movements to improve the lives of the poor, the oppressed, and the disenfranchised are clear examples of the importance of mutual consent. In capitalist industrial societies, organizing refers to efforts to build forms of purposeful social collaboration among relatively weak individuals. The focused collaboration of many individuals gives each power none could muster alone. As members of a union, precinct, club, or other association, participants can threaten to undermine the routines the powerful rely on to pursue their own purposes. By threatening to strike, to protest police brutality, to boycott hazardous products, or conduct other such coordinated actions, the weak may force the powerful, who otherwise rely on their complicity and consent, to negotiate changes to remedy some of the injustices.

Of course, the powerful usually resist the organized efforts of the weak. Thus, organizing is usually perceived as an adversarial political activity. In the United States, dramatic confrontations between the powerful and the weak have signalled turning points in efforts to extend democracy. They give evidence that self-interested individualism is neither pervasive nor inevitable.

The organizer who is trying to pull together individuals into a coalition must rely on more than appeals to their self-interest. Bruce, the aggressive planning director, does not possess enough power to change the zoning ordinance to accommodate affordable housing, so he tries to organize support from those whose interests would be served by the changes he has in mind. Though the developers are attentive and respectful, their primary interest is in the salability of the homes. They cannot promise Bruce the support he needs to develop a coalition to lobby the mayor to change development standards and procedures. Bruce's ultimate aim, of course, is to get enough amendments to the rules to force other municipal departments to negotiate with the planning director to get their way. However, collaboration based solely on the self-interest of the developers offers only modest hope as a support for institutional change. Betty and Hal speak longingly of the former CD director who used his powers to make the system work in their favor. They want a sympathetic CD director, rather than new rules. The struggle for efficiency and affordability represent important planning objectives, but they are secondary issues in Bruce's efforts to organize support for institutional changes that will enhance the authority of planning.

While Bruce appeals to self-interest, Darlene promotes a mix of career development and group cooperation. Darlene hopes to foster the spirit of collaboration within her newly formed research and development department. She believes that planners can better advance the reform agenda if they collaborate with their coworkers as a team. She also believes that this collaboration will enhance their prospects for professional and career development. The links between reform and advancement, however, are not realized in her account. The spirit is willing, but the institution is weak. Darlene's advice reflects the lessons of solidarity she learned in the Civil Rights movement and the professional standing she has acquired in corporate positions. For her subordinates, the lessons can be confusing and contradictory.

Jean, Darlene's faithful admirer and an experienced community organizer, perceives the ambiguity. When a bureaucracy fails to function as a political democracy, efforts at internal reform cannot succeed without the support of adversarial organizing from the outside. Darlene knows this, but still believes that her department has received sufficient authority from the new municipal leaders to realize some of the reform programs. Jean understands that because of longstanding indifference and antagonism between the staff and clients internal reform will fail. Instead, clients must be organized to challenge staff routines. Jean perceives that these organizing efforts among the clients must be based on more than professional expertise. Rather, the reform-minded staff must build relationships of mutual respect and reciprocity among the clients to help them develop organizational strategies that will increase uncertainty for the indifferent and hostile service providers and thereby enhance the discretion of client groups.

Jean also perceives that if the reformers expect professional payoffs in such a venture, genuine client empowerment will likely be undermined. Darlene wants to believe that professionals can share their powers with clients and retain, and even improve, their special status. Jean disagrees. If professionals successfully share their powers with clients, the professionals lose their status. They become redundant outsiders, as the clients become empowered to control and shape their own lives. Needleman and Needleman (1974) and Hoffman (1989) described this phenomenon among community planners in the 1970s. Jean, as a committed egalitarian, cares little for professional status. She uses the symbols of her professional training and experience to project an image of respect and to legitimize the struggle to keep the focus on the clients in the agency's bureaucratic hierarchy.

Neither Stelian nor Alice had to cope with institutional resistance or suspicion. Stelian represents an interesting hybrid of adversarial and unitary politics. He neither thinks of himself nor acts as a conventional professional. His competent planning work for a community-based non-profit industrial development corporation challenges the ideological assumptions of local developers and industrialists. Stelian is successful because he has worked hard to find common cause with his board members. He does not publicize his more radical ideological beliefs. Stelian avoids having an identity crisis by drawing on his intellectual and personal ties with other activists and reformers to keep his purposes on track. Stelian is not an infiltrator—an agent of the left working covertly against the right. Rather, he belongs to several communities from which he draws a meaningful set of practical ideas for conducting plans to aid the inner city and retain industrial jobs there.

Alice also belongs to several communities, which give her the knowledge and experience to maintain the quality of her work. She is a practical contradiction—a democratic bureaucrat. Although she started out in the trenches of adversarial politics, she does not pursue adversarial democracy on the job. She introduces deliberative democracy to tame the excesses of bureaucratic coercion and incompetence. She does not wage war, but uses her authority selectively and attentively to encourage collaboration and reconciliation among potential enemies.

Adversarial organizing, which usually provokes confrontation and conflict, does not leave much room for the conduct of professional planning. Collaborative and cooperative organizing, however, can play an important role in the efforts planners make to pursue common objectives with the community and to reduce shared uncertainty. Organizing works best for those who place secondary importance on their professional standing. Even for the selfless organizer, this activity is not a panacea for the ills of our communities and the failures of the profession. Institutional limits remain and can shift in ways that upset even the most successful organizing efforts. These limits remind professionals that in a liberal capitalist society the conduct of planning is difficult, contentious, and challenging.

9

Racism and Planning

RACISM AND THE PLANNING PROFESSION

Most planning professionals, like most Americans, do not give racism much thought. Planners rarely study racism or write about it in their professional journals, even though the rare analysis has uncovered evidence of continuing racial discrimination despite civil rights reforms (Catlin 1993). The low priority that planners assign to injustice may stem from the demographic makeup of the profession. Fewer than 16 percent of the APA membership are racial minorities and only 3 percent are African-Americans. The racial composition of the profession appears to be just as imbalanced as the nation's newer middle-class suburbs.

Many African-Americans lead relatively marginal socioeconomic lives in segregated neighborhoods. Therefore, contact between middle-class whites and less prosperous African-Americans is minimal. The legacy of geographic segregation, socioeconomic discrimination, and cultural oppression continues to insulate the majority of whites from the African-American population, even after the significant political and legal reforms of the Civil Rights movement. The boundaries are no longer as thick, nor the gatekeepers as violent as in the past, but the barriers remain.[1]

According to Andrew Hacker:

America has always been a "multicultural" nation, although events elsewhere should remind us that we are not the only such society. Where we differ from most other countries is the degree to which we impose an apartheid on our

major minority race. Even successful middle-class black Americans find they
have a narrow choice of neighborhoods and few social contacts with members of other races. When all is said and done, black children and adults
spend more of their lives among themselves than almost any other group,
including recent immigrants. To be sure, this isolation is to some degree voluntary; yet the central reality is that white America wants black America
kept apart (1992, 30).

The planning profession did not embrace the pursuit of racial justice
until the 1960s. A rogue group of advocate planners, calling themselves
Planners for Equal Opportunity and led by Paul Davidoff (1965), actively
participated in the Civil Rights movement and proposed standards for
racial justice. Some of the group's proposals were incorporated within
the professional prototype of the good planner. The AICP amended its
code to include norms that supported the principles of racial fairness
already incorporated in the national civil rights legislation of the 1960s.
The code, however, is a passive instrument. It has not provoked among
planners an ongoing public commitment to social justice, as the advocate planners had proposed. It is not as if professional planners carry the
code around with them at the ready. The code matters less as a source of
moral inspiration and more as a useful rhetorical protocol. When critics
question professional planners' support for racial justice, they can hold
up the code and say, "See! We support racial justice."

Federal measures to outlaw the use of local police powers for purposes
of racial discrimination have not eliminated the more subtle and indirect
forms of exclusion. Jurisdictions still cloak the exclusion of low-income
minorities in justifications that appeal to other planning goals. For example, officials might argue for the retention of large lot zones to ensure
the character of a residential community. In spite of the persistence of
these subtle forms of discrimination, the issue of race has moved to the
margins of professional concern. The implementation of civil rights legislation slowed in the 1980s and critics of liberal race relations programs
shifted policy debates away from questions of institutional reforms and
toward an emphasis on personal responsibility and moral desert (Wilson 1987).

Few members of the planning profession would deny that local public
officials have used government zoning and permit approvals to enforce
racial segregation. Overt political efforts to maintain the racial character
of a municipality now violate federal law. Conflict, however, remains.
The various moral claims of competing public authorities complicate the

issue. The defense of states' rights and the protection of racial discrimination, if no longer synonymous, still remain intertwined.

Consider the infamous public housing case in Yonkers, New York (Feld 1989, 67). A federal judge ended up imposing heavy fines and other legal sanctions on a group of Yonkers elected officials who resisted a federal mandate to include predominantly white neighborhoods in the siting of public housing. Local elected officials fought against the imposition of federal authority by narrowly circumscribing the range of acceptable siting alternatives that planners could consider and propose. As a result, the municipal planners ultimately complied (some more willingly than others) with the exclusionary policies of their employer—the City of Yonkers. The federal judge eventually preempted the local authority and appointed a planning consultant to select desegregated public housing sites for Yonkers.

The Yonkers case does not represent exceptional practice, merely an exceptional episode of public debate and censure. Many planners, whether they are on the staff of or serve as consultants for government agencies, engage in the de facto exclusion of minorities—especially African-Americans—either in their employment policies or client services. In these cases, the responsibility of planners is nebulous; the demands for racial justice are not very compelling. What do planners do in such settings? What concepts of racial justice do planners use, especially minority planners?

INTERPRETING RACIAL JUSTICE

Annette: Discrimination and Equal Opportunity

Annette first appeared in chapter 5, where she told about serving as a consultant for an inner city redevelopment project. In the interview, she also shared her experience as an African-American and some difficulties she had faced due to racial discrimination.

> I feel I can make a difference. There are many black people in business and law that don't impact the [black] community that much. I want to use my planning knowledge to do something good [for this community]. I'm still not sure what it is, though, that I want to do.
>
> Being black has increased my sensitivity to the injustice of discrimination. Racism is still pervasive. I am taking architectural classes at a college in a black neighborhood and a white student from Germany insisted that the black neighbors were all angry and dangerous. His views are not exceptional. White people still hold stereotypical views of black neighborhoods.

We [the family consulting firm she works for] face greater obstacles than white firms when we bid on contracts. Our firm has been in business for twenty-five years and has performed successfully on a variety of contracts, yet we still find that we are treated as the "minority firm." Institutional discrimination is the most frustrating and damaging.

In one recent incident, a federal agency had hired us to do some interior design planning for a new building it was constructing. The same agency put out a bid for a space plan. We had experience doing this sort of work and a staff capable of doing it, but a much smaller white firm got the contract. When I met with the representative to ask why we were turned down, she told me it was because we had not worked for the agency before in that capacity. I pointed out to her that we were already working for her agency in another related capacity and that we were more qualified than the agency they selected on all the criteria they had requested. I also told her that if previous experience were the crucial factor in allocating jobs, then it means that the same firm will always get the contracts. She simply ignored my arguments and protest.

In another instance, I was coordinating a design competition for a large civic structure in Central City with the department of planning. The liaison person with the city, however, refused to inform me of crucial organizing meetings, although everyone else was properly notified. Then, when I didn't show up, the liaison would call and ask why I didn't show up. Meanwhile, when I called other members of the coordinating group, they told me that the city liaison was accusing our firm and me of incompetence. I had to meet with the planning director and take all sorts of time-consuming steps to deal with this discrimination.

Annette dealt with racial discrimination in the familiar terms of liberal moral debate: Professional planners who happen to be African-Americans should be treated just like white professionals. She appeals to a color-blind application of the law to all citizens. In practice, this means removing the social and political barriers that place African-Americans at a disadvantage, usually through the courts and sometimes through legislation. The liberal imperative says: Uncover unfair institutional practices and outlaw them. Ensure equal opportunity.

Annette did not recall any incidents of clear and purposeful racial domination. The racial exclusion she describes in her professional encounters is opaque, appearing in the guise of an inadequate fit or incompetent performance. The ambiguity generated by such institutional racism frustrates Annette. This unfairness escapes formal identification and, hence, the legal liability public exposure would likely produce. Civil rights legislation has fostered greater public respect for the equal treatment of African-Americans, but racial prejudice remains embedded in the established contracts, agreements, and social expectations that make up the social environment of professional planning.

Annette perceives the problem of race as an obstacle to successful social mobility and occupational competence. Ignorant and bigoted white people use their institutional ties and position to undermine selectively the access of African-Americans to important contracts, information, and other resources. Racism persists and must be snuffed out by minorities gaining access to political power and using this authority to oppose and make illegal these subtle, but debilitating forms of discrimination.

Francesco: Affirmative Action

Francesco speaks with a mild Hispanic accent. His words rush out in a lyrical staccato, first stretching, then bunching together, ending a sentence in a suspended, mild interrogatory. He dresses impeccably. Gold cufflinks, tasseled loafers, and wrinkle-free suit on his trim figure produce an image to challenge any *GQ* model. Yet, Francesco's movements and speech do not convey any executive machismo.

He works in the regional office of a federal agency. He reviews proposals requesting federal funds and evaluates the outcomes of the programs. He has held this job for about a year. A first generation Central American immigrant, he came to the United States as a young boy. Work and mobility comprise the central themes of his interview. Asked about the relationship between planning and politics, he turns immediately to his own story and the worry he has about his own worth.

> I never felt that being Hispanic was the reason I got my jobs. Yesterday, I was talking with my present supervisor about my probable promotion. He put it like this: "Look, you're qualified and your Hispanic background gives you great potential for advancement." He made it clear that my qualifications were crucial, including my ability to get along with my coworkers. At least for the most part, but later the same day I asked myself, "What else could he have said?"
>
> I don't like to think that I got my present job because I'm Hispanic. I think that fact was important, but not the deciding factor. I remember when I had been on the job for only a few days at the Central City transportation division, the job I held before coming here. Other workers (mainly blacks) came up to me and said I got the job because I was Hispanic. I went to my boss who had hired me and told him what people were saying. I asked him di-

rectly, "Did you hire me because I am an Hispanic or because I was the most qualified?" He told me it was because of my qualifications.

I left the Central City transportation division because I was constantly criticized by my coworkers. There were two blacks—one male and one female—who had over twenty-five years experience. They constantly complained that they were not promoted like the whites. Neither had degrees. The guy really got to me. He would come over and interrupt my work as an interagency contract manager with his complaints. I'd point out that I had a college degree and was making $29,000, while he was making $40,000 without a degree and having less responsibility. He wanted to get to a particular supervisory position, but had a strong and aggravating sense of entitlement. He was given a chance for a position, but turned it down when it didn't meet his desires. They [the management] ended up offering a supervisory position to a qualified, but inexperienced, black woman.

The blacks didn't act the same way toward their white coworkers [as they did toward their minority coworkers]. They thought that since I am a minority that we would share the same basic outlook, but when they learned that I didn't share the same sense of entitlement they would get upset. That's when the trouble would start. Sometimes I feel like we're overpaid relative to the amount of work we do. Let's be realistic. People in public bureaucracies where I've worked put in only about five hours a day. I know how hard people work in the food business. They put in a full day's work. They work harder than people here.

The public civil service works just like the private sector bureaucracy. I've worked for years as a manager for a large grocery chain. I moonlight for the money. It's who you know that makes the difference in hiring. The way I got my job here was through a friend who, when he found out about the opening, thought I would be good for the job and he called me. Although the deadline for official application had passed, I was able to get the forms and submit them in time. Applying for a high-level federal job like this takes filling out a lot of paperwork.

Plenty of minorities like me have been given breaks, and if you know how to use them, you can benefit. I have benefited, but there is a downside. When I started at my present job, I shared an office with a black female coworker. She kept asking how I got the job in a challenging way. I explained how my friend helped me learn of the application and about my background. She was angry that I had gotten it. She thought I had a big ego. I don't work that way, but she wouldn't listen. She didn't have any degrees and had worked her way up in the system, but had ambitions to go higher. "Here the whites get all the promotions and not the blacks," she said.

I disagreed with her and told her that you have to work hard and get the right background to get the promotion. "Look!" I said. "My family came here from Latin America when I was just a kid in 1968. I had to learn a new language and work nights to help keep the family alive. I went to school and worked full time all the way through high school, college, and graduate school. You can still go to college." She said I didn't have a kid. She wanted to blame the system and I didn't.

Those who believe that minorities have been forced to bear unequal socioeconomic burdens due to institutionalized forms of favoritism and prejudice are likely to approve of efforts to compensate for or remove the inequalities that undermine the ability of minorities to get good paying jobs, to secure good housing, and to achieve social standing. Justice here requires the reform and revision of institutional and cultural conventions, such as traditional hiring practices, which appear normal or natural to the majority, who rely on them as both a source of employment and of social mobility. Instead of merely sanctioning acts of discrimination, the proper and just approach would be to take affirmative steps not only to remove them, but to rectify the discriminatory consequences of established practices.

Affirmative action poses problems not only for those who feel left out, but also for those who benefit. Francesco wonders deeply about his own accomplishments. His upward mobility, fueled by his ambition, his political connections, and the affirmative action policies, has given him status and position, but has set him at odds with his coworkers and raised self-doubts about his competence. He chides skeptical African-American coworkers with stories of hard work and self-improvement, knowing full well that his own rapid promotion has been tied to color. Francesco, who finds fulfillment in hard work, also wants a sense of solidarity with his coworkers. However, his upward mobility in the ranks of the bureaucracy has diminished both. His supermarket moonlighting may be less for the money and more for the camaraderie and sense of hard work well done that he has yet to find in the public bureaucracy.

The conflict between a first generation Hispanic immigrant and African-Americans over the distribution of jobs and promotions testifies to the peculiar burden of African-Americans. In interviews with middle-class blacks, Benjamin found frequent examples of racial favoritism in which Asians or Hispanics were selected for jobs or promotion over blacks (1991). Few African-American interviewees reported the kind of ambivalence that haunts Francesco. They did not worry about their competence or hesitate to take a promotion. Francesco perceives their sense of entitlement to jobs, promotions, and other goods as illegitimate. Francesco considers affirmative action an important supplement to making good on the promise of equal opportunity. In contrast, many African-Americans, whose efforts to survive and prosper in the white community have long been burdened with numerous racial indignities, perceive these benefits to be long overdue compensation. It is not enough that benefits be distributed fairly, but that they be offered in ways to repair the injury of racial stigma. When we apologize to and feel concern for those we have injured, we do not expect them to have to earn our respect. We demonstrate this respect when we acknowledge our responsibility and offer compensation.

Norma: Racial Resistance, Solidarity and Dignity

It is mid-morning and bitter cold. In her office, Norma (who first appeared in chapter 4) is busily completing a mailer, occasionally interrupted by phone calls. Norma is a large African-American woman, sporting a magnificent explosion of frosted blonde hair embraced by a brilliant green headband. The luster of her plump brown cheeks enhances her sensuous bright red lips. They seem liquid. Any hint of alluring femininity or vulnerability, however, is lost in meeting her gaze. Her look penetrates, sizing and testing. Her manner is powerful and imposing, yet strangely hesitant and even shy. Her voice is rich and deep, resonating with free-flowing and lyrical words. Her volume and pitch push well beyond the conventions of bureaucratic talk, while her vocabulary and tempo maintain a semblance of conformity. Mixing idioms and slang from urban African-American and white bureaucratic culture, she presents a formidable composition of contrasts.

> I would like to be a writer some day and get a children's story published. Of course, no eight year old is going to get all the complex relations I'm talking about. I want to write about the black experience, but without making it only accessible to blacks. I want it to be human.
>
> I've always neglected to accept the authority of others. I decide who the bad guys and good guys are. People say they can read me easily. [Laughing] I have a face with a lot of stuff to read.
>
> [On politics, planning, and doing good] Racism isn't good or bad. It's a factuality. They didn't put Jackie Robinson on the team because he was black. You got to be able to review policy in terms of consequences. Did the policy do what we wanted it to do? If we're way off the mark, then we need to review the whole policy, the whole point of it all.

Fair is subjective. For white males, fair housing means the ability to go into a bank or S & L and negotiate a mortgage based on job security and income. Black women can't do that. First of all, if they have a job (a great percent are unemployed and on welfare), they don't have savings and security. Getting good housing for black women means getting on the list for public housing. They negotiate to get on and then get some. Black men are even worse off.

I'm not saying there is injustice, but everyone is not being treated the same. When I went to kindergarten, it was the first time I was separated from my mother. I didn't want to go. She threatened me. I went. The first person who came to me was a white girl with a ponytail and a bow. I had no knowledge of racism. We became friends. One day, we came in from playing outside. It was windy and our hair had come undone and our bows were untied. The teacher pulled my friend aside and said, "Let me braid your ponytail." She did and I sensed the care that that teacher gave that child. I just knew that she was going to turn around and do mine next, but when she turned around her facial expression changed. I didn't know what the expression meant at the time, but I felt the hate. I felt hateful myself, but I was persistent. I said, "Here's my bow." She snapped at me, "Go sit down!" I knew something was wrong. I sat down because she frightened me. Before the day was over I tried again. This time she threatened me: "If you don't sit down and shut up I'm going to tell your mother that you've been a bad girl." Even more painful than her words was the feeling of being marked and bad.

We've been initiating a series of downzoning efforts in older, mainly Afro-American neighborhoods that are zoned for too high density. We told the owners, "You might have difficulty selling (at least for the price you want) after downzoning." This guy called and he was pissed. He gave the staff who answered the phone a hard time. Eventually, they passed him on to me. I understood his rage. I allowed him to play it out. I listened. When he had finished I said, "Sir, if you would reread the line in the third paragraph of the letter we sent, you will see that you have no real concern." He had misread our warning and thought it was a threat. After he reread the paragraph, his whole temperament changed.

People don't believe fair applies to them. Being a minority and a woman, you soon realize that if you allow yourself to believe in the rights of the individual, you'll find life frustrating. You can't afford to forgo the meaning of those rights. They may not get passed out to you, but you can't allow yourself to accept the judgments others have about you. So, all the policy stuff like fair housing laws are ultimately subjective.

The perverse and profoundly damaging legacy of slavery continues to foster contempt for African-Americans by others in the United States.

This contempt reinforces a powerful stigma not shared by other minorities. The African-American experience of social marginality and subjugation generates feelings of self-doubt and hatred. The injustice of racial practices not only limits opportunity, but narrows and distorts the expectations African-Americans hold. The exclusion, segregation, subordination, and discrimination that African-Americans experience in the mainstream educational and employment institutions damage their self identity. Making rules fair and offering compensatory opportunities will not by themselves heal the wounds to individual identity that racial practices inflict.

The small incident of an irate citizen's call to complain illustrates how even the most mundane everyday communication gets shaped by race. Norma tells her story not out of outrage, but as her most recent example of the countless institutional indignities suffered by African-Americans. Her ability to placate the irate citizen with simple information reflects her compassion, which enables her to grasp the caller's experience of injustice and painful fear. She listens patiently, not as an altruistic or long-suffering public servant, but as a fellow human being who understands the pain of exclusion and who hopes to offer reassurance. She takes a small, but important action to heal the ongoing rupture between white institutions and black lives.

Healing these deep wounds is a formidable task. Racial practices against blacks may be institutional, but those who suffer injustice are individuals. Legal and programmatic remedies alone are not sufficient. Full citizenship in a liberal democracy requires a sense of civic trust and of self-respect. Individuals expect reciprocity with their fellow citizens in everyday settings (Marris 1982b; 1987). Members of the white majority need to listen to the stories of racial oppression and identify with the suffering to recognize its painful and perverse contingency and to understand how white majority cultural beliefs and moral practices impose stigma and shame on African-Americans. More ambitiously, members of the majority should change the customs and traditions of neighborhood, ethnic, class, and professional identity to rid them of racial separation and exclusion (Lukas 1985).

PLANNING AND RACE

Annette, Francesco, and Norma do not experience injustice in the same way. Although they all argue for fairness, their orientations and interpretations differ in important ways. All three approaches to racial justice seem to have merit in the face of pervasive and stultifying racism. Yet to give them equal weight overlooks the different demands these moral interpretations place on the majority. Equal opportunity (Annette) asks the majority to allow minorities to participate without prejudice. Affirmative action, according to Francesco, removes historical handicaps imposed on minorities, while his African-American coworkers expect such action to compensate for the burdens of racial injustice. Racial inclusion (Norma) asks the majority to change its customs and institutions and embrace a multicultural, multiracial human identity.

Equal opportunity and affirmative action have obtained legitimacy, if not wholesale acceptance, in the United States. Racial inclusion and multicultural identity have not. Equal opportunity and affirmative action rely on principles of distributive justice, but racial inclusion raises more difficult questions about cultural membership and identity. Changing the white majority's deep-rooted beliefs that stigmatize and subject African-Americans may seriously challenge even the most ardent white, liberal reformers.

The next section presents three planning stories in which racial issues predominate. In the first, Michael uses clever political maneuvers to get racial and ethnic politics out in the open in the suburban municipality where he works. He challenges discrimination in ways that accommodate political relationships. Ralph, a dedicated liberal, sees racism as an unacceptable and ugly social condition. He works hard with his colleagues to take practical steps to reduce and alleviate the consequences of discrimination. For him, reform occurs through the redistribution of scarce resources in ways that respect the moral fabric of the community and the claims of its members who lead marginal lives. By contrast, Norma reflects on problems of identity and the risk faced by African-American planners who try to conduct reforms on the job. Ralph works from the inside out. He draws on a contentious set of moral values about distributive justice. Norma works from the outside in. She cannot rely on the conventional forms of distributive justice because they have too often proven deceptive and perverse to African-Americans.

Michael: Accommodation over Confrontation

Michael works as planning director for an old working-class industrial suburb with a largely Italian population. I first introduced him in chapter 6 in the zoning meeting with Andrew and Pat. A second generation Mexican immigrant, he grew up in an inner city Italian neighborhood.

Although bilingual, he has no accent. He projects warmth and openness, yet his jerky gestures and rapid speech suggest impatience, perhaps even anger. He seems to be agitated about the slow response of the director of public works to the water damage that recently spoiled his office. A peeling ceiling and torn-up carpet do little to impress visitors or shore up morale.

I liked planning for the older suburbs and learned of the planning job here in Fair Oaks at my old job. At that time [about 1986], the Fair Oaks village board had created a new job of zoning administrator. I did some homework on the place. I asked around about the reputation of the village staff and political leadership. I am Mexican and learned that the village had no minority staff. Furthermore, the village had a small Mexican community, which was quite poor. I was interested in trying to improve the living conditions of these residents.

I decided to apply for the job. Anticipating discrimination, I wrote my name as Michael instead of Miguel. When I interviewed I was Michael. The interviews went quite well for several reasons. I was competent and had experience administering CD [community development] programs. The trustees wanted someone to get their CD program running well. However, even more crucial was the fact that I had grown up in an Italian neighborhood in nearby Central City—the same neighborhood where many of them had grown up or where their parents had grown up. Furthermore, since most were Catholic, they were especially impressed that I had studied with the Jesuits. The trustees who interviewed me just presumed I was an Italian with the added advantage of being able to speak Spanish. I got the job.

After being hired, I appeared before the village board to express my gratitude for being hired and introduce myself to those whom I had not met during the interview. One trustee asked me about my nationality. I told him the truth. I'm Mexican. I don't think what I did was dishonest. It was a strategy designed to neutralize racism and give me an opportunity to have my selection based on competence and a sensitivity to the kinds of values the citizens and I shared. We really did have the same urban neighborhood social roots.

I take every opportunity I can to combat the racism among staff and citizens. For example, one staff member referred to Italians as "spics." I told her this was no way to speak of others. Thinking I had been offended, she explained that she didn't think I was a low-life Mexican, but I insisted that she not speak that way about anyone. Little stuff like that is important to change the bigotry people have.

I can recall one instance where a local home owner called my office complaining about the misbehavior of a Cuban neighbor. The person spoke of the neighbor using racist stereotypes. I decided to visit the resident, listen to the complaint in person, and then serve as a mediator between the two. I also knew that by going in person that I might be able to teach the resident that he could overcome racial prejudice to resolve a dispute. The Cuban was in the wrong, but the mediation worked out. The complaining resident is still a bigot, but he knows he can change his behavior and that it will work in his favor.

Unlike my former job, in this position I do not report to a manager, but directly to the mayor. I like the mayor. We have a close relationship. The mayor has enabled me to pursue projects that improve the village. I can identify with this community because the mayor gives me sufficient discretion to do planning. The mayor and I both benefit.

For instance, because of its longstanding bigotry, the village had for years failed to allow any low-income housing units within its boundaries. Hiring me, however, was part of a larger effort initiated by the mayor to put an end to this practice. A nonprofit regional housing agency dedicated to providing affordable housing, however, did not know about these recent changes and was organizing a campaign to shame the village. I arranged a meeting with the agency advocates who came in with a chip on their shoulders—convinced the city was incorrigibly bigoted. I told them about our plans and the steps we were taking to improve the low-rent housing we had and to take whatever steps necessary to open the village to some subsidized units. The mayor was there and clearly pleased that I had defused a tense situation. The city council did eventually pass a fair housing ordinance as a result of my efforts.

I have grown closer to the mayor over time because he cares about the entire community. I feel a loyalty to him because we share this concern for the public good. For example, there is this four-block subdivision that the city annexed some twenty years ago. It consists of large low-rent apartment buildings, which were poorly built and lack adequate parking and street improvements. I told him that the village needed to get the mainly Mexican residents involved in efforts to improve their neighborhood.

The subdivision is a small geographic pocket, bordered on two sides by industrial land and on the other two sides by major four-lane arterial roads. Given the area's proximity to the village, it presents serious social concerns to the residents and trustees, who fear the possibility of gang incursions. The decaying physical appearance and obvious poverty fuel racial stereotypes.

I wanted to improve the area and knew that long-term success would hinge crucially on developing a group of local activists. Getting these people to act would be greatly assisted by the mayor's support of a local initiative.

I set up a public meeting that was billed as a community needs meeting. Come and tell the mayor what your problems and needs are. This was the first time in over thirty years, when the area was annexed, that a mayor had visited the area. At first, when I asked the mayor, he balked. I emphasized that such a meeting was crucial to build community morale and an attachment to the village. Other trustees advised the mayor against such a visit. They felt it would backfire. "You'll be crucified! The press will tear you apart when issues come up that you are not prepared to address," they said. Other advisers feared that a visit to the Mexican neighborhood would upset the residents in other parts of the city who would consider such an initiative to be pandering to the bad elements. Despite this, he finally decided to go.

I prepared him for the meeting by briefing him about what problems the residents were most likely to mention. I had already met with numerous residents of the area to find out their complaints. I also gave him some concrete proposals to make. The things he could do to address some resident concerns included beginning a program to monitor and improve police response time to calls, promising that the area would be given priority for CD funds, and directing inspectors to enforce the building code more diligently to confront disinvesting absentee landlords.

The night of the meeting, I arrived early and encouraged the people to express their concerns. The meeting began. About fifty people showed up and complained about poor police service and a lack of public improvements, the very issues we had anticipated. This went on for a couple of hours. The mayor was prepared to offer specific actions that addressed their concerns. When he told them that he would represent their interests, he was believable. The residents left satisfied and the event launched the formation of a small group of local activists dedicated to seeing that the promises are kept and that residents keep trying to improve their neighborhood.

I have gone out of my way to introduce these people to the different department heads so that they know whom to contact to get certain questions answered or services provided. This has made me popular among the Mexicans, who told me that if my job should ever be threatened, that they would get two hundred people to protest. I was grateful and flattered, but not interested in becoming specialized. Helping this neighborhood is important because the residents have been treated so unfairly, but I still care about the whole community.

There has to be a detached approach to my role. I am culturally tied to the Mexicans. The relationship is special and I feel a kind of kinship, but I also want to remain detached enough to fulfill the needs of others whose cultural values I don't share. I don't want to become the mediator for or patron of the neighborhood. That's why I work with them to build their own neighborhood organization. I have been especially active helping get the residents registered as voters. The area is quite dense and could have a significant effect on local elections. I also helped many residents get in touch with amnesty officials to obtain citizenship under the recent changes in the immigration laws. Finally, I worked closely with census officials to make sure everyone was counted.

I have been here less than five years, but I have managed to create a professional versus patronage-based planning department. I hired the first black employee in the village and hired two women staff as well. I encourage quality work and the competence of the department has given us a good reputation.

Unlike Francesco, Michael avoided affirmative action issues. He maneuvered his way around any potential censors by turning his light complexion to his advantage. Drawing on his boyhood experience of the neighborhood values he shared with the board, he had no difficulty acting Italian. He did not tell lies, since the values he spoke of were his own. He did not, however, provide the village board with the opportunity to confront any prejudice that its members might hold.

Michael avoids confrontation. He does not lack courage, but understands the vulnerability of minorities and the risks of a frontal assault. He adopts a politics of accommodation. Instead of forcing elected officials to take public stands favoring racial justice, he finds ways to obtain concessions that benefit minority residents and employees while minimizing the political risk to white politicians. He is proud of his efforts to establish a color blind merit system in the planning department, but he still plays community politics to obtain improvements for resident minorities. Professionalism and patronage coexist for him as part of an ongoing tension. He manages this tension through acts of mediation and negotiation that reduce the indignities of racial discrimination one at a time.

Ralph: Practical Redistribution

Ralph is the executive director of a small nonprofit local housing development corporation (LDC), which just finished rehabilitating two old apartment buildings. One building has eighteen two-bedroom units and the other has three one-bedroom, six two-bedroom, and nine three-bedroom units. All of the units have been improved to house low-income households through a mix of public and private subsidies.

A bespectacled white, middle-class male, Ralph does not fit the stereotype of an inner city reform activist. His bare bones basement office is well organized and efficient. Slow to argue and quick to compliment,

Ralph focuses on practical action. Trained as a transportation planner and educated partly in Europe, he shows an intelligent and critical commitment to rebuilding inner city neighborhoods. His effortless speech shows his sensitivity to his audience.

Ralph is meeting with two African-American staff members (the tenant selection committee) to discuss the allocation of the recently rehabilitated apartment units. The staff had sent notices of availability to people who had applied for but had not received units in residential projects completed earlier. Because federal funds had been used to build the projects, only applicants who held Section 8 certificates, federal housing vouchers, or who were on the official housing authority waiting list were eligible for consideration. The guidelines required that these applicants' income fall below 80 percent of the city's median household income.

Ralph explains that his board wants to provide housing for the eligible members of the LDC who live in the neighborhood. The LDC also wanted to protect the neighborhood's ethnic and racial diversity by integrating the buildings. He proposes a quota scheme for allocating the units among different racial and ethnic groups, based on the existing distribution of the groups in the local community and the mix achieved in previously rehabilitated buildings. The board also wants to ensure that large households get large units and small households the small units. Also, there should be some income mix in the buildings. Thus, some of the one-bedroom units should be allocated to tenants who could pay market rents. The committee is to select tenant households using these criteria.

The tenant selection committee has a randomly ranked list of three hundred neighborhood applicants from the housing authority list. Next to each applicant rank and name is information on income, household size, and race/ethnicity. Ralph goes down the list with the two staff members, rationalizing the selection or rejection of each household until the committee decides on the thirty-six tenants needed for the units. Most assignments are straightforward, but occasionally Ralph also takes into account additional circumstances. For example, he asserts that a household of African refugees is more vulnerable than other recent emigrés, most notably the Vietnamese. He argues that they are more deserving because of the double burden of immigration and racial prejudice. This household should take precedence over other blacks. Ralph notes that the local refugee association will remember this step favorably. Furthermore, he adds, the household would enhance the mix of residents in the buildings. Thus, a large Sudanese family with a Section 8 certificate gets a three-bedroom unit.

Ralph puts the vulnerability criterion to use again later in considering a single applicant from a local halfway house. Ralph argues that this handicapped person, whom he and the staff know, is more vulnerable and so more deserving of a unit than other poor single people without handicaps. A staff member responsible for building management objects. He points out that the presence of seriously handicapped people may lead to housekeeping and building management problems. He wants to ensure that there is some level of competence among the tenants. Another staff member states that the vulnerability that makes the tenant deserving also puts him at risk in living alone in a poor neighborhood where he might be a target for exploitation. Ralph, unconvinced, drops the vulnerability argument and returns to the diversity criterion. The handicapped man is white and would therefore contribute to the goal of racial diversity in the building. The staff agree.

Having considered the long list of applicants, the staff select one Asian, one Sudanese, and three Hispanic households with follow up checks to be made on the handicapped white person and four other Hispanic households. The committee had a difficult task. More than 95 percent of the low-income households holding federal certificates or on the housing authority waiting lists were African-Americans. Ralph and the tenant selection committee wanted to meet the obligation incurred by the LDC in using federal funds to help pay for the rehabilitation of the units, but they also saw a conflict. Ralph acknowledged that it would be illegal to violate the federal requirements, but he also wanted to meet the LDC's goals of promoting diversity. The committee started using competing concepts of justice to allocate the units.

Clearly, the goal of achieving a racial mix was not feasible as long as the staff picked tenants solely from the list of eligible federal subsidy applicants. Furthermore, the allocation effort was hampered by the absence of information on race on a third of the applicants' forms. Ralph assigned a staff member to get this information to be used in a second round of allocations, in which they would try to increase the number of nonblack households in the final roster of tenants. These steps, however, do not yield the desired diversity. Ralph revises the team's allocational priorities: 50 percent of the units are to be allocated to blacks from the neighborhood rather than to white, Asian, or Hispanic households from outside the area. In effect, community membership is to count more than racial mix in the second round of tenant selection.

The staff adopted a systematic rational method for ranking and sorting applicants. They had assessed each household according to predefined criteria presumed to be commensurate. During the discussion, reliance on the rational method as a source of fair-minded judgment ("Let's not be arbitrary.") gave way to practical reasoning that drew heavily on personal experience and beliefs. The rational method became less analytical and more rhetorical, responding to the particular context and relationships (Forester 1989; Throgmorton 1992). The committee adopted selection criteria and then violated them in favor of undiscussed criteria. In evaluating the applicants they knew, the staff related personal accounts that either enhanced or diminished the suitability of the household as potential tenants by introducing issues of honesty, character, competence, and other moral factors.

The board and staff clearly wanted to house minorities, but did not want to foster ghettos of poor African-American households. Ralph would have preferred to follow his own criteria in the allocation of units, but the formal obligations imposed by the use of federal funds meant that he had to develop procedures that combined elements of both. The staff did not disagree with the legitimacy of the federal fairness requirement, but simply introduced additional moral criteria in their decision making. Ralph respected civil rights, but also hoped to respond to local moral claims as well.

As the staff labored to turn policy into practice, their actions were both exclusionary and inclusionary. It is important to consider context in analyzing this scenario. This is not a middle-class suburban community with elected officials enforcing racial homogeneity. This inner city residential community is already substantially integrated. No racial or ethnic sector accounted for as much as 50 percent of the local residents; whites are a minority. However, the staff's effort to replicate the community's diversity undermines the fairness principle that guides the housing authority policy, which suggests that evenhandedness and favoritism cannot occur simultaneously.

Staff judgment, however, was not arbitrary. The committee did not simply pick friends or people like themselves. Ralph and the staff members used various concepts of moral justice in their practical deliberations. They evoked such criteria as vulnerability, membership, proximity, poverty, and household size in trying to assign housing fairly among different racial groups. Some households easily recommended themselves because they met multiple moral criteria, but others raised conflicts between different values.

As this scenario shows, deliberations about racial quotas need not be superficial or simplistic ideological debates that end up frustrating efforts to change unfair practices. The story reminds planners to be wary of holding too firmly to one concept of racial justice, as it may be not only impossible, but foolhardy to live up to it fully. The history of racial justice efforts in the United States documents examples of well-intentioned liberals whose moral righteousness has actually encouraged cynicism and a self-serving distance from the practical conflicts that make up the politics of racial difference—especially for African-Americans. Furthermore, the imposition of an ideologically conceived corrective may produce undesirable and unpredictable costs and suffering.

Norma: Countering Deception

> The old industrial city I work for wants to attract the middle class back. So, they don't want to go after multiunit affordable housing for inner city minority residents. Middle-class whites imagine all affordable housing to be dilapidated projects. The City of Burgess is currently undertaking downzoning efforts. What does this do to the existing multiunit housing stock except put it in trouble?
>
> Perhaps the planning commission and city council members don't realize the ramifications, that significant downzoning can actually encourage displacement. The city ought to anticipate this sort of outcome. You can't go about just attacking a piece of the problem, you've got to take a holistic approach.
>
> Fred, my boss, trusts me as a good person, but I still have to present my stuff carefully. It has to be in a form he can accept. Sometimes I just try and overwhelm him with some outrageous proposals, and just hope for something better than what is. [Speaking to herself] OK, Norma, this is your thing and you really want it. So, go get it. It's OK if I can do something for my folks, even if it's just a little. Then the effort is worthwhile.
>
> Sure it's risky, but I will not compromise my good name. Look, I never stop looking for work. I'm always sending out applications. I'm the first Afro-American professional staff person they've had in Burgess. Professional appointments are not held by blacks here. Look, white people seem to have this innate fear of black people. I work hard to overcome these groundless fears.
>
> Planners, like most people, aren't willing to act on their convictions. In part they can't afford to do what they think is right. They aren't like a Su-

preme Court justice who enjoys the protection of law and position. Planners don't have the power to enjoy such freedom. When you take a stand for justice as a planner, you're taking a big risk. Working as a real planner is tough.

When I first got here, I asked about the housing situation for low-income people and minorities. I wrote a fair housing analysis of the area for HUD, which uses this to judge the eligibility of the city for federal funds. I was asked by the city manager to change significant conclusions that might threaten the city's eligibility. For instance, I pointed out how black households (some 70 percent of whom live in public housing) had not been told about the subsidized elderly housing that was available and for which they were eligible. The city did not want to deal with the racial segregation between the two forms of subsidized housing. The manager wanted me to soften the finding. I took the decision to Fred and told him I wouldn't do it. He said, "You've got to live with your convictions. So go with it." I did. Fred was supportive.

You keep getting your nose smashed from time to time, but this doesn't happen every day. I keep making modest accomplishments in the face of intermittent adversity. If you're not willing to make arguments and stick to them in order to pursue difficult agendas, then don't get involved in planning. We don't need any hang nails on the fickle finger of fate.

One of the things I saw here, soon after I came, was a lack of time and effort given to develop relations between inner city neighborhood organizations and city hall. A meeting was planned for an inner city neighborhood to discuss community downzoning plans. "Take me to the meeting," I urged Fred. He agreed. Fred is a native of Burgess. He grew up here and feels at home, but I was at the meeting for only ten minutes and was able to establish a rapport that included the minority Afro-American neighbors as our partners, not our clients. Fred was careful, still the politician. I was enthusiastic. A brief meeting went on for three hours with residents voicing their concerns and needs.

One resident challenged me: "What's your background?" I gave her my own story (from poverty to professional). "Oh!" she said, impressed. "You've been around. You've been put here for your expertise."

"No," I said. "I want to develop a closer relationship with your community. What you got in mind?" Once I asked, she could hardly stop talking.

Amazing how people have the same concerns and how we need to help them voice them and learn about their shared concerns, rather than always emphasizing differences. Her fear was that absentee landlords were buying up single-family dwellings and apartments and converting them to rental units. The landlords would rent to riffraff and provide no oversight or maintenance. She mistrusted the city because the plan adopted twelve years earlier had offered promises the city did not keep. She was suspicious of any new city plans.

I'm working on the downzoning plan for the area. I intend to keep their trust. I gave anyone interested my card. When they call with questions, I get right back to them and work to find the information. I don't like double-talk.

My sister has a male coworker who wasn't feeling too well. He went to the doctor. He goes in for a routine check and is diagnosed as having an enlarged heart. His response? "What do you expect, Doc? I'm a black man."

Look! You just have to survive. You have to know who you are and how to avoid the definitions of others about fairness, which are used against you in so many ways. So when you get dealt cards, the deal ain't fair, but you play your hand. It's the only one you got.

Norma's vignettes illustrate the multiple incommensurable social expectations that burden her daily life as an African-American planner. In contrast to Michael and Ralph, these are not criteria for rational judgment, but painful indignities. She refuses to appeal to conventional concepts of justice because these criteria have been used as weapons to categorize and subject her. The indignity of racism produces uncertainty, doubt, and skepticism in all her relationships—with city officials, her boss, citizens, and colleagues. No matter that she has an obvious affection for Fred, she cannot rely on this bond. She considers his actions with a vigilant surveillance. Her work against injustice is not a liberal practice, like Ralph's, but is a means of gaining self-respect and obtaining greater fairness for African-American communities.

Norma's view of racial justice is not based on abstract ambiguities, but on her own experience. Her professional protocol is her armor, but she refuses to entrust her moral identity to either her profession or to her employer. Her calls for justice reject the words the professional and bureaucratic cultures use to define justice. Her description of her experiences are so profound that they render conventional concepts of justice both ephemeral and dangerous. The huge cultural gulf that racism engenders between minorities and the dominant culture raises serious questions about professional identity and membership.

BEYOND THE CODE

In the Yonkers case, the judge imposed rules to implement a fair share, rational redistributive scheme. The planners in Yonkers did not champion racial justice. Most stayed within the conventional moral boundaries of municipal government, although some were more critical than others of the city's recalcitrance. How should planners, committed to racial justice, have acted in Yonkers?

Should planners take public stands that oppose the city council and side with a federal judge? Most professional planners possess only modest institutional authority. Planners who publicly advocate for racial justice in ways that challenge conventional practices will likely generate conflict and the imposition of sanctions. It is easier to fire a planner than it is to reform longstanding institutional practices. Committing occupational suicide for racial justice may seem morally correct in the abstract, but foolish to the working planner on the job.

Consider this. Yonkers, New York, unlike most of its neighboring municipalities, was already providing housing to low-income blacks when the city became nationally famous for its conflict on the siting of additional public housing. Ironically, this suburban municipality that made room (albeit inadequately) for low-income African Americans was punished for its failure to achieve housing integration throughout the community, while municipalities that have successfully excluded the African-American poor have received no sanctions at all.

Institutional constraints, however, do not excuse planners from diligent moral reflection. Planners who share with Ralph institutional support in the pursuit of racial justice must still deal with the conflicting moral demands of their personal beliefs, professional ties, and occupational obligations. The awkward calculus of allocation and its uneven outcomes in Ralph's story do not mean such efforts are foolish or futile. Rather, they represent the limitations of liberal reforms. They do not address the cultural differences that divide and inspire racist beliefs about and practices toward African-Americans. Proponents of liberal reforms unrealistically expect consensus and harmony to follow quickly and easily from the implementation of these schemes.

Any serious and sustained effort to alter the distributional status quo in ways that rectify or remedy racial inequalities will incite resistance and conflict, especially when such efforts require the white majority to change their beliefs. Professional planners will likely avoid such efforts because they threaten their livelihood. Norma understands this, as seen in her emphasis on the courage it will take to overcome the racial inertia she encounters every day. Norma's story raises serious questions about white professionals' willingness and ability to form sufficiently deep attachments to minorities to take the risk involved in pursuing racial justice. Can only those who have endured the indignity of racial discrimination find sufficient reason and motivation to pursue vigorously racial reforms?

Well-intentioned planners with institutional support still make imperfect practical judgments about racial justice. In practice, rights are respected unevenly. Unfortunately the professional protocol of the expert advice giver and dutiful public servant does not acknowledge the complexity of racial justice issues and, in fact, seems to simplify the problem. The established professional protocol keeps practitioners from considering and proposing advice and actions that would challenge established conventions of racial discrimination. The protocol gives planners moral legitimacy and imposes conservative limits on what constitutes a legitimate moral justice claim. Norma's story challenges the appropriateness of using conventional rational planning methods to improve the fairness of practical planning judgments. Simply revising the AICP code will not address this difficulty, nor will workshops on professional ethics.

Studs Terkel's *Race* (1992) offers some hope. The white middle-class voices in the book articulate an emerging sense of moral doubt about the norms and customs that minimize or ignore racial injustice. These uncertainties are beachheads for renewed assaults on institutional racism. After all, when individuals become ambivalent about the legitimacy of the occupational and bureaucratic rules, the support for these rules may begin to shift. Members of the white majority may not know what it means to suffer the indignity of growing up as an African-American, but they know what injustice means. All citizens share certain vulnerabilities imposed on them in their roles as consumers, clients, and employees of corporate and government organizations. Unfortunately, the institutional expectations fostered by conventional white, liberal culture and the moral values integral to the various social classes, races, and groups make efforts to build solidarity across such affiliations quite difficult, but not impossible.

Planners seeking to promote modest racial reforms within their institutional terrain can find moral support for their efforts by drawing on civil rights legislation, administrative precedents, and the popular moral language of individual rights. Implementing fair share practices provides real benefits to those minorities who would otherwise be disadvantaged. Small reforms may not remedy the institutional and cultural sources of injustice, but they set precedents and offer examples, while improving the lives of minorities. However, professionals acting alone to reduce racial discrimination should not expect that their efforts will change the cultural and social traditions that support or benefit from racial injustice.

The liberal language of human rights does not adequately address the problems imposed by the stigma of race. Professional norms are not a source of moral guidance here. Instead, planners must turn to examples of democratic citizenship and civility exhibited by those who resist racial injustice and who try to find practical ways to make the boundaries of conventional ways of American life more inclusive. Individual actions and judgments matter, but they alone do not bridge the racial divide. Changing established conventions and familiar expectations requires participation in organized social and political reforms to reshape the cultural expectations of *both* whites and African-Americans. Professional planners may (and should) participate in such efforts, but the impetus and inspiration will come from citizen activism and not professional norms.

NOTE

1. Residential segregation decreases for most ethnic minorities when their income, education levels, and occupational status rise. Not so for African-Americans. "At the rate the country is going, it will take more than six decades for blacks to achieve even the minimal levels of integration with whites that Asians and Hispanics have now" (Ballard and Feagin 1991, 61–62).

10

Research on
Effective Planning

Earlier in my teaching career, I often found myself coming to cynical conclusions about the efficacy of planning. These fits of despair arrived when I scanned the horizon for large and important consequences of plans. The more abstract my viewpoint and demanding my hopes, the more trivial planning impacts appeared to be. At other times, however, when I turned my attention to what particular professionals were saying and doing, I experienced the opposite reaction: I observed meaningful and useful consequences of planning activities. Although modest and largely incremental, these efforts and their results filled me with hope.

For many years, I ignored this tension, teaching students to adopt a critical understanding of grand-scale planning failures (e.g., urban renewal). I encouraged them to develop a morally engaged, politically astute, and technically sound planning vocation on the small scale. Midway in the 1980s, however, I began searching for a way to reconcile these two views. I discovered, as I surveyed the literature, that others had traveled this path of inquiry. This chapter summarizes this research. It examines the methodological and ideological issues that have shaped research on planning effectiveness.

Research conducted in the past six decades on planning practice and its effectiveness in the United States has focused primarily on the activities and organizations of planner bureaucrats, analyzing how they plan in different political settings. Walker's national survey of the profession in 1939, Meyerson and Banfield's study of the Chicago Housing Authority in the early 1950s, and Altshuler's study of planning in Minneapolis and St. Paul ten years later are pivotal examples of research examining the effectiveness of the rational comprehensive planning process in the face of local political resistance. Numerous studies conducted since then have explored how planners cope with local politics and bureaucracy in their efforts to plan for the public interest.

Dalton's review (1989a) of this literature testifies to the profession's central concern with the effectiveness of different planning actions and methods in diverse political and organizational environments. A central theme in all the research studies has been to determine if planners have found ways to resolve the tension between the requirements for rational competence, the demands of political allegiance, and the hopes for democratic reform. I argue that the measure and meaning of effective planning has changed over time in response to the shifting institutional fortunes of the planning profession and changing fashion in research methods. Research that confidently started out as a test of how well and to what extent politicians and citizens follow the rational plans made by professional planners has ended up questioning whether rational planning is even a useful and reasonable approach to resolving urban problems.

THE STUDY OF PLANNING INSTITUTIONS

Planning as an Executive Function

Robert Walker conducted a national survey of planning activity in over thirty U.S. cities to evaluate the structural organization and functions of city planning. He was dismayed with how municipalities were using their planning commissions, physical development regulations, and master plans. An avid supporter of New Deal reforms, Walker asserted that the real estate boom of the 1920s had fostered city planning as a probusiness activity. His survey indicated that the independent planning commissions were neither independent nor particularly competent. Their members overwhelmingly represented the local business community (52 percent) and the wealthier professional residents (33 percent) (Walker 1941, 150). The commissions mainly employed zoning and subdivision controls to ensure against the fall of property values. This emphasis on securing the value of development meant that the commissions generally ignored issues of housing, employment, and health. According to Walker:

Planning commissions actually have devoted an overwhelming proportion of their time to zoning, streets, and parks, whether or not they have had comprehensive plans prepared involving other elements.... In several cities high officials admitted never having looked at comparatively recent and readily available plans prepared supposedly for their guidance and in general they expressed an uncomplimentary opinion of the comprehensive plan prepared by an outside consultant (1941, 33).

Furthermore, Walker stated, the consultants who drew up the plans were mainly engineers and architects, who focused on physical design and not on socioeconomic factors or organizational conditions. City planning, "both in its sponsorship [by local business interests] and in its technical applications [by architects and engineers]...was guided more or less rigidly along lines of physical reconstruction until brought to a shaking halt by the impact of economic depression" (1941, 36). He observed that the reliance on consultants posed a serious obstacle to the widespread employment of planners as civil servants. Consultants could deliver a physical blueprint, but, as outsiders, did not have the administrative authority to turn the plan into action.

Walker urged staff planners to use social and economic analysis in the formulation of city plans. He stated that effective planning coordinates and integrates the purposes, programs, and operations of different municipal departments:

Planning in the determination of policy can mean little more than the marshaling of available information and the presentation of alternative courses to be followed. Thus, it is essentially a research function. The final decision as to specific policies rests with elected representatives, i.e., with the council or with the executive and council together. If the only function of a planning agency were to make recommendations as to general policy, it might be attached to the council as well as to the executive. But, as we have observed, the full usefulness of a planning staff can be realized only if it is in a position to aid the executive in implementing the execution of policies and to aid in coordinating the planning done by several departments. Plans for the future can be realized only if daily decisions are influenced by them and if each operating agency is guided by consideration of overall planning (1941, 175–76).

Walker's ideas show the influence of the New Deal planning advocates who had worked on the National Resources Planning Board and other agencies that had promoted the institutionalization of planning as part of the executive powers of government. Charles Merriam (his thesis adviser) and Chicago School sociologists Louis Wirth (1964) and Ernest Burgess (1974) argued that linking comprehensive planning and regional government would overcome the fragmentation, political bias, and inefficiency of local planning institutions, which had been captured by business interests and were relying on planning consultants. Walker wanted to institutionalize planning as an executive branch function at the local level as it had been at the national level during the New Deal.

The Failure of the Federal Ideal

Walker had looked to the New Deal for his inspiration. The efficacy of executive-based planning at the federal level, however, proved far more limited than he and his colleagues had supposed. Martin Meyerson and Edward Banfield's case study (1955) of public housing in Chicago in the late 1940s and early 1950s illustrated how planning within the federally funded housing authority foundered on the rocks of racial prejudice, conflicting local political interests, the fragmentation of power, and, most significantly, the marginality and irrelevance of rational planning methods. The researchers observed:

> As the case study shows, the Authority made little use of social science or of any technical knowledge regarding social phenomena.... The knowledge the Authority most needed was not the kind that social scientists as such could supply. There was no reason to believe that a social scientist, or a planning technician using social science, would be better equipped, or even as well equipped as an administrator like Miss Wood [the executive director] or a lawyer like Fruchtman to chart the agency's opportunity area, to clarify and order its end-system, to delineate the alternative courses of action that were open to it, or to identify and evaluate the consequences that would probably attend each course of action (1955, 279, 281).

It is not surprising that Meyerson and Banfield's conclusions led them to eschew Progressive planning reform. Their work raised serious questions about the feasibility and even the desirability of using the comprehensive rational planning model to guide public decisions. Banfield remained the more skeptical of the two, as evidenced by his later work (1970). Meyerson, however, called for a middle-range policies planning approach, which he believed could bridge the gulf between planning ideas and local politics (1956). He felt that planners needed to be able to recognize the institutional and political realities of development and adapt to them.

Political Limitations of Comprehensive Planning

Altshuler's case study of Minneapolis–St. Paul planners asserts that their lack of institutional authority limited their efficacy. Planning, to be effective, must take on controversial and difficult problems. He observes that the tendency to equate the good plan with the successful plan—that is, the plan based on consensus—leaves important public goals unfulfilled. If planning focuses only on problems that lend themselves to consensus, the controversial issues will be ignored. Planners should not be deluded into thinking that the successful implementation of routine and noncontroversial planning actions means that effective planning has taken place (Altshuler 1965).

Altshuler holds that the biggest impediment to effective, comprehensive planning is citizen mistrust of government power. Although Americans supported the federal urban renewal and highway development programs of the late 1950s and early 1960s as efforts to strengthen the free market and to encourage local growth, they resist local projects that are not of obvious and direct benefit to them. Planners encountered three obstacles: the resistance of politicians and directors of other departments; the laws and fiscal constraints of local government; and their lack of executive authority.

Altshuler observes that the planning department was susceptible to the political sanction of elected officials, who did not hesitate to employ it, especially when planners proposed actions that would expand their influence and power.

> The Minneapolis planning budget...was cut back in 1960 after five years of rapid rise. The planners believed that they had been disciplined, in part for engaging in a jurisdictional dispute with the city engineer over who would do major streets planning, and in part for neglecting informal City Hall relationships in favor of the cultivation of outside groups and the local press.... Most city officials looked with disfavor on planners' assertions that their view was comprehensive. The heads of other agencies generally said without hesitation that they had no quarrel with planners so long as the planners did not try to tell them how to run their own departments (1965, 369).

Altshuler reports one interview in which "the city engineer of St. Paul told me that while he had no objection to letting city planners comment on his proposals for public works, he had no intention of working with them in the conception stage of project planning" (1965, 369).

Other local government agencies had greater discretion and authority than the planning agencies precisely because they had limited responsibilities and well-defined constituencies. By contrast, planning sought to shape the overall order and structure of city programs and development. Says Altshuler:

> Politicians dealt with this threat of competition by defining the planners' specialties as narrowly as possible. Again and again I was told that planners were specialists in the maintenance of property values by land-use regulation and/or that they were specialists in civic design (1965, 373).

Altshuler discusses the strategies that city planners pursued to reach their objectives. His focus shifts from the planning agency to the planning directors, and how they defined their jobs to achieve a sense of accomplishment. He tells how one planning director took the political risk of offending some city council members, but did not battle the private interest groups that held political influence. Another director found ways to do well the important tasks that no other agency was willing to do, such as conducting facility location studies and street improvement plans. Another director organized and reported information about the municipality's pressing problems, while emphasizing optimistic views of future solutions and growth. These efforts, however, neither met the comprehensive ideal nor placed planning on the public agenda. Local political practices, customs, and bureaucracy were too formidable an obstacle for local planners to launch serious initiatives.

Altshuler argues that planners were also blocked from implementing a comprehensive plan because of their contradictory beliefs:

> On the one hand, we have seen, planners believe that they should present crucial alternatives for public choice; on the other, they feel that they court political failure by acknowledging uncertainty. They preach that all problems and solutions are interrelated, and emphasize the virtues of honest comprehensiveness; yet they think that political success is possible only if they think optimistically and ignore areas of intense controversy (1965, 392).

According to Altshuler, planners overlook the contradictions by simultaneously praising the virtues of comprehensiveness and boasting of their grasp of political feasibility.

Altshuler's critique questions the efficacy of all planning activity. His observations of the Minnesota planners made them seem not only politically inept, but doomed from the outset. He observes that the lack of institutional and political authority for comprehensive planning under-mined the professional planners' efforts, while the language and beliefs of planning reflected a devastating political naiveté. In conclusion, Altshuler urges planners to enter into the politics of interest and com-promise as members of a moral community of professional planners with a clear vision of the specific principles that should guide practice.

FROM PLAN TO PLANNER

From Cynicism to Hope

Francine Rabinowitz conducted survey research in New Jersey in the 1960s on the relationship between organizational structure and planning effectiveness—the same concern that Walker had pursued two decades earlier. Her survey analysis (1969) uncovered that differences in organi-zational authority generated only modest differences in the conduct of planning, in contrast to Walker's findings. In part, this shift reflected the widespread adoption of planning as a staff function of municipal gov-ernment in the 1950s and 1960s.[1]

Having concluded that organizational structure has little influence on planning efficacy, Rabinowitz introduces the concept of social roles. She argues that the differences in planning effectiveness can be traced to the roles planners choose to play in three different kinds of political settings: the executive-centered, the competitive, and the fragmented. These set-tings foster three kinds of roles: technician, broker, and mobilizer, re-spectively. Her message is clear: To achieve effectiveness planners should adopt the role that fits the political environment. Rabinowitz ignores the broader issues of planning as an institutional activity and as a contribu-tor to urban reform. Traditional planning goals no longer serve as stan-dards of good planning. The success of practitioners depends on their ability to achieve the goals they have set for themselves and to adopt the appropriate role in their particular political setting.

Rabinowitz also analyzes the resources available to planers and the constraints they face in each of the roles. As resources, she lists expertise, time, position, and access to others. She perceives only two constraints: the ability of the planner to act politically (as either broker or mobilizer) and the norms of the planning community, which discourage adopting political roles. Rabinowitz's assessment offers a clear path for the im-provement of planning effectiveness. She wanted to put to rest the then common image of the planner as the expert offering advice independent of the political interests and deliberations of the city council. Planners need to receive better theoretical and methodological preparation and also need to learn how to assume the roles that will allow them to put this knowledge to use in political deliberations. Rabinowitz's call for a politicized planning fails, however, to explore the tension between such a call and the demands of professional socialization. Her account projects a too-neat separation between the local political system and the professional's role and too abstract a notion of effectiveness.

Shifting the focus from institutional efficacy to individual action enabled Rabinowitz to avoid the skepticism exhibited by Meyerson and Banfield and Altshuler. Optimism was the pervasive mood in the profession at the time she was conducting her research. Planning employment was rapidly increasing and confidence in the promise of regional and national planning was still widespread. Hence, her decision to shift the research focus from planning organization to planners reflected both a change in method and a shift within the profession from a skeptical to a hopeful outlook. Her definition and measure of effectiveness emphasize the functional contributions of individual planners:

> Effective participation may be defined as the intervention of the expert at all levels where decisions vitally affect the course of a city's development. The planner's ability to modify the system of people and space in favor of the preferred alternative is also a mark of his effectiveness. The effectiveness of planning can be determined in three situations: (1) when the expert initiates a planning policy that meets no opposition, and it is enacted; (2) when the planner prevents a policy he opposes from being enacted; and (3) when the planner initiates a policy that meets with opposition but that is nevertheless enacted (1969, 7).

Rabinowitz's analysis of effectiveness ignores traditional planning issues and focuses instead on the planner's achievement of his or her own purposes. The shift in research attention from effective planning institutions to effective role performance makes the study of individual planning actions more compelling as a source of evidence for judging effectiveness. The shift also makes professionals the main audience for the research, because they are both the subjects of study and the agents of change. Although Rabinowitz criticizes professional socialization for being too narrow and unpolitical, she constricts the definition of planning to the activities of individual professionals.

Rabinowitz argues that the mature professions, like medicine, possess a set of norms that define membership and practice independently of the practitioner's occupational setting. Planners do not yet have a core of professional values:

> There is little information on the factors leading to differential effectiveness in the expert's participation in decision-making in different cities. There is not even agreement on what they are. Most practicing professionals explain effectiveness in terms of factors peculiar to specific situations. In large part, their failure to draw generalizations can be attributed to the fact that most urban experts are members of professions that have not yet become fully professionalized (1969, 7).

Rabinowitz presumes that the planner's discretion flows only partially from a shared discipline. Lawyers and doctors meet certain minimum standards and protocols of practice on which they are formally and informally tested. These protocols legitimize their authority. Because planners do not yet enjoy a protocol that exists independently of their organizational position, their professional judgments are constrained by their political context. Rabinowitz believes, however, that one day planners will share in the autonomy of the more established professions.[2] She urges planners to engage in political activity to enhance the profession's status.

The research discussed so far relied on theoretical and professional norms to evaluate the actions and responses of practitioners. However, as Perloff (1957) observed, the profession was still in its adolescence, and the standards of efficacy were nebulous. Hence, analysts adopted a comparative approach to understanding planning effectiveness.

Two Sides of the Story

Wright's survey (1970) of planning directors and city executives (mayors and city managers) in several hundred U.S. cities with populations of 25,000 to 250,000 residents compared responses on characteristics of directors and executives, on descriptions of planning activities, on assessments of planning performance, and on preferences for planning change. Like Rabinowitz, Wright controlled for type of planning organization and type of municipal government, but unlike her, he treated these institutional arrangements as either aids or obstacles to the actions of planning directors.

The study showed a high degree of similarity in the responses of planners and executives to the questions. Only modest differences emerged in response to questions about the value of planning. Fifty-three percent of the executives rated local planning to be very good or excellent, compared to only forty-two percent of planning directors. The results were the same for the ratings of planning commission performance. Slightly more than half the executives (56 percent) claimed they considered it a primary obligation to support the planning director on controversial issues, but only 43 percent of the planning directors perceived that they had full executive support. Half of the planners felt that their primary source of support was the planning commission. Wright observes:

> These results suggest that the planner is caught in an institutional cross-fire between chief executives and planning commissions. The secular movement toward executive-centered planning has been extensively and solidly sold and executives see planning as a general function for which they have an important responsibility. But from the planner's perspective and institutional position the vestiges of independence as exemplified in a commission orientation still holds an honorable heritage.... The heritage is not only honorable but highly practical and politic. The shifting personnel and preferences among municipal executives dispose the planner to hedge his bets in terms of institutional support (1970, 85).

Wright found that most of the differences in the perception of planning's role were determined by the structure of the local municipal government rather than by the institutional structure of planning. City managers were more likely than mayors to agree that comprehensive planning was the most important activity of planning staff and that the staff should be involved in presenting planning proposals to the city council. Wright held that the institutionalization of planning had led to a shared view of planning priorities among city managers and planners, but it has also preempted the institutional authority of planners (1970, 94–95). Wright was hopeful that planners could find ways to turn their institutional incorporation to advantage. Ten years later, this optimism would wear thin.

The Survival of Rational Planning

Research in the late 1970s and early 1980s on planner attitudes and beliefs raised serious questions about whether members of the profession still believed in rational planning. Galloway and Edwards (1982) measured attachment to the values of rational planning within a large national sample that included both city planners and city managers. Like Wright, they discovered few differences in the responses of the two groups. However, they found one startling response: City managers valued comprehensive planning much more than the planners did. Galloway and Edwards concluded that the organizational and occupational expectations of the respondents as public bureaucrats appear to shape their beliefs about planning, rather than the respondents imposing their sense of professional purpose on the bureaucracy (1982, 193). This finding challenged the prevailing view among planning analysts and theorists that expert knowledge played a crucial role in shaping professional planning practice.

Rabinowitz did not explore the commitment of planning directors to rational planning. She was more concerned with how their adoption of various different political roles enhanced or limited their efficacy. By the mid-1970s, however, comparative survey research results showed how the institutionalization of planning within local bureaucracies and the limitations of government employment were shaping the expectations planners entertained and even undermining their belief in the viability of the professional norms that a decade earlier seemed to be developing as a powerful source of legitimacy.

The research shift from questions of effective planning to effective planners occurred as the profession grew in numbers, but not in power. Analysts offered advice on how planners might adopt roles and strategies to inform, lobby, and organize interests and constituencies for planning objectives, but their robust belief in the possibility that planners could be fully empowered participants in the local political arena did not realistically address the efficacy issue. Many planners still considered the politics of interest either illegitimate or heavily weighted against them and the disenfranchised, whose interests they embraced.

ADVOCACY PLANNING

Research findings documenting the antagonism between the rational planning method and planners' endorsement of political action raised serious questions about the efficacy of the profession. Evidence that planners believed in rational comprehensive planning less than their manager bosses did undermined hopes for profession building. The identity crisis was exacerbated by the doubts raised from the left. Advocacy researchers, influenced by the radicalism of the New Left, championed a militant version of Progressive reform. They evaluated the federal freeway construction, urban renewal, and public housing programs and determined that they had fostered social injustices (Gans 1982; Hartman 1964; 1971a; 1971b).

The advocate planners criticized their colleagues for acquiescing in the use of government support to enact the plans of the powerful. In their professional positions as state employees, planners were misusing the rational model and its public interest rationale to legitimize urban redevelopment and suburban expansion policies that displaced the poor and excluded minorities (Hartman 1975). The advocates called for a more widespread and persistent commitment to social justice. They shared with their mainstream colleagues a confidence in professional expertise, but disagreed with them on whose interests should be served through the use of rational planning knowledge. Advocates conducted research that uncovered the abuse of power and the ideological use of plans. Altshuler had claimed that the powerful often ignore the plans made by professional planners. Advocacy research showed that when the powerful do use these plans, it is often to achieve the insidious goal of justifying private and political interests as public goods.

Community Planning

The research influenced by the advocacy approach focused primarily on policies, programs, and politics, but not on planners, with the exception of *Guerrillas in the Bureaucracy* (1974) by Carolyn and Martin Needleman. The Needlemans studied community planners in nine big city planning agencies and found three out of four "acting as administrative guerrillas or insurgents" (1974, 158). The authors recount brief tales of political organizing and institutional finagling among seventy-seven planners who took the side of community groups while still working as city employees.

In their brief historical introduction, the Needlemans assert that the failure of urban renewal programs caused city planners to question their beliefs. Deeply involved in these renewal efforts, city planners could not easily avoid sharing responsibility for the often uneven and unjust results:

> For them, urban renewal marked an end of innocence for city planning. The casualties of urban renewal included not only the poor and the minorities whose needs were deferred and homes demolished, but also the planners' concept of the "general public interest." The program had purported to improve the city as a whole, but its benefits and burdens were clearly distributed very unevenly among those who lived in and used the city.... Once stripped of the mask of "serving the public interest," all the activities of city planners can be seen as service to a particular set of clients, with other poten-

tial clients losing out.... The traditional beneficiaries of city planning have been the city's white, affluent, business elite. Therefore, according to this argument, planning departments should try to balance the profession's activities by extending advocacy services to those groups neglected in the past— the city's residents, especially the poor and the minorities. In this way the conflicting interests of all groups will be represented in contests over specific planning proposals (1974, 30–31).

Advocacy planning offered a compelling agenda for the rejuvenation of the Progressive reform spirit that had inspired analysts like Walker. Only in this version, government was not an ally, but the arena for political competition and struggle that had for too long been captured by the interests of wealthy elites. Advocacy planning championed reforms to make the politics of local planning work fairly for all.

The Needlemans' research, however, revealed more dilemmas than clear-cut success stories. Efforts to encourage professional planning bureaucrats to be advocates for poor, minority neighborhoods produced mixed results for both residents and planners. The Needlemans' analysis outlined the impediments to effective advocacy that existed in most institutional settings. Despite their skepticism, the Needlemans hoped that community planning efforts would endure. The fact that most did not further convinced many left-wing critics that advocacy planning was a well-intentioned, but misguided attempt to counter the larger structural forces making for unfair urban development. The critics asserted that the government institutions that the advocates hoped would serve the poor, serve the interests of the rich by design. Therefore, the promise of a truly rational planning that responds to the needs of all people can be realized only through the removal of class distinctions. They believed that professional planners employed in the bureaucracy could contribute little to this revolutionary effort.

Many liberal analysts, convinced of the legitimacy of the advocates' criticisms, looked for ways to assimilate them into the profession. Thus, they redefined advocacy as a political role available to the practitioner, in contrast, for example, to the Needlemans, who defined planners' roles in relation to the institutional challenges of advancing the needs of minority and working-class communities in different political settings. The liberal analysts believed that planners could assimilate the critical insights of the advocates without abandoning their belief in the rational legitimacy of planning or changing the institutions of local government. Individual professionals could reconcile the political and the rational.

ASSIMILATING THE POLITICAL AND THE RATIONAL

A False Dichotomy

Michael Vasu introduced his national survey of planning professionals by assuring his readers that the commitment to planning, even national social planning, enjoyed widespread support. He asserted that the demand for professional planners would continue to increase and that the problems in the profession rested not with planners' institutional powers, but with their individual power:

> In other words, regardless of any lofty goals conceived and formulated by any planning structure or law that might be enacted, one essential theoretical perspective that endures is the role orientations of the planners themselves. It is difficult to underestimate the capacity of planning professionals to implement preexisting ideas regardless of the legal-structural framework established by government (1979, 5).

Like Rabinowitz, Vasu saw individual planners and their roles as proper objects of study. His survey revealed that fewer than 8 percent of planners agreed that plans were neutral technical documents, while an even smaller portion (fewer than 4 percent) claimed that planning was a strictly technical activity. In contrast, almost three out of four concurred that planning was value oriented.

Vasu classified planners by using an index that was "conceptually organized to form a continuum reflecting two diverse poles: specifically, the traditional conception of the planner as technician and the converse, a role definition that rejects this position for a more policy oriented perspective" (1979, 84).[3] The classification revealed that only about 20 percent of the planners preferred advocacy as a professional role, compared to 48 percent who favored a technical role and 32 percent who adopted a moderately political role. Furthermore, when Vasu asked about attitudes toward comprehensive planning, he found that only slightly more than half thought government-sponsored comprehensive rational planning was possible in a pluralistic society. However, when Vasu asked respondents if the United States should establish a federal agency responsible for comprehensive planning on a national basis, 65 percent agreed.

The results are more ambiguous than Vasu suggests in his commentary. They downright contradict the conventional model of rational comprehensive planning, which Vasu is attempting to measure. The vast majority of Vasu's respondents admitted that neither planning documents nor planning processes were the products of detached technical analysis. However, fewer than 30 percent preferred the role of political advocate. Vasu sets up a false dichotomy. Planners' rejection of advocacy does not automatically make them technocrats, as his classification suggests. Planners reluctantly perceive themselves to be expert technicians, because this fits their institutional realities. They must play the part of the competent expert to ensure the legitimacy of their plans and advice. Planners, however, do not use the rational planning model as a guide for their practical planning activity, but rather as a rhetorical protocol to legitimize their activity within the city and county government institutions where planning occurs in the United States. The planners who Vasu found were harboring doubts about government-sponsored comprehensive planning were not so much questioning the efficacy of planning comprehensively as expressing their frustration with their lack of institutional power to make effective comprehensive plans at the local level. This explains why so many who would adopt a technical role in one portion of a survey could also favor forming a national planning agency in another.

Bridging the Gap

Beth Howe and Jerome Kaufman (1979) used social science survey methods to explore how planners cope with the gap between the rational and the political. They designed their interview questionnaire to distinguish among planners committed mainly to the application of rational expertise (technicians), those concerned primarily with putting their knowledge to use serving (and advocating for) the public good (politicians), and those seeking both (hybrids).

> The former type is supposed to be technically expert, value neutral, and responsible to the public through the political decision-makers he serves.... The latter [the politician], as an ideal type, is more value committed, more responsive to the groups or issues he thinks are particularly related to the public interest, and more willing to work actively through the political system to see that plans are implemented (1979, 246).

Howe and Kaufman divided their respondents into groups of ideal types with distinct social roles. They ignored the traditional dichotomy between the independent commission whose members decide on the technical merits of a proposal and the executive-serving planning department in which good plans are those that serve the purposes of a political regime. Rather, Howe and Kaufman examined the functional roles that practitioners chose to adopt. This left them free to tie the quest for planning effectiveness to individual learning, innovation, and adaptation, rather than to institutional reform or professionalization. According to Howe and Kaufman, technicians worry about rationality (Did we do it right?), while politicians tend to care more about political relationships (Did we do much good?). Howe and Kaufman found that most planners—the hybrids—worry about both sorts of issues.

Howe and Kaufman found similar results as Vasu, despite differences in their methodology. Planners classified as politicians or hybrids approved such activities as lobbying, building political support, working covertly, and increasing government authority for planning more frequently than did technicians (1979, 249). Although they do not explicitly rate the desirability of the different roles, their classification scheme tends to favor the center over the extremes. The predominance of hybrids indicates a preference among respondents for practice that combines political and technical skills. The Howe and Kaufman classification implies that effective planners are likely to be hybrids whose role mixing bridges the gap between theory and practice; rationality and politics. Planners can learn to adopt hybrid roles that will allow them to apply theoretical knowledge to the complex and risky demands of politics.[4]

Expectation and Reality

James Mayo (1982) used the Howe and Kaufman classification to assess the relationship between work roles and job satisfaction among a national sample of professional planners. He tested (controlling for the statistical effects of many other variables) whether the relationship between expectations and ability in technical and political roles would predict job satisfaction. He found that the degree of organizational constraint on the pursuit of important political activities was the best predictor of job dissatisfaction for all types of planners. Job satisfaction was strongly tied to the fit between the political roles planners expected to play and the actual roles organizational circumstances allowed them to play. The capacity to play technical roles was much less significant in predicting satisfaction. Mayo's results were similar to those produced by Galloway and Edwards and echoed the findings of the earlier case studies by Meyerson and Banfield and Altshuler.

Mayo's findings provide evidence of the frustration planners were feeling over the institutional marginality of the profession in the late

1970s. His work gives reason to revise the functional optimism of Howe and Kaufman's classification of the hybrid planner. Mayo's findings suggest that the hybrids were not combining rational detachment and political advocacy to better achieve planning goals, so much as adopting this mix to cope with the organizational constraints on their political authority. Hybrid and advocacy roles proved satisfying to those few planners whose organizational setting allowed them political authority, but most planners who adopted some sort of political role expressed frustration and dissatisfaction with their ability to achieve planning objectives.

The failure to obtain executive authority for planning, combined with the fiscal crises and growing conservative attacks of the late 1970s, made meaningful occupational commitments to a political role, whether as advocate, insider, or hybrid, increasingly unrealistic for most planning practitioners. Vasu's optimism about the advent of national planning was way off the mark. Even the Needlemans' guarded hope for increasing the political influence of planners proved excessive.

A NEW LOOK AT INSTITUTIONS

Liberal theorists like Harvey Perloff (1974) had presumed that planning was a useful and important activity that informed, organized, and justified government actions. Generally, American society shared a belief in the egalitarian principles and purposes of the modern welfare state. Analysts and practitioners drew on this consensus to justify their actions. The hope for the introduction of rational comprehensive planning in the United States rested precariously on continued public support for and belief in the expanding welfare state. Both radicals and conservatives cut short the celebration of this consensus.

From the Left

The intellectual ferment of the New Left spread among the analysts and students of urban problems in the late 1960s. Advocacy planning was an important predecessor for this more radical critique of the liberal welfare state urban and of the suburban policies initiated in the New Deal. The efforts by the liberal Kennedy and Johnson administrations to increase the redistributive impact of welfare state programs, especially the aid programs for urban areas, had increased expectations of what government could provide and, subsequently, criticism of the limits of the programs.

Radical analysts took longstanding populist critiques and imposed on them Marxist rationales. They deployed the instruments of rational analysis with vigor. Conventional analysts and even the more militant advocates, they argued, were blinded by social and political assumptions that only a critical social science could expose. The radicals argued that the rational model was not a truth-seeking method, but an ideological scaffolding that cloaked biased inquiry as objective analysis. Overcoming subtle and pervasive class bias required the faithful application of critical, usually Marxist-inspired, social science.

The leftists argued that capitalist accumulation and class struggle shaped the problems of cities and regions. They discredited the hopes of planning professionals for reform and innovation. Empirical studies analyzed how the liberal state (and the planners its employed) created spatial policies to protect the system of accumulation from the consequences of its own excess (Harvey 1975; Roweis and Scott 1978; Roweis 1983; Smith and Feagin 1987), channeled capital into infrastructure and real estate investment to accommodate cyclical crises in capital accumulation (Harvey 1982), and fragmented class conflict into local political conflicts (Tabb and Sawers 1978). Some analysts described urban renewal in big city cores and the rapid development of mixed use urban centers on the suburban periphery in terms of class conflicts, compromises, and coalitions (Beauregard 1978; Fainstein and Fainstein 1983; Gottdeiner 1985; Logan and Molotch 1987). These radical analysts criticized the pluralist beliefs held by many professional planners that justice gets distilled through political compromise and the competition of diverse interests. Study after study heaped up evidence of the exploitation, cooptation, and subordination of the powerless by urban policies that were producing uneven development and social inequality (Katznelson 1981; Mollenkopf 1983; Smith 1984).

Despite numerous and important differences in theory and method, these diverse research studies led to a common criticism of planning: Planning schemes to do good end up helping the rich and powerful get more wealth and power, while policing or buying off the dispossessed. The radicals observed that liberal planning analysts, in adopting models of bourgeois social science, were naturally blind to this process. Because of the ideological assumptions of conventional analysis, they failed to consider the capitalist institutional practices that were setting the urban development agenda. The Marxists offered a theoretical alternative that tied the emancipation of the capitalist city from injustice to the rigorous application of a pure social science. They argued for the objectivity of their ideological position, which opposed the interests of capital. They offered class struggle as the engine of change and the working class as the agent of emancipation.[5]

This research left little room for planning reforms and virtually no room for meaningful professional action. For the most part, the leftists either dismissed the influence of professional planners as marginal (Beauregard 1983; Fainstein and Fainstein 1978; Harvey 1978) or elevated planning to a menacing ally of the wealthy and powerful that tirelessly supports and orders capitalist spatial development (Kravitz 1970; Roweis and Scott 1978). A few radical analysts observed that planners, as relatively low-paid and exploited urban managers, were closer to the proletariat than the capitalists whose interests their employers served. They asserted that planners' commitment to professional ideology had blinded them to their real class roots (Angotti 1978).

The structural claims of class analysis dismissed traditional planning and professional planners as impediments (either major or marginal) to the sort of progress and justice that liberals had claimed to be offering. Questions about the efficacy of professional planning were irrelevant within this framework. The Marxist critics quite unintentionally supplied powerful explanations for the frustration and dissatisfaction survey researchers like Mayo had documented among planning professionals in the 1970s. The lesson was clear, even if the strategy was not: Stop trying to work from within to reform the system. Change it.

The legacy of positivism haunted critical Marxist social science research. The left-wing analysts presumed that scientific and practical knowledge were dialectically commensurate, not paradoxical and antagonistic. Tied to the scientific method of analysis, the Marxist researchers applied criteria of success based on rational expectations that cut across cases, individuals, and settings in ways that abstracted from the particular and the practical. They relied on their own dialectical version of the rational prototype. Although the Marxist researchers wanted changes in the entire system, rather than in the roles professional planners chose within the system, the analysts still expected their ideas to inspire practical efforts among planners—in this case—to resist and change established class relationships. Activists and organizers were expected to judge the efficacy of their practice against the rational standards of scientific class analysis.

Lily Hoffman (1989) studied the compatibility of leftist-inspired political activism and professional work. Comparing left-leaning activist planners and doctors over twenty years (1968–1988), she identifies three distinct political stages experienced by members of both radical reform movements. Generally, professional activists first conduct service delivery to the poor and disenfranchised; then they develop empowerment strategies; and then they finally enact theoretically inspired efforts at social transformation.

Hoffman reluctantly concludes that the radical planners were not very effective. The planners' early service delivery and advocacy strategies were criticized by community activists as being out of touch. Their efforts at empowering the poor met with similar criticism:

> Attempts to mobilize communities to demand their rights; to collapse distinctions between professionals, paraprofessionals, and clients; to transfer expertise; and to create community control through participatory democracy and decentralization were satisfactory neither to the activists, the community, nor the sponsors of reforms (1989, 196).

When activist planners adopted political roles to transform the system, they lost their client and organizational supports. Community members perceived the professionals' efforts to be cooptive, while sponsors perceived them to be misdirected:

> Activists discovered that their legitimacy before their clients was based on their narrow and "relevant" technical knowledge; before their sponsors, on their "apolitical" role and general social acceptance. This meant that in rejecting technical aid and adopting nontechnical roles on political grounds, activists undermined their legitimacy and thus their ability to act (1989, 198).

The activists had turned to social theory to guide them beyond the limits of service delivery and empowerment, but the radical explanations of structural contradictions and social injustice failed them as well, because these analyses served to draw the activists away from direct action by promoting "renewed claims to knowledge, increased social distance from clients, and professionally defined service objectives" (1989, 198). The compelling analysis of systematic class inequality undermined the legitimacy of liberal reform and cast into serious doubt the entire planning enterprise. Despite their attractiveness as a rationale for basic social change and improvement, these structural claims had difficulty finding their way into practice. Peter Marris explains the dilemma:

> In the Marxist tradition of social analysis the agent of change is, of course, the working class as a whole, as it grows into self awareness. But if capitalist

relationships can be represented as sustaining themselves by a mutually re-inforcing structure of economic, political and ideological control, then the working class appears to be incorporated in that structure, its institutions and ideology manipulated into compatibility with the requirements of capitalism. Combining a dialectic of class struggle with a structural analysis produces an ambiguous conception of the working class as at once inside the capitalist structure, captive, and yet capable of reconstituting itself outside it. This ambiguity tends to make radical strategies seem ineffectual: they set out to help people grasp their position within a capitalist society and organize to change it, but the analysis is so overwhelming in the scope and control of the forces it describes as to make any local, countervailing response seem futile (1982b, 112).

The imperatives of radical structural reform proved more demanding than those proposed by liberals, which instilled a gap between leftist theory and the professional's practical judgment. The leftists asked practitioners to throw away the protective protocol of technical objectivity and embrace a prototype of rationality that challenges the legitimacy of society's most central and powerful institutions, including the organizations that empower and employ planners.

Left-wing arguments that detailed the systemic ties between private corporate interests and public policy gave rise to cynical assessments of the possibility of change. Activist planners turned passive and gave up devising practical and relevant proposals based on the structural critiques. Practitioners began to be attracted to the schemes of the neoconservatives, which began to take practical shape with the election of conservative regimes in the 1980s. Conservative ideas began permeating planners' employing institutions. The federal withdrawal of its fiscal and administrative commitments to planning undermined the institutional support and legitimacy of government planners. What were liberal planners to do?

From the Right

Neoconservative planning critics from within the field echoed the ideas of Hayek (1944), complaining about the abandonment of physical planning by the university and by professionals pursuing social reform objectives in the expanded welfare state. To the neoconservatives, the tradition of artistry and design had been sullied by the imposition of a social science logic and the desire for reform. They believed that planning education and research should again focus on issues of land use. Planning should remain sensitive to social and economic consequences, but it should reject the critical notions of those "social science Ph.D.'s—who invaded the field of planning in the last twenty years believing that the world responds predictably to buttons and levers, and that they really knew which buttons to push and which levers to pull" (Raymond 1978, 1).

The neoconservatives emphasized the freedom of individuals within the operation of markets. The powers of the state that merit support are those that sustain market institutions. State policies that pursue the objectives of public welfare—for example, redistributive welfare programs and social insurance schemes—undermine the foundations of liberty because they erode the market. Even modest efforts to redistribute public goods and private wealth can threaten the integrity of the competitive market. Government should lay down the property and exchange rules, but should not play favorites.

Whereas, back in the 1940s, Hayek believed that government planners should use the modest powers of land use control to cope with the frictions and externalities that accompany change in local land markets, more recent neoconservatives were less tolerant. Some, like Edward Banfield, contemptuously dismissed planned reforms (1970). They held that instead of making for a fairer distribution of public goods, comprehensive planning schemes actually introduce new inequities.

Some neoconservatives portray planners as relatively powerful ideologues who use their sinecures in government bureaucracy to expand the influence of the state over the affairs of private citizens. Kristol (1977; 1983), Glazer (1988), and Berger (1987) blame planners (along with other related professionals) for contributing to the proliferation of welfare state institutions, established to "solve" social problems. They see planners as part of a new class of liberal and left-wing intellectuals threatening the integrity of capitalist democracy (Bruce-Briggs 1979). They assert that the futility of comprehensive planning rests in the inability of planners to grasp the complexity of the problems. Their efforts to do so have imposed an ever-expanding, but useless, bureaucracy of experts and research.[6]

These neoconservative ideas, which shaped the federal policies of the Republican regimes of the 1980s and early 1990s, have long been popular at the state and local levels in the United States. Locally elected officials tend to approve of the use of police and tax powers to support local markets and to promote private business ventures that promise to foster economic growth. The widespread adoption of such policies, especially by suburban municipalities, has long encouraged possessive individualism and privatization. Some municipalities have even tried to bring the virtues of competitive markets to professional planning (Savas 1981; Tiebout 1956; Warren 1964). The liberal schemes for public-private partnerships were replaced with the conservatives' proposals for privatization, deregulation, and cutback planning. Entrepreneurship began to displace public service as the guide for public planners and administrators (Hoch 1985).

Planning consultants began to fashion packages of planning policies for the growing marketplace of local government. Instead of preparing comprehensive plans subsidized by the federal government, they conducted fiscal analyses of annexation proposals or proposed development impact fees. The public interest and the bottom line converged. Many in-house staff planners had to find conservative justifications for their existence. The roles of cop and broker, rather than advocate and technician, dominated in planning circles. Liberal talk was out and business talk was in. Planners were called on to implement local regulations to help police the local land market against extreme forms of speculative and environmental abuse and unwanted land uses. They were asked to market the environmental qualities of the local jurisdiction to attract business and residential wealth. They justified their activities with the rationale that obtaining valuable development improves the community's fiscal health by enhancing land values and increasing tax revenues. Liberal planners felt the squeeze.

PLANNERS IN CONTEXT

Planners in search of their identity were caught between the cynical conclusions of both left- and right-wing analysts. Planning practitioners Bruce McClendon and Ray Quay offered a plucky response. They cleverly sidestepped the ideological debates with a compromise strategy.

The Business of Government

Mastering Change (McClendon and Quay 1988) is an excellent example of practitioners' redefining effectiveness by pasting together liberal and neoconservative ideas about how planning should be organized and how planners should function. They revise the professional protocol to help planners come to grips with their increasingly marginal and precarious institutional position. McClendon and Quay address planners as individuals (not as members of a professional community, social class, political community, party, or coalition). Their assumed audience is planning directors with authority over a part of the local government bureaucracy, whose attachment to the old has left them unable to cope with the new. These planners went into the profession expecting to exercise government authority over private powers, but are faced with a period of fiscal retrenchment in which governments are cutting back budgets and asking planners to find new sources of revenue and pursue business growth. Local governments now must compete with other jurisdictions for a solvent tax base and must anticipate and respond to the rapidly changing uncertainties of economic cycles and political shifts. This changing and competitive environment requires public sector agencies to adopt the management style of private sector organizations:

> Competition is the American way, and the planning profession has suffered because the competitive spirit hasn't been instilled in enough public sector planners and managers. Competition heightens awareness and sensitivity to changes in the environment; that is one of the reasons why the private sector is quicker and more aggressive than the public sector in changing its mix of products and services (McClendon and Quay 1988, 4).

McClendon and Quay point to the commonality of problems faced by planners and by private sector managers. They conclude that the management innovation schemes that work for the private manager should also be useful to the public sector planner, though admittedly business and government are not the same:

> Under a government, individuals relinquish authority over some of their rights and, in return, the government promises to ensure that all of their rights will be protected.... The important point is that the basis for the trust between government and those being governed is not monetary, but individual rights.
>
> Of course, government cannot protect these rights without some monetary exchange, and this is why government is like a business. To provide this protection, and fulfill the trust, it does with those rights as it believes is best. One thing it does is exert its authority over the right of personal possession so that in order to own or use property, individuals must pay a tax. But a government is not a business and it is the nature of its trust that makes it different (1988, 237).

They argue that public sector bureaucracies provide a set of organizational opportunities that parallel those in the private sector. However, these public agencies have languished because practitioners adopted inefficient bureaucratic modes of action in public agency work, rather than the more efficient forms of management of the competitive corporate world. McClendon and Quay conceive of government as the mediator between competing individual rights. Planners, like corporate managers, should shape their practice to understand and direct the competition. The planner should think of the developer who complains about the burdens of local regulation and the citizen who organizes against the proposed group home as customers with rights. The planner's job is to help meet the customers' desires, but, of course, without giving the store away. Thus, the planner should charge fees and cut deals for the municipality to get a piece of the action.

McClendon and Quay show planners how to repackage everyday bureaucratic practice into simple and specialized chunks of action that meet the needs and demands of the various public customers who show up at city hall. As they sell bits of long-range hope wrapped around short-range projects, planners can adapt to changing political demands in a way that satisfies both their bosses and customers, while enhancing their own organizational importance. Instead of using the protocol of the objective civil servant serving the public interest, planners should adopt the protocol of the public entrepreneur serving the full range of citizen-customer desires.

This effort to resolve the longstanding antagonism between liberal and conservative values is not fully successful. McClendon and Quay provide a list of "25 components of a winning strategy for personal success" (1988, 246), which are mainly self-improvement guidelines. The authors fail to see the numerous contradictions within their list. For instance, one imperative urges planners to adopt the boss's value system, while another tells planners to become a leader. There are many such conflicts: deliver quality versus doing more with less; being sensitive to the political considerations of superiors versus listening and attending to citizen clients. Each maxim on its own may have merit, but as a group they point to contradictory choices and dilemmas. McClendon and Quay avoid the conflict by urging planners to use the maxim that is most appropriate for a particular situation. The maxims are not moral or theoretical concepts, but elements of a rhetorical strategy for enhancing the persuasiveness of the planner and for fostering an acceptance of the need for multiple professional identities. The planner should tailor her style to meet the needs and desires of various clients in the competition for public goods.

McClendon and Quay state that planners can increase their power by shifting their commitments to meet the changing needs and desires of subordinates, clients, and superiors. Effective professional planners enhance the efficiency of their organizations by reducing the conflict inherent to competitors vying for their objectives. Planners should sell planning, not a plan. The McClendon and Quay concept of planning effectiveness differs greatly from that of Robert Walker in 1941. Planners no longer guide the executive authority, but are quasi-privatized public managers.

McClendon and Quay overlook the profound differences between government organization and business corporation. They use the conservatives' emphasis on market to transform political disputes into competition among preferences. The planner as departmental entrepreneur and salesperson offers practitioners who are feeling the squeeze between conservative public officials and a fragile organizational position a new rhetorical defense. It is unlikely that planners putting the authors' maxims into practice will get better results than their colleagues who are committed to public service, but they will be able to reassure themselves and others of the appropriateness of the actions they feel compelled to take.

WHEREFORE DEMOCRATIC PLANNING?

By the 1980s, the prototype of the rational plan had lost most of its appeal and luster. The rational model showed great promise when the federal government was subsidizing programs grounded in the model and academics were busy refining and expanding its meaning. Though early research on planning effectiveness and on planners found little fit between rational plans and practical policies, students and professionals could still find room for the improvement of and innovation in rational planning. The case studies of Meyerson and Banfield (1955) and Altshuler (1965), which focused on the relationship between planning and politics, gave way to research that focused on the role performance of individual planners and their effectiveness (Howe and Kaufman 1985; Rabinowitz 1969; Vasu 1979). As political and institutional support for planning diminished, analysts narrowed their focus to what planners could control—their own actions.

The shift in focus to the individual professional was accompanied by serious criticism of rational planning. In the early 1960s, advocate planners had raised questions about rational planning, which challenged its presupposition of consensus. Radical criticism in the 1970s went much deeper, questioning the value of government planning in a capitalist society. This critical tradition, which flourished in university planning programs, raised doubts about the legitimacy of professional planning. The crises among academics had very little to do, however, with the practical world of planners in their local government bureaucracy.

When the conservatives won the presidency in 1980 and quickly dismantled many federal fiscal and program supports for planning, many practitioners were cast adrift from the liberal institutional moorings that justified their efforts to push local reforms. Advocate planners, who had been the planning heroes of the 1960s and early 1970s, were portrayed by the neoconservatives as self-serving parasites who lobbied the liberal state to provide programs that would make use of their expertise. To the conservatives, these champions of redistributive justice constituted a particularly insidious special interest group in that they claimed that they acted for the good of others. While right-wing cynicism had little impact on the ranks of the faithful, it did reinforce the public's ambivalence about the role of experts in public affairs.

Some practitioners hastily scrambled to cobble together an eclectic hodgepodge of liberal and conservative beliefs in handbooks of hope that rationalized the retreat from advocacy planning and planning engaged in municipal reform. Planner-entrepreneurs adopted the language and practices of the traditional enemies of planning to formulate the imperatives of the 1980s. Rational comprehensive planning became corporate strategic planning. Cities were firms and planners their middle managers offering schemes for besting the institutional bottom line. An effective planning department was one that enhanced city revenues; an effective planner, one who satisfied the powerful patron or wealthy customer.

In the 1980s, as Americans turned their backs on the disenfranchised, planners could no longer rely on the consensus support of welfare reform as a source of legitimacy. The introduction of the conventions of the capitalist marketplace, combined with neoconservative rationales, obscured the antagonisms between many public and private activities and threatened to eliminate the pursuit of a common good based on shared purpose. How might planning practitioners better understand their mission in the era of retrenchment? What counts as effective democratic planning in this setting?

NOTES

1. B. Douglas Harman conducted a detailed survey of planning activity for 954 cities in the United States. He found that 71 percent had planning staff, although only a few of the municipalities with 50,000 or more residents did so. This lack of planning staff on the part of smaller municipalities reflected their inadequate budget or insufficient need. Exclusive reliance on independent planning commissions continued to drop off. Between 1960 and 1970, the proportion of municipalities relying solely on planning commissions without staff declined from 42 percent to just 21 percent (1972, 56).

2. Rabinowitz failed to see the dilemma raised later by Hoffman, who observed that when planners become mobilizers and political actors they lose their legitimacy within the profession and can no longer command attention or offer advice that other planners consider appropriate (1989).

3. Vasu used four statements (paraphrased here) to classify respondents' role preferences: Planners should not openly seek to sell their plans politically. Planners should ultimately accept the goals submitted by elected officials. Urban planners should base recommendations on professional rather than political criteria. Urban planners, by virtue of their training, are in the best position to be neutral judges of the public interest. A planner was classified as technical who agreed strongly with three or more of these statements. Those who disagreed strongly on three or more were classified as advocates. Those falling in between were classified as moderates (1979, 196).

4. Howe later conducted a detailed analysis of factors influencing the choice of role (1980). Although she claims her evidence does not show the hybrids as integrating the technical and the political, she favorably cites Rabinowitz (1969), Jacobs (1978), and Meltsner (1976), who show less restraint. These analysts argue that a combination of technical competence and political savvy makes for a better planner than either technical or political skills alone. Hence, effective planners are those who balance and integrate the technical and political roles.

5. This simplifies what represents a contested concept at the heart of intellectual debates about the crucial causes of basic revolutionary social change in capitalist societies.

6. Albert Hirschman's *The Rhetoric of Reaction* (1991) compares and contrasts three conservative arguments against purposeful efforts at social change: perversity (efforts to build will destroy), futility (efforts to improve will not succeed), and jeopardy (efforts to improve will generate unexpected and unacceptable consequences).

11

Planning Deliberation and Politics

For several decades, professional planners depended on the rational model to explain and justify specific policies and programs. It provided a solid foundation for the kinds of knowledge planners put to practical use (Perloff 1961; Mann 1972). They confidently believed that the rational model tied together their quest for truth and for the good. When Henry Hightower surveyed planning theory courses at North American university planning schools in the late 1960s, he observed that the rational model was strongly in place, taming the emerging theoretical diversity (1969). By the early 1970s, however, many analysts were beginning to express serious doubts not only about the efficacy of the rational model in practice, but about the possibility of rational planning altogether (Lindblom 1959; 1979; Webber and Rittel 1973). These doubts stimulated a diverse and conflicting variety of planning theories. Some analysts worked hard to revise the rational model in ways that would displace doubt and deflect criticism (Alexander 1984; Faludi 1973; 1986; Lim 1986). Others, adopting ideas from such diverse fields as language philosophy, phenomenology, pragmatism, psychoanalysis, and critical theory, abandoned the quest for rational planning altogether.[1]

FROM THE RATIONAL MODEL TO PRACTICAL REASON

As theoretical arguments multiplied, planning students were no longer taught the rational model as a guide for practice, but received a variety of ideas about what counted as theory. Richard Klosterman's analysis (1992) of planning theory course outlines in 1979 and 1989 reveals a greater range of theoretical diversity than Hightower had documented. The rational model retains a central place in today's planning curriculum, but as a touchstone, rather than as a guide. Practitioners longing for a theory that will buttress their attachment to the rational protocol find little cause for reassurance.

When planners make a case for their advice, combining evidence and interpretation to compose and justify their plans, they want to know that their judgments are right and correct. The rational model helped justify such claims by offering a firm, truthful foundation—at least in theory. Political theorist Benjamin Barber calls faithful adherents to rationality "foundationalists":

> The foundationalist wishes to establish unimpeachable epistemological foundations for political and moral knowledge in a bedrock composed of either irreducible empirical data (empiricism, positivism, behavioral science) or indefensible a prioris (rationalism, idealism, analytic philosophy). His goal is to render political knowledge certain by associating it with the putative certainties of prepolitical knowledge.... Indeed, there may be little for the foundationalist to choose between the metaphysics of rationalism and the metaphysics of empiricism: the object in both cases is to ground politics in something less contingent and less corrigible than politics itself tends to be (1988, 6).

The political and moral complexity planners encounter, however, seldom follows the logical routes laid out by rational analysis. Uncertainty and contingency in practical affairs resist the application of rational procedures and the scientific method. Unfortunately, the continued popularity of the professional protocol has blinded practitioners to the limits of this sort of expertise.

The promise of detached objectivity may make sense in a community of scientists, but not in the political communities in which planners work. Scientists conduct research using procedures that are indifferent to the desires of the analyst and to the historical meaning of the inquiry. Planners, however, are confronted with problems that are shaped by and cannot be isolated from the expectations, relationships, and methods of the political community composed of elected officials, citizens, and other professionals. Planners who claim scientific expertise to rationalize their judgment mislead themselves and others. The scientific rationality that they embrace as a uniform and coherent model of understanding broke apart decades ago in the academy. Historians and philosophers of science had successfully challenged rationalist and positivist claims to a method of inquiry that transcends the historical and contingent conditions of human life (Bernstein 1983).

Planning theorists have conducted similar critiques of the rational planning model as a coherent account of human action and as an effective moral and political guide. For instance, such disparate analysts as Charles Lindblom (1959; 1979), Seymour Mandelbaum (1979; 1988), and John Forester (1989; 1992c) have all warned against trusting rational analysis as a source of predictable and comprehensive knowledge for planning. Each, in his own way, describes planning as advice-giving based on practical judgments. Planning does not require necessary and certain knowledge, but simply coherent reasons for advice that others can recognize, understand, and use. The planner's claim to a comprehensive understanding need not encompass (nor can it) knowledge of everybody and everything. It is enough that the planner know what is relevant and important for the problem at hand. This is the emphasis of pragmatic planning theory.

Theorists and practitioners who harbor rational expectations criticize pragmatism for being relativistic. Good rational arguments, they assert, transcend the contingent circumstances of history and context. How, they ask, does a professional planner justify the rational superiority of her judgment if she cannot appeal to higher standards of rationality? If no one viewpoint proves more rational than another, are not all equally compelling? These questions presume that professional planners make better judgments than others because the planners' advice better corresponds with the truth. The rationalists would have planners compare competing arguments according to certain principles and standards of rational inquiry, believing that it is possible to find a common denominator for evaluating social, political, psychological, and other differences in outlook. For pragmatists, however, the meaning of rationality shifts from testing correspondence to evaluating consequences.

> For the pragmatists the pattern of all inquiry—scientific as well as moral—is deliberation concerning the relative attractions of various concrete alternatives. The idea that in science or philosophy we can substitute "method" for deliberation between alternative results of speculation is just wishful thinking.... The great fallacy of the tradition, the pragmatists tell us, is to think that the metaphors of vision, correspondence, mapping, picturing, and representation which apply to small, routine assertions will apply to large and debatable ones. This basic error begets the notion that where there are no

objects to correspond to we have no hope of rationality, but only taste, passion, and will (Rorty 1987, 164).

Planners can believe in one set of community purposes and values and still recognize the validity and merit of competing purposes without suffering mental and moral confusion. The intellectual vertigo of relativism makes planners dizzy only if they believe they are standing on a tower of rational expertise. The pragmatists urge planners to step off the tower. Instead of committing the suicide they fear, planners will discover they are walking along a path of inquiry, whereas previously they had been standing still.

Pragmatic theorists imagine planners taking actions with others who hold competing notions of community. For the pragmatists, effective planning requires tolerance, freedom, and fairness—characteristics of liberal democracies at their best. The pragmatists replace the model of the planner as an expert offering truthful advice to the public with that of the planner as a counselor who fosters public deliberation about the meaning and consequences of relevant plans with those who will bear the burdens and enjoy the benefits of purposeful change (Dewey 1927).

Instead of treating technical and political values as mutually exclusive and even antagonistic domains, pragmatism recasts the two as different aspects of advice giving. Sometimes conflict emerges between the technical and the political aspects of a plan. For instance, Nancy in chapter 4 refused to calculate the estimate of citywide tax savings by household because she felt that doing so would have offered a misleading representation of benefits. She would not change data to fit the expectations of one or another political adversary. In most cases, however, planners make practical judgments about different problems using both technical knowledge and political values. Most of the stories in this book fall in this category. Donald adjusts the criteria for selecting a land fill in chapter 5. Ralph balances incommensurable values as he allocates scare housing units in chapter 9.

The rationalists offer refined arguments about the scientific integrity of the planning method; the pragmatists advance a revised understanding of liberalism, placing questions of justice and democracy at the center of their evaluations of planning effectiveness. The rationalists build grand conceptual models based on objective detachment; the pragmatists describe and evaluate what planners do in context. Pragmatists study the relationship between planners and their organizational settings, exploring how misleading ideas (Krieger 1981), inappropriate socialization (Marris 1982b; 1987), unconscious psychological fears (Baum 1983a; 1983b; 1987), and rhetorical manipulation (Forester 1989; Throgmorton 1990; 1992) distort efforts to conduct democratic and egalitarian planning. Pragmatists ask: What is the relationship between planners and the social institutions they inhabit and serve? How do the actions of planners hamper or improve democratic planning in different institutional and political settings?

Pragmatic theory studies the relationship between power and reason. For planners to be effective in liberal democratic societies, they must draw on power relationships of coercion, craft, and consensus. The problems professional planners encounter in advising civic leaders and in developing plans emerge less from conflicts between the technical and the political and more from their sense of conflicting allegiance on the job to the competing demands of different democratic constituencies. Hence, pragmatic analysts study the relationship between power and technical expertise to determine how the profession can best foster democratic planning. The liberal pragmatist seeks to discourage the administrative dogmatism of the commissar and the specialized provincialism of the technocrat, although order and efficiency do play important roles in coping with complex uncertainty. The pragmatist encourages consensus as a melding of professional expectations about control and craft with different forms of democratic politics.

Imagine professional expectations arrayed along a continuum with autonomous judgment at one end and collaborative judgment at the other. Tim, the design-oriented planner from chapter 1 who believes in the efficacy of professional autonomy, falls at one end of the continuum. Fred, the planning director for Burgess, convinced that effective professionals must build plans from a base of shared responsibility, sits at the opposite end. Next, picture a political continuum with adversarial competition at one end and unitary cooperation at the other. Rancorous and divisive debates at a legislative session fall at the adversarial pole of the continuum, while the reasoned deliberations of citizens at a New England town meeting would fit at the unitary end of the democratic spectrum. Both dimensions have relevance for planning.

THE PROFESSIONAL CONTINUUM:
FROM AUTONOMY TO SHARED RESPONSIBILITY

As planners pursue private fulfillment on the job through the expression of their powers of craft, design, and artistry, they rub up against the institutional boundaries that shape how organizations settle matters of justice. The planner crafts beautiful and fair-minded advice, only to find that bosses, clients, or colleagues are indifferent or disagree. Planners who want their self-expression to find flower in the commonweal can get testy here, grumbling about the irrational and immoral views of others. The planner may be tempted to use persuasion, but this can lead all too easily to pressuring or manipulating others to follow advice that actually reduces their freedom (Throgmorton 1992). Bruce in chapter 6 took this tack when he used his insider knowledge to sidetrack the banker's plans to ignore the setback requirements.

Inherent to the rational model is the protocol of the independent professional as the proper standard of conduct. The protocol, however, simultaneously overstates the powers of expertise and disguises them as matters of technique. The rational planning model deals with the politics of uncertainty by either ignoring the reality of political relationships or taming them with technical guidelines. This imposes a serious impediment. Planners who adopt the model as a practical guide blind themselves to the power relationships that permeate their work. They hold a naive notion of science, failing to see how the social organization and political use of scientific and technical knowledge contributes to new risks and new domains for the exercise of power.

The danger of technocratic rationality comes not from the commitment to reason, but from the use of technical findings to discredit the legitimate purposes of others as irrelevant, self-interested, and stupid. The rational technocrat offers advice that may be used to dispel and silence the questions of those worried about the uncertainty they face. Planners, along with other professionals working in organizations to create a public good, must navigate between the autonomy of expertise and their responsibility to others. The grip of their dilemma flows from the tendency of conventional theory to separate the technical and the political and the planner as a member of a profession and of society. What if the dilemma were both more complex and less rigid?

THE DEMOCRATIC CONTINUUM:
FROM ADVERSITY TO UNITY

The pursuit of the public interest regains practical respectability when liberated from universal claims. The pragmatist's vision rejects the notion of the public interest as a utopian condition discovered through the rigorous application of rational method and portrays it as the outcome of a contingent and fragile social union. The pragmatist holds that there can be no one exclusive spokesperson for reason. Hence, multiple authorities, reasons, and beliefs should compete for attention and public standing (Bernstein 1983; Rorty 1989).

This pragmatic sensibility is most appropriate for liberal democracies, which, in theory, elevate and protect the purposes of individual citizens. A liberal moral order relies on citizens to self-consciously shape their own destiny, making informed choices based on reflective moral inquiry. Ideals and reality, however, rarely match up. Class, race, and gender discrimination prevent many citizens from realizing and exercising their interests. The process of identifying public problems and determining solutions can be easily sabotaged by those who refuse to respect the purposes of others and by free riders, who benefit from others' efforts and refuse to contribute their own.

Democracy Through Adversity

Classical liberals suggest that the public arena should emulate the adversarial politics of market institutions (Mansbridge 1983). For market institutions, the best outcome is achieved through the free competition of members, regulated only to protect fairness. The competitors make rational choices, calculating how to achieve their own interests. In the political arena, the competition for votes among candidates echoes the competition among entrepreneurs for sales. Adversarial politics complements and supports the laissez-faire market approach to the public good: The best public good emerges through the competitive sorting through of equally weighted individual preferences. In this process, individual purposes, preferences, and interests remain separate from each other.

Adversarial politics accommodates conflicting interests, but has some negative side effects. Adversarial competition fosters cynical social relationships. It locks citizens into fixed positions and discourages debate. Observes Mansbridge:

> It replaces common interest with self interest, the dignity of equal status with baser motives of self protection, and the communal moments of face-to-face council with the isolation of a voting machine (1983, 18).

Planning undertaken in a setting of adversarial democracy results in citizens' drawing up special plans to match their own interests and spending time and energy campaigning for majority approval. Both insider log rolling and outsider public advocacy foment adversarial relations in which the like-minded view opposing plans as being irreconcilable with their own.

Democracy Through Cooperation

Planning theorists have been misguided in their reliance on the model of adversarial democracy. Meyerson and Banfield (1955) and Altshuler (1965) based their dismissal of rational planning efforts as ineffective on the standards of liberal adversarial politics. By these standards, the actions of city planners pursuing the public interest appeared to be apolitical, naive, and inept. Advocate planners gave the adversarial model even more credence. Reacting against the widespread belief of the 1950s and 1960s that rational planning was politically neutral, the advocate planners revealed how comprehensive plans tended to rationalize the interests of the powerful as if these were the interests of all citizens. The advocates proposed reforms to expand planners' participation in adversarial practices to help remedy the unjust exclusion of the poor, women, and minorities from the planning process (Davidoff 1965). Many planning analysts and practitioners, seeking to understand the politics of injustice, have relied heavily on the concept of adversarial democracy, which is at the center of the advocacy approach.

For instance, Howe and Kaufman's measures of political action include only adversarial activities (1985). They classified as politicians planners who advocated partisan positions and labeled as apolitical technicians those planners who sought a unitary concept of the public good. This dichotomy retained the discredited rational model and projected it on planners who did not engage in adversarial politics. They were the technicians. At best, planners could be hybrids, working to maintain a precarious balance between the competing claims of expertise and political interest. Howe and Kaufman overlooked those forms of political action that planners take to reconcile their technical expertise and political purpose. Organizations and communities possess shared as well as antagonistic interests. These common interests provide the grounds for democratic power relationships that are based on respect and consensus (Mansbridge 1983).

Planners pursue various kind of political activity: the politics of vision, interest, advocacy, and deliberation. Planning theory has tended to concentrate exclusively on the relationships and activities of the first three kinds of politics. The pragmatic approach emphasizes the politics of deliberation.

The Politics of Vision

Today's views on the proper place of politics in professional planning have been shaped by the legacy of reform, which sought to separate the profession from the politics of interests, especially the patronage relationships of big city political machines. Most accounts mark the 1893 Columbian Exposition in Chicago as the birth of planning. This fair with its towering neoclassical facades and its grand public landscape sparked the City Beautiful movement. Reformers prepared visual plans that projected monumental vistas and scenic parkways on the nasty and congested grids of industrial cities, hoping that their vision would inspire public investment and regulations. This visionary aesthetic sought to implant a unitary order on America's physically fragmented and socially diverse cities. The reformers believed that the imposition of the symbols and images of civic identity on the chaos of urban life would render an order so efficient and a beauty so compelling that popular consensus in the creation of a new social order would follow. Good planning, as part of civic reform, would follow the rules of good design and efficient administration in the service of the broad public interest.

Professional planners spend a good deal of time learning about the causes of urban problems. The visionary approach to planning draws on the traditions of physical design in architecture and landscape architecture. The talents and imagination of the designer inform the work, which is composed by individual effort, rather than through shared enterprise and communication. Planners wedded to this tradition see their role as making plans that others will read, discuss, and adopt. The visionaries, however, encounter serious difficulties in politically charged settings. Many planners, like Tim in chapter 1, believe deeply in the quality of their professional judgment about the right design. They tend to oversimplify any political opposition to their judgment as being corrupt.

The visionary's deep faith in the rational comprehensive plan relies on the marriage of the scientific method and professional design expertise. Although decades of critical research have eroded the respectability of the comprehensive plan, even the agnostics remain faithful to the protocol of rational planning in their daily work for want of an acceptable option. From blueprint to spreadsheet, from master plan to public policy, the image of the rational designer who stands above the political fray remains at the center of the professional protocol and of professional education (Dalton 1986).

The Politics of Interest

Soon after its formulation, the rational planning model was found wanting as a guide for practice. Research studies revealed that actual planning activity did not fit the model. The skeptics asserted that the model's view of the social order was too idealistic. Some critics claimed the model was perverse, while others argued that it was misleading and infeasible (Lindblom 1959; Simon 1957; 1976).

Edward Banfield, once a true believer in rational planning, outlined a pluralistic concept of politics that belittled the model. In his analysis of public housing in Chicago, Banfield described and classified areas of political competition, observing that the conflicting desires of the many different participants could only be resolved through politics, not planning (Meyerson and Banfield 1955, 304–305). Instead of blaming the failure of public housing on political corruption, Banfield described politics as a social reality over which planners have no effective influence.

In the 1950s and 1960s, Banfield and other analysts abandoned the Progressive tradition of moral reform and pursued the founding of conceptual systems based on the applied social sciences. Whereas their reform predecessors had maintained a practical separation between their values and corrupt politics, the scientific analysts gave the separation theoretical weight. They advised planners to keep their scientific objectivity unsullied by biased commitments to particular political values. Skepticism replaced institutional reform as the approach to evaluations of the political situations that planners faced.

In the past thirty years, analysts have amply documented the political situations that trump the efforts of planners who have been too elitist, naive, or scrupulous to deal. In these accounts, political participants bring their purposes and interests to the public domain and through contestation, bargaining, and adjudication these individuals, groups, and organizations—including government—achieve some of their purposes. Altshuler (1965), Bolan and Nuttal (1975), Catanese (1974; 1984), Judd and Mendelson (1973), Rabinowitz (1969), and others have used insights from the social sciences to demonstrate how private interests shape the political terrain within which planning takes place. Despite their differences in method, style, and ideological orientation, these analysts emphasize that planning cannot build master plans independent of political interests and relationships. The problem for planners is to be able to act politically without becoming cynical competitors or elitist snobs (Benveniste 1989).

The Politics of Advocacy

The shift to advocacy planning in the 1960s reflected a break with the traditional model of comprehensive planning as advice giving independent of politics. Perceiving that issues of social and economic justice were tied to the competition and conflict among interests, both policy and advocate planners were now advised to understand, analyze, compare, and assess the politics of planning. They differed, however, on the issue of the proper involvement of planners in politics. The policy analysts endorsed the objective application of the methods of the social sciences to the analysis of contentious public policy issues (Friedmann 1987, 137–80). They studied interests not as skeptical analysts, but as expert advisers seeking compromise and consensus. The advocates took sides, mainly with the liberal left (Davidoff 1965; Heskin 1980). The advocates, many influenced by the Civil Rights and New Left social movements, reacted against what they perceived to be the rigidity and elitism of visionary planning. They hoped to inject adversarial political relationships into the heart of the planning enterprise to rectify the uneven playing field of local politics. The left-leaning advocates pushed an adversarial agenda to make plan making more competitive and to overcome the biased exclusion of minorities and the poor as effective political competitors.

The advocates' efforts at democratic reform drew heavily, if selectively, on the organizing efforts of the Civil Rights movement. Militant planners organized protests and other confrontational activities to challenge traditional political arrangements. They challenged planning processes and procedures that failed to identify and prioritize the needs of poor and minority residents (Davidoff, Davidoff, and Newton 1970). They pushed for plans that would capture public attention and support against what they perceived to be the cooptive plans of government bureaucrats serving local special interests and elites. Their efforts at militant polarization and direct action got public attention, but they also instilled a cynical suspicion of rational comprehensive planning.

The advocates dismissed efforts to foster a common vision of the public good as elitist, cooptive, and naive. The cynicism inherent to adversarial politics left even the most ardent proponents wondering about the meaning of their own reforms. The Needlemans (1975) and Hoffman (1989), who studied the reports of radical advocate planners about their own work, found them expressing frustration over the behavior of the recently empowered. Instead of engaging in struggles for social justice

and building coalitions with other disadvantaged groups, the newly en-
franchised participants would often engage in the same sort of competitive and exclusionary politics that had previously excluded them. Some
planners wondered how they could overcome this cynical detachment
and offer up plans that would incorporate the interests of the broader
public.

The Politics of Deliberation

The politics of deliberation allows planners to put the formal conventions—argument, conversation, debate—of unitary liberal democracy to
practical use. Political actors rarely engage in deliberations in highly
charged adversarial settings. However, the routines of governance, especially in large organizations, cannot survive sustained adversity. Political opponents involved in complex and longstanding conflicts surrounding such planning policies as land use regulation, energy conservation, public housing, and public health cannot withdraw like prize
fighters to their corners to get relief, but must carry on in public, seeking
compromises and mutual support. When adversarial relations prove
exhausting, perverse, or inconclusive, then the prospects for deliberation improve. The pursuit of the public interest need not be a pipe dream
or a byproduct of political competition.

Deliberative democracy requires participants with different purposes
and from different spheres of influence and authority to listen and reconsider their own views based on what they hear from others whom they
trust. Through mutual discussion and evaluation the participants learn
from each other. These activities replace logrolling and deal cutting. The
politics of deliberation requires planners to attend to the needs and goals
of participants and to avoid coercion and political competition.

REVISING LIBERALISM

Conventional liberal guidelines do not help planners resolve the contradictory requirements of achieving professional fulfillment and social responsibility. Either they have to choose between political competition
and apolitical consensus or adopt an awkward combination of the two.
The professional protocol of detached expertise presumes clear boundaries between the obligations to oneself and to others, but in practice the
separation breaks down. The portrayal of professionals as detached experts hinders planners from understanding their political roles and blinds
them to practical opportunities to achieve effective and egalitarian goals.
The research reviewed in chapter 10 showed that planners who relied

solely on rational planning methods were unable to meet effectively competing political expectations. Planners who embraced adversarial politics did not fare much better, even when they replaced liberal rationality for a more radical version.

The pragmatic analysts concerned with planning effectiveness have revised the liberal concepts of adversarial democracy to incorporate the unitary concepts of democratic politics. They place professional success at adversarial politics within a broad array of possible democratic political relationships. Unlike earlier analysts, they publicly acknowledge the various kinds of practical democracy that planners tacitly use or strive to implement. Their approach does not offer a new synthesis of the profession's enduring dilemma, but rather asserts that unitary democracy is a practical possibility in the planning arena of competing communities of interest.

The pragmatists' studies recast the meaning of planning. Good planning is not so much a reflection of rational purpose as the popular adoption of democratic reforms in the provision of public goods. Instead of accommodating or resisting the conservative turn, the analysts adopted revised versions of liberalism that cut across the conventional ideological split between left and right. Keenly aware of the limits of scientific rationality and its dangers when applied to public policy through government bureaucracy, these analysts used surveys, interviews, and observation to study how planners coped with political ambiguity (Baum 1983a; 1987; Forester 1986; 1987b; 1989; Schon 1982) and conflict (Dalton 1990; Hoch 1988; Hoch and Cibulskis 1987). Others used case studies to describe how planners introduced risky innovation (Adler 1990; Krumholz and Forester 1990) or local reform programs (Clavell 1986; Marris 1987) in the pursuit of modest democratic planning improvements.

Conventional liberal ideals and the professional protocol encourage planners to adopt a skeptical instrumental rationality. They use social science methods to tally and evaluate economic, social, and political interests. Detached objectivity spills over from the domain of inquiry (where it makes sense) into the domain of judgment (where it proves restrictive and misleading). The rational method tends to treat expressions of passion and desire as suspect. Revised liberalism encourages planners to limit their employment of detached objectivity to research and analysis and to find the appropriate expression of their passion in their judgments and advice. The revisionists advise planners that they need not identify wholesale with the role of the disinterested and unfeeling expert. The planner need not resolve the tension between the technical and design aspects of planning and the political demands for compromise, cooperation, and conflict by permanently separating the technical and the political. Rather, they can undertake shifting involvements, learning to form and to fulfill multiple attachments and commitments. Instead of ignoring competing interests or taking sides, planners can experience and articulate each interest in turn.

This shifting relies on a detachment that differs from that of the objective scientist. The planner's detachment must be one that allows her to recognize and respect the varieties of individual purpose and their mutual limitations. Planners with this sense of detachment can integrate their own desires with those of their many audiences by defining problems and creating policy options that weave together the many purposes into a complex plan. Planners do not win their audiences' respect by having no opinions, but rather by offering alternatives that acknowledge the participants' hopes and desires. Planners must be able to grasp empathetically and express emotionally the significance of diverse and conflicting beliefs.[2]

Howell Baum, John Forester, and Peter Marris have studied how professional planners cope with the challenges of democratic politics. Each offers a revised view of liberalism, describing how planners can balance the tension between professional autonomy and the public interest through the politics of deliberation. Baum reminds planners that they need not act as dispassionate bureaucratic gatekeepers, development brokers, or technical visionaries. Professional autonomy can include passionate as well as utilitarian sensibilities. Planners can earn political respect as active and committed participants in the democratic community. Marris asserts that planners should embrace a robust set of professional protocols that enables them to mediate between their expertise and the public's need and between adversarial interests and unitary goals. Planners can learn to engage in shifting involvements, adopting a professional pluralism that is based on ironic solidarity rather than skeptical detachment. Solidarity demands shared commitment; irony inspires critical separation. Together they give order and meaning to the ambiguity and conflict that shifting involvements evoke. Forester claims that if planners can move beyond the technocrat-politician split, they will be free to foster deliberations among different communities over shared interests and values. Instead of harnessing the complexity of practical life to the strictures of rational authority, planners should design ways for diverse communities to respect one another, even as their purposes conflict.

Feelings Matter

In his interviews of professional planners, Howell Baum discovered that they had a strong desire for personal efficacy, but felt powerless. Baum stated that planners responded to this tension in one of two ways. Some planners complained about the unwillingness or failure of the political participants to respond to good ideas. (Howe and Kaufman called these planners technicians.) Other planners became involved in the organizational and political details of turning ideas into action. Baum believed that these planners expressed less ambivalence and dissatisfaction with their work than did those who complained about political lassitude. Although most planners spoke of good planning as free of political influence, they still desired the power that is expressed in organizational settings through political persuasion and influence.

Baum has extensively explored the relationship between what he calls unconscious and conscious thought in the work of planners (1983b; 1987; 1990). Drawing on psychoanalytic and social theory, he discusses the sources of ambivalence and ambiguity in planners' accounts of organizational relationships. Unresolved fears, anxieties, and other painful experiences from early childhood shape the adult feelings of professional planners and foster unconscious defenses. When planners handle relatively routine problems their conscious deliberations proceed without tension. However, faced with organizational uncertainty and ambiguity, the planners' unconscious defenses profoundly influence what they say and do. They may be only dimly aware of or even oblivious to their ambivalence.[3]

Baum found that few planners expected to become bureaucrats. They turned to a career in planning, expecting to become entrepreneurial problem solvers—rugged individuals skillfully pursuing a useful public service. The planners also expected to obtain status and recognition from their occupational prowess. They wanted to achieve a positive sense of identity through their work performance (Baum 1987, 16–17).

Baum asserts that planners view their work symbolically, as the result of problem solving efforts. However, problem solving requires working with others, listening to their troubles, and offering advice about solutions. The planner may actively try to formulate the problem in relationship to a particular client, but conflicts are likely to emerge.[4] In the face of these conflicts, planners must exercise power, which Baum treats as a form of organizational collaboration rather than the exercise of coercion.[5] Baum advises participants to make commitments to each other in their effort to overcome or cope with shared uncertainty. If planners have difficulty forming emotional attachments or fear that others will exploit them, cooperation will break down and collaborative problem solving will suffer. It takes courage to overcome such fears, especially unconscious ones.

Many planners long to voice their deepest sentiments about public problems and what should be done. Ironically, many practitioners look to the professional protocol of detached objectivity as the source of personal expression and self-fulfillment. Instead of passionately embracing objectivity, these professionals should perhaps consider how their advice can be both an expression of their passion and a practical and useful resource for community building.

Baum defends the need for participatory community. He believes that democratic political activity requires public thinking that focuses on the meaning of public actions. Strong democracy offers planners an antidote to the self-sacrificial burnout of adversarial advocacy and to ritual professionalism. It discourages solitary professionals from trying to change longstanding community practices through the clever or politically correct deployment of their expertise. It discourages adversaries from using expert testimony to define a policy debate, thus, eliminating or sidetracking informed public discussion. Good public judgment about complex technical issues does not hinge solely on the quality of expertise, but also on the experience and wisdom of those involved in the deliberations. Planners acquire such wisdom on their own, through their active participation with colleagues and clients.

Shifting Involvements: Linking Meaning and Action

Peter Marris offers a conventional, commonsensical definition of planning. It is the effort to control social or collective uncertainty, "either by taking action now to secure the future, or by preparing actions to be taken in case an event occurs. Both make the future more predictable and manageable in terms of present purposes." As planners work to manage the future, the quality and scope of rational argument and evidence matter less than the meaning these efforts offer to those involved in making the plans and to those most likely to experience the consequences of the plans (1982b, 126). The meaning of the plans includes much more than just the instrumental connection between purpose and outcome. Meaning embraces the context within which purposes develop and actions get played out.[6]

For Marris, the source of both practical and theoretical insight is individual experience, which is created and channeled by social conditions, institutional settings, emotional attachments, and the purposes of others. To create meaningful plans, planners must take into account individual purposes and attachments in preparing to deal with social uncertainty. Planning that does not take into account these complex and interrelated sets of attachments undermines the legitimacy of the plan for those people whose attachments are threatened. The image of planners as unfeeling social engineers or technocrats expresses this fear.

For Marris, understanding does not *reflect* an empirical meaning, but involves inquiry that weaves together causes, intentions, and feelings to *make* meaning. In recognizing, respecting, and incorporating the attachments of others in defining problems, setting purposes, and working up alternative actions, planners should acknowledge the particular histories of the participants. For Marris, planning is a complex social effort to institutionalize and justify political reforms, conceived to eliminate or reduce the uncertainties produced by the institutions and policies of advanced industrial societies. The burdens of poverty, slums, unemployment, and congestion—the whole repertoire of urban problems—fall most heavily on the weak, whose purposes get displaced by the plans of the powerful. Marris uses a moral and historical framework to describe planning. He asserts that the priorities and plans of the powerful have undermined opportunities for those subjected to the plans to achieve freedom, justice, autonomy, and solidarity. For Marris, the unjust and uneven results of the plans of the powerful call into question the effectiveness of these plans.

Marris perceives that instrumental rationality imposes too narrow a judgment on meaningful planning practice. It excludes important aspects of practice—the emotional, experiential, and intentional relationships that make practical action useful and meaningful. He advises planners to eschew the rational model and focus instead on how people in contemporary societies cope with the patterns of change that inform everyday life.

Baum offers strong democracy to counter the ambivalence planners experience when they believe they must choose between adversarial politics and the professional protocol. He urges planners to *create* organizational communities that support democratic deliberation. In contrast,

Marris argues that planners should *reclaim* democratic aspects of social collaboration that have been displaced by adversarial economic and political relationships.

When planners in liberal societies meet to discuss the scope of a problem, the merits of different schemes of action, and the potential benefits of different resource allocations, they draw on tacit standards of tolerance and respect for mutual deliberation and individual choice as a test for good advice. Unfortunately, adversarial expectations and institutions frequently undermine and belittle these efforts. Ambiguity emerges as planners seek to make egalitarian ideals practical through the use of professional understanding in adversarial settings. Instead of responding to this ambiguity as gatekeepers or visionaries, Marris suggests they work as mediators.

Marris describes four groups of professionals who seek egalitarian social reform: reformers, community organizers, social scientists, and planners:

> All these play the part of intellectual mediators. They interpret particular situations and needs in the light of broader conceptions from which collective definitions of purpose and action can arise; and their authority to do this comes from their intellectual vocation, as people trained in the articulation of general ideas. So, for instance, they take up the claims of inner city residents for better housing, more jobs, less degraded surroundings, and justify them in terms of ideals and principles which the institutions of society claim to represent as a whole (1982b, 3).

These professionals first identify the disparities between the social and democratic ideals and the realities of modern society and then offer schemes to remedy the inequalities. They enjoy sufficient ideological autonomy to carry out their critical assessments, but find that their policies for change do less to solve the problem and more to enhance the ambiguity of their roles as mediators.

In his studies of various professional teams at work, Marris discovered that the members were prepared to criticize the liberal system of welfare policies,

> but they could not agree upon an alternative ideology of social action, because they were still preoccupied with rival definitions of their professional authority, all derived from the ideology that they were explicitly or implicitly rejecting. Planners, researchers, community workers, management consultants depend on an understanding of their moral responsibility, and therefore their right to intervene, to seek clients and claim support, defined by

liberal conceptions of the legitimate structure of power. Once you see that structure as inescapably dominated by relationships which create the problems you are trying to solve, you cannot adopt an accepted professional stance within it (1982b, 35).

Marris does not provide a guide for professional practice. Rather, he shows how individuals tried to make sense of various problems and to achieve social change by moving back and forth between specific attachments and broad public purposes. Marris reveals his democratic and egalitarian hopes as he explores how people in bureaucracies, community organizations, and political institutions can take meaningful actions to correct the unfair and uneven distributions of uncertainty.

The planner as mediator does not reconcile adversaries—the rich versus the poor or the powerful versus the weak. The effective planning mediator shifts between egalitarian planning ideals and the specific desires, needs, hopes, and beliefs of the people burdened with uncertainty. The shifting is made possible by the preexisting respect for democratic deliberations among people willing to modify their expectations in light of the planner's advice. Unfortunately, because organizational settings and cultural expectations seem to favor adversarial competition rather than cooperative deliberation, planning deliberation may appear to be superfluous or foolish:

> Because plans are so often ignored, whenever they attempt to set priorities and guarantees in the interests of the most vulnerable, or constrain the freedom of actions of those more powerful so as to reach some resolution which is both fair and practicable, planning even at its best often comes to seem merely a distraction from more effective forms of political protest, and so cooptive. But the lesson of this is not to reject planning in favour of political struggles, but to incorporate into these struggles a demand for effective, open, collective planning, as a crucial part of carrying out any practical ideal of social justice. Otherwise, the struggle does not lead towards any resolution except competitive bargaining between different kinds of interests, and that cannot protect the weaker and more vulnerable members of society (1982b, 126–27).

Marris argues that the adversarial liberalism that creates social inequality and fosters individual autonomy relies on unacknowledged relationships of social solidarity and interdependence. Planners can use these relationships to help remedy this lopsided liberalism by mediating between the two domains.

Shift Share Planning

In his early theoretical work, Forester criticized the formal and instrumental qualities of rational planning (1980; 1982; 1985). He combined insights from critical theory, phenomenology, pragmatism, and language philosophy to argue for practical reasoning. He convincingly demonstrated that the planner who aspires to technical objectivity can offer little of use in the complex social and political process of project review. From a theoretical base, Forester exposes how the planner who uses technique as a moral guide distorts and undermines democratic deliberation, which he, like Marris, believes should guide public policy (1983; 1987b; 1989).

Using observations of professional planners, Forester constructs detailed cases to show how the allegedly technical judgments of practitioners conducting development reviews incorporate normative and cultural judgments as well (1987b; 1989; 1992a; 1992b). His cases illustrate the inseparable bonds that link technical knowledge and practical judgment in organizational settings. Forester shows how the conversations of planners echo the norms of efficiency and order, but also resonate with concepts of justice, based on the planners' political experiences in multiple overlapping communities.

Forester argues that in the world of practical affairs, planners rarely, if ever, separate the technical from the political. Efforts to do so usually lead to no good. Forester focuses primarily on understanding the complex moral and political activities planners engage in to pursue their various goals, rather than on how efficiently and predictably planners achieve their goals. He rejects his predecessors' search for a rational model that neatly separates means from ends, thought from action, and feelings from reflection. To Forester, effective planning can not be defined solely as the achievement of purposes established by bosses or planners. Rather, the effective planner offers advice in a manner that anticipates complex and competing purposes. Sensitive to the bureaucratic environment in which most planners work, Forester recognizes the tension between efforts to conduct democratic planning and the undemocratic pressures of organizational life. Effective planners use democratic deliberations to challenge the unjust use of power.

Forester is well aware that political conflicts that involve adversarial power relationships do not lend themselves easily to practical deliberation. He proposes steps that planners can employ as mediators to help antagonists reason together. First, planners can listen carefully to learn about what's important to the people you're working with; try to avoid being blinded by your own prejudgments of what they care about. Such listening might help you gain trust, too, because it demonstrates a respect for others rather than presumptuousness (Personal communication 1993).

Second, they can foster deliberations that enable the disputing parties to reconsider their fixed attachments to a particular outcome. Third, they can change relations of antagonism (e.g., the enemy) into relations of mutual, if grudging, respect (Forester 1992b).

In one article, Forester describes six mediated negotiation strategies local land use planners might adopt to anticipate and handle disputes among planners, developers, and neighborhood residents. He skillfully demonstrates how successful planning involved democratic mediation efforts that reduced antagonisms and established common ground. The planners used their limited discretion to "challenge existing inequalities of information, expertise, political access, and opportunity" (Forester 1987b, 312). In these conflicts developers, planners, and residents agreed to negotiate. Forester concedes that in situations in which a disputant enjoys unilateral power, mediated negotiation will not enhance the discretion of the planner and may be used to coopt the weaker parties. In the face of this kind of adversity, organized resistance is likely to be the more effective strategy.

Forester criticizes liberal adversarial democracy and embraces a cooperative democracy of citizenship and participation (1992a). His empirical research reveals planners striving to practice cooperative democracy in their daily work, but burdened with the intrusion of adversarial competition and bureaucratic maneuvering. Forester refers to the ideas of social theorist Jurgen Habermas to identify the norms that planners rely on as they communicate their advice. According to Habermas, all human communication makes four validity claims: sincerity, truthfulness, legitimacy, and comprehensibility (1987). Forester uses these distinctions to show the moral and political significance of practical planning judgments. For instance, a planner reviewing the impacts of a proposed development does not just report the probability of flooding, but must decide whether to advise that the risk is modest or serious and how he will offer this advice. The protocol of the rational professional often discourages such moral refection in its misguided effort to legitimize planning as the work of experts.

Forester believes that the proliferation of professions throughout the twentieth century has kept the articulate citizen from receiving society's expanding cultural capital. The specialized and exclusionary limits of professional disciplines have "colonized" the "life-world" (Habermas's phrases) into domains of expertise. Forester urges design professionals to abandon the forms and conventions of their practice that distance them from their clients. Planners should nurture and apply both direct and latent forms of democratic community.

Direct democracy builds cooperative agreements in a competitive world. Latent democracy revives preexisting, but moribund forms of social cooperation that have been displaced by adversarial relationships. In chapter 8, Stelian helped build an economic development organization that directly fostered cooperative democracy among industrial competitors. He drew on the latent solidarity of these competitors when he organized opposition to the closing of the Acme factory. The Acme executive earned their scorn and censure, not for closing the plant, but for his lies, which violated the common trust they had all shared.

In his study with Norman Krumholz of the Cleveland planning department, Forester uncovered examples of democratic planning that drew on both latent and direct forms of communitarian democracy. He showed how Krumholz, as director, violated many conventions of bureaucratic power by introducing forms of participatory democracy both inside and outside the department (Krumholz and Forester 1990). Krumholz helped found a community of planners whose shared commitment to social equity outweighed their commitments to the protocols of expertise. The planners in this community maintained and perhaps even elevated the profession's standards of competence, but they did not rely on them for their sense of professional identity. Rather, they cared most about how well their technical work improved the equitable distribution of city services and resources.

Most important, the staff's actions to enhance equity were not the result of individual initiative, but of their ongoing collective deliberations. Their struggle to achieve greater justice through the workings of the local bureaucracy and electoral politics was based on participatory democracy. Shared deliberations enabled the staff to view conventional professional, bureaucratic, and political norms as means rather than as ends. Under Krumholz's guidance, planning expertise was no longer an exclusive good employed by the powerful to meet their own ends. The staff worked hard to foster deliberations within the local government bureaucracy over improvements in the just distribution of public goods. They built relationships that nurtured the informal powers of unitary rather than adversarial democracy. These same planners, however, also promoted adversarial advocacy in the public arena of political competition by pushing blatantly and consistently for the interests of poor and working class residents. Krumholz and his colleagues shuttled back and forth between the realm of advocacy and inquiry, drawing on a community of care and deliberation.

Forester asserts that democratic deliberation takes the form of stories that planners tell each other and their clients (1993b). He analyzes snippets of planning conversation to illustrate that planners not only describe events, but make moral, political, and emotional judgments about the importance and value of actions they might avoid or take. These judgments do not constitute conclusions, but are part of a process of mutual story telling that eventually leads to decision making. When planners tell stories about their practical work, they weave together description, perception, analysis, and evaluation—activities to which most theorists give separate attention. In the planner's complex everyday conversation, scientific objectivity represents a minor rhetorical ploy, rather than a guiding norm. The specialized language of scientists cannot adequately address the ambiguities, nuances, and pressures that fill a practicing planner's day.

The attention and sensitivity to one another's tales determines the quality of the deliberations. Forester argues that useful, practical deliberations occur best among friends. Friends tell each other stories that lead to greater self-understanding. Friends can be supportive critics, helping each other to see what is missing in each other's lives and what is being misunderstood. Friends help each other sort out what really matters in complex situations (Forester 1993b). Forester holds up Aristotle's notion of public friendship—the friendship of reciprocal care—to indicate the sorts of relationships planners need to foster to lead to useful democratic deliberations. Krumholz established a planning community in Cleveland that relied heavily on the solidarity of friendship, rather than on the skepticism of technical know-how.

Forester urges researchers to study the complex practical deliberations and judgments that planners exercise. Studies should be structured to acknowledge that planners are moral improvisers, moving back and forth between principles and specific details. Planners use narrative to impose order on their activity. At their best, planners tell stories that show they are both listening to their audience (and to themselves) and persuading them to take certain actions. To avoid manipulation, the planners must recognize and respect the purposes, attachments, and interests of their audience. Their stories about particular planning problems and strategies for solving them should reflect these concerns. Planners should tell their stories and listen to those of citizens in deliberations that engage and involve the entire audience.

Forester urges planners to pay attention to their powers of reason, judgment, and persuasion as resources for planning. Once planners abandon the false dichotomy between the technical and the political, they can put these powers to practical use by offering technical advice infused with the values of democratic deliberation. Planners should rely less on the protocol of expertise and more on the tacit norms of communication that they share with superiors, coworkers, and clients.

THE POLITICS OF DELIBERATION AS AN INTERPRETIVE FRAMEWORK

Baum, Marris, and Forester all propose a revised liberalism that embraces the politics of deliberation. All care a great deal about reviving the notion of power as collaboration based on mutual communication, choice, and action. They study planners engaged in adversarial politics, not to offer theories and strategies that will help planners reach victory, but to show how planners adopt liberal presuppositions and expectations to guide and justify their practice. All three hold as ideal the individual who draws on community-based democratic participation and collaboration to reduce shared uncertainties. Baum appeals to the powers that evolve from self-exposure and trust in others; Marris relies heavily on the notion of the latent community that informs moral choice; and Forester emphasizes the importance of direct political participation in deliberating communities.

Planners seeking how-to advice for getting ahead are likely to find the work of these authors intellectually stimulating, yet disturbingly difficult to assimilate into their practice. These works, however, fill in an important and overlooked dimension for understanding planning effectiveness: the politics of deliberation. The communitarian planning ideas of Baum, Marris, and Forester allow for planners to engage in both unitary and adversarial politics. They propose that planners practice a form of politics that presumes that common interests can be realized through equal respect among participants who seek consensus through face-to-face deliberations (Mansbridge 1983). The research by these analysts shows that rational plans and planning can be reasonable and practical guides for public action. Some plans are merely rationalizations for the desires of the powerful and these deserve critical review and counterplans by advocates for the weak. However, many plans end up making good political sense in unitary settings where consensus plays a central role.

Analysts with an adversarial notion of politics tend to treat planning efforts that do not generate controversy as apolitical "technical" activity. Marris and Forester suggest that this is a kind of political activity that cannot be understood through adversarial lenses. Take, for example, the African-American in chapter 4 who insisted on treating Esteban, the director of research in a large planning agency, as an antagonist. Although Esteban had gone out of his way to alleviate suspicions and foster deliberations about the proposed census participation process, the antagonist's adversarial convictions made finding a common ground impossible. Donald in chapter 5 offers an example of a practitioner alternately anticipating and resenting the limits of adversarial land use procedures and politics, as he tries to bring practical reason to bear on the selection of a new land fill site. Esteban and Donald made politically informed technical judgments, but avoided taking sides among competing political partisans.

Professional planners are seldom either party hacks or civic saints. On the one hand, they try hard to craft and support their judgments and advice using appeals to shared ideals. They make rational claims on public attention and expect a fair hearing. On the other, they realize that public attention is fragmented and specialized, focusing on the needs and problems of specific populations. Analysts have tended to overemphasize the scope of adversarial relationships in planners' work and to underestimate the social significance of their technical activity. The analysts have fostered commitments to distinctions that not only miss the complexity of planners' activity, but also offer categories of moral interpretation that blind practitioners to the importance and value of their actions.

Planners can give passionate expression to their talents and desires, not by projecting their rational or aesthetic visions on the public, but by imagining and constructing advice that members of different communities can comprehend, find useful, discuss, try, and evaluate. Rendering advice in this way requires that planners be members of several communities. Seymour Mandelbaum says:

We are simultaneously members of many mythic communities whose claims overlap—some competitive, some complementary, some largely independent of one another. We assess the implications of affiliation with one of these communities—place, sex, family, religion, profession, class or club—by locating it within the dense fabric of the entire set. We move within this fabric—now emphasizing one group of claims and then another, leaving one identity and adopting a new one—without usually encountering a charge of apostasy (1988, 21-22).

Planning that respects difference and yet serves the public good will exist in a setting of ambiguous and contentious relationships. By shifting their involvements, planners can move between adversarial and unitary settings without taking sides, engaging in what Jerome Kaufman calls "boundary spanning" (1987). Planners are not only gatekeepers, but path breakers; not simply visionaries, but counselors; not just power brokers, but public servants; not experts, but teachers.

Adopting the insights of critical pragmatists like Baum, Marris, and Forester does not require that planners dismiss the earlier research and the rational model. Rather, the pragmatists seek to shift attention from theoretical analysis to practical interpretation. The pragmatists draw attention to the forms of democratic deliberation that planners adopt in nonadversarial political settings. These somewhat unfamiliar ideas challenge the dualisms that have informed planners' professional identity.

Planners may engage in the politics of vision, interests, and advocacy and do well. Planning thrives, however, in the political domain of deliberation and consensus. The planners introduced in this text had little success in local political battles, in advocacy campaigns, and in convincing clients of their irresistible expertise. My interpretations of their efforts are based on concepts and distinctions central to the politics of deliberation. The accounts and episodes of individual planners are intended to help the reader to discover how failure in the conventional arenas should not be cause for alarm. The effectiveness and practical meaning of what planners do might be better understood if judged as efforts to establish, expand, and refine deliberations.

Deliberations are usually identified with private life, shared mainly with friends, family, and neighbors. The interpretive framework of this chapter shows that planners dedicate much of their time and effort to making way for public democratic deliberations about collective problems and desirable solutions. Most planners do this hoping to make a living and to render advice that others will agree to amend and adopt in useful ways.

NOTES

1. The intellectual debts here could easily fill a large volume. Works by Martin Krieger (1981), Judith DeNeufville (1983; 1987), and Richard Bolan (1980) provide excellent examples of the impact of phenomenology. John Forester offers the best example of an analyst adapting critical theory to the study of planning (1989; 1993a). Psychoanalytical ideas are most prominent in the work of Howell Baum (1983a; 1987) and Peter Marris (1974). James Throgmorton (1990; 1992) routinely applies the insights of rhetoric and language analysis. My own work (Hoch 1984a; 1984b) draws from pragmatism, a philosophy whose influence has shaped several generations of planning theorists.

2. Liberal theory recast to emphasize separate spheres and shifting involvements has powerful political and psychological implications. First, it draws more attention to questions of opportunity than does liberalism as a bourgeois ideology or doctrine of formal rights. This is true whether the romantic notion of possibility is one of ecstatic plenitude or somber self-protection.... The second implication of shifting involvements is a correspondence between the romantic sense of self and the external world of liberal pluralism.... Romantic sensibilities are many-sided and resist the claims of any one sphere: the external world is similarly complex and differentiated. Romantics can feel at one with liberal society precisely because it is not unified or homogeneous (Rosenblum 1988, 147).

3. The empowerment of planners must be a political process. Yet few planners perceive any contradiction between calling for depoliticization of the planning process and simultaneously calling for more power for planners. Further, most of the planners calling for more power do not refer in definitive ways to the organizational setting in which they presently work with less than the desired support. Nor do they specify organizational strategies that could bring them power (Baum 1987, 292).

4. Differences may be the product of conflicting interests, what is a problem to some may be a source of benefit to others. Interested persons may have different information about a situation, or they may evaluate similar information differently.... Their work requires negotiation. As much as possible, they must attempt to create agreement about how a situation is to

be perceived. Further, they must attempt to negotiate a commitment to do something about whatever is troublesome about the situation. Only then is it possible to consider initiating some action that may solve a problem. Quite clearly, giving advice on solving problems entails collaboration—working together (Baum 1987, 21).

5. [P]eople create power when they work together to do things collectively that no one could do alone. Significantly, power brings gains and costs, and the latter many deter people from attempting to wield power, or even from thinking about it. Power brings control, but it also gives participants new responsibilities. Because power comes out of a relationship among people who struggle with and against one another to satisfy their interests, success requires that they care for one another when they attempt to act together. Caring involves not only an abstract intellectual commitment but also an emotional closeness in which parties reveal their needs and take others' needs seriously. This intimacy promises to lead to new agreements, but it also presents risks.... In negotiation, people must expose their commitments to groups, places, or ideals with the uncertainty of whether others will join and strengthen these commitments or decline and devalue the objects of the commitments (Baum 1987, 21).

6. But at any level, a structure of meaning attempts to organize the relationship between three aspects of reality: the observable associations between categories of events; the emotions these events provoke; and the purposes they entail. That is, it provides a framework in which to think about what is likely to happen, what it would feel like, whether we want it to happen and how we can influence it. Each of these questions involves the others: our intentions affect how we categorize events, these categories define the predictable relationships in whose terms we think about the future and so, reciprocally, influence our intentions; just as the feelings which events provoke at once reflect and shape our intentions, colouring the categorical language through which we represent experience (Marris 1982b, 5).

12

Professional Authority: Craft, Character, and Community

The two stories that opened this book represented the extremes of professional orientation. Tim, the planner designer, believed his aesthetic judgment should rule, while Fred, the planning director, was willing to trade off elements of his plan to obtain public support and commitment to downtown improvements. The conventional interpretation, which I hope planners will abandon, casts Tim as the technical expert and Fred as the political advocate. Such typecasting misleads because it fails to recognize the complex nature of planning in a liberal society. Worse, it encourages planners to take sides, dismissing one approach as morally inferior to or less effective than the other.

Tim and Fred do not represent types, but rather they adopt different approaches to the deep and persistent tensions between the authority of the professional planner and the politics of public authority in the United States. Each planner connects with the public good through the exercise of power. Tim finds his power in his craft, the aesthetic efficacy of his design judgments; while Fred relies on the efficacy of public persuasion, the power of consensus. Although both play professional roles, neither identifies with the protocol of expertise. As Tim seeks public expression and form for his artistry, he does not rely on rational or instrumental theories of planning, but on intuitive and contextual designs, in this case, for a riverfront. He wants to replace the landscape of banality with visual features that evoke a credible past and leave a positive imprint on the passerby. In contrast, Fred wants to produce a plan in which local officials, business people, and residents will recognize their hopes. He tries to create a plan for the future that people will adopt as their own, because it is neither unfamiliar nor strange.

Our culture and the planning profession play off fact and value, the public and the private, and reason and emotion as mutually exclusive opposites. The profession, through its protocol based on the rational planning model, tries to synthesize the poles. The good planner, the effective planner, balances the conflicting demands by making plans that integrate expertise and service. This portrayal of the good planner as the objective professional who applies techniques, makes judgments, and imposes regulations that render a public good glosses over the tensions embedded in the profession. The rational model and the professional protocol encourage planners to separate expertise from politics and politics from the public good. Many planners who have identified with the image of the expert expect that the comprehensiveness, objectivity, and rationality of their work will displace and diminish the inherently provisional and contingent qualities of their own practical reasoning and judgment. Their expectations do not adequately or accurately account for the complexity and ambiguity of the problems they face.

The planners in this book report routine and unexceptional circumstances. I have identified the impediments to planning, not to discourage students and practitioners of planning, but to show the breadth of moral and political imagination that planners exercise to guide and justify their own work. Both skepticism and hope permeate these stories.

The stories illustrate that questions of planning efficacy need a new interpretive framework. A pragmatic orientation emphasizes how these planners, despite their different interests, styles, beliefs, and backgrounds, share a practical approach to identifying and evaluating plans and their consequences. Each tries, like Tim and Fred, to reconcile American individualism and concepts of social responsibility. I do not believe we should judge the efficacy of their efforts by framing the dilemmas of liberal society into a single continuum with freedom on one end and responsibility on the other. Gaps exist. Tensions prevail. The language of duality tends to overlook the many ways that individual freedoms and public responsibilities conflict in practice. The stories in this book are intended to reintroduce an awareness of the complexity of practical experience into professional interpretation. Tim and Fred are neither good nor bad planners, but some of both.

Ironically, adherents of the professional protocol often blame theorists for failing to offer useful theory, not realizing how the legitimizing force of their professionalism—the protocol—relies on the abstract ideas they deplore. For instance, the professional protocol contrasts the objective rationality of planners with the adversarial irrationality of politicians. When adherents of the professional protocol are challenged or criticized, their only resource for justifying their expertise are theories that ignore or place planners above political purposes and relationships. This handicaps practitioners in two ways. First, it prevents planners from taking organized political actions to anticipate and cope with threatening conflicts. Second, the protocol blinds adherents to opportunities for political collaboration and consensus building. The professional protocol promotes a cynical view of public life, because it makes planning deliberations appear hopeless.

The tales here from the everyday lives of practicing planners show how the conventional beliefs that separate moral vision, technical expertise, and adversarial politics do not adequately explain what planners do. None of the planners had discovered a singular method of practice that resolved the complex tensions and ambiguities that accompany planning. Some identified more closely with the conventions of competent inquiry, while others cared more about political strategy. However, they all composed responses to the problems of planning that combined elements of vision, interest, advocacy, and deliberation.

Instead of describing planning analysis and design as instrumental techniques, planners should consider using the language of craft, which emphasizes how individuals apply skills. Instead of treating power and politics as mainly adversarial, planners should recognize and nurture forms of communication and practice that build on reciprocal and unitary modes of democratic action. Instead of trying to reconcile the tension between autonomy and responsibility through acts of professional prowess, planners should consider forming "open" moral communities that cut across established lines of bureaucratic authority and community affiliation (Mandelbaum 1988). Members of these communities would share the burden of political defeats and celebrate their victories. This need not lead to passivity in the face of adversity or threats, but could help all participants prepare for such episodes on a regular basis.

CRAFT AND CHARACTER

Too often, in their debates over the rules of good social science inquiry, analysts separate the technical from the political. This distinction has unwittingly spilled over into guides for planning practice. A more useful distinction for grasping how planners put their knowledge to use in their everyday practice is that between craft and rhetoric. Craft refers to the competent application of skilled inquiry and composition to the creation of a useful product: a design, ordinance, or plan. The proper judges of such competence are other professionals, designers, and skilled craftspeople who possess experience making the product. Rhetoric refers to the judgments planners make and the deliberations they engage in with local officials, municipal employees, citizens, and businesses about purposes, alternatives, and means. In strong professions, like medicine and law, which carry a good deal of authority in our society, the elements of craft frequently define the rhetoric. For instance, the terminology doctors use to make a diagnosis—their language of expertise—not only informs their judgment, but shapes how their diagnosis is communicated and discussed among others. However, in a marginal profession like planning, the rhetoric tends to define the craft. Planners emphasize a professional protocol of expertise precisely because their craft does not enjoy substantial institutional legitimacy and support. Planning craft proves vulnerable in the face of powerful local institutions, interests, and civic and business leaders who believe they can make their own worthy plans.

Planners take up many different purposes, worries, concerns, and issues and deploy causal knowledge and professional lore about them, but in the context of the particular relationships and attachments that make up local authority. In other words, planners try to use their expertise to convince local officials and citizens of the necessity and importance of planning. In their stories to members of the community, planners carry on planning traditions, but rarely develop a plan independent of the purposes at hand, the situations they face, or their relationships with others.

The planners I interviewed did not cast their work in terms of formal theory, but rather found authority for their reflections on the meaning of their actions from the communities with which they most identified. For instance, Tom (the sacked suburban planning director in chapter 3) identified with the profession, while Bill (the suburban planning director in chapter 6 who found room for the portable toilets) turned to other municipal employees to check his bearings. Alice (the federal bureaucrat in chapters 6 and 8) shifted among her allegiances to community residents, local officials, and federal regulations without suffering moral anguish or engendering incoherent advice.

The ways planners talk and think about the future of the community intersect with the oral traditions of growth and prosperity promoted by local boosters, developers, investors, consumers, and community activists. Like other professionals, planners do not impose rules, but rather make judgments about causes, reasons, behavior, and consequences on a case-by-case basis. They offer interpretations and arguments to justify their judgments and to set historical precedents that they can use over time to build recognition of and support for the policies that they favor. Consider Donald's careful orchestration of the landfill siting plans in chapter 5 or Fred's efforts to build support for the downtown redevelopment plan in chapter 1.

John Forester, in writing about planning activity that brings craft and rhetoric together, argues that planners engage in anticipatory analysis:

> First, the analyst must *envision* possible futures of the (implemented) project in its physical, institutional, and cultural contexts. Second, the analyst must *prepare* and *manage* arguments both supporting the proposal (the analyst thus seems to assist the developer) and seeking to modify the proposal (the analyst thus sets the stage for the comments of the Public Works director and others). Third, the analyst must seek effectively to *present* (and perhaps *negotiate* with his or her own formal analysis of) a final proposal and alternatives to it (1987a, 163).

Forester contrasts the planning analyst with the social scientist. The scientist seeks to explain or interpret; the planner, however, must do more—she must also anticipate:

> The planning or policy analyst is engaged with a prospective project; the analyst must not only present the facts of what may happen, not only interpret and explain what is likely, but he or she must try to respond practically to anticipated problems and so seek directly to influence, alter, and shape what will happen (1987a, 164).

Planning craft uses practical reasoning to combine expert knowledge and moral judgment. The protocol of the professional expert, however, tends to emphasize only one aspect of this craft—the discovery, analysis, and representation of the facts (truth). Methods of rational analysis and assessment enjoy pride of place. By contrast, planning craft draws on the principles, models, and images of good planning that planners use to judge the relative merits of different proposals. It draws on moral frameworks to select, compare, and evaluate these proposals. For instance, the longstanding reform tradition of plan first, then regulate may shape

324 What Planners Do

the judgments planners make about land development proposals, but planners do not proclaim moral principles or scientific findings without anticipating the practical consequences of different development schemes. The lack of political authority and cultural standing provokes caution and inspires rhetorical innovation.

Planners must balance their craft and rhetoric because of the difficulties they face when they try to talk shop to developers, citizens, and elected officials. Planners adopt rhetorical conventions that respect the social, emotional, and cultural background of the participants. For example, planners work hard to determine what arguments and actions will prove meaningful to the different participants in the development of a neighborhood plan or the review of a development proposal. At times, in searching for a common language of deliberation, planners fall back on the cynical politics of cronyism or of special interests, turning the process into a masquerade. Local officials and developers often pressure planners to abandon the moral conventions of the planning tradition and apply the planning rationale as a justification for individual gain. These are the sorts of pressures that Tom and Martin tried unsuccessfully to cope with in chapter 3 and that George and Bruce encountered in the setback battles in chapter 6.

Bruce Jennings argues that overreliance on the professional protocol of the objective expert actually contributes to the cynical abuse of expertise. As each interest group hires a certified expert to argue the merits of its case, rational expertise serves to enhance the divisions between the various political interests, rather than seek a common good. Jennings proposes advice that emphasizes artistry and craft:

> Its aim is to demonstrate the interconnections among the various conventions that make up the cultural context within which actions take place and to show how the agent's intentions in any particular action are related to the overall pattern of projects and roles that make up his or her self-identity (1987, 145).

Planning as craft seeks to promote deliberation within the community about what counts as meaningful development, now and for the future. Unfortunately, the pursuit of planning deliberations about the regulation of development encounters considerable resistance. Too often, regulations appear attractive to local officials only when they have a narrow or even perverse planning impact and are unacceptable when they promise significant public benefit.

One planner offered an especially reflective account of his craftsmanship. His story describes how he balances the pursuit of professional desires with the fair and faithful service to the public good. He describes difficult, but routine challenges. He struggles to balance the demands of competence with the complex expectations of the community by redefining local problems.

Craft: Andrew

Andrew is the zoning administrator from chapter 6 who tried unsuccessfully to constrain the property interests of Mr. Trimble, the manufacturer. Andrew understands the political nature of his work and has no illusions about his powers. However, he sustains his planning imagination and his desire to find ways to tie together and balance the fragmented and often divisive communities of the municipality for which he works.

> A lot of planning professionals leave school thinking they know what's best for a community, despite what the residents think, but I think this is a mistake. In fact, I believe it is very important to respect and use the experience of residents, even in cases of profound moral disagreement. Even when residents raise blatantly racist ideas, I am reluctant to protest, not because I agree with them, but because I do not want to violate the community solidarity.
>
> I don't think people should pave backyards. First, paving increases run off and the hazard of flooding. Second, paving is ugly, compared to grass or other natural ground cover. When people call to ask permission to pave, I can exercise discretion in interpreting the reg. I can tell them the rule—no pavement allowed on more than 50 percent of the yard—or I can negotiate to help encourage a more beautiful and aesthetically pleasing job. Although I don't want them to do any paving at all, I also respect their right to use their property as they please. I suspend my personal values, become sort of detached, because these sorts of individual uses do not pose a serious risk to the public good.
>
> This community includes people whose values differ from mine. One of these is paving backyards and putting up patios and decks. I don't think I should use my authority as zoning administrator to impose my personal aesthetic values on these people. The homeowners in this old suburb don't have much space. Most of the lots in the city are 35 by 120 feet. It's natural that they would want to use this small space more intensely. Look, I don't think there is good and evil—clear, fixed standards. So everything, each case I review, is kind of a back and forth, a give and take situation.

I think there are levels of competence in a regulatory job. At the first level, you simply listen to someone's request and try to figure out a way to meet it, although if you don't like it, there are plenty of ways to make the same proposal illegal. The second level moves from knowledge of the rules to knowledge of the policy. You understand the purpose of different elements of the code and then interpret ambiguous rules or particular cases in light of these policies.

I get at the policy by trying to figure out the legislative intent. When I can't figure out a rule, I search the minutes of council meetings to find out the purpose of the rule. I don't go back too far. I concentrate mainly on recent amendments and decisions. I use the record of the public will, at least as expressed by the elected officials, to interpret how to apply the regulations. The final level is to go beyond deciphering intent to developing arguments based on my own experience and values, which not only reflect but inform the public will.

Andrew then illustrates how he uses his craft with the following story:

Residents in a Hispanic suburban neighborhood were using the vacant backyard behind some large apartment buildings for parking. The yard was not paved and was a muddy and unsightly area that could pose dangers. The director of health, who was a racist, wanted to instigate action. He wanted the backyard fenced off from auto parking, insisting that the drivers violated a city traffic ordinance that prohibited driving over curbs.

However, the police department found no curbs separating the yard from the street, so the ordinance did not apply. The health inspector turned to me as zoning administrator and insisted that I do something to put the parking to an end. The health official pounced on a zoning ordinance that required all parking areas greater than 1,200 square feet be paved and used it to pressure me to enforce a ban on parking.

I acknowledged the law and on inspection found the yard unsightly and in need of paving, but I also knew there were some serious obstacles. First, the owners were absentee and hard to contact. Delay was inevitable. Second, when I analyzed the feasibility of paving, I discovered that a utility easement prohibited it. Third, the buildings were constructed in an area whose zoning had not originally required adequate parking. As a result, the high-density area was plagued by a serious parking shortage. The backyard offered an important source of parking in a congested area. I figured that the unsightly yard would pose less of a burden on residents than the removal of parking. So, I simply began to drag my feet. I waited a month and then sent a letter to the owners of the buildings informing them that, unless it was paved, parking in the yard was illegal. So far I've received no response.

My next step was to circulate a draft of the letter to various department heads and invite them to a meeting to offer their advice. The health official has made it clear that he wants the police to ticket the auto owners. He keeps nagging me, but I want the burden of improvement to fall on the shoulders of the owners who undermaintain their property.

By calling the meeting, I can turn the regulatory problem into a planning issue. Furthermore, by bringing in other department heads, I can shift responsibility from my shoulders and share it. Finally, I hope to buy time to develop a longer term solution to the parking problem that residents face. I am anticipating getting some of the city CDBG funds to use for paving and street improvements. I have already scouted about for alternative parking sites and explored some of the costs of placing a curb along the road bordering the backyard where illegal parking is occurring. So far, the steps are modest and no formal plan has been developed, but the punitive health official is not having his way.

I feel ambivalent about my role. On the one hand, I'm something of a libertarian when it comes to property rights. I don't want to intrude unless there is serious cause. However, I find racism intolerable and sufficient reason to intrude. For the most part, I'm response oriented unless an issue emerges that plays to my bias.

Andrew describes his part in the regulatory process. In this ongoing activity he tries to introduce elements of fairness and efficiency that other municipal bureaucrats will tolerate and local citizens will respect. His story, however, illustrates his misgivings about the regulations and his reluctance to enforce paving restrictions, which good planning policies favor, but which local residents do not want. He shifts back and forth between the values of environmental quality and of citizens using their property as they please.

Andrew acknowledges the inherent ambiguity and tension between freedom and justice, the public and the private, the individual and the rule. He seeks neither the power of rules nor of political persuasion as desirable approaches to ensuring the public order. Rather, he engages in an internal dialogue in which he empathizes with the positions and interests of different parties in a regulatory dispute. He believes rules are important, but treats them as social products that need constant review.

Andrew tries to turn an adversarial regulatory action into planning deliberations. Where the health inspector saw only deviance, Andrew saw injustice and intolerance. Andrew did not engage in a principled struggle, however, but rather used the powers of his bureaucratic turf to generate delay and interdepartmental uncertainty. Buying time gave him the opportunity to redefine the issue from a police problem to a community development priority.

Andrew's description of the planning process does not outline methodical steps for good planning. In learning about a problem, he takes a developmental rather than a technical approach. He takes the time to learn about the needs, expectations, and history of others before making judgments. Andrew does not view his work as a zoning administrator as a technical activity, but as a craft that he has acquired through practice and reflection. He does not seek to employ cleverness, but to acquire a practical wisdom that combines technical knowledge with an empathic knowledge of the locale and its residents. Andrew's doubts and ambivalence about his powers do not reflect technical incompetence or a lack of smarts. His honest self-appraisal tempers the hubris of his professional ambitions, without curbing his willingness to exercise moral courage.

Character

It is the planner's incremental visions that inspire the public to recognize and accept his interpretation of the consequences that will likely ensue from particular plans. The public's belief that these plans are comprehensible and plausible and that the planner's judgment is trustworthy does not rest on the planner's certain knowledge of the future. No one, including planning experts, knows how the future will turn out. Belief in the credibility of planning advice relies heavily on the assessment of the moral character of the planner. The moral integrity of the planner determines the public's willingness to believe her arguments.

Whether planners embrace particular rules of conduct or behavioral consequences as a moral guide matters less than the meaning of the relationships that they form with the people they are advising. Tom, the suburban planning director in chapter 3 who tried unsuccessfully to educate the village board, and Ken, the planner whose impassioned defense of planning vision was ridiculed in chapter 5, both exhibited ethical behavior and moral character. The officials, however, did not share their outlook. Tom and Ken remained faithful to the moral values of the professional protocol, but in so doing, sacrificed their credibility with their audience, who held a different moral interpretation of the problems.

Planning advice not only reflects moral character, but establishes and nurtures that character in relationships with others. The professional protocol provides too narrow and restrictive a moral outlook to allow for the robust development of the planner's character. To cultivate relationships with superiors, colleagues, and potential adversaries, planners must listen well, give reliable information, and keep promises. And, they must do this in ways that evoke respect from the members of the community that they hope to advise. In the absence of institutional power, planners cannot expect that their words and ideas will automatically command attention and assent. They must take great care to cultivate relationships that will establish an appreciation of their moral character and, thereby, enhance the authority of their advice. Such community-based character building makes way for planning advice based on shared judgment, rather than expert advice based on impeccable moral authority.

Fred: Community as a Source of Character

Fred, the optimistic and politically active planning director for Burgess, worked his way up through the ranks of the local municipal bureaucracy. Planning started out as a job and only later became a vocation.

> I finished my undergraduate degree in 1976. CETA was still in place then and I got my first job working in the Burgess planning department as an engineering aide. I worked in the department for five years and without much ambition worked up to the position of landscape architect.
>
> When the depression hit in 1981, the city laid off some one hundred employees. My boss at the time was a cold man and withdrawn. He called me into his office and told me that I was laid off. Usually you can tell ahead of time when something like this is going to happen. I had no idea it was coming. I was the only one from the planning department laid off.
>
> I was married with a child. I owned a home. I panicked and feared being a failure. The lack of money didn't bother me as much as this fear and sense of failure, but my family was very supportive. I hustled and found a job working for the park district. I had done work for them before in my planning job, so they knew my work. It turned out that I didn't miss a single day of work after being fired.
>
> Within two years, I had become assistant superintendent of parks. The park district had a five-member board, the chair of which took an active involvement in the day-to-day administration of the district. If you were to bad mouth a board member in conversations with your department colleagues, word would quickly get back to that board member and you'd be called in to explain what you said. I tried to mind my own business and do a good professional job, but then the superintendent was unexpectedly fired and I became superintendent. I could no longer ignore or avoid the political involvement of the board chair in the administration of the parks.

The board chair would frequently insist that the superintendent hire someone who was not well qualified for an open position, and then later chastise the superintendent for the incompetence of the person he had urged the superintendent to hire. I didn't like this. When I took over, I tried to be honest. I told him what I felt outright. I refused to hire unqualified applicants.

The board had manipulated my predecessor and I did not want to go along. The board wanted to do it all—make decisions and implement them, but without taking the responsibility. Our differences came to a head when I discovered a thirty-year employee stealing gas. I wouldn't overlook this theft because I wanted to maintain my credibility and integrity as an administrator. So I took the case to my boss, the administrator of the parks. He took the issue up with the board and they told him to forget it. He in turn told me to forget it. I couldn't and didn't. I postponed making a decision for about four months and was absolutely miserable.

I spoke about it with my wife and together we decided I should quit and go back to school for my master's degree in planning. She offered to go to work while I went to school. I could never quit if she hadn't made it possible. It was an important turning point. I overcame my fear of failure and found out I was able to act on my convictions. I also learned important political lessons that I still use.

I had been naive about professional work. For years I simply did not understand how political authorities would and could manipulate and control bureaucratic staff like me. I was very private then. I turned inward and tried to rely on my competence and character. But that wasn't enough. Now I constantly work to build a base of public support for my plans and actions. I work openly in a public arena and try to foster a sense of the public good that can be achieved through planning.

Fred became a civic activist, through a kind of conversion experience. He changed from being a defensive and self-centered professional to becoming an outgoing and innovative public professional. He treats planning as a vocation marked by a vivid sense of community commitment. He bases his work on the depth of his experience with a place and its people, rather than on an allegiance to technique. He works enthusiastically to foster community in his workplace and in the city. It would be hard to imagine Fred as a rootless consultant, offering advice to different clients.

The character and integrity of Fred's planning have developed through his relationship with a particular geographic community—his home town. Instead of identifying with the norms of professional practice, he turns instead to the values of the community activists and reformers.

Fred rejected the unfair politics of patronage and finds inspiration and support for his own planning work through a more just social reciprocity. He rejects patronage, with its self-serving and cynical system of unequal exchanges, and embraces collaboration, with its emphasis on sharing and fair exchange. The next story examines how consultants establish credibility and authority with an audience of strangers and in the absence of long-established relationships.

Diane: A Consultant's Integrity

Diane seems demure and innocent. She sits with her hands folded. Her long, brown hair is clasped neatly in a barrette. Her bangs and thick eyebrows seem to protect the vulnerability of her eyes. Her soft voice and high cheekbones convey steely shyness. Vulnerable? Yes. Weak? No. She works as a consultant traveling across the United States conducting prison site plan studies. Unlike Fred, she must build relationships of trust and open channels of communication from scratch each time she visits a new place.

> I work for a firm that does what's called prison development consulting. My job is to visit different states that are planning to build new prisons and to determine the best site. My first step is to analyze the demographic makeup of the state's counties. I do a social and economic analysis to determine the need for the prison jobs and target a small number of the neediest counties, usually about five. Then, I have to take political bias into account. After I conduct my initial analysis, county officials begin pressuring me to make their county be selected as the site. This usually occurs in the big urban states like California, Florida, and New York. The prison means jobs and getting them is kind of a patronage payoff.
>
> I basically visit each of these counties and attend public meetings about the prison. I want to find out what proportion of the residents favor or oppose a prison locally. What are the sorts of reasons they give for wanting or not wanting the prison? What is the general feeling about the presence of a prison?
>
> I record the responses to these questions and prepare a brief report that suggests priority locations among the top four or five counties. I present these to the state prison board and discuss the findings with them. Occasionally the governor's staff will come right out and tell me what the governor wants, even before I conduct the research. Others will try to persuade me at the meetings. In one midwestern state, a county official approached me and said that the governor had promised his county a prison to provide jobs.
>
> I said, "There are a lot of counties like yours that deserve the employment benefits of a prison."

He replied, "The governor and I were speaking the other day and he said that our county was the best site."

"It's not my decision," I said. "I just make proposals about priorities."

In disbelief he said, "I'm sure the governor will decide my way, one way or another."

I snapped back, "Well, if that's the case, then why bother talking with me?"

"I thought it might be easier for you if you knew where you'd eventually be putting it."

I was speechless. In fact, the prison did end up there. It was the most blatant and overt example of political pressure I've experienced in two years on the job. Usually the pressure I receive is more subtle.

You know, my job is only to propose and not dispose, but nine out of ten times the state prison boards and governors choose the site I select as the top priority. I think they listen to me because I pay attention to what the citizens have to say. I spend usually a week traveling to each of the prospective counties and attending the public meetings. These are required by law in most states. The feedback at these meetings is very different than what I get when I first meet with officials in the state capital. I listen closely to what people say. When I finish the public meetings, I go back to the office and begin working out the details. I combine the demographic, geographic, and economic information with what the citizens and officials told me about local needs and desires. I try to assess the potential economic and social benefits of the prison for each county.

I make an emotional and intuitive judgment based on both the demographic needs and my sense of citizen interest. The more articulate the community residents and representatives are, the more information I have to go on, and this usually gives such places a better chance of being a high priority site. For instance, I especially remember the testimony of citizens in one county that focused not just on how the prison would serve them, but how they could serve the prison. That scored high for me.

I do use political criteria in my judgment, but it only comes into play when the differences between potential sites is close. In some states, the governor steps in after I identify the final five and I don't have an opportunity to set priorities. Governors use any number of electoral and political criteria to pick the final site.

A few weeks ago, I was at a community meeting in which everyone who came brought children. They wanted me to see that the prison would have a potentially harmful effect on their children. I checked this tactic out with my colleagues. It was new to everyone. It worked, too. I didn't recommend putting a prison in that county.

They reminded me of an important point. It's easy to lose sight of who will be affected by a prison. It bothers me that I could be so short-sighted and not see who's going to be affected. But I have to make my judgments quickly—in just two to four weeks—seldom longer than a month. Sometimes I feel it is not a very complete planning process.

I'm not sure there is a good way to plan for prisons. The demand for the employment that prisons provide greatly exceeds the supply. There are lots of places to choose from and little time to conduct a thorough assessment.

I think I do a much better job than my coworkers. They don't do any of the social and economic analysis that I do. They don't really care about citizen input and feelings. I do a lot more than is required. All you have to do is visit the handful of prospective sites, attend the meetings, take notes, and offer priorities. I spend a lot of time and effort collecting and assessing the needs and desires of each place.

I was amazed when I first started working for the firm that so little was actually required, but I wasn't going to do the minimum. I am willing to admit that I don't know things. Most of my colleagues won't. I try to learn. I put myself in the place of the local residents and officials. I try to get an accurate sense of their feelings about the prison and its consequences for them. The prison is full of bad people. Would I want to live near a prison?

I tell the truth. I say, "No, I wouldn't." However, there's more to it than just that risk. The prison brings jobs and economic development. You don't have to identify your community with the prison. Of course, this is hard to pull off when the prison gets built across the street.

At some point, I usually point out to residents fearful about the prison that they already turn a blind eye to undesirable activities and buildings in their community. You could learn to do the same with the prison. Most people don't say anything after that.

I'm thinking to myself, could I really not notice it everyday? I have a hard time saying yes to that question. I try avoiding this question, but when someone puts it to me, I'm honest. I say no. I used to think that if you lied to people it wouldn't make that big a difference, but I could never bring myself to do it. When I went on my first site visit, I traveled with a colleague who stood before the people and lied. He'd say whatever he thought they wanted to hear. He said things like, "It'll really not be that bad," and, "The governor will think you're an important place. You'll get political attention." He wanted them to believe that the prison was a good thing. The people left, it seemed to me, a lot more afraid than when they first came. Many seemed resigned and defeated. They felt the coming of the prison was inevitable. They lost the sense that their participation mattered.

At least when you're honest, the residents will trust you and listen to what you say. I guess the fact that I'm female helps. I do feel a sense of maternal concern. Partly, they have no other choice but to trust me, since I'm their only opportunity to make their participation count, but they also trust me because I speak sincerely and honestly. I tell them that what they say matters and then I make every effort to take what they say into account—use it in setting priorities.

My predecessor used political criteria to make the first cut of counties in the state. He said, "You need to know who's paying your salary. Politics is central," but I haven't found that to be true.

I face more frustrations taking my approach. My colleagues leave work whistling, carefree. I carry this stuff home with me. I spend sixty-hour weeks thinking about the people. What's going to be best for them? What's the best choice? Am I exceeding my authority? Did I leave something important out? Maybe I should do something more?

I make these huge charts on my walls at home and I divide them into five parts, one for each county. Then I put up all the information I've collected for each county from the census, reports, and my own notes and memory. I especially include the fears and hopes of residents. After it's all listed, I read and compare them, weighing the good and bad consequences. What people have said tends to be the most important influence on me, I think. If the differences between two finalists are small and both are geographically adjacent, I will urge a location at or near the border.

I don't like making the final recommendations, because I always have doubts. I'm never really sure. I get scared that I'm recommending a choice that won't really prove beneficial. Once the final choice is made, I go away feeling bad that choices B, C, D, and E didn't get the prison. Getting to know the places and people in some detail means that I feel the frustration of not helping the places that deserve a prison, but didn't get one.

It's my sense that people want a prison for the benefits it provides—the jobs and resources. When I first started graduate school, I thought only about what people wanted and not about what they needed. Now I find my work involves me in consideration of both.

You can't solve everyone's problems. What's best for the whole? I always listen to everyone, but still feel bad when the wants of the few get pushed aside to meet the needs of the many. I can't separate myself from these feelings yet. It would make my job much easier if I could. I try to separate myself, but find myself still getting involved in these peoples' lives. I don't want to hear another resident tell me a story of misery. Yet, I still listen. I ask them how they feel and they tell me. I hear their stories and feel bad.

My colleagues don't really offer any support. I don't see things the way they do. I'm the youngest person on the staff. There's a competitive atmosphere. The big payoff is getting contracts with states. Everyone is supposed to improve their track record in the siting process, so as to improve prospects of getting more contracts. The competition pits us against each other and takes away any incentive to share.

In one case, my colleagues knew I was going to a state whose governor was notorious for politicizing the siting process. They let me run head on into this mess without warning me. They laughed when I got back and told them about the political maneuvers. I asked them why they didn't tell me. They just laughed some more and said, "You've got to find out by yourself."

I am the only female at the office who does this sort of site planning. The men resent me because it had up until my coming always been a man's world. Of the twenty-five companies nationwide that do this sort of work, there are only two other women involved. The men laugh because I feel and care for the people I plan for.

When I come back to the office and conduct my assessments, my colleagues will say things like, "Hasn't the Good Samaritan made a decision yet?" They say it in a joking way, but it's a put down. At first I doubted myself. I thought they might be right. But after two years, I have developed the best track record of anyone in the office. The next guy above me has over ten years' experience! I'm quite new, a woman, and I've done great. This fuels their resentment. It's no fun, but I care much more about my work and the people I serve than what my coworkers may think about me.[1]

Diane holds out hope for prison development to small, mainly rural towns, desperate for economic activity. Her older and much more experienced colleagues express a more cynical view of their work. They adopt an adversarial conception of the political process. Although Diane recognizes the politics of interests, she tries to understand the desires and needs of local communities. She does not deceive or manipulate, but sincerely tries to pull together the evidence of need and community desires.

She composes judgments that combine quantitative and qualitative information. Her empathic inquiry, in which she shuttles between the analysis of social need and the understanding of individual burdens, prepares her to speak convincingly to the diverse political audiences about the communities she selects as priorities. Her success, however, hinges as much on the relationships she establishes as the arguments she makes. Diane does not rest her authority on the application of a standard method that would allow her to claim objectivity. She tries to grasp meaning as well as the facts. She takes up the competing purposes and makes judgments, drawing on a wide variety of complex and often incommensurable arguments.

According to Diane, her gender plays an important role in distinguishing her from her male colleagues, particularly in the contentious community meetings and in the consultations with the governors' staff. The envy and resentment she senses from her coworkers reflects some sex discrimination, but also a fundamental misunderstanding of her nurturing and yet risky style. I can easily imagine cynical and seasoned male veterans being angered by a young woman who is able to inspire successful deliberations, while their own efforts to manipulate adversarial politics and competing self-interests tend to backfire. A colleague is disappointed when a competitor obtains greater success using the same approach. Diane's colleagues become angry because they neither understand nor respect her successful methods.

Although Andrew, Fred, and Diane used different methods in different settings with different audiences, they all built and projected a strong moral character. They all believed that their plans would matter only if they could persuade others to grasp the moral significance of the problems as they have framed them. Each, in offering advice about what should be done to serve the public interest, relied on their professional integrity, centered in relationships of trust and mutual communication, rather than on a morality of expert authority. Andrew did not like either paving or racism, but he developed practical judgments that both reflected and resisted public desires. Fred earned the community's trust through carefully nurtured, longstanding social ties, while Diane fostered trust by adopting a nurturing style that downplayed adversarial relations and emphasized participation and respect.

While all three planners exhibited moral integrity and professional competence, their stories tell how they pushed against the institutional and political boundaries that diminished their hopes that public officials and other department staff would share their commitment to planning. Andrew puts off the health official; Fred continues to work in the local bureaucracy even though it has caused him grief; and Diane faces the pressures of political lobbying and the rejection of her male colleagues. Despite these difficulties, each planner takes moral responsibility for matters that extend well beyond the boundaries of the professional protocol. These planners do not separate fact and value. Their judgments and actions go beyond the technical instrumentalism of the professional protocol, as they seek ways to offer useful, critical, and democratic advice.

COMMUNITY

The planning accounts in this book reflect my belief that professional planners work at the institutional margins of society, handicapped by social and cultural customs and expectations that rarely recognize or respect the importance of shared independence and of public goods. Respect for the public interest cannot be adequately grasped by those dedicated to possessive individualism. This respect requires a concept of individualism that is based on social reciprocity and responsibility. Ideological debates too often contrast possessive individualism with collective socialization, echoing the cold war battle between democratic capitalism and state socialism. Debates about democracy and planning in the United States should go beyond this narrow dichotomy and consider a broader spectrum of views concerning individualism and social relations. Especially important to planners are views of democratic organization that can complement and challenge the adversarial schemes that fragment and exclude the commonweal (Barber 1984; Bellah et al. 1985; Bryson and Crosby 1992; Nussbaum 1990; Wolfe 1989).

The planning stories in this book are intended to offer some reassurance. Professional planners work in an institutional order of competitive and hierarchical relationships, which, despite their adversarial and instrumental qualities, require some cooperation. Many professional planners regularly try, in imaginative, incremental, and occasionally grand ways, to shift attention from the adversarial to the deliberative. Their persistence testifies to the effort they are making in our competitive liberal society to keep alive the practical possibility and the hope of responsible, free, and informed deliberation. One respondent offered an articulate account of the ambiguity and challenge of democratic planning in the United States.

Ralph: Community Empowerment

Ralph, the planner implementing racial quotas in chapter 9, worked for a decade as the executive director of an inner city community development corporation (CDC), helping organize neighbors to rehabilitate aging apartment buildings. He has since joined a nonprofit organization that helps fund CDCs in Central City. He conducts evaluations of local nonprofit development corporations and provides them with technical assistance and funds for decent and affordable housing. We meet in his office in a rehabilitated commercial building on the edge of downtown.

> One of the tensions in this job is the affinity I feel for CDC practitioners and the obligations and constraints I experience in my role as a funder and reviewer of CDCs. I expect CDCs to perform. I have high expectations. I don't like it when the directors mess up. I know that CDC direc-

tors work without adequate resources in dark basements, but they still need to get the job done.

In my present job, I have to show results and the CDC directors do, too, for their own credibility, but this emphasis on performance makes me appear unsympathetic and too bottom line oriented in the eyes of many CDC directors. I have less difficulty accepting the failure to meet deadlines and get successful project results when the problem is due to financial hardship than if CDC staff are incompetent or sloppy. Too many people in the nonprofit world cloak their incompetence in radical rhetoric, blaming poor results on an unjust system, but there are plenty of radical groups that are competent.

For instance, the local Acorn group will demonstrate in front of city hall in the name of social justice for the poor, and when they do a project, their pro formas won't have errors. They know how to make clear, convincing, and persuasive presentations to funders. I do whatever I can to aid them, not only because I care about justice, but because I can trust their numbers.

I may sound too tough, but I really want these efforts to work. In my mind, the whole notion of community-based development could be just a footnote to U.S. social policy in the late twentieth century or it could become the primary method for delivering affordable housing. For CDCs to play this role we have to convince federal policymakers that there's a technology for building these organizations.

We are really trying to build local institutions that don't exist at present. The CDCs I envision will combine democracy and business, reconciling the two with a budget between $100,000 and $200,000. I want to see how far we can take this idea nationwide.

Here's what I look for. First, I like a CDC whose director and board have a clear strategy. Even if I don't like the strategy or I think it is unrealistic, it's better than no strategy at all. I don't think you can measure the success of CDCs by using a simple measure of productivity, like how many deals you've done.

There's this one CDC director whom I really admire. He's director of a CDC in an area that straddles black and white neighborhoods that have been segregated for decades. At a gut level he struggles with the issue of racial change in all the CDC's development efforts. He tries to develop projects and programs that whites can accept without either leaving or turning to violence against the black inmigrants. This is the high-water mark of performance.

I suppose that the single most important asset for CDCs is leadership. There really aren't enough good leaders to go around. I am not sure if this is inevitable, or the result of cultural and institutional barriers preventing this leadership from emerging. We aren't reaching out to minorities. We don't offer enough salary. We aren't doing enough to entice capable leadership into this kind of work.

Part of the reason I left my job as a CDC director to take this job was that I wanted to develop different viable CDC models. If you look at my experience as a director, you will find I was a good administrator, but that the organization was poorly governed. The planning and management functions were in tension with the organizing and empowerment activities. Ten years ago, CDC administrators and organizers emphasized social objectives that placed heavy burdens on the development activities.

It turns out that successful CDCs were those that focused on particular functions, such as job training or real estate development. They did not try to do everything. That's the reason I look for and encourage CDCs to follow plans—CDCs that follow a strategy, set priorities, and follow them. A successful CDC eventually has to say no to some objectives. As the CDC I worked for became more successful and wealthy as a real estate development and management organization, the members started to make increasing claims on its resources. As director, I wanted to continue doing development, but others on the board and in the membership wanted to pursue social policy and organizing activities. So I left.

A CDC strategy embodies not only what is needed in the area. Most of the neighborhoods have plenty of needs. The strategy should address issues of empowerment based on participatory democracy, as well as the development of feasible and useful projects. I usually consider three issues: governance, participation, and development.

I want to see actual results in each of these areas, but, of course, it is much easier to assess development outcomes than the other two. We do use objective criteria when we assess the performance of the CDCs we fund and advise. For instance, in assessing participation we ask questions like: "Is the board reflective of the race and ethnicity of the neighborhood?" For governance: "How often does the board meet?" We have a whole list of such questions to get at effective participation and good governance.

The really important issues are more difficult to assess. I think it is the presence of a culture that promotes participation in decision making. For instance, we had one CDC that was very good at implementing development projects, but top heavy in their board. We pointed this out and they hired a CDC director with a good track record at encouraging participation to show them some processes they could adopt to invite and use participation from the membership. His suggestions were interesting, but for the proposals to take hold, the executive director must take the initiative and set the mood. Leadership remains crucial.

When I visit the CDCs as part of the evaluation, I look for processes and procedures that share power rather than consolidate it. I face problems with this idea here at work. Many of my coworkers resist discussing their ideas and judgments with others. For instance, we have these quarterly meetings with all our CDC constituents. One of my program supervisors is terrified of these meetings. I think she's afraid of being criticized by all the directors, many of whom have unrealistic expectations about what our staff can do. My feeling is that if you're honest and competent, then you have nothing to fear.

Look, power is not a zero sum equation. When you learn how to share and do give and take, then all the participants can find real success. I cringe when I hear my coworkers sound like foundation bureaucrats: "Just call them on the phone or send a memo. Use your power as a funder to make them do what you want instead of taking some risks."

[On reciprocal empowerment] In one case, the director of a CDC was a lousy administrator. I was in the position of having to decide what was possible versus what I wanted. I called a staff meeting to discuss our options after the first year of little action. Do we drop the program entirely? Impose more stringent conditions? Make them hire an in-house technical assistance person? Step up monitoring? Each option had serious problems and risks. After discussion, it occurred to me that we might use a training program to both structure the monitoring (the stick), but provide at the same time the in-house support needed to carry out development projects (the carrot). This arrangement was based on reciprocal agreements and incentives, enabling us to keep track of the CDC's progress while contributing to its development.

I did this, even though I didn't like the director. You can't let personality get in the way of this work. There are a lot of people you won't like. You need to understand the other person's self-interest and their intentions. Where are they coming from? I don't mean by this that you become a manipulator who develops the perfect political persona—the charming liar.

I learn the interests of others so as to focus on opportunities for reciprocity. I try to get a sense of the different parties' goals and the situation, but without making them meet my goal. This is what I call negotiation. This director was not bad. He was a good organizer in a position that required an experienced development administrator. Instead of blaming the guy, I tried to figure out the reasons for failure and then figure out ways to get the CDC back on track rather than side-tracked.

My experience as a CDC director helps. I'm much less likely to get engaged emotionally over this sort of frustrating failure. Learning how to conduct useful mediation and negotiations is the key. This is hard work. What I learned after working for ten years as an executive director of a CDC is that you should not be so closely identified with your work. A lot of stuff can go wrong for no good reason and independent of your influence. If you identify with these results, your whole identity is thrown into question.

I have learned to do what I can during my time at work and then to let go at the end of the day. This works. The more difficult challenge is remaining hopeful. I get depressed a lot with the economic situation. Our work with CDCs looks good when put under a magnifying glass, but the overwhelming fact that poverty keeps getting worse haunts me. The social and demographic trends reshaping the society, with the rich getting richer and the poor getting poorer, defies our present schemes. Even though I was successful as a CDC director in providing many units of decent affordable low-income housing, the conditions in the neighborhood where I worked got worse during the ten years I was there. When I came there were no homeless. By the time I left I had accepted their presence as routine.

Ralph empathizes with the CDC directors, but he is also detached. He knows how hard it is to build affordable housing. He knows the sacrifices of time and effort it takes to mobilize resources and skills. Yet his desire to achieve significant results leads him to criticize incompetence and inefficiency on the part of many CDC directors. Ralph clearly wants CDCs to prosper as a major form of housing development in urban communities. He recognizes that pressures from a competitive economy, scarce social capital, and local political interests allow little room for organizational slack. He believes that to be able to provide decent housing for the poor, the CDCs must excel in organizational competence and development acumen.

Ralph believes in community empowerment, based not on adversarial politics, but on the unitary politics of reciprocity. In his efforts with other organizers, planners, and leaders to provide decent housing in poor neighborhoods, he experiences kinship and empowerment. However, when he tries to link up these local efforts with large-scale institutions, the performance principle takes center stage. In shuttling between kinship and performance, Ralph has developed his capacity to move among many communities, using his sense of detachment to mediate among multiple and sometimes incompatible solidarities.

Ralph understands the important relationship between power and planning. He recognizes the salience of adversarial political relationships, but does not embrace them. He nurtures his competent craftsmanship to be able to render practical judgments that others can put to good use. He exhibits ironic solidarity. His detachment enables him to compose strategies that offer alternative courses of action, while his empathy allows him to frame these options in terms that are meaningful to the client.

Ralph was exceptional among those I interviewed in being able to conceive of and implement ideas for building community institutions that foster democratic leadership and competent performance. Some of the

other planners wanted to bridge the adversarial and collaborative relationships of their situation, but had very little support. Ralph labored in
nonprofit institutions that were relatively small and organized to respect
consensual over adversarial democracy. Nancy, Annette, Alice, and Stelian
viewed the interdependencies of their situations not as a problem to be
eliminated or escaped, but as an opportunity for innovation and collaboration. Their efforts, however, to avoid adversarial procedures were
compromised and frustrated by their organizational settings. By contrast, Esteban, Donald, Kathleen, and Diane were able to engage in activities that at least represented marginal improvements within the
adversarial arena. All the planners, however, had to rationalize their own
achievements. In only a few instances (Annette, Nancy, Fred, and Ralph)
did the planners enjoy a network of colleagues who were a source of
moral inspiration and constructive criticism and who served as able and
willing consultants and useful political allies. Planners need to create
communities of support.

BUILDING THE REFORM COMMUNITY

The activities of professional planners remain on the margin of social
importance, even though the problems they address increasingly touch
the lives of almost everyone. Such pressing and grave problems as environmental degradation, social injustice, and untamed land development
underscore our interdependence, even as many of us seek escape as free
riders, huddling together in havens of suburban privilege. The fragmented system of government authority, the monopoly of adversarial
politics, and the primacy of cultural individualism sustain and support
policies that ignore this interdependence and intensify the uneven distribution of social, economic, and political uncertainty. The prominence
of these conditions makes many planners receptive to the professional
protocol of expertise as a source of guidance and legitimacy for their
work. The good planner offers expert knowledge, free of moral and political bias. The individual professional "speaks truth to power"
(Wildawsky 1979).

    The stories I tell here are typical of the experiences of many planners, if
not representative of most. Some planners design and regulate the growth
and development of settlements, so as to expand individual choice and
mobility. Others negotiate and organize agreements that foster joint responsibility for solving difficult and unpopular problems. I have emphasized the latter theme, because I believe the United States needs more

people willing, prepared, and able to carry out purposeful deliberations about the complex interdependencies that we experience as social and environmental problems. Responsible and informed citizenship is not the exclusive domain of professional planners. In fact, as I have argued, efforts to emphasize professional status and expertise are an impediment to nurturing and expanding planning deliberations among citizens with different occupational, ethnic, racial, and religious affiliations.

Planners have long debated how to professionalize the field. The broad scope of planning activity has frustrated efforts to bind planning to a single professional domain. The American Planning Association (APA), for example, includes members who have very different perceptions of the field. Some see planning as a practical activity tied to public service and occupation; others see planning as a form of professional expertise.

For decades, these two traditions were represented by separate organizations: the American Association of Planning Officials (ASPO) and the American Institute of Planners (AIP). These two associations merged in 1978 to become the American Planning Association to be better able to draw on their common strengths to promote planning to a largely indifferent world. The merger proved an organizational success, but it has tended to forthrightly embrace the tradition of professionalization and expertise, while extending a more ambivalent handshake to the tradition of liberal reform. The APA leadership, in leaning toward the professional orientation, tends to worry excessively about questions of turf, expertise, and legitimacy, which concern members seeking to enhance their authority and standing. Much effort goes into lobbying federal and state legislatures to approve laws that favor professional planning. These concerns merit attention, but should not dominate the association's agenda.

Planning offers an important means for institutionalizing the politics of deliberation within government. Democratic planning acknowledges the interdependencies of our social problems, too often overlooked in the adversarial arena of legislative and executive politics. The executive branch of government at all levels has expanded enormously in the twentieth century, seeking to manage, regulate, and coordinate the growing U.S. welfare state and its economy, but without seriously incorporating the culture and knowledge of planning that many early reformers believed were needed to overcome the powers of self-interest and competitive advantage. We need to conduct planning at all levels of government, but without encouraging additional specialized, fragmented, and powerful bureaucracies. To avoid this, leaders must assimilate the useful and democratic planning innovations that emerge when reformers put forth new programs. The APA can take an important step by developing, supporting, and publicizing the planning activities of the liberal reform movements that nurture these leaders and reform policies.[2]

I am not proposing, however, that the APA become a liberal advocacy organization like the American Civil Liberties Union. I have already discussed the risks of nondeliberative advocacy for the planning enterprise. Planners should give up the misleading dichotomy between expertise and advocacy and between professionalism and reform. Instead of building a bridge between the poles, planners should revise the language of liberal reform. Planning deliberation offers a way of persuading ourselves and others about how to conduct purposeful collective change without relying on adversarial conflict or detached expertise.

The APA should take advantage of its ambiguous self-definition, rather than impose a more uniform professional definition. Its ambiguity makes the association accessible to planning recruits from a wide array of occupations, avocations, and social movements. The APA should emphasize the value and promise of planning for reform-oriented public activists. More Americans will appreciate the value and importance of planning if the APA and its members offer planning as an accessible and useful resource for guiding and advancing liberal reform programs, rather than promoting planning as an exclusive professional good. For example, the APA should invite the leadership of the various liberal reform movements to speak and conduct formal discussions, seminars, and joint educational events at national and regional conferences. The association should provide a forum for liberal reformers pursuing purposeful deliberations about how to understand and solve such pressing problems as environmental pollution, inner city decline, natural disasters, educational reform, land conservation, and farmland preservation.

The professional protocol appears to render the embrace of liberal reform illegitimate. Planners who publicly display their liberal commitments forfeit their claim to objectivity and lose standing as experts in adversarial competition with political adversaries. The protocol, however, exaggerates both the powers of expertise and the efficacy of planning in adversarial settings. Adversarial politics do shape much of the discussion and debate about the problems planners hope to solve, but if planning remedies require collaboration and consensus, selling planning through adversarial means will likely backfire.

Planners should seek out, promote, and engage in liberal political deliberations that put forth responsible collaborative solutions to public problems. Planners should not foolishly enter adversarial political disputes, urging everyone to deliberate, nor should they avoid engaging in adversarial political debates altogether. Instead of trying to obtain respect for planning experts in adversarial politics, planners should identify, invent, and nurture political deliberations in which planning plays an important role. In such cooperative political settings, good professional practice comes less from the application and display of expertise and more through the clarity, efficacy, and popularity of planning visions and arguments shaped through political deliberation.

NOTES

1. In a letter written on June 22, 1993, commenting on her story several years later, Diane wrote:

   It has been four years since I started my job. My task has not gotten any easier but my understanding of how to politically persuade a governing body has become finely tuned.... My role (as those people who are concerned with what happens in their area see it) is to be the voice through which their *choice* is reflected. It is as if in some odd way they have finally begun to realize that I can only *suggest* the most suitable location for a detention facility, not pick it.... The emotional impact of my decisions does not follow me around as it used to. The emotional contribution of local residents plays an important role in my deliberation process, but my own no longer justifies my own feelings on the matter without losing sight of who I am responsible to.... The role of politics is even greater.... Governments are scrambling for money to protect their communities from the "potentially harmful situations" that felons create. In other words, political favors are being traded for governmental support of detention facility projects. Instead of one out of ten facility sites being determined by politics, four out of ten projects I work on are decided that way. It is a tough business to be in right now.

   As far as my career is going though, it couldn't be better. I have out survived many of my colleagues and am now training all new hires.

2. I am not reviving New Dealer Rexford Tugwell's proposal for a revision of the Constitution that would include planning as the fourth power of government. I share his belief in the crucial importance of planning for the guidance of modern societies, but recommend a more diverse and widespread institutionalization.

REFERENCES

Abrams, Charles. 1967. *The City Is the Frontier.* New York: Harper and Row.

Ackerman, Fredrick L. 1919. Where Goes the City Planning Movement? *Journal of the American Institute of Architects* 7: 418–520.

Adams, Thomas. 1927. *Planning the New York Region.* New York: Committee on Regional Plan of New York and Its Environs.

Adler, Seymour. 1990. Environmental Movement Politics, Mandates to Plan, and Professional Planners: The Dialectics of Discretion in Planning Practice. *Journal of Architectural and Planning Research 7, 4: 315–29.*

Advisory Commission on Intergovernmental Relations (ACIR). 1974. *The Challenge of Local Government Reorganization: Substate Regionalism and the Federal System,* vol. 3. Washington, DC: U.S. Government Printing Office.

Alexander, Ernest. 1984. After Rationality, What? A Review of Responses to Paradigm Breakdown. *Journal of the American Planning Association* 50, 1: 62–69.

Altshuler, Alan. 1965. *The City Planning Process: A Political Analysis.* Ithaca, NY: Cornell University Press.

American Institute of Planners. 1967. *AIP Newsletter* 218 (August).

Anderson, Charles. 1990. *Pragmatic Liberalism.* Chicago, IL: University of Chicago Press.

Angotti, Thomas. 1978. Planning and the Class Struggle: Radical Planning Theory and Practice in the Post-Banfield Period. In *The Structural Crisis of the 1970s and Beyond: The Need for a New Planning Theory,* edited by Harvey Goldstein and Sara Rosenberry. Blacksburg: College of Architecture and Urban Studies, Virginia Polytechnic Institute and State University.

Ballard, Robert D., and Joe Feagin. 1991. Racism and the City. In *Urban Life in Transition,* edited by M. Gottdeiner and C. Pickvance. Newbury Park, CA: Sage.

Banfield, Edward. 1970. *The Unheavenly City.* Boston: Little, Brown.

Barber, Benjamin. 1984. *Strong Democracy.* Berkeley: University of California Press.

___. 1988. *The Conquest of Politics: Liberal Philosophy in Democratic Times.* Princeton, NJ: Princeton University Press.

Baum, Howell. 1983a. *Planners and Public Expectations.* Cambridge, MA: Schenkman.

___. 1983b. Autonomy, Shame and Doubt: Power in the Bureaucratic Lives of Planners. *Administration and Society* 15, 2: 147–84.

___. 1987. *The Invisible Bureaucracy: The Unconscious in Organizational Problem-Solving.* New York: Oxford University Press.

___. 1990. *Organizational Membership and Personal Development in the Work Place.* Albany: SUNY Press.

Beard, Charles. 1927. Conflicts in City Planning. *Yale Review* 17: 65–77.

Beauregard, Robert. 1978. Planning in an Advanced Capitalist State. In *Planning Theory in the 1980s,* edited by Robert Burchell and George Sternlieb. New Brunswick, NJ: Center for Urban Policy Research.

___. 1983. Planners as Workers: A Marxist Perspective. In *Professionals and Urban Form,* edited by Judith Blau, Mark LaGory, and John Pipkin. Albany: State University of New York Press.

___. 1985. Occupational Transformations in Urban and Regional Planning, 1960 to 1980. *Journal of Planning Education and Research* 5, 1: 10–16.

Beckman, Norman. 1964. The Planner as Bureaucrat. *Journal of the American Institute of Planners* 30, 4: 187–92.

Bellah, Robert, Richard Madsen, William W. Sullivan, Ann Swindler, and Steven Tipton. 1985. *Habits of the Heart.* Berkeley: University of California Press.

___. 1991. *The Good Society.* New York: Knopf.

Benjamin, Lois. 1991. *The Black Elite: Facing the Color Line in the Twilight of the Twentieth Century.* New York: Nelson Hall.

Benveniste, Guy. 1989. *Mastering the Politics of Planning.* San Francisco, CA: Jossey-Bass.

Berger, Peter. 1987. *The Capitalist Revolution: Fifty Propositions About Prosperity, Equality and Liberty.* New York: Basic Books.

Bernstein, Richard. 1983. *Beyond Objectivism and Relativism: Science, Hermeneutics and Praxis.* Philadelphia: University of Pennsylvania Press.

Bolan, Richard. 1980. The Practitioner as Theorist: The Phenomenology of the Professional Episode. *Journal of the American Planning Association* 46, 3: 261–74.

Bolan, Richard, and Ronald Nuttal. 1975. *Urban Planning and Politics.* Lexington, MA: Lexington Books.

Boyer, Christine. 1983. *Dreaming the Rational City.* Cambridge, MA: MIT Press.

Branch, Melville. 1983. *Comprehensive City Planning: General Theory and Principles.* Pacific Palisades, CA: Palisades Publishers.

____. 1990. *Planning: Universal Process.* New York: Praeger.

____. 1992. *Planning and Human Survival.* New York: Praeger.

Bruce-Briggs, B., ed. 1979. *The New Class?* New Brunswick, NJ: Transaction Books.

Bryson, John, and Barbara Crosby. 1992. *Leadership for the Common Good.* San Francisco, CA: Jossey-Bass.

Burgess, Ernest. 1974. In *The Basic Writings of Ernest W. Burgess,* edited by Donald Bogue. Chicago, IL: University of Chicago Press.

Burnham, Daniel, and Edward H. Bennett. 1909. *Plan of Chicago.* Chicago: The Commercial Club.

Caro, Robert. 1974. *The Power Broker.* New York: Vintage.

Catanese, Anthony. 1974. *Planning and Local Politics: Impossible Dreams.* Beverly Hills, CA: Sage.

____. 1984. *The Politics of Planning and Development,* vol. 156. Beverly Hills, CA: Sage.

Catlin, Robert. 1993. The Planning Profession and Blacks in the United States: A Content Analysis of Academic and Professional Literature. *Journal of Planning Education and Research* 13, 1: 26–33.

Chapin, F. Stuart. 1965. *Urban Land Use Planning.* Urbana: University of Illinois Press.

Chapin, F. Stuart, and Edward Kaiser. 1979. *Urban Land Use Planning.* Urbana: University of Illinois Press.

Clavell, Pierre. 1986. *The Progressive City: Planning and Participation 1969–1984.* New Brunswick, NJ: Rutgers University Press.

Coles, Robert. 1989. *The Call of Stories.* Boston: Houghton Mifflin.

Connolly, William. 1987. *Politics and Ambiguity.* Madison: University of Wisconsin Press.

Dalton, Linda. 1985. Politics and Planning Agency Performance. *Journal of the American Planning Association* 51, 2: 189–99.

____. 1986. Why the Rational Paradigm Persists—The Resistance of Professional Education and Practice to Alternative Forms of Planning. *Journal of Planning Education and Research* 5, 3: 147–53.

____. 1989a. Emerging Knowledge About Planning Practice. *Journal of Planning Education and Research* 9, 1: 29–44.

____. 1989b. The Limits of Regulation: Evidence from Local Plan Implementation in California. *Journal of the American Planning Association* 55, 2: 151–68.

____. 1990. Planners in Conflict: Experience and Perception in California. *Journal of Architectural and Planning Research* 7, 4: 284–302.

Danielson, Michael. 1976. *The Politics of Exclusion.* New York: Columbia University Press.

Davidoff, Paul. 1965. Advocacy and Pluralism in Planning. *Journal of the American Institute of Planners* 31, 4: 103–15.

Davidoff, Paul, Linda Davidoff, and Neil Newton. 1970. Suburban Action: Advocacy Planning for an Open Society. *Jour-*

nal of the American Institute of Planners 36, 1: 12–21.

De Neufville, Judith. 1983. Planning Theory and Practice: Bridging the Gap. *Journal of Planning Education and Research* 3, 1: 35–45.

___. 1987. Knowledge and Action, Making the Link. *Journal of Planning Education and Research* 6, 2: 86–92.

Dewey, John. 1927. *The Public and Its Problems.* New York: Henry Holt.

Dykman, John. 1973. What Makes Planners Plan? In *Readings in Planning Theory*, edited by Andreas Faludi. Oxford, UK: Pergamon.

Erickson, Kai. 1976. *Everything in Its Path.* New York: Simon and Shuster.

Fainstein, Norman I., and Susan Fainstein. 1978. New Debates in Urban Planning: The Impact on Marxist Theory. In *The Structural Crisis of the 1970s and Beyond: The Need for a New Planning Theory*, edited by Harvey Goldstein and Sara Rosenberry. Blacksburg: College of Architecture and Urban Studies, Virginia Polytechnic Institute and State University.

Fainstein, Susan, and Norman Fainstein, eds. 1983. *Restructuring the City: The Political Economy of Urban Redevelopment.* New York: Longman.

Faludi, Andreas. 1973. *Readings in Planning Theory.* Oxford, UK: Pergamon.

___. 1986. *Critical Rationalism and Planning Methodology.* London: Pion.

Feld, Marsha. 1989. The Yonkers Case and Its Implications for the Teaching of the Practice of Planning. *Journal of Planning Education and Research* 8, 3: 169–76.

Fisher, Roger, and William Ury. 1983. *Getting to Yes.* New York: Penguin Books.

Fishman, R. P., ed. 1978. Appendix 5-1: State of the Art in Local Planning. In *Housing for All Under Law.* Cambridge, MA: Ballinger.

Fogelsong, Robert. 1986. *Planning the Capitalist City.* Princeton, NJ: Princeton University Press.

Forester, John. 1980. Critical Theory and Planning Practice. *Journal of the American Planning Association* 46, 3: 275–85.

___. 1982. Towards a Critical Empirical Framework for the Analysis of Public Policy. *New Political Science* 2: 145–64.

___. 1983. Critical Theory and Organizational Analysis. In *Beyond Method: Strategies for Social Research*, edited by Gareth Morgan. Beverly Hills, CA: Sage.

___. 1985. *Critical Theory and Public Life.* Cambridge, MA: MIT Press.

___. 1986. Critical Theory and Public Life: Only Connect. *International Journal of Urban Regional Research* 10, 2: 185–206.

—. 1987a. Anticipating Implementation: Normative Practices in Planning and Policy Analysis. In *Confronting Values in Policy Analysis: The Politics of Criteria*, edited by Frank Fischer and John Forester. Beverly Hills, CA: Sage.

—. 1987b. Planning in the Face of Conflict: Negotiation and Mediation Strategies in Local Land Use Regulation. *Journal of the American Planning Association* 53, 3: 303–14.

___. 1989. *Planning in the Face of Power.* Berkeley: University of California Press.

___. 1992a. Envisioning the Politics of Public Sector Dispute Resolution. In *Studies in Law, Politics and Society*, edited by Austin Sarat and Susan Silbery. Greenwich, CT: JAI Press.

___. 1992b. On the Ethics of Planning: Profiles of Planners and What They Teach Us About Practical Judgment and Moral Improvisation. Paper presented at the American Planning Association Conference, Washington, DC, 9–13 May.

___. 1992c. Critical Ethnography: On Fieldwork in a Habermasian Way. In *Critical Management Studies*, edited by Mats Alverson and Hugh Wilmott. Newbury Park, CA: Sage.

___. 1993a. *Critical Theory, Public Policy, and Planning Practice.* Albany: State University of New York Press.

___. 1993b. Learning from Practice Stories: The Priority of Practical Judgment. In *The Argumentative Turn in Policy Analysis and Planning*, edited by Frank Fischer and John Forester. Durham, NC: Duke University Press.

Forstall, Richard L. 1975. Annexations and Corporate Changes Since the 1970 Census: With Historical Data on Annexation for Larger Cities for 1900–1970. *Municipal Yearbook*. Washington, DC: International City Managers Association.

___. 1976. Annexations and Corporate Changes, 1970-74: With Historical Data on New Incorporations, 1950–74. *Municipal Yearbook*. Washington, DC: International City Managers Association.

Fowler, Robert B. 1991. *The Dance with Community*. Lawrence: University of Kansas Press.

Frieden, Bernard. 1979. *The Environmental Protection Hustle*. Cambridge, MA: MIT Press.

Friedmann, John. 1987. *Planning in the Public Domain*. Princeton, NJ: Princeton University Press.

Galloway, Thomas, and James Edwards. 1982. Critically Examining the Assumptions of Espoused Theory: The Case of City Planning and Management. *Journal of the American Planning Association* 48, 2: 184–95.

Gans, Herbert. 1982. *The Urban Villagers*. New York: The Free Press.

___. 1991. *Middle American Individualism*. New York: Oxford University Press.

Glasmier, Amy, and Terry Kahn. 1989. Planners in the '80s: Who We Are, Where We Work. *Journal of Planning Education and Research* 9, 1: 5–18.

Glazer, Nathan. 1988. *The Limits of Social Policy*. Cambridge, MA: Harvard University Press.

Goodman, William I., and Eric C. Freund, eds. *Principles and Practices of Urban Planning*. Washington, DC: International City Managers Association.

Gottdeiner, Mark. 1985. *The Social Production of Urban Space*. Austin: University of Texas Press.

Habermas, Jurgen. 1987. *The Theory of Communicative Action*. Translated by Thomas McCarthy. Boston, MA: Beacon Press.

Hacker, Andrew. 1992. The New Civil War. *New York Review of Books* 34, 8 (April): 30–34.

Hall, Peter. 1988. *Cities of Tomorrow*. Cambridge, MA: Blackwell.

Harman, B. Douglas. 1972. City Planning Agencies: Organization, Staffing, and Functions. *Municipal Yearbook*. Washington, DC: International City Managers Association.

Hartman, Chester. 1964. The Housing of Relocated Families. *Journal of the American Institute of Planners* 30, 4: 266–87.

___. 1971a. Relocation: Illusory Promises and No Relief. *Virginia Law Review* 57, 5: 745–817.

___. 1971b. The Urban Field Service. *Architectural Forum* 135, 2: 50–53.

___. 1975. The Advocate Planner: From "Hired Gun" to Political Partisan. *Social Policy* 1, 2: 37–39.

Harvey, David. 1975. The Geography of Capital Accumulation. *Antipode* 7, 2: 9–21.

___. 1978. On Planning the Ideology of Planning. In *Planning Theory in the 1980s*, edited by Robert Burchell and George Sternlieb. New Brunswick, NJ: Rutgers Center for Urban Policy Research.

___. 1982. *The Limits to Capital*. Oxford, UK: Basil Blackwell.

Hayek, Fredrick A. von. 1944. *The Road to Serfdom*. London: Routledge & Kegan Paul.

Hays, Samuel P. 1964. The Politics of Reform in Municipal Government in the Progressive Era. *Pacific Northwest Quarterly* 55, 4: 157–69.

Healey, Patsy. 1992. A Planner's Day: Knowledge and Action in Communicative Practice. *Journal of the American Planning Association* 58, 1: 9–20.

Hecimovich, James. 1983. Planners' Salaries and Employment Trends, 1989. *PAS Report* 382. Chicago, IL: American Planning Association.

___. 1989. Planners' Salaries and Employment Trends, 1989. *PAS Report* 423. Chicago, IL: American Planning Association.

Hemmens, George. 1988. Thirty Years of Planning Education. *Journal of Planning Education and Research* 7, 2: 85–92.

Heskin, Alan. 1980. Crisis and Response: A Historical Perspective on Advocacy Planning. *Journal of the American Planning Association* 46, 1: 50–63.

Hightower, Henry. 1969. Planning Theory in Contemporary Education. *Journal of the American Institute of Planners* 35, 5: 326–29.

Hirschman, Albert O. 1991. *The Rhetoric of Reaction: Perversity, Futility, Jeopardy.* Cambridge, MA: Belknap Press.

Hoch, Charles. 1984a. Doing Good and Being Right. *Journal of the American Planning Association* 50, 3: 335–45.

___. 1984b. Pragmatism, Planning and Power. *Journal of Planning Education and Research* 4, 2: 86–95.

___. 1985. Make No Large Plans. *Plan Canada* 25, 3: 80–87.

___. 1988. Conflict at Large: A National Survey of Planners and Political Conflict. *Journal of Planning Education and Research* 8, 1: 25–34.

___. 1990. Power, Planning and Conflict. *Journal of Architectural and Planning Research* 7, 4: 272–83.

___. 1992. The Paradox of Power in Planning Practice. *Journal of Planning Education and Research* 11, 3: 206–15.

Hoch, Charles, and Ann Cibulskis. 1987. Planning Threatened: A Preliminary Report of Planners and Political Conflict. *Journal of Planning Education and Research* 6, 2: 99–107.

Hoffman, Lily. 1989. *The Politics of Knowledge.* Albany: State University of New York Press.

Hofstadter, Richard. 1955. *The Age of Reform: From Bryan to FDR.* New York: Alfred A. Knopf.

Hommans, Mary. 1993. *City Planning in America.* Westport, CT: Praeger.

Howe, Beth. 1980. Role Choices for Planners. *Journal of the American Planning Association* 46, 4: 398–410.

Howe, Beth, and Jerome Kaufman. 1979. The Ethics of Contemporary American Planners. *Journal of the American Planning Association* 45, 3: 243–55.

Hubbard, Henry, and Theodora Hubbard. 1929. *Our Cities, Today and Tomorrow, a History of Zoning and Planning Progress in the United States.* Cambridge, MA: Harvard University Press.

Innes, Judith. 1992. Group Processes and the Social Construction of Growth Management: Florida, Vermont, and New Jersey. *Journal of the American Planning Association* 58, 4: 440–54.

Jacobs, Alan. 1978. *Making City Planning Work.* Chicago, IL: ASPO.

Jennings, Bruce. 1987. Interpretation and the Practice of Policy Analysis. In *Confronting Values in Policy Analysis,* edited by Frank Fischer and John Forester. Newbury Park, CA: Sage.

Judd, Dennis, and Robert Mendelson. 1973. *The Politics of Urban Planning.* Urbana: University of Illinois Press.

Kartez, Jack. 1989. Rational Arguments and Irrational Audiences: Psychology, Planning and Public Judgment. *Journal of the American Planning Association* 55, 4: 445–56.

Katznelson, Ira. 1981. *City Trenches: Urban Politics and the Patterning of Class in the United States.* New York: Pantheon.

Kaufman, Jerome. 1987. Teaching Planning Students About Strategizing, Boundary Spanning and Ethics: Part of the New Planning Theory. *Journal of Planning Education and Research* 6, 2: 108–15.

Kaufman, Sanda. 1990. Neighborhood Redevelopment: The Planner's Role in Conflict Management. *Journal of Architectural and Planning Research* 7, 4: 303–14.

Kendig, Lane, with Susan O'Conner, Cranston Byrd, and Judy Heyman. 1980. *Performance Zoning.* Washington, DC: Planners Press.

Kent, T. J. 1964. *The Urban General Plan.* San Francisco, CA: Chandler.

Klosterman, Richard. 1992. Planning Theory Education in the 1980s: Results of a Second Course Survey. *Journal of Planning Education and Research* 11, 2: 130–40.

Kravitz, Alan. 1970. Mandarinism.... In *Planning and Politics: Uneasy Partnership,* edited by Thad Beyle and George Lathrop. New York: Odyssey Press.

Krieger, Martin. 1981. *Advice and Planning.* Philadelphia, PA: Temple University Press.

Kristol, Irving. 1977. *Two Cheers for Capitalism.* New York: Meridian.

___. 1983. *Reflections of a Neo-Conservative: Looking Back, Looking Ahead.* New York: Basic Books.

Krueckeberg, Donald. 1984. Planning and the New Depression in the Social Sciences. *Journal of Planning Education and Research* 3, 2: 78–87.

Krumholz, Norman, and John Forester. 1990. *Making Equity Planning Work.* Philadelphia, PA: Temple University Press.

Levin, Melvin. 1979. Bumpy Roads Ahead. *Planning* 45, 7: 28–35.

Ligget, Helen. 1991. When They Don't Have to Take You In: The Representation of Homelessness in Public Policy. *Journal of Planning Education and Research* 10, 3: 201–208.

Lim, Gil Chim. 1986. Toward a Synthesis of Contemporary Planning Theories. *Journal of Planning Education and Research* 3, 2: 75–87.

Lindblom, Charles. 1959. The Science of Muddling Through. *Public Administration Review* 19, 1: 79–88.

___. 1979. *Usable Knowledge.* New Haven, CT: Yale University Press.

Logan, John, and Harvey Molotch. 1987. *Urban Fortunes: The Political Economy of Place.* Berkeley: University of California Press.

Longhini, Gregory. 1980. Salaries and Tenure of Professional Planners 1980. *PAS Report* 355. Chicago, IL: American Planning Association.

Lowi, Theodore. 1979 [1969]. *The End of Liberalism: The Second Republic of the United States.* New York: W. W. Norton.

Lukas, J. Anthony. 1985. *Common Ground.* New York: Knopf.

McClendon, Bruce, and Ray Quay. 1988. *Mastering Change.* Chicago, IL: Planners Press.

Mandelbaum, Seymour. 1979. A Complete General Theory of Planning Is Impossible. *Policy Sciences* 11, 1: 59–71.

___. 1985. The Institutional Focus of Planning. *Journal of Planning Education and Research* 5, 1: 3–10.

___. 1988. Open Moral Communities: Theorizing About Planning Within Myths of Community. *Society* 26, 1: 20–27.

Mann, Lawrence. 1972. Social Science Advances and Planning Applications: 1900–1965. *Journal of the American Institute of Planners* 38, 4: 346–58.

Mansbridge, Jane. 1983. *Beyond Adversary Democracy.* Chicago, IL: University of Chicago Press.

Marris, Peter. 1974. *Loss and Change.* London: Routledge and Kegan Paul.

___. 1982a. Social Change and Reintegration. *Journal of Planning Education and Research* 2, 1: 54–61.

___. 1982b. *Community Planning and Conceptions of Change.* New York: Routledge and Kegan Paul.

___. 1987. *Meaning and Action.* New York: Routledge.

___. 1990. Witnesses, Engineers, or Storytellers? Role of Sociologists in Social Policy. In *Sociology in America,* edited by Herbert Gans. Newberry Park, CA: Sage.

Marsh, Benjamin. 1953. *Lobbyist for the People: A Record of Fifty Years.* Washington, DC: Public Affairs Press.

Mayo, James. 1982. Sources of Job Dissatisfaction: Ideal Versus Realities in Planning. *Journal of the American Planning Association* 48, 4: 481–98.

Meltsner, Arnold. 1976. *Policy Analysis in the Bureaucracy.* Berkeley: University of California Press.

Meyerson, Martin. 1956. Building the Middle Range Planning Bridge for Comprehensive Planning. *Journal of the American Institute of Planners* 22, 1: 58–64.

Meyerson, Martin, and Edward Banfield. 1955. *Planning, Politics and the Public Interest.* Boston, MA: Free Press.

Milroy, Beth. 1991. Into Postmodern Weightlessness. *Journal of Planning Education and Research* 10, 3: 181–88.

Mollenkopf, John. 1983. *The Contested City.* Princeton, NJ: Princeton University Press.

Morris, Marya. 1992. Planners' Salaries and Employment Trends, 1991. *PAS Report* 439. Chicago, IL: American Planning Association.

Mumford, Lewis. 1932. The Plan of New York. *New Republic* 71, 2: 121–26.

Needleman, Martin, and Carolyn Emerson Needleman. 1974. *Guerrillas in the Bureaucracy: The Community Planning Experiment in the United States.* New York: John Wiley and Sons.

Nicholas, James, Arthur Nelson, and Julian Juergensmeyer. 1991. *A Practitioner's Guide to Development Impact Fees.* Chicago, IL: Planners Press.

Nussbaum, Martha. 1990. *Love's Knowledge.* New York: Oxford University Press.

Perloff, Harvey. 1957. *Education for Planning: City, State and Regional.* Baltimore, MD: Johns Hopkins University Press.

Perloff, Harvey, ed. 1961. *Planning and the Urban Community.* Pittsburgh, PA: University of Pittsburgh Press.

Perloff, Harvey, with Frank Klett. 1974. The Evolution of Planning Education. In *Planning in America: Learning from Turbulence,* edited by David Godschalk. Washington, DC: American Institute of Planners.

Peterson, Paul. 1981. *City Limits.* Chicago, IL: University of Chicago Press.

Pettergill, Robert, and Jogindar Uppal. 1974. *Can Cities Survive? The Fiscal Plight of American Cities.* New York: St. Martins Press.

Rabinowitz, Francine. 1969. *City Politics and Planning.* New York: Atherton Press.

___. 1989. The Role of Negotiation in Planning, Management, and Policy Analysis. *Journal of Planning Education and Research* 8, 2: 87–96.

Raymond, George. 1978. The Role of the Physical Urban Planner. In *Planning Theory in the 1980s,* edited by Robert Burchell and George Sternlieb. New Brunswick, NJ: Rutgers Center for Urban Policy Research.

Rorty, Richard. 1987. *Consequences of Pragmatism.* Minneapolis: University of Minnesota Press.

___. 1989. *Contingency, Irony, and Solidarity.* New York: Cambridge University Press.

Rosenblum, Nancy. 1988. *Another Liberalism.* Cambridge, MA: Harvard University Press.

Roweis, Shoukry. 1983. Urban Planning as Professional Mediation of Territorial Politics. *Environment and Planning D* 1, 1: 139–62.

Roweis, Shoukry, and Alan Scott. 1978. The Urban Land Question. In *Urbanization and Conflict in Market Societies,* edited by Kevin Cox. Chicago, IL: Maaroufa Press.

Savas, E. S. 1981. *Privatizing the Public Sector.* Washington, DC: American Enterprise Institute.

Schon, Donald. 1982. Some of What a Planner Knows: A Case Study of Knowing-in-Practice. *Journal of the American Planning Association* 48, 3: 351–64.

___. 1983. *The Reflective Practitioner: How Professionals Think in Action.* New York: Basic Books.

Scott, Mel. 1969. *American City Planning Since 1890.* Berkeley: University of California Press.

Segoe, Ladislaus. 1964. The Planning Profession: Its Progress and Some Problems. *Planning 1964.* Chicago, IL: American Society of Planning Officials.

Simon, Herbert. 1957. *Models of Man.* New York: Wiley and Sons.

___. 1976. *Administrative Behavior.* New York: Free Press.

Smith, Michael, and Joe Feagin. 1987. *The Capitalist City.* Oxford, UK: Basil Blackwell.

Smith, Neil. 1984. *Uneven Development.* Oxford, UK: Basil Blackwell.

So, Frank, and Judith Getzels, eds. 1988. *The Practice of Planning.* Washington, DC: International City Managers Association.

So, Frank, et al. 1979. *The Practice of Local Government Planning*. Washington, DC: International City Managers Association.

Solnit, Albert. 1988. *The Job of the Practicing Planner*. Chicago, IL: Planners Press.

Spencer, James. 1979. Planning Agency Management. In *The Practice of Local Government Planning*, edited by Frank So et al. Washington, DC: International City Managers Association.

Tabb, William, and Lawrence Sawers. 1978. *Marxism and the Metropolis*. New York: Oxford University Press.

Terkel, Studs. 1992. *Race*. New York: The New Press.

Throgmorton, James. 1990. Passion, Reason, and Power: The Rhetorics of Electric Power Planning in Chicago. *Journal of Architectural and Planning Research* 7, 4: 330–50.

___. 1992. Planning as Persuasive Storytelling About the Future: Negotiating an Electric Power Rate Settlement in Illinois. *Journal of Planning Education and Research* 12, 1: 17–31.

Tiebout, Charles. 1956. A Pure Theory of Public Expenditures. *Journal of Political Economy* 64 (October): 416–24.

United States Department of Housing and Urban Development (HUD). 1978. *Statistical Yearbook*. Washington, DC: U.S. Government Printing Office.

Urban Land Institute (ULI). 1940. *Decentralization: What Is It Doing to Our Cities*. Chicago, IL: ULI.

Vasu, Michael. 1979. *Politics and Planning*. Chapel Hill: University of North Carolina Press.

Walker, Robert. 1941. *The Planning Function in Urban Government*. Chicago, IL: University of Chicago Press.

Warner, Sam Bass. 1966. Urban Constraints and Federal Policy. In *Planning for a Nation of Cities*, edited by S. B. Warner. Cambridge, MA: MIT Press.

Warren, Robert. 1964. A Municipal Services Market Model of Metropolitan Organization. *Journal of the American Institute of Planners* 30, 2: 193–204.

Webber, Melvin. 1973. Comprehensive Planning and Social Responsibility: Toward an AIP Consensus on the Profession's Roles and Purposes. In *Readings in Planning Theory*, edited by Andreas Faludi. Oxford, UK: Pergamon.

Webber, Melvin, and Horst Rittel. 1973. Dilemmas in a General Theory of Planning. *Policy Sciences* 4, 2: 155–69.

Weinstein, James. 1968. *The Corporate Ideal in the Liberal State*. Boston, MA: Beacon Press.

Wildawsky, Aaron. 1979. *Speaking Truth to Power: The Art and Craft of Policy Analysis*. New York: Little, Brown and Company.

Wilson, William J. 1987. *The Truly Disadvantaged*. Chicago, IL: University of Chicago Press.

Wirth, Louis. 1964. *On Cities and Social Life: Selected Papers of Louis Wirth*. Chicago, IL: University of Chicago Press.

Wolfe, Alan. 1989. *Whose Keeper?* Berkeley: University of California Press.

Woods, Robert. 1961. *1,400 Governments*. Cambridge, MA: Harvard University Press.

Wright, Deil. 1970. Governmental Forms and Planning Functions: The Relation of Organization and Structures to Planning Practice. In *Planning and Politics: Uneasy Partnership*, edited by Thad Beyle and George Lathrop. New York: Odyssey Press.

INDEX

DATE DUE